Lecture Notes in Computer Science   8212

Commenced Publication in 1973
Founding and Former Series Editors:
Gerhard Goos, Juris Hartmanis, and Jan van Leeuwen

Albert Ali Salah   Hayley Hung   Oya Aran
Hatice Gunes (Eds.)

Human Behavior Understanding

4th International Workshop, HBU 2013
Barcelona, Spain, October 22, 2013
Proceedings

 Springer

Volume Editors

Albert Ali Salah
Boğaziçi University, Istanbul, Turkey
E-mail: salah@boun.edu.tr

Hayley Hung
Delft University of Technology, The Netherlands
E-mail: h.hung@tudelft.nl

Oya Aran
Idiap Research Institute, Martigny, Switzerland
E-mail: oaran@idiap.ch

Hatice Gunes
Queen Mary University of London, UK
E-mail: hatice@eecs.qmul.ac.uk

ISSN 0302-9743   e-ISSN 1611-3349
ISBN 978-3-319-02713-5   e-ISBN 978-3-319-02714-2
DOI 10.1007/978-3-319-02714-2
Springer Cham Heidelberg New York Dordrecht London

Library of Congress Control Number: 2013950178

CR Subject Classification (1998): I.5, I.2, H.5, H.3, I.4, H.4

LNCS Sublibrary: SL 6 – Image Processing, Computer Vision, Pattern
Recognition, and Graphics

Typesetting: Camera-ready by author, data conversion by Scientific Publishing Services, Chennai, India

Printed on acid-free paper

Springer is part of Springer Science+Business Media (www.springer.com)

Preface

Domains where human behavior understanding is a crucial need (e.g., robotics, human–computer interaction, affective computing, and social signal processing) rely on advanced pattern recognition techniques to automatically interpret complex behavioral patterns generated when humans interact with machines or with others. This is a challenging problem where many issues are still open, including the joint modeling of behavioral cues taking place at different time scales, the inherent uncertainty of machine-detectable evidences of human behavior, the mutual influence of people involved in interactions, the presence of long-term dependencies in observations extracted from human behavior, and the important role of dynamics in human behavior understanding.

The 4th Workshop on Human Behavior Understanding (HBU), organized as a satellite to ACM Multimedia (ACM MM 2013, Barcelona), gathered researchers dealing with the problem of modeling human behavior under its multiple facets (expression of emotions, display of relational attitudes, performance of individual or joint actions, imitation, etc.). The HBU Workshop, previously organized jointly with the International Conference on Pattern Recognition (ICPR 2010, Istanbul), International Joint Conference on Ambient Intelligence (AMI 2011, Amsterdam) and IEEE/RSJ International Conference on Intelligent Robots and Systems (IROS 2012, Algarve), highlights different aspects of this problem since its inception. The 4th HBU Workshop focuses on applications of human behavior analysis for interactions in creativity, arts, entertainment, and edutainment. There are tremendous social and societal implications of creating human-centered, adaptive, and responsive systems in these areas.

The workshop featured two invited talks. The first talk by Dr. Antonio Camurri (Casa Paganini InfoMus Research Centre, DIBRIS, University of Genoa) was entitled "Multimodal Systems for Embodied Experience of Music and Audiovisual Content." Dr. Camurri, in his talk, remarked that the adoption of the embodied cooperation paradigm opens new perspectives for social applications in future user-centric media. At the same time, mobile technologies enable us to share experiences in an easier and faster way, using multiple modalities and media. By combining these aspects, Dr. Camurri and colleagues proposed mobile systems integrating real-time analysis of movement and of non-verbal expressive gesture and social behavior. This keynote presented an overview of recent research results at Casa Paganini-InfoMus in these directions, including the EyesWeb XMI software platform, focusing on socio-mobile embodied experience and retrieval of music and audiovisual content, and on teaching autistic children to recognize and express emotions by non-verbal full-body movements and gestures. The research of Dr. Camurri is partially funded by the European Projects ASC INCLUSION (7 Framework Programme ICT) and MetaBody (EU Culture).

The second keynote talk was by Dr. Pushmeet Kohli (Microsoft Research Cambridge, UK), as a part of the ACM Distinguished Speakers Program. In his talk entitled "Learning to Interact (Naturally) with (All) Users," Dr. Kohli discussed the development of "natural" user interfaces that can understand the intent and preferences of users and are easier to use. Making machines understand human intentions and preferences is an exceptionally challenging problem for the AI community. Part of this difficulty lies in capturing the large variability in preferences and behavior of different users. In his talk, Dr. Kohli discussed some steps taken by his research group at Microsoft Research Cambridge to overcome this problem in the context of two application scenarios: interaction/activity recognition using the Kinect, and information retrieval. Dr. Kohli described their recent work on human pose estimation using the Kinect sensor and the challenges of developing a system that is supposed to work on "everybody." He then elaborated on the problem of personalization in the context of information retrieval and discussed how traits like the personality of users can be inferred from their online behavior.

This proceedings volume contains the papers presented at the workshop and a summarizing paper. We have received 50 submissions in total, and each paper was peer-reviewed by at least two members of the Technical Program Committee. Twelve papers were accepted as oral presentations, and eight papers were presented as posters.

We would like to take the opportunity to thank our Program Committee members and reviewers for their rigorous feedback, our authors and our keynote speakers for their contributions, Maja Pantic, Vladimir Pavlovic, and Nicu Sebe from the ACM MM Organizing Committee for their help. We thank the ACM Distinguished Speakers Program, the InfoMus Research Center, the EPSRC MAPTRAITS Project (Grant Ref: EP/K017500/1), Swiss National Science Foundation (SNSF) Ambizione fellowship project PZ00P2_136811, and the BAP 6531 project of Boğaziçi University for their support.

October 2013

Albert Ali Salah
Hayley Hung
Oya Aran
Hatice Gunes

Organization

Conference Co-chairs

Albert Ali Salah   Boğaziçi University, Turkey
Hayley Hung   Delft University of Technology,
     The Netherlands
Oya Aran   Idiap Research Institute, Switzerland
Hatice Gunes   Queen Mary University of London, UK

Technical Program Committee

Elisabeth André	University of Augsburg, Germany
Nick Bryan-Kinns	Queen Mary University of London, UK
Carlos Busso	University of Texas at Dallas, USA
Rafael E. Calvo	University of Sydney, Australia
Antonio Camurri	University of Genova, Italy
Jeffrey Cohn	University of Pittsburgh, USA
Simon Colton	Imperial College London, UK
Fernando de la Torre	CMU, USA
Hamdi Dibeklioğlu	Delft University of Technology, The Netherlands
Thierry Dutoit	University of Mons, Belgium
Gwenn Englebienne	University of Amsterdam, The Netherlands
Jordi Gonzalez	UAB-CVC Barcelona, Spain
Daniel Gonzalez-Jimenez	Gradiant, Spain
Zakia Hammal	CMU, USA
Christian Jacquemin	LIMSI-CNRS, France
Dinesh Jayagopi	Idiap Research Intitute, Switzerland
Kostas Karpouzis	National Technical University of Athens, Greece
Cem Keskin	Microsoft Research Cambridge, UK
Ben Kröse	University of Amsterdam, The Netherlands
Dana Kulic	University of Waterloo, Canada
Matei Mancas	University of Mons, Belgium
Louis-Philippe Morency	USC, USA
Florian 'Floyd' Mueller	RMIT, Australia
Frank Nack	University of Amsterdam, The Netherlands
Hiroshi Okuno	Kyoto University, Japan
Isabella Poggi	Roma Tre University, Italy
Thierry Pun	University of Geneva, Switzerland
Francis Quek	Virginia Tech, USA

Ben Schouten   Eindhoven Technical University,
                                        The Netherlands
Björn Schuller   Technical University of Munich, Germany
Alan Smeaton   Dublin City University, Ireland
Koray Tahiroğlu   Aalto University, Finland
Reiner Wichert   Fraunhofer IGD, Germany

Additional Reviewers

Enrique Aragones-Rúa   Derya Özkan
Sharon Chu   Fumihide Tanaka
Wen-Sheng Chu   Esteban Vazquez-Fernandez
Raquel Dosil-Lago   Kazuyoshi Yoshii

Table of Contents

Facial Behavior

Social Signals

Affective Signals

Creative Applications of Human Behavior Understanding

Albert Ali Salah[1], Hayley Hung[2], Oya Aran[3], and Hatice Gunes[4]

[1] Boğaziçi University, Department of Computer Engineering,
Istanbul, Turkey
salah@boun.edu.tr
[2] Delft University of Technology, Intelligent Systems
2628 CD Delft, The Netherlands
H.Hung@tudelft.nl
[3] Idiap Research Institute, Social Computing Group
Martigny, Switzerland
oaran@idiap.ch
[4] Queen Mary University of London, School of Elect. Eng. & Computer Science
London, U.K.
hatice@eecs.qmul.ac.uk

Abstract. The role of computer science in the creative industries is becoming recognised as an important way to bring forward progress in both domains. There is a need for smarter applications that sense and adapt to their users in arts, creativity, entertainment and edutainment domains. Understanding human behavior in this area is challenging because it forces practitioners to engage in both creative, and perhaps counterintuitively, analytic processes of understanding how people engage with creative phenomena. The systems constructed for this purpose promise to enhance and redefine the scope of creative industries significantly. This paper discusses scientific and technological factors that make this a challenging topic to address, provides a brief survey of related work in this area, and identifies active topics of research. Since arts, creativity, entertainment and edutainment all contribute to significant social and societal benefits, it is vital to tackle the problem of measuring and evaluating the success of automatic behavior analysis solutions as a social and human phenomenon.

1 Introduction

The important relationship between artistic creativity and science has existed for centuries, perhaps since the Ancient Greek mathematicians' scientific approach to aesthetics in what became the golden ratio, producing along the way people of genius like Leonardo Da Vinci. While there were periods in which arts and science drifted apart, the 20th Century saw attempts to bring them together in different forms, for instance with the establishment of the art science journal Leonardo[1],

---

[1] http://www.leonardo.info/

A.A. Salah et al. (Eds.) : HBU 2013, LNCS 8212, pp. 1–14, 2013.

international conferences such as Ars Electronica[1] and SIGGRAPH[2], institutes like Numediart[3] and special sessions in major conferences like the Interactive Arts Programme[4] in ACM Multimedia, which celebrates its 10th year in 2013.

Obviously, science is instrumental in delivering artists new tools of artistic expression. More that than, it can provide systematic evaluation of the success of creative works, which remains an often taboo subject in the creative industries. For the consumer of art, the implications are very direct, as they expect to be stimulated intellectually, socially, or simply, to be entertained.

With arts and entertainment extending their scope to include societal themes, as well as with the proliferation of digital and computerized art forms, the intermingling of these domains increased. It is now commonplace to encounter artists that produce exclusively on digital medium, or interactive artworks that use state-of-the-art sensing technology to involve their spectators. With such technology becoming easily accessible, it is even possible for ordinary people with no specialized formation to grab a few sensors, and transform experiences, including daily living routines, into digital experiences, where data can be collected, analyzed, visualized, and acted upon [59]. In this paper, we investigate how human behavior understanding contributes to creative enterprises technologically.

Under the term *human behavior understanding* (HBU), we understand pattern recognition and modeling techniques to automatically interpret complex behavioral patterns generated when humans interact with machines or with other humans [46]. These patterns can involve actions, activities, attitudes, affective states, social signals, semantic descriptions, and contextual properties. Taken together, they define multimodal ways of enhancing human-computer, human-robot, and even human-human interactions [53].

We investigate the theme of HBU in relation to the arts, creativity, entertainment and edutainment under the following categories:

- HBU in the presence of passive entertainment systems: These analyze peoples' behavioral responses to stimuli from systems that do not require continuous input from a human.

- HBU in interactive systems: These systems inherently analyze people's behavior as input and respond accordingly.

- Multi-party HBU for systems that function as social spectacles: This refers to the analysis of the social element of audience participation in such systems where the awareness of reactions from others in the audience is part of the experience of the spectacle.

We proceed by looking at each of these categories in turn.

---

[1] http://www.aec.at/
[2] http://www.siggraph.org
[3] http://www.numediart.org/
[4] http://acmmm13.org/submissions/call-for-artworks/

2   HBU in the Presence of Passive Entertainment Systems

In its most traditional form, arts and entertainment are about providing visual, auditory, or haptic stimuli for a human observer. HBU can be used to observe the participant's implicit (e.g., physiology) and explicit behavior (e.g., emotional expressions), either to improve the quality of presentation, or to gain a better understanding of the participant's response.

Let us give the example of films, which are rich in audiovisual and emotional stimuli. People watching movies go through a variety of experiences, engineered to some extent by the director of the movie, and their expressive responses during the course of the movie can be analyzed using HBU techniques. For instance Smeaton and colleagues previously looked at heart rates, Galvanic skin response, and the amount of movement in spectators watching films in a special movie theatre equipped with smart chairs [50]. They found that group psychology affects people watching movies together, and they have highly correlated emotional responses. Similarly, Baumgartner et al. investigated emotions evoked by still pictures and classical music, and demonstrated that emotional responses are strongest when audio and vision are combined [3].

In this volume, Tarvainen et al. investigate stylistic features of movies in visual, aural and temporal modalities, and correlate these features with perceived and felt affect [52]. While it is difficult to sort through idiosyncratic variations of affective experiences of different subjects, this kind of analysis, beyond engineering an emotional experience, can serve pragmatic purposes, like summarization of a movie by its emotional peaks, or for customized recommender systems.

3   HBU in Interactive Systems

This topic refers to the role of human behavior as a trigger for interactive systems. Representative applications are the ones where a person directly interacts with a system that displays an artistic message, encourages creativity, play, or learning.

For some interactive art pieces, the humans' behavior towards the work becomes part of the narrative of the piece [51,23]. In interactive arts, a key issue is the mode of interaction. HBU essentially provides artists with new tools, and with new interaction possibilities. In the absence of analysis, a clever setup may permit the use of simple sensors in a reactive application scenario. The Piano Stairs installation at Odenplan Station in Stockholm[1] is a well-known example of how an innovative behavior sensing system can be made to change people's daily routines: by converting an ordinary stair into a musical instrument via pressure sensors and loudspeakers, it was possible to get more people to take the stairs over the escalator.

Peter Beesley's *Hylozoic Soil* is an example of a responsive architectural geo-tactile space, made up of a network of micro-controllers, proximity sensors and

---

[1] http://www.thefuntheory.com/

shape-memory alloy actuators [5]. Its layers move in response to the presence of human occupants. Samadani et al. illustrated that movement in such frond-like structures can easily create the perception of affective states in their users [47]. The Sissy (Sound-driven, Interactive, Self-conscious SYstem) installation at the STRP festival was made of 700 flip dots with white and black colored sides, and it slowly responded to visitor movements that it sensed via its camera [8]. It was perceived as "shy," which is an unusual attribute for seemingly random dot patterns. In [35], an interactive playground was designed for children, indicating that through context-awareness, adaptability, and personalization, rich game experiences can be created.

In this volume, several works illustrate that responsive and interactive spaces can create stimulating and engaging experiences. Morgan and Gunes [36] introduce an installation designed to let people represent their "mood" by controlling the lights around the rim of the London Eye. Over 800 people participated, taking control of the lights using their heart rates and hand gestures. Affective and behavioral computing inspired techniques applied for analysing the physiological and motion capture data showed that during the interaction with the Eye people's heart and kinematic behavior differed according to the content style they were interacting with, and gestures were predominantly performed with extended arms. In [30], a pressure sensing floor prototype for detecting human actions is described. Once human presence is sensed at a certain location, it can be connected to an event in an interaction scenario. The authors describe several such applications, including a memory game, a virtual piano, foot painting, and a position-controlled media player.

A key insight in interaction design is that the nature of interaction between a person and a computer system is dictated both by the affordances of the system, and by the cognitive and physical limitations of the interacting person [44]. Accurate models of the latter can be used to steer the former for improved interaction. In this volume, Fourati et al. present an analysis of walking and turning tasks based on shoulder, hip and head activity [18]. Their results show that the emotional state expressed by the subject strongly determines the style of head gestures and walking and turning behavior. Marchegiani and Fafoutis conduct a behavioral study to investigate the listening capabilities of subjects under challenging conditions, with rock music playing in the background [32]. Their results indicate that the subjects' familiarity with the music acts as an emotional trigger that attracts the subject's attention. It has been previously shown that emotions play a significant role in driving user's attention in a system [39]. Subsequently, automatic analysis of emotions has an additional potential in shaping interactions, i.e. by helping to estimate the user's attention.

4   Multi-party and Social HBU

HBU in the context of multiple receivers becomes an interesting social phenomenon in its own right. An entertaining public spectacle becomes a social event, where the response of other audience members is a vital part of the experience of an event, heightening its value to the people receiving it. In some cases the spectacle becomes talking point for strangers, which was referred to as triangulation by Whyte [58] and similarly as collaborative sense-making by Hook et al. [24]. The behavior of performance artists and audience as a collaboration in creating and eliciting spectacles in public spaces has also been studied by Gardair et al. [19]. Similar research has been carried out on understanding the social behavior of people in front of a painting, and as mentioned in Section 2, while watching movies.

HBU with multiple receivers is not only about human-arts interaction, it also extends to situations where the focus is directed towards collaborative creativity and performance. Understanding the social behavior of people and enhancing the interaction between them when they are engaged in a creative activity, promises great potential for linking HBU with new media art and computational creativity research [37]. Recent works on the analysis of groups show that the collective intelligence of a group, while performing several cognitive tasks, ranging from brainstorming to video game playing, not only depends on the average member intelligence, but also on the way the members interact with each other [60]. Computer supported systems have been proposed to ensure the equal participation from the group members for various occasions such as collaborative learning [2] and social events [40]. In this volume, [42] proposes a real-time system that automatically analyzes the audio recordings of two-person dialog to assess several social constructs such as interest, agreement and dominance.

Several other works look at musical performance and focus on the analysis of interaction between the members in musical groups, investigating the emergence of several social constructs such as leadership [54] and dominance [20]. Varni et al. [54] also investigated the synchronization of the affective behavior within the group and showed that the synchronization and leadership measures are effective and reliable in supporting social active music listening applications, such as Sync'n Move [55].

Education and edutainment also involve interactions that are essentially of a social nature. The keys to successful education are ensuring engagement (or activation) of the student, and providing educational material that has the appropriate level for the student. Both tasks require real-time monitoring of the student and estimation of engagement and comprehension levels. Computer games for students have been recently used in education for ensuring better engagement and comprehension, and it has been shown that children are more engaged if multimodal interaction systems are enabled [25,26]. Interactive tabletops has also been used to support collaborative work in education [13].

The interaction between the teacher and student is also of great importance for successful outcomes in education, and several works have investigated this interaction from the HBU perspective either in classroom settings to detect the influence of one party on another via automatic analysis of facial movements, face and hand gestures, and speech loudness [57] or in dyadic teacher-student interaction settings to detect helping and over-helping [11].

Recently, robots are being increasingly employed to engage children in educational scenarios [16]. There is significant evidence that robots can enhance learning [6], or can induce behavioral change, for instance in helping autistic individuals improve their social skills [10]. One such robotic application is described in this volume. The ALIZ-E Project[1] targets behavior change for children suffering from diabetes or obesity. In their work, Ros and Demiris propose to use robots as creative dance tutors [45]. In their experiments with 8 and 9-years-old children, the authors observe that a robot that displays non-verbal signals of interaction successfully engages children in a joint dance session, where children imitate the robot, and expect to be imitated by it. Similar engagement scenarios have been deployed for other socially assistive robotics applications, including fitness coaching for the elderly [21], and post-stroke rehabilitation [17], where the robot needs to observe and guide human subjects through imitation-based interactions. Towards the generation of multimodal behavior for a humanoid robot engaged in a collaborative task with a human partner, Mihoub et al. present a probabilistic approach based on hidden Markov models in this volume, using multimodal speech and gaze data from computer-mediated dyadic conversations [34].

Coaching systems come in many flavors, and robotic variants are relatively marginally used. Pfister and Robinson described a public speaking skills coach that is based on the analysis of affective states from nonverbal features of speech [41]. In this volume, Baur et al. present the NovA (NOnVerbal behavior Analyzer) system that automatically analyzes and interprets social signals from posture, gestures, facial expressions and others in the context of a job interview, which constitutes a starting point for social coaching in human-human interaction settings [4].

5   Open Challenges of HBU for Creative Applications

HBU for creative applications has an enormous potential that brings along a number of challenges. In what follows we attempt to focus specifically on three challenges that we group under the headings of behavioral experimentation, ecological validity, and data collection for analysis and validation.

5.1   Behavioral Experimentation

The rigors of experimental science, where conditions can be controlled for while varying one parameter, and the proof of a hypotheses is required based on measurable outcomes, may not be practically achievable "in the wild", outside of a clean lab environment. Sometimes, the real world imitates the lab. For instance, there can be striking similarities between galleries and exhibition spaces and the controlled lab environments. The gallery environment is purposefully designed to be clear of the clutter of the outside world so all attention can be focused on the artwork itself. Rooms are often curated into themes, which enables people to be exposed to a common aspect relating to a set of works, stimulating

---

[1] www.aliz-e.org

certain ideas while de-emphasizing others. Such controlled setups may also pose the Observer's Paradox problem identified by Labov as a situation where data gathering is influenced by the presence of the experimenter [28]. Even in "the wild" experimentation settings are not fully exempt from this dilemma - participants are still aware of placement of the sensors and their locations which tend to affect their (expressive) behavior [36].

An interesting case can be made for sports games, which constitute rich settings particularly suited for measuring affective states like excitement, triumph, disappointment, joy, and pride in naturalistic conditions. Matsumoto's well-publicized research investigated spontaneous facial expressions of medal winners in Olympic games [33], focusing on the moment when the gold medal winner triumphs, and the silver medal winner (despite a tremendous achievement) faces the agony of defeat. Analysis of such moments presupposes that the recorded individual is either not aware of a detailed analysis that will take place, or is in an emotional state that is so intense, that the cameras pointed at the subject do not matter much.

The trade-off then is in capturing detailed information about a phenomenon, as opposed to capturing the information naturally. A recent example that illustrates this is the Multimodal and Multiperson Corpus of Laughter in Interaction (MMLI), described in this volume [38]. This corpus captures different laughter types, in different contexts, and with full body movement information in addition to audio and facial video recordings. The subjects are equipped with 17-19 inertial sensors placed on Velcro straps, in addition to recordings with two personal microphones close to the mouth, one room microphone, four webcams, two high-rate color cameras, two RGB-D cameras and one respiration sensor. The MMLI scenario illustrates the data intensive recording extreme of the spectrum, providing a much clearer picture of what happens at the expense of a natural setting.

5.2 Ecological Validity

In recent years, ecological validity has become a prerequisite for research studies focusing on human behavior understanding. Given the level of subjectivity in creativity, entertainment, and edutainment, it is certainly not possible to talk about the ability of the studies conducted in this field, and their results, to *generalize* (i.e., external validity). Would these studies that are meant to encourage originality, ambiguity, and even incongruity at times, be able to claim ecological validity? How closely do the settings, the conditions and the methods used in these studies replicate the actual look, feel and procedure of the so-called *real-world*? Is it possible to conduct research studies in these fields without disrupting levels of creativity and playfulness? These are key questions that cannot be approached and discussed by researchers alone, requiring input from artists and practitioners.

Interactive and new media art technologies have the potential to take human behavior research into the wider world, serving as a valid and a genuine context in which to conduct user-centered tests [12]. When using technologies as an ecological testbed for research, there is a need to achieve a balance between the accuracy of hypotheses testing in experiments and the naturalness of the experience and situation. Ideally, the contextual and aesthetic aspects of the artwork should guide the participant with respect to the purpose of the experiment, without limiting the overall experience [12]. In order to strike a balance between the functional needs of a given artistic context and assess the artistic purpose of the technology, Deweppe et al. [12] advocate the use of new media festivals (e.g. Ars Electronica, Transmediale) as ecological testbed for the above-mentioned type of research. In this volume, the London Eye Mood Conductor project, with its design, outdoor setup and participants appears to form a good example - it meets the functional and the experimental needs of the artwork as well as participant experience, providing an ecologically valid case study of human affective behavior in new media art [36].

5.3   Data Collection for Analysis and Validation

A major challenge for creating rigors experimental conditions is obtaining some level of "understanding" about the data through an evaluation process that can then be subsequently used for analysis and validation. Participant evaluation can be obtained either explicitly or implicitly. Explicit evaluations typically provide self-report measures obtained by interviewing participants explicitly using surveys and questionnaires, as well as some standard evaluation and labeling techniques (e.g., the Self Assessment Mannequin (SAM) [29]). Implicit evaluation instead is obtained by recording the participants' visual, auditive and physiological behavior while they are experiencing the interaction. When recording multiple cues for implicit evaluation, it is important to keep in mind that not all recorded cues might be correlated with the displayed stimuli equally. Due to this, different results may be obtained with different types of data.

When it comes to behavior analysis of people interacting with art installations, special circumstances apply. Needless to say, art installations are subjective phenomena, therefore, should ideally be evaluated by self-report. However, self-report measures have their own limitations: they may be inconsistent, variable, and depend on past experience. Obtaining participant self-report might be easier in indoor and gallery environments where variables such as entry, number of participants, and access can be monitored and controlled. This in turn allows for the systematic exclusion of confounding factors and generally make data analysis more straightforward and the results more compelling. If the digital artwork moves outdoors, attempting to obtain implicit measures might be more appropriate. This certainly appears to be one of the reasons for the London Eye Mood Conductor project, introduced in this volume, to opt for implicit evaluation [36]. However, data with implicit measures also presents new challenges when it comes to validation, analysis and extraction of meaningful results. Tackling these challenges is a necessary step if human behavior understanding is to be fully incorporated into new media art applications.

Different sets of sensors can be used in tandem when observing people. In [49], the authors use the audio modality and investigate the usage of functional meanings of discourse particles for emotion recognition. They present methods to extract the pitch-contour of the discourse particles and link them with emotions. While audio is seen as the more reliable modality in recognition of affect, the visual modality is predominantly used for identification of people, particularly from their faces [14]. Face analysis is also used to classify facial actions, which can give clues about affective states of a person [61,15], and for gaze estimation, which can indicate the focus of attention of a person during interactions. In [31], an eye-gaze framework is proposed for capturing the dependence of eye-gaze on visual stimulus, intent and person.

When detailed information of individuals is not available, it may still be possible to sense collective emotions via the analysis of more general audiovisual cues. In one of the earliest papers on automatic detection of excitement in videos, Hanjalic used overall motion activity (measured at video frame transitions), the rhythm (via the changes in shot lengths along the video), and the energy (computed from the audio track of a video) to highlight segments with high expected excitement levels [22]. In this volume, Conigliaro et al. use image segmentation to measure excitement levels of groups of people during the 2013 IIHF Ice Hockey U18 World Championship [9]. This kind of analysis can be used for automatically segmenting groups of people among the spectators or players of a game, to monitor student engagement in edutainment applications, or to change game experience as the excitement levels are translated into visualizations and sonifications that encourage the spectators to be more active.

For interactive systems that sense human body positions, the recently developed RGB-D cameras (like Microsoft Kinect) quickly became standard. Thanks to specialized hardware support, RGB-D sensors make tracking a human body skeleton accurately in real-time possible, after which a number of gestures can be automatically recognized. Such devices made a whole new set of entertainment applications possible [48]. One example in this volume is the work on iconic gestures used by first person shooter games (e.g. crouch, shoot, throw, kick, etc.) and metaphoric gestures (e.g. raising hands to increase volume) that are recognized via rapid random forest feature selection and gentle AdaBoost classifiers on such depth camera images [7]. In [56], Wang et al. present an approach for real-time continuous emotion recognition from body movements. They extract both low level and high level 3D postural features to represent dynamics of body movements and train a random forest classifier to obtain their model, which has been tested on continuous Kinect data.

State-of-the-art gesture classification approaches (including random forest based methods) require large sets of training samples for accurate representation of each gesture class. For this reason, innovative methods are sought to help in training generalizable and flexible models. In [27], a 3D hand model is used to synthesize many hand scans taken from different angles to train a hand gesture recognition system. In this volume, a transfer learning procedure is proposed to take advantage of the fact that some human body poses are shared among actions, and key poses can be trained from external sources [43]. Most action and activity recognition systems target a specific set of behavior classes (e.g. pre-determined gaming gestures for a gesture-sensing game, as in [7]), which reduces the number of classes and simplifies the training procedure. Avcı and Passerini use correlations in multiple sensor streams to detect change points, and to automatically segment behavior classes [1]. While this is a more challenging scenario, the idiosyncratic variations in behavior classes make it also a potentially more powerful approach.

6   Conclusions

This paper highlights research on analysis of human behavior under its multiple facets (expression of emotions, display of complex social and relational behaviors, performance of individual or joint actions, etc.), with particular attention to interactions in arts, creativity, entertainment and edutainment.

With advances in pattern recognition and multimedia computing, it has become possible to analyze human behavior via multimodal sensors, at different time-scales and at different levels of interaction and interpretation. This ability opens up enormous possibilities for multimedia and multimodal interaction, with a potential of endowing the computers with a capacity to attribute meaning to users attitudes, preferences, personality, social relationships, etc., as well as to understand what people are doing, the activities they have been engaged in, their routines and lifestyles. Re-defining the relationship between the computer and the interacting human, moving the computer from a passive observer role to a socially active participant role and enabling it to drive different kinds of interaction has implications across multiple domains, including arts, creativity, entertainment and edutainment. In these domains in particular, modes of interaction are highly variable and so observing, analyzing and interpreting behaviors systematically is a challenge.

Acknowledgments. The work of Albert Ali Salah is supported by Boğaziçi University project BAP 6531. The work of Hatice Gunes is partially supported by the EPSRC MAPTRAITS Project (Grant Ref: EP/K017500/1). The work of Oya Aran is supported by the Swiss National Science Foundation (SNSF) Ambizione fellowship under the project "Multimodal Computational Modeling of Nonverbal Social Behavior in Face to Face Interaction"(SOBE).

References

1. Avci, U., Passerini, A.: A fully unsupervised approach to activity discovery. In: Salah, A.A., Hung, H., Aran, O., Gunes, H. (eds.) HBU 2013. LNCS, vol. 8212, pp. 77–88. Springer, Heidelberg (2013)
2. Bachour, K., Kaplan, F., Dillenbourg, P.: An interactive table for supporting participation balance in face-to-face collaborative learning. IEEE Transactions on Learning Technologies 3(3), 203–213 (2010)
3. Baumgartner, T., Esslen, M., Jäncke, L.: From emotion perception to emotion experience: Emotions evoked by pictures and classical music. International Journal of Psychophysiology 60(1), 34–43 (2006)

4. Baur, T., Damian, I., Lingenfelser, F., Wagner, J., André, E.: NovA: Automated analysis of nonverbal signals in social interactions. In: Salah, A.A., Hung, H., Aran, O., Gunes, H. (eds.) HBU 2013. LNCS, vol. 8212, pp. 160–171. Springer, Heidelberg (2013)
5. Beesley, P.: Hylozoic soil. Leonardo 42(4), 360–361 (2009)
6. Benitti, F.B.V.: Exploring the educational potential of robotics in schools: A systematic review. Computers & Education 58(3), 978–988 (2012)
7. Bloom, V., Makris, D., Argyriou, V.: Dynamic feature selection for online action recognition. In: Salah, A.A., Hung, H., Aran, O., Gunes, H. (eds.) HBU 2013. LNCS, vol. 8212, pp. 64–76. Springer, Heidelberg (2013)
8. Boerman, H., Bergman, T., Pieters, J., Reitsma, L., van den Hoven, E.: Sissy: an interactive installation with a personality. In: OZCHI Workshop Proceedings - The Body In Design, pp. 1–4 (2011)
9. Conigliaro, D., Setti, F., Bassetti, C., Ferrario, R., Cristani, M.: ATTENTO: ATTENTion Observed for automated spectator crowd monitoring. In: Salah, A.A., Hung, H., Aran, O., Gunes, H. (eds.) HBU 2013. LNCS, vol. 8212, pp. 102–111. Springer, Heidelberg (2013)
10. Dautenhahn, K., Werry, I.: Towards interactive robots in autism therapy: Background, motivation and challenges. Pragmatics & Cognition 12(1), 1–35 (2004)
11. D'Errico, F., Leone, G., Poggi, I.: Types of help in the teacher"s multimodal behavior. In: Salah, A.A., Gevers, T., Sebe, N., Vinciarelli, A. (eds.) HBU 2010. LNCS, vol. 6219, pp. 125–139. Springer, Heidelberg (2010)
12. Deweppe, A., Diniz, N., Coussement, P., Leman, M.: A methodological framework for the development and evaluation of user-centered art installations. Journal of Interdisciplinary Music Studies 5(1), 19–39 (2011)
13. Dillenbourg, P., Evans, M.: Interactive tabletops in education. International Journal of Computer-Supported Collaborative Learning 6(4), 491–514 (2011), http://dx.doi.org/10.1007/s11412-011-9127-7
14. Dornaika, F., Bosgahzadeh, A., Raducanu, B.: Efficient graph construction for label propagation based multi-observation face recognition. In: Salah, A.A., Hung, H., Aran, O., Gunes, H. (eds.) HBU 2013. LNCS, vol. 8212, pp. 124–135. Springer, Heidelberg (2013)
15. Drira, H., Amor, B.B., Daoudi, M., Berretti, S.: A dense deformation field for facial expression analysis in dynamic sequences of 3D scans. In: Salah, A.A., Hung, H., Aran, O., Gunes, H. (eds.) HBU 2013. LNCS, vol. 8212, pp. 148–159. Springer, Heidelberg (2013)
16. Druin, A., Hendler, J.A.: Robots for kids: Exploring new technologies for learning experiences. Morgan Kaufmann (2000)
17. Eriksson, J., Mataric, M.J., Winstein, C.J.: Hands-off assistive robotics for post-stroke arm rehabilitation. In: 9th International Conference on Rehabilitation Robotics, ICORR 2005, pp. 21–24. IEEE (2005)
18. Fourati, N., Pelachaud, C.: Head, shoulders and hips behaviors during turning. In: Salah, A.A., Hung, H., Aran, O., Gunes, H. (eds.) HBU 2013. LNCS, vol. 8212, pp. 223–234. Springer, Heidelberg (2013)
19. Gardair, C., Healey, P.G., Welton, M.: Performing places. In: Proceedings of the 8th ACM Conference on Creativity and Cognition, pp. 51–60. ACM, New York (2011), http://doi.acm.org/10.1145/2069618.2069629
20. Glowinski, D., Coletta, P., Volpe, G., Camurri, A., Chiorri, C., Schenone, A.: Multiscale entropy analysis of dominance in social creative activities. In: Proceedings of the International Conference on Multimedia, MM 2010, pp. 1035–1038. ACM, New York (2010), http://doi.acm.org/10.1145/1873951.1874143

21. Görer, B., Salah, A., Akın, H.: A robotic fitness coach for the elderly. In: Int. Joint Conf. on Ambient Intelligence (2013)

22. Hanjalic, A.: Adaptive extraction of highlights from a sport video based on excitement modeling. IEEE Transactions on Multimedia 7(6), 1114–1122 (2005)

23. Hara, K., Takemura, N., Iwai, Y., Sato, K.: Table-Top Interface Using Fingernail Images and Real Object Recognition. In: Keyson, D.V., et al. (eds.) AmI 2011. LNCS, vol. 7040, pp. 21–30. Springer, Heidelberg (2011)

24. Höök, K., Sengers, P., Andersson, G.: Sense and sensibility: evaluation and interactive art. In: Proceedings of the SIGCHI Conference on Human Factors in Computing Systems, CHI 2003, pp. 241–248. ACM, New York (2003), http://doi.acm.org/10.1145/642611.642654

25. Jovanovic, M., Starcevic, D., Minovic, M., Stavljanin, V.: Motivation and multimodal interaction in model-driven educational game design. IEEE Transactions on Systems, Man and Cybernetics, Part A: Systems and Humans 41(4), 817–824 (2011)

26. Kannetis, T., Potamianos, A.: Towards adapting fantasy, curiosity and challenge in multimodal dialogue systems for preschoolers. In: Proceedings of the 2009 International Conference on Multimodal Interfaces, ICMI-MLMI 2009, pp. 39–46. ACM, New York (2009), http://doi.acm.org/10.1145/1647314.1647324

27. Keskin, C., Kıraç, F., Kara, Y.E., Akarun, L.: Hand pose estimation and hand shape classification using multi-layered randomized decision forests. In: Fitzgibbon, A., Lazebnik, S., Perona, P., Sato, Y., Schmid, C. (eds.) ECCV 2012, Part VI. LNCS, vol. 7577, pp. 852–863. Springer, Heidelberg (2012)

28. Labov, W.: Field Methods of the Project in Linguistic Change and Variation. In: Language in Use, pp. 28–53. Prentice-Hall (1984)

29. Lang, P.: The cognitive psychophysiology of Emotion: Anxiety and the anxiety disorders. Lawrence Erlbaum, Hillside (1985)

30. Lombardi, M., Pieracci, A., Santinelli, P., Vezzani, R., Cucchiara, R.: Human behavior understanding with wide area sensing floors. In: Salah, A.A., Hung, H., Aran, O., Gunes, H. (eds.) HBU 2013. LNCS, vol. 8212, pp. 112–123. Springer, Heidelberg (2013)

31. Ma, K.-T., Sim, T., Kankanhalli, M.: VIP: An unifying formal framework for computational eye-gaze research. In: Salah, A.A., Hung, H., Aran, O., Gunes, H. (eds.) HBU 2013. LNCS, vol. 8212, pp. 209–222. Springer, Heidelberg (2013)

32. Marchegiani, L., Fafoutis, X.: A behavioral study on the effects of rock music on auditory attention. In: Salah, A.A., Hung, H., Aran, O., Gunes, H. (eds.) HBU 2013. LNCS, vol. 8212, pp. 15–26. Springer, Heidelberg (2013)

33. Matsumoto, D., Willingham, B.: The thrill of victory and the agony of defeat: spontaneous expressions of medal winners of the 2004 athens olympic games. Journal of Personality and Social Psychology 91(3), 568–581 (2006)

34. Mihoub, A., Bailly, G., Wolf, C.: Social behavior modeling based on incremental discrete hidden Markov models. In: Salah, A.A., Hung, H., Aran, O., Gunes, H. (eds.) HBU 2013. LNCS, vol. 8212, pp. 172–183. Springer, Heidelberg (2013)

35. Moreno, A., Reidsma, D., van Delden, R., Poppe, R.: Socially aware interactive playgrounds: Sensing and inducing social behavior. IEEE Pervasive Computing 12(3), 40–47 (2013)

36. Morgan, E., Gunes, H.: Human nonverbal behaviour understanding in the wild for new media art. In: Salah, A.A., Hung, H., Aran, O., Gunes, H. (eds.) HBU 2013. LNCS, vol. 8212, pp. 27–39. Springer, Heidelberg (2013)

37. Morgan, E., Gunes, H., Bryan-Kinns, N.: Measuring affect for the study and enhancement of co-present creative collaboration. In: Proc. of Int'l Conference on Affective Computing and Intelligent Interaction, ACII (2013)
38. Niewiadomski, R., Mancini, M., Baur, T., Varni, G., Griffin, H., Aung, M.S.H.: MMLI: Multimodal multiperson corpus of laughter in interaction. In: Salah, A.A., Hung, H., Aran, O., Gunes, H. (eds.) HBU 2013. LNCS, vol. 8212, pp. 184–195. Springer, Heidelberg (2013)
39. Öhman, A., Flykt, A., Esteves, F.: Emotion drives attention: detecting the snake in the grass. Journal of Experimental Psychology: General 130(3), 466–478 (2001)
40. Otsuka, Y., Inoue, T.: Designing a conversation support system in dining together based on the investigation of actual party. In: 2012 IEEE International Conference on Systems, Man, and Cybernetics (SMC), pp. 1467–1472 (2012)
41. Pfister, T., Robinson, P.: Real-time recognition of affective states from nonverbal features of speech and its application for public speaking skill analysis. IEEE Transactions on Affective Computing 2(2), 66–78 (2011)
42. Rasheed, U., Tahir, Y., Dauwels, S., Dauwels, J., Thalmann, D., Thalmann, N.: Real-time comprehensive sociometrics for two-person dialogs. In: Salah, A.A., Hung, H., Aran, O., Gunes, H. (eds.) HBU 2013. LNCS, vol. 8212, pp. 196–208. Springer, Heidelberg (2013)
43. Martínez, M.F.R., Medrano, C., Herrero, E., Orrite, C.: Transfer learning of human poses for action recognition. In: Salah, A.A., Hung, H., Aran, O., Gunes, H. (eds.) HBU 2013. LNCS, vol. 8212, pp. 89–101. Springer, Heidelberg (2013)
44. Rogers, Y., Preece, J., Sharp, H.: Interaction Design. Wiley & Sons 2011 (2007)
45. Ros, R., Demiris, Y.: Creative dance: an approach for social interaction between robots and children. In: Salah, A.A., Hung, H., Aran, O., Gunes, H. (eds.) HBU 2013. LNCS, vol. 8212, pp. 40–51. Springer, Heidelberg (2013)
46. Salah, A.A., Gevers, T., Sebe, N., Vinciarelli, A.: Challenges of human behavior understanding. In: Salah, A.A., Gevers, T., Sebe, N., Vinciarelli, A. (eds.) HBU 2010. LNCS, vol. 6219, pp. 1–12. Springer, Heidelberg (2010)
47. Samadani, A.-A., Gorbet, R., Kulić, D.: Gender differences in the perception of affective movements. In: Salah, A.A., Ruiz-del-Solar, J., Meriçli, Ç., Oudeyer, P. (eds.) HBU 2012. LNCS, vol. 7559, pp. 65–76. Springer, Heidelberg (2012)
48. Schouten, B.A., Tieben, R., van de Ven, A., Schouten, D.W.: Human behavior analysis in ambient gaming and playful interaction. In: Salah, A.A., Gevers, T. (eds.) Computer Analysis of Human Behavior, pp. 387–403. Springer, Heidelberg (2011)
49. Siegert, I., Hartmann, K., Philippou-Hübner, D., Wendemuth, A.: Human behaviour in HCI: Complex emotion detection through sparse speech features. In: Salah, A.A., Hung, H., Aran, O., Gunes, H. (eds.) HBU 2013. LNCS, vol. 8212, pp. 246–257. Springer, Heidelberg (2013)
50. Smeaton, A.F., Rothwell, S.: Biometric responses to music-rich segments in films: The cdvplex. In: Seventh International Workshop on Content-Based Multimedia Indexing, CBMI 2009, pp. 162–168. IEEE (2009)
51. Snibbe, S.S., Raffle, H.S.: Social immersive media: pursuing best practices for multi-user interactive camera/projector exhibits. In: Proceedings of the SIGCHI Conference on Human Factors in Computing Systems, CHI 2009, pp. 1447–1456. ACM, New York (2009), http://doi.acm.org/10.1145/1518701.1518920
52. Tarvainen, J., Westman, S., Oittinen, P.: Stylistic features for affect-based movie recommendations. In: Salah, A.A., Hung, H., Aran, O., Gunes, H. (eds.) HBU 2013. LNCS, vol. 8212, pp. 52–63. Springer, Heidelberg (2013)

53. Turk, M.: Multimodal interaction: A review. Pattern Recognition Letters (2013)
54. Varni, G., Volpe, G., Camurri, A.: A system for real-time multimodal analysis of nonverbal affective social interaction in user-centric media. IEEE Transactions on MultiMedia 12(6), 576–590 (2010)
55. Varni, G., Mancini, M., Volpe, G., Camurri, A.: Sync'n'Move: Social Interaction Based on Music and Gesture. In: Daras, P., Ibarra, O.M. (eds.) UCMedia 2009. LNICST, vol. 40, pp. 31–38. Springer, Heidelberg (2010)
56. Wang, W., Enescu, V., Sahli, H.: Towards real-time continuous emotion recognition from body movements. In: Salah, A.A., Hung, H., Aran, O., Gunes, H. (eds.) HBU 2013. LNCS, vol. 8212, pp. 235–245. Springer, Heidelberg (2013)
57. Watanabe, E., Ozeki, T., Kohama, T.: Extraction of relations between behaviors by lecturer and students in lectures. In: 2011 IEEE International Conference on Automatic Face Gesture Recognition and Workshops (FG 2011), pp. 945–950 (2011)
58. Whyte, W.H.: The Social Life of Small Urban Spaces. Project for Public Spaces Inc. (2001)
59. Wolf, G.: The data-driven life. The New York Times 28 (2010)
60. Woolley, A.W., Chabris, C.F., Pentland, A., Hashmi, N., Malone, T.W.: Evidence for a Collective Intelligence Factor in the Performance of Human Groups. Science 330(6004), 686–688 (2010), http://dx.doi.org/10.1126/science.1193147
61. Yüce, A., Arar, N.M., Thiran, J.P.: Multiple local curvature Gabor binary patterns for facial action recognition. In: Salah, A.A., Hung, H., Aran, O., Gunes, H. (eds.) HBU 2013. LNCS, vol. 8212, pp. 136–147. Springer, Heidelberg (2013)

A Behavioral Study on the Effects of Rock Music on Auditory Attention

Letizia Marchegiani[1] and Xenofon Fafoutis[2]

[1] Language and Speech Laboratory, Faculty of Arts,
University of Basque Country
l.marchegiani@laslab.org
[2] Department of Applied Mathematics and Computer Science,
Technical University of Denmark
xefa@dtu.dk

Abstract. We are interested in the distribution of top-down attention in noisy environments, in which the listening capability is challenged by rock music playing in the background. We conducted behavioral experiments in which the subjects were asked to focus their attention on a narrative and detect a specific word, while the voice of the narrator was masked by rock songs that were alternating in the background. Our study considers several types of songs and investigates how their distinct features affect the ability to segregate sounds. Additionally, we examine the effect of the subjects' familiarity to the music.

Keywords: Auditory Attention, Speech Intelligibility, Cocktail Party Problem.

1 Introduction

Colin Cherry coined the term *Cocktail party effect* to indicate the human ability to pay attention, in particularly noisy acoustic scenarios (like a cocktail party), to the speech of only one of the present talkers, ignoring the other sounds and voices around [6]. Knudsen defined attention as a filter between all the incoming stimuli, "selecting the information that is most relevant at any point in time" [14]. A long debate about the collocation of this filter along the perception process has raged for many years and several studies and experiments have been performed to understand how attentive mechanisms decide on the saliency of a stimulus.

Bregman claimed that the perceptual process is articulated in two phases: a preliminary separation of all the signals of the mixture in segments, on the base of the generating source, and a following grouping of the segments in streams [3]. Cusack *et al.* [7] and Carlyon [5] confirmed Bregman's findings and proved that the way in which the stimuli are organized as part of the same audio flow and the level of analysis performed on each of them, is broadly affected by attention. These assertions reduce the cocktail party effect mainly to a sound source segregation problem, opening a new perspective of investigation on which factors could influence the segregation procedure and how this ability is related to the concept of saliency.

A.A. Salah et al. (Eds.) : HBU 2013, LNCS 8212, pp. 15–26, 2013.

Cherry proposed that some specific cues could help the mental ability of isolating a single sound from the environment, such as different speaking voices, different genders of the competitive talkers (see also [9]), different accents and previous knowledge. The voice features which could facilitate the segregation process, like difference in the fundamental frequency, phase spectrum or intensity, are illustrated in [19]. The spatial location of the source also plays a crucial role (the so called *spatial unmasking*), as shown in [1] and [2]. Depending on to the nature of these factors, it is possible to analyze human attentive behavior under two different angles: a bottom-up and a top-down one. According to the bottom-up perspective, the sounds which pop out of the acoustic scene, such an ringing alarm, result to be salient. In the top-down perspective, on the other hand, saliency is driven by acquired predispositions, the presence of a task or a specific goal.

We are interested in top-down attention in a simulated cocktail party scenario, in which the listening capability is challenged by the presence of rock music in the background. We chose to begin our investigation with rock music because, in addition to its popularity, it is shown to be distracting from performing a task [18]. Studying how attention is influenced by music has significance in several domains. From one perspective, organizers of social events or DJs can choose background music with respect to its effect on the ability of the participants to communicate. Up to some extend, they might be able to direct their attention and their behavior. Furthermore, music composers can incorporate in their compositions features that attract the attention of their audience. Parente [22] explored the distracting efficacy of rock music and the influence of music preference, showing a positive effect of music liking on task performance. Later, North and Hargreaves [20] confirmed these results, making subjects play computer motor racing games either while accomplishing a backward-counting task or in the absence of it. They also demonstrated that arousing music determines a bigger confusion than less arousing music. The impact of loudness has been investigated in [26], while the effect of music tempo on reading abilities has been studied in [11].

In this paper, we analyze the distribution of attention in a noisy environment, in which the voice of interest is masked by alternating songs with specific features. In order to understand how these features affect speech intelligibility and the performance in a listening task, we carried out some behavioral experiments, asking our subjects to follow a narrative and push a button each time they hear a specific word. In particular, we investigate the influence of soft and hard rock songs, along with songs with high dynamics. The latter are songs that frequently alternate between soft and hard states multiple times throughout their duration. The effect of familiarity to the music is also examined. Our analysis is twofold. First, we investigate the influence of the temporal and spectral overlap of the narrative to the background music to exclude the case that the performance doesn't depend on auditory attention, but on the inability of the subjects to listen to the speaker. Then, we analyze the influence of the songs.

The remainder of the paper is structured as follows. Section 2 presents the selected songs and the behavioral experiments. Section 3 analyses the experimental results. Lastly, Section 4 concludes the paper.

2   Experiment Setup

The experiment aims to identify how rock music influences the performance in tasks that require attention. In a nutshell, the participants were asked to focus their attention on a narrator and identify a specific word, while in the background different songs were alternating.

The narrative was a fairy tale, entitled *The Adventures of Reddy Fox* [4]. Specifically, we used the 14 minutes out of the first five chapters of the audio-book[1]. Since it is targeted to children, the fairy tale uses simple language that is relatively easily understood by non-native English speakers. Since it is relatively easy to lose attention while performing a trivial task, the subjects were asked to identify the word *'and'*. The selected word is very common and it can be easily missed. Thus, the participants' full attention is required to successfully perform the task. Furthermore, with such a common word we avoid bottom-up cues that depend on the rarity of the sound and the possible "surprise effect", as described in [10]. The duration of the narrative was 14 minutes. During the first 2 minutes of the narrative, there was no background music. During the remaining 12 minutes, 6 songs were alternating in the background. Each song played for 2 minutes. The original story was slightly modified so that the target word, *'and'*, appears 9 or 10 times in each 2-minute time slot, resulting to a total amount of 67 word appearances.

The carefully selected songs had particular properties that affect the attention in different ways. Our primary goal, is to identify the effect of dynamics in the songs. Since unexpected sensory stimuli tend to attract the attention [10], background music with high dynamics is expected to significantly disrupt the subjects. Additionally, we consider two categories of rock music with low dynamics. The former is soft rock songs, that are characterized by low emotional intensity, clean vocals, peaceful drumming and guitars without distortion sound effects. The latter is hard rock songs, that are characterized by high emotional intensity, high-pitched screaming vocals, intense drumming and guitars with distortion sound effects. Rock songs with high dynamics tend to alternate between soft and hard states multiple times throughout their duration. We note that the terms *soft* and *hard* do not refer to particular properties of the audio, such as the volume, but rather on the aggressiveness of the performance, as this is indicated by the musical terms *piano* and *forte*. The selected songs represent these three classes of rock music, that for the remainder of the paper will be referred to as *HD* (High Dynamics), *ND* (No Distortion) and *D* (Distortion).

Apart from the song properties, we expect the subjects' familiarity to the songs to significantly affect the task performance. Such influence can be of various

---

[1] http://www.booksshouldbefree.com/book/
the-adventures-of-reddy-fox-by-thornton-w-burgess

Table 1. The rock songs selected as background music and their respective properties

Song Code	Artist	Song Title	Listeners	Dynamics	Soft / Hard
HD-NP	The Pixies	Gouge Away	320228	High	Both
HD-P	Nirvana	Smells Like Teen Spirit	1589584	High	Both
ND-NP	The National	Runaway	203268	Low	Soft
ND-P	Radiohead	Karma Police	1285583	Low	Soft
D-NP	Mother Love Bone	This is Sangrila	72672	Low	Hard
D-P	Guns 'n' Roses	Welcome to the Jungle	981998	Low	Hard

natures. For instance, a subject might feel the tendency to sing along with a favorite song or might have associated the song with specific memories. In order to identify this influence, we have selected two songs of each class, a popular and an unpopular. The unpopular songs aim to identify the influence of the song properties clean from the effects of familiarity. Then, the relative comparison to the popular songs will indicate the effects of the subject's familiarity to the songs. The popularity of the songs was assessed based on the statistics of the *Last.fm*[2] music social network. In particular, the popular songs were selected among songs that have more than 900000 unique listeners. The listeners of the unpopular songs are one order of magnitude less than the respective popular song. In an attempt to verify the validity of the song selection, the subjects were questioned to characterize their familiarity to the songs. For the remainder of the paper, a suffix on the code name of each song indicates its popularity. Specifically, *-P* indicates a popular song and *-NP* indicates an unpopular song.

Table 1 summarizes the selected songs with their respective properties. The fourth column shows the unique listeners in *Last.fm* at the time of the song selection. All songs are available in common audio / video streaming services. When mixed with the narrative, the volume of the songs was adjusted to the same level and the transition between two consecutive songs was smoothed out using fading. In particular, we adjusted the peak volume of all songs to $-6dBFS$ (while the narrative was adjusted to $-3dBFS$). Furthermore, we made sure that no word *'and'* appears in the transition between two different songs. The songs were mixed in two different orders between which, the subjects were divided. The purpose of this is to mitigate the influence of the subjects' fatigue on the results. Table 2 shows the song order as mixed with the narrative. The last column shows the total number of appearances of the word *'and'* for each 2-minute slot.

Prior to the actual experiment, the subjects were asked to do a 1-minute test experiment to get familiar with their task. The test experiment was using a different narrative and song from the actual experiment. During the actual experiment, the time the subject was clicking the button was recorded. Lastly, the subjects were allowed to pause the experiment. After the completion of the experiment, the subjects were asked to characterize their familiarity to the songs. In particular, they were asked to choose from the following options:

– Not familiar. I have never listened to the song before.
– Barely familiar. It reminds me something, but I'm not able to recognize it.

---

[2] http://www.last.fm

Table 2. Song order as mixed with the narrative

Narrative Time	Oder 1	Order 2	Words
0:00-2:00	No Music	No Music	9
2:00-4:00	HD-P	ND-P	9
4:00-6:00	ND-NP	HD-NP	10
6:00-8:00	D-NP	D-P	9
8:00-10:00	D-P	D-NP	10
10:00-12:00	ND-P	ND-NP	10
12:00-14:00	HD-NP	HD-P	10

- Quite familiar. I have listened to the song enough times and I know it sufficiently.
- Very familiar. I know the song very well and I'm able to recognize it. I have listened to it many times.

According to the answers of each subject, $0 - 3$ points were assigned to each song (0 represents zero familiarity). The normalized average value among all the subjects defines the *Familiarity Index (FAM* $\in [0, 1]$*)* of each song.

A total amount of 22 subjects (similarly to previous works on selective attention [8][23][7][17]), between $25 - 35$ years old, with no hearing, language or attentional impairment, participated in the experiment (11 subjects per song order). Their task performance, their answers to the post-questionnaire and occasional short interviews suggest that all the subjects understood their task at a sufficient level and conducted the experiment in silent environments using headphones.

3   Experimental Results and Analysis

For each subject, we consider as hits any word identification that has a timestamp within 3 seconds from the actual word appearance in the narrative. All other word identifications are considered false alarms and are excluded from the results. Figure 1 shows the total number of appearances of the target word in the narrative, as well as the total number of hits and false alarms for each song, aggregated over all the 22 subjects. The relatively high performance when no background music was present, shows that the subjects were able to perform the task. For each one of the 67 word appearances, Figure 2 shows the ratio of subjects who successfully identified the word over the total number of subjects. The analysis of the results continues as follows. First, we aim to identify if there is a significant correlation between the subjects' performance and the temporal and spectral overlap of the narrative and the background music. Assuming that such correlation doesn't exist, the relative performance variation in presence of different music can only depend on the properties of the songs.

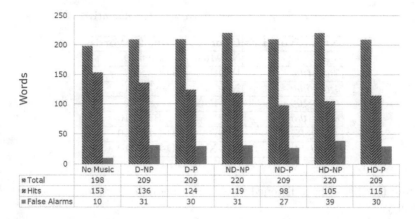

	No Music	D-NP	D-P	ND-NP	ND-P	HD-NP	HD-P
▨ Total	198	209	209	220	209	220	209
▨ Hits	153	136	124	119	98	105	115
▨ False Alarms	10	31	30	31	27	39	30

Fig. 1. Total number of word appearances and number of hits and false alarms per song aggregated all over all the subjects

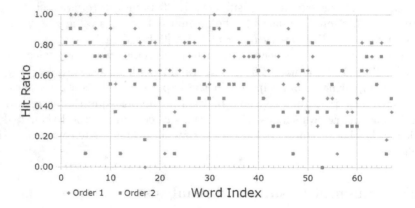

Fig. 2. Hit ratio over the total number of subjects for each of the 67 word appearances

3.1 Audibility: Spectral and Temporal Overlap

We compute the spectral and temporal overlaps introduced by the musical background, making use of the concept of Ideal Binary Mask (IBM). Wang [24] first proposed the idea of IBM as the aim of Computational Auditory Scene Analysis (CASA), in terms of extrapolation of a target signal from a mixture. Further investigations [25][13] have shown that these masks can be exploited to improve the speech reception threshold and, more generally, speech intelligibility, both in impaired and normal-hearing listeners. In [15] these results has been confirmed by exploring in more detail some of the factors which could affect these improvements. As highlighted in [24], IBMs are defined according to the nature of the signal of interest and their performance is similar to the way the human auditory system functions in the presence of masking. These characteristics are crucial for the perceptual representation and analysis of different acoustic

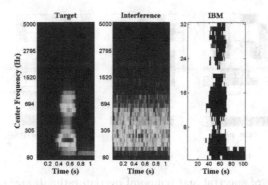

Fig. 3. Example of IBM, obtained with SNR=0 dB, LC=-4 dB, windows length=20 ms, frequency channels=32. The ones are indicated by the black bins, the zeros by the white bins.

scenarios. In [17], IBMs are used to calculate the masking between two narratives uttered by a speech synthesizer in a monaural combination. We follow the same approach to estimate spectral and temporal overlaps between the story and the songs and their relative effect on speech intelligibility.

A binary mask is a binary matrix in which 1 represents the most powerful time-frequency regions of the target signal compared to an interference signal, according to a local criteria (LC). If $T(t, f)$ and $I(t, f)$ denote the target and interference time-frequency magnitude, then the IBM is defined by the following formula.

$$\text{IBM}(t, f) = \begin{cases} 1, & \text{if } T(t, f) - I(t, f) > LC \\ 0, & \text{otherwise} \end{cases} \tag{1}$$

In Figure 3, an example of the IBM relative to one of the 'and' in the story is shown. The spectrograms of a target sound signal (the story) is compared to an interference signal and the regions of the target with the highest energy are kept in the resultant IBM. As interference signal, we use a Speech Shaped Noise (SSN) of reference. The time frequency (T-F) representation is based on the model of the human cochlea, by the use of gammatone filtering (see [16]). The parameters controlling the structure of the binary masks are, apart from the LC, the windows length (WL) and the number of frequency channels (FC).

We estimate the masking between each audio frame containing the word 'and' in the story and the respective frame in the song sequence. We use the definition of overlaps given in [17], which are based on the comparison between the IBMs correspondent to each pair of frames. The spectral overlap is determined by the co-occurrence of black bins in the two binary masks over the total number of time-frequency bins. The temporal overlap is obtained by compressing the IBMs over frequency, assigning value 1 if there is at least a black slot in one of the relative frequency bins and 0 otherwise (0 is considered as silence). The resulting binary vectors, named Compressed Ideal Binary Masks (CIBM) are

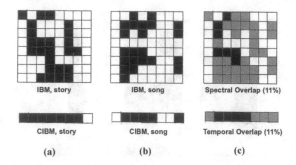

Fig. 4. An example of spectral and temporal overlap estimation. Only black regions represent overlapped parts on (c).

compared and the amount of temporal overlap is given again by the number of co-occurrence of black bins on the CIBMs over the total number of bins in the vectors. Figure 4 illustrates the temporal and spectral overlap definitions.

Initially, we compute the overlap between each word 'and' and the background music using IBMs with the following parameters: $SNR = 0\ dB$, $LC = -4\ dB$, $WL = 20\ ms$ and $FC = 32$. We consider the total number of times each word 'and' has been correctly detected as a measure of speech intelligibility. The results suggest small positive correlation between the spectral overlap (0.08 for the first order and 0.056 for the second) and the subjects' performance, as well as small negative correlation between the temporal overlap (-0.103 for the first order and -0.056 for the second) and the subjects' performance. The results are validated using a permutation test with 10000 resamples, at 5% significance level, which indicates no significant correlation ($p > 0.22$). We, then, optimize the parameters of the IBMs (LC, WL and FC) keeping $SNR = 0$ to maximize the correlation and apply again a permutation test with 10000 resamples at the same significance level. The test shows no significant correlation even in the case of optimized parameters ($p > 0.11$). Therefore, there is no significant correlation between the masking level and the ability of the subjects to identify the requested words and the difference in the performance of the subjects can only be attributed to the song properties.

3.2   Analysis of Song Influence

Using the answers of the post-questionnaire regarding the familiarity of each subject to each song, we calculate the *Familiarity Index (FAM)* of each song, as described in Section 2. Table 3 shows the familiarity index of each song in comparison to the number of unique *Last.fm* listeners that we used to define their popularity. The results suggest that our subject's familiarity to the songs matches their popularity. An ANOVA test on FAM shows significant ($p < 10^{-10}$) difference between popular and unpopular songs.

Table 3. The familiarity of the subjects to the songs matches their popularity

Song Code	Listeners	FAM
HD-NP	320228	0.41
HD-P	1589584	0.8
ND-NP	203268	0.33
ND-P	1285583	0.55
D-NP	72672	0.15
D-P	981998	0.79

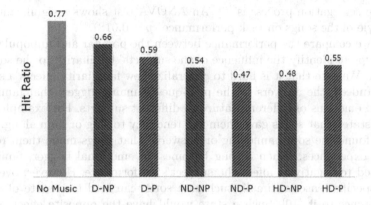

Fig. 5. Average hit ratio of the subjects for each song

Figure 5 shows the average hit ratio of the 22 subjects for each song. We note that the performance variation between different songs is at the same order of magnitude as the difference of the performance between no music and music, which indicates its significance. Furthermore, we performed an ANOVA test which shows that the difference between the various backgrounds is significant ($p < 0.0001$).

Since the unpopular songs can be characterized as unfamiliar to the subjects, a comparison between them would expose the influence of background music on attention solely based on the song properties. Observe that the subjects' performance in the song with high dynamics (HD-NP) is significantly lower than the respective songs with low dynamics (D-NP and ND-NP). High dynamics in music are shown to attract significantly the attention of the subjects. Since the subjects are unfamiliar with the song, the frequent and sudden changes in the song's dynamics are unexpected and, thus, distract the subjects from their task. The relative comparison between the two songs with low dynamics suggests that hard rock music (D-NP) attracts the attention at a lower level compared to softer rock music (ND-NP). This phenomenon happens because distorted music is perceived by the human mind as more noisy. Thus, the human mind is significantly more capable to differentiate it from the narrator's voice and ignore it. On the soft song, on the other hand, the background music is much more

Table 4. List of common mistakes

Time	Subjects	Actual Text
6:03	12	"End of"
12:28	11	"in broad"
5:00	9	"As she"
8:19	8	"that he"

similar to the narrator's voice and it is harder for the human mind to separate them. Indeed, the greater the difference between the features of two sounds, the easier the segregation process is [6]. An ANOVA test shows a significant effect of the style of the songs on task performance ($p = 0.018$).

Next, we compare the performance between the popular and unpopular song of each type to identify the influence of the subjects' familiarity to the songs on attention. We note that it is hard to generalize how familiarity affects a specific subject. Indeed, the answers to the post-questionnaire suggest that familiarity generated emotions of different nature to different subjects. For example, some subjects stated that songs gave them the tendency to sing or hum along. Other subjects found the songs annoying or answered that songs made them remember past experiences. When a song becomes an emotional trigger, familiarity is expected to negatively affect the subject's performance. However, overexposure to specific sensory stimuli, such as a song, can lead to a state of apathy or indifference to it [10]. Such a state would have the opposite effect on task performance. Nevertheless, our results indicate that in the songs with low dynamics (D-NP, D-P, ND-NP, D-NP), the subjects' familiarity to the music acts as an emotional trigger that attracts the attention. Interestingly, the results in the songs with high dynamics (HD-NP, HD-P) indicate the opposite. Given the subjects' familiarity to the song (HD-P), the frequent and sudden changes in the song's dynamics cannot be considered unexpected. Contrary to the respective unpopular song (HD-NP), the sudden changes in the dynamics are anticipated by the subjects who are more capable to keep their attention on their task.

Lastly, we noticed that there are some common mistakes among the subjects. Table 4 summarizes how many subjects did the specific common mistake. The last column indicates what the narrator actually said instead of the word 'and' as perceived by some of the subjects. The coherent confusion, that can be attributed to the phonetic similarities of the words, suggests that some subjects were focused on catching words, rather than semantically interpreting the meaning of what they were listening to. Attentive mechanisms are responsible of allocating resources, assigning saliency and deciding on the level of analysis required for each stimulus, according to task difficulty. Therefore, it would be interesting to understand if subjects' behavior was a strategy to better accomplish the task or if the complexity of the task did not allow them to follow the story. It should be also noted that there were no common mistakes that were associated to the appearance of the word 'and' in the lyrics of the songs.

4 Conclusion and Future Work

We performed behavioral experiments to investigate the distribution of attention in a simulated cocktail party scenario, characterized by the presence of rock music in the background. The subjects were asked to identify a specific words from a narrative while different songs were sequentially playing in the background. We showed that some specific features of the songs result to be more confusing than others while performing the assigned task, giving hints about the distracting power of some particular kinds of songs (D, ND, HD). Further analysis could be carried out in the future to analyze more specifically the nature of these features. Moreover, previous works (e.g. [21]) proved that attention can be highly influenced by the emotional state induced in the subject by a stimulus. With regards to arousal aspects, for example, provocative stimuli that are able to induce surprise or fears, are easily detectable even in situations in which the subject is exposed to a strong cognitive load because of another task that requires attention. Other investigations [12] provided a characterization of emotional associations which could be generated by music and triggered by particular acoustic features, drawing to a classification of songs on the base of these associations. Therefore, we plan to explore how the emotional character of the songs (considering both arousal and valence effects) can influence task performance. Such a study would also provide more conclusive results regarding the effects of familiarity.

References

1. Arbogast, T.L., Mason, C.R., Kidd Jr., G.: The effect of spatial separation on informational and energetic masking of speech. J. of the Acoustical Society of America 112, 2086 (2002)
2. Arbogast, T.L., Mason, C.R., Kidd Jr., G.: The effect of spatial separation on informational masking of speech in normal-hearing and hearing-impaired listeners. J. of the Acoustical Society of America 117, 2169 (2005)
3. Bregman, A.S.: Auditory Scene Analysis: The perceptual organization of sound. The MIT Press (1994)
4. Burgess, T.W.: The Adventures of Reddy the Fox. Little Brown and Company (1923)
5. Carlyon, R.P.: How the brain separates sounds. Trends in Cognitive Sciences 8(10), 465–471 (2004)
6. Cherry, E.C.: Some experiments on the recognition of speech, with one and with two ears. J. of the Acoustical Society of America 25, 975 (1953)
7. Cusack, R., Deeks, J., Aikman, G., Carlyon, R.P., et al.: Effects of location, frequency region, and time course of selective attention on auditory scene analysis. J. of Experimental Psychology-Human Perception and Performance 30(4), 643–655 (2004)
8. Darwin, C.J., Brungart, D.S., Simpson, B.D.: Effects of fundamental frequency and vocal-tract length changes on attention to one of two simultaneous talkers. The Journal of the Acoustical Society of America 114, 2913 (2003)

9. Drullman, R., Bronkhorst, A.W.: Multichannel speech intelligibility and talker recognition using monaural, binaural, and three-dimensional auditory presentation. J. of the Acoustical Society of America 107, 2224 (2000)
10. Itti, L., Baldi, P.: Bayesian surprise attracts human attention. Advances in Neural Inform. Process. Syst. 18, 547 (2006)
11. Kallinen, K.: Reading news from a pocket computer in a distracting environment: effects of the tempo of background music. Comput. in Human Behavior 18(5), 537–551 (2002)
12. Kim, Y.E., Schmidt, E.M., Migneco, R., Morton, B.G., Richardson, P., Scott, J., Speck, J.A., Turnbull, D.: Music emotion recognition: A state of the art review. In: Proc. ISMIR, pp. 255–266. Citeseer (2010)
13. Kjems, U., Boldt, J.B., Pedersen, M.S., Lunner, T., Wang, D.: Role of mask pattern in intelligibility of ideal binary-masked noisy speech. J. of the Acoustical Society of America 126, 1415 (2009)
14. Knudsen, E.I.: Fundamental components of attention. Annu. Reviews Neuroscience 30, 57–78 (2007)
15. Li, N., Loizou, P.C.: Factors influencing intelligibility of ideal binary-masked speech: Implications for noise reduction. J. of the Acoustical Society of America 123, 1673 (2008)
16. Lyon, R.: A computational model of filtering, detection, and compression in the cochlea. In: Proc. IEEE Int. Conf on Acoust., Speech, and Signal Process (ICASSP), vol. 2, pp. 1282–1285. IEEE (1982)
17. Marchegiani, L., Karadogan, S.G., Andersen, T., Larsen, J., Hansen, L.K.: The role of top-down attention in the cocktail party: Revisiting cherry's experiment after sixty years. In: Proc. 10th Int. Conf. on Machine Learning and Applications and Workshops (ICMLA), vol. 1, pp. 183–188. IEEE (2011)
18. Mayheld, C., Moss, S.: Effect of music tempo on task performance. Psychological Rep. 65(3f), 1283–1290 (1989)
19. Moore, B.C., Gockel, H.: Factors influencing sequential stream segregation. Acta Acustica United with Acustica 88(3), 320–333 (2002)
20. North, A.C., Hargreaves, D.J.: Music and driving game performance. Scandinavian J. of Psychology 40(4), 285–292 (1999)
21. Öhman, A., Flykt, A., Esteves, F.: Emotion drives attention: detecting the snake in the grass. J. of Experimental Psychology: General 130(3), 466 (2001)
22. Parente, J.A.: Music preference as a factor of music distraction. Perceptual and Motor Skills 43(1), 337–338 (1976)
23. Shinn-Cunningham, B.G., Ihlefeld, A.: Selective and divided attention: Extracting information from simultaneous sound sources. In: International Community for Auditory Display, ICAD (2004)
24. Wang, D.: On ideal binary mask as the computational goal of auditory scene analysis. Speech Separation by Humans and Machines 60, 63–64 (2005)
25. Wang, D., Kjems, U., Pedersen, M.S., Boldt, J.B., Lunner, T.: Speech intelligibility in background noise with ideal binary time-frequency masking. J. of the Acoustical Society of America 125, 2336 (2009)
26. Wolfe, D.E.: Effects of music loudness on task performance and self-report of college-aged students. J. of Research in Music Educ. 31(3), 191–201 (1983)

Human Nonverbal Behaviour Understanding
in the Wild for New Media Art

Evan Morgan and Hatice Gunes

School of Electronic Engineering and Computer Science
Queen Mary University of London, Mile End Road, E1 4NS, London, U.K.
{evan.morgan,hatice.gunes}@eecs.qmul.ac.uk

Abstract. Over the course of the London 2012 Olympics a large public installation took place in Central London. Its premise was to enable members of the public to express themselves by controlling the lights around the rim of the London Eye. The installation's design and development was undertaken as a collaborative project between an interactive arts studio and researchers in the field of affective and behavioural computing. Over 800 people participated, taking control of the lights using their heart rates and hand gestures. This paper approaches nonverbal and affective behaviour understanding for new media art as a case study, and reports the design of this installation and the subsequent analysis of over *one million frames* of physiological and motion capture data. In doing so it sheds light on how the intersection of affective and behavioural computing and new media art could be beneficial to both researchers and artists.

Keywords: New media art, affective behaviour understanding in the wild, gestural interaction, mood, nonverbal behaviour.

1 Introduction

New Media Art is defined as art that utilises new media, such as digital electronics, computer animation, interactive interfaces or networked communication [1]. In many cases, these media comprise the very same tools that affective and behavioural computing researchers are adopting for the computerised recognition and expression of human nonverbal behaviour and affect. Despite this plurality, there is currently very little exploration or utilisation of affective and behavioural computing techniques in artistic practices. This is surprising, given the important roles that nonverbal behaviour and affect play in creative expression and experience [2]. As affective and behavioural computing starts to migrate from the laboratory and into the wider world, the question of whether artists will welcome affective and behavioural computing based technologies as a positive addition to their new media palettes is likely to come to the fore.

During the summer of 2012 we undertook a collaborative project with Cinimod Studio - an interactive arts studio based in London. The project involved both artists and researchers in affective and behavioural computing and led to

A.A. Salah et al. (Eds.) : HBU 2013, LNCS 8212, pp. 27–39, 2013.

the design and analysis of a high profile interactive installation called the Mood Conductor. Our work was conducted *in the wild* (non-laboratory settings) and consequently this paper approaches nonverbal behaviour analysis as a case study, when subjective evaluation of the user experience cannot be obtained. We report the design of the installation and the subsequent *unsupervised* analysis of over *one million frames* of physiological and motion capture data. By presenting and discussing the processes, challenges and results of this study, we hope to provide valuable insights into the nature of the intersection of affective and behavioural computing and new media art practices.

2   Background

Physiological measurement and gesture recognition are two techniques that have been adopted by technologists, artists and researchers in order to enrich the ways we interact with computers, artworks and creative installations. However, there has been little cross-pollination of ideas between the commercial and academic worlds. While researchers attempt to identify affective states from measurable components of nonverbal behaviour and physiology, artists and technologists are creating entities that enable new forms of expression. The project discussed in this paper combined both physiological and gestural measurements in an attempt to bring an affective and behavioural dimension to a large public installation.

2.1   Heart Rate Measures, Affect and Art

In the field of psychophysiology many studies have been carried out which attempt to quantify the physiological aspects of different emotions [3–5]. The most commonly measured variables are galvanic skin response (sweating), breathing rate, muscle contraction, pupil dilation, and cardiac output (e.g. heart rate, blood pressure, heart rate variability) [6]. Heart related measurements are particularly attractive to affective and behavioural computing researchers due to the fact that changes in cardiac output occur very quickly in response to external stimuli. In a study of emotional reactions to video game events Ravaja et al [7] found that phasic heart rate changes occurred in response to specific game events. Rewarding and positive game events were accompanied by an increase in heart rate, whilst the authors suggested that decreases in heart rate could be associated with a rise in attentional engagement. In relation to sadness, a study of emotion during musical performance observed a decrease in average heart rate when musicians performed under the condition of induced sadness relative to performances in which they merely expressed sadness [8]. Heart rate changes in response to negative emotional stimuli have also been found to be more prolonged when compared to equivalent exposure to positive stimuli [9]. The main challenge in using heart rate as a reliable indicator of affect is that it is necessary to control for the numerous variables that can affect a person's heart rate. These include health factors, physical exertion and the influence of drugs such as caffeine. In laboratory based experiments it is possible to account for these extra variables using controlled settings, subject profiles and questionnaires. However, if we are to use heart rate measures in media and arts applications *in the wild* there is a much greater challenge in extracting meaningful data from heart rate measures alone.

2.2   Hand Gestures, Affect and Art

One of the first gestural interfaces was the Theremin [10], a musical instrument which creates sound oscillations with varying frequency and amplitude according to the position of the player's hands relative to two antennas. The Theremin serves as a good example of the design considerations that should be made when using gestural input as a control interface. Sturman and Zeltzer [11] formalise these considerations and organise them as sequential stages in the design process. The initial stage involves assessing the *appropriateness* of whole hand input as a method of interaction by considering its distinguishing features - naturalness, adaptability, coordination and real-time control. The second stage concerns *taxonomy* - distinguishing which styles of whole-hand input will fit the application. Sturman and Zeltzer organise the expressivity of the hand into two categories - *continuous features*, which concern quantifiable measurements of the physics of the hand (e.g. force applied, and degrees of rotation); and *discrete features* that refer to symbolic 'input tokens' such as postures (e.g. thumbs-up) or gestures (e.g. waving). The third and final stage involves the matching of 'task primitives' to particular hand actions. In the case of the Theremin the primitives are pitch and amplitude adjustment, and the actions are the continuous movement of the hands in three dimensions.

In more recent years the release of open source drivers for the Microsoft Kinect has provided an accessible way for artists and interaction designers to work with motion capture based gesture recognition. When looking at examples of the use of the Kinect in these contexts (see [12] and [13] for specific works), a common feature is that less defined input to output mappings are used, an approach which puts more creative freedom in the hands of the person using the interface. The LEAP motion sensor, released in July 2013, purports to be able to measure finger movement to a resolution of 0.01 millimetres. Technologies like this will undoubtedly contribute towards on-going advances in the measurement of fine-grained gestures.

The Component Process Model (CPM) [14] breaks emotion down into five components - cognitive, neurophysiological, motivational, motor expression and subjective feeling - each with associated functions and 'organismic subsystems' [15]. The study of affective gestures relates to the motor expression component of this model - the movement of joints, muscles and limbs. In a study of the perception of affect from arm movement, Pollick et al. [16] used point-light displays to represent knocking and drinking movements, each performed with ten different affects (afraid, angry, excited, happy, neutral, relaxed, sad, strong, tired, and weak). They found that the arousal dimension [17] of each affective state had a strong correlation to kinematic features of the movement such as velocity, acceleration and jerk. Similar experiments have since supported this link between emotional arousal and motion [18, 19].

3 Design and Development

Cinimod Studio[1] were commissioned to create an installation which would enable members of the public to represent their *mood* by taking control of the lights on the London Eye. Participants would be invited free-of-charge to step onto a podium for roughly one minute, during which they would be able to use the motion of their hands to control the 320 lights which line the rim of the Eye.

3.1 Design

Simplicity was one of the main concepts that guided the design process. Given the potentially short amount of time that each participant would have to interact with the installation, the following were identified as prerequisites: (i) ensuring that the participants would not spend a majority of the time trying to understand how their movements affected the lights, and (ii) making the sense of *control* clear and powerful by focusing on direct mappings of hand and arm movements to lighting changes, as opposed to recognising and responding to specific symbolic gestures.

The Kinect SDK was used to track the position of each of the participants' hands and the centre of their body (torso). The angles between each hand and the torso (along the coronal plane) were then directly mapped to the angular positions of two segments of lighting content on the perimeter of the Eye (see Fig. 1). In order to create a robust motion tracking system the Kinect data was passed through three stages of processing: (i) detecting the current user and extracting joint coordinates (shoulder, elbow, hand, etc.), (ii) filtering to discard false participants based upon coordinate positions and quantity of motion, and (iii) smoothing the motion data and calculating hand-torso angles to be used by the lighting content generator.

Three *distinct lighting content styles* were designed in order to give some aesthetic variation to the artwork. We also wanted the variation in these styles to be somewhat representative of different mood states. The three styles were named Wave, Fire and Spectrum (see Fig. 2). *Wave* had a sense of calmness (a low arousal, high valence mood), simulating the fluidic motion caused by waving your hands in a pool of water. *Fire* gave the impression of juggling with flaming torches, which we associated with high arousal moods. *Spectrum* was the most colourful of the three and had a sparkling appearance that gave it a sense of representing high valence (positive) moods. Since the Eye was rotating during the installation, a gyroscope (positioned on the rim of the Eye) was used to sense the angle of rotation and correct the orientation of the lighting content so that it did not appear to move with the Eye.

---

[1] http://cinimodstudio.com/

The inclusion of a pulse rate sensor was intended to provide an additional, symbolic means of representing the participants' moods through the lights on the Eye. We built a custom heart rate monitor, which used a photo-plethysmographic ear-clip sensor coupled with an analog switch. The signal from this was then transmitted wirelessly (using XBee modules). The resulting device was small enough to be worn around the neck, and could be quickly transferred between participants. An additional lighting content feature was developed, allowing the participants to view their heart beats as a pulsing red strip of lights at the top of the Eye. The feature was triggered when a participant held their hands still for longer than three seconds. The software for processing the inputs from the Kinect and pulse monitor was developed using VVVV, a visual programming environment which has inbuilt support for Kinect, as well as DMX protocol lighting output. An overview of the full system is given in Fig. 1.

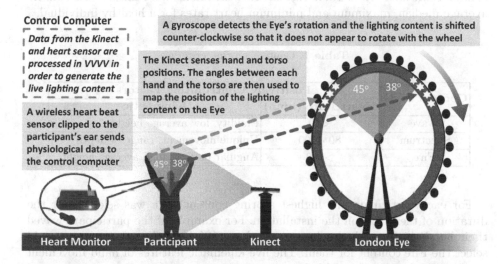

Control Computer

Data from the Kinect and heart sensor are processed in VVVV in order to generate the live lighting content

A wireless heart beat sensor clipped to the participant's ear sends physiological data to the control computer

A gyroscope detects the Eye's rotation and the lighting content is shifted counter-clockwise so that it does not appear to rotate with the wheel

The Kinect senses hand and torso positions. The angles between each hand and the torso are then used to map the position of the lighting content on the Eye

45°   38°

45° 38°

Heart Monitor   Participant   Kinect   London Eye

Fig. 1. System diagram detailing the basic setup and functioning of the installation

Fig. 2. Content styles: (from left) Wave, Spectrum, Fire, Wave with heart pulse feature

3.2 Mood Profiling

We decided to assign a fixed content style to each participant. It would be confusing if the content style changed, especially given the short time people had to explore the installation. As previously discussed, heart rate and kinematic features of gesture have been shown to be linked to the arousal dimension of affect. By analysing each participant's initial motion and heart rate data, we created a snapshot profile of their mood state which was then used to select the content style.

The profiling was performed at the beginning of each participant's turn (first 5 sec). Content choice was implemented by assigning a score to each of the three content styles based upon weighted contributions of six features: the *average heart rate* and five kinematic variables - *fluidity, angular motion, range of depth, average height and unique movement.* The contribution of these factors to each content score is shown in Table 1. Heart rate thresholds were chosen based on the average median, maximum and minimum heart rates for a healthy individual.

Table 1. Content scoring criteria

Content Style	Positively Contributing Factors	
	Heart Rate (bpm)	Kinematic
Wave	<80	Fluidity, low average height
Spectrum	80 - 100	Unique movement, range of depth
Fire	>100	Angular motion, high average height

For each participant the highest scoring content style was selected for the duration of their turn on the installation. For example, if the participant waved their hands high and had a heart rate above 100 bpm then the system would select the Fire content for them. The five kinematic features of hand movement are described in more detail below.

1. **Fluidity(flu):** A measure of the uniformity of motion [18], calculated based upon the variance in the first n velocity values for each hand,

$$flu = \frac{1}{n} \sum_{i=1}^{n} (v(i) - \mu)^2 \qquad (1)$$

   where μ is the average velocity over first n samples and $v(i)$ is the *velocity* at sample i:

$$v(i) = \frac{\sqrt{(x_i - x_{i+1}))^2 + (y_i - y_{i+1})^2 + (z_i - z_{i+1})^2)}}{t_{i+1} - t_i} \qquad (2)$$

   $(x_i, y_i z_i)$ are the $3D$ coordinates of the hand at sample i, and t_i is the time at sample i.

2. **Angular motion** (m_α): A measure of amount of rotational movement of the arms, calculated by finding the range in the first n angle values.

$$m_\alpha = \max_{i=1}^{n}(\alpha(i)) - \min_{i=1}^{n}(\alpha(i)) \tag{3}$$

where $\alpha(i)$ is the angle value for the ith sample:

$$\alpha = \arctan 2(y_h - y_t, x_h - x_t) \tag{4}$$

(x_h, y_h) is the $2D$ position coordinates of left or right hand, and (x_t, y_t) is the $2D$ position coordinates of the torso.

3. **Range of depth**(rd): Calculated as the maximum range in the first n depth range values along the Z axis (depth) for each hand.

$$rd = \max_{i=1}^{n}(z(i)) - \min_{i=1}^{n}(z(i)) \tag{5}$$

4. **Average height**(h): Calculated as the average of first n height values along the Y axis (vertical) for each hand.

$$h = \frac{1}{n}\sum_{i=1}^{n} y(i) \tag{6}$$

5. **Unique movement**: A measure of the uniqueness of the hand movement during a given sampling period. This was calculated using a function in *VVVV* which outputs the number of unique coordinates in an array containing all of the hand coordinates over n samples. For example, if someone kept their hand still for the duration of the sampling period then there would only be one unique coordinate value (uniqueness = 1), whereas if they waved their hand between multiple positions the uniqueness value would be greater, reflecting the number of positions their hand covered.

4   Data Analysis and Results

Due to the restrictions of collecting data *in the wild* we were aware that our ability to draw significant conclusions from our data analysis would be somewhat restricted. For example, we were unable to collect video data or subjective feedback from participants. Consequently we approached our data analysis with an intention to broadly investigate the outcomes of applying affective and behavioural computing inspired techniques in a real-world interactive media and arts context. More specifically, the goal was (i) to explore the potential of using unsupervised data analysis techniques for new media art and design, and (ii) to contrast the embedded intentions in the design of this specific installation to the actual outcomes of it, in terms of recorded participant behaviours. The data collected over the course of the installation amounted to over *one million frames* of motion capture and physiological data from over *800 individuals*.

In the following section we analyse the data acquired under (i) spatial analysis, (ii) physiological and kinematic analysis, and (iii) gestural analysis categories.

4.1 Spatial Analysis

The goal of the spatial analysis was to obtain an overview of how the motion capture data was spread spatially. We achieved this by using histogram images to represent the spread of data in both the X-Y (face-on) and Z-Y (side-on) planes. The histogram images were generated by (i) separating the coordinate space into a two dimensional grid and creating a corresponding array (where the row and column numbers corresponded to the centre coordinates of each grid element), (ii) summing up the number of times that hand coordinates appeared in each grid element, and (iii) plotting the array as an image to distinguish them in terms of different intensity values. To account for variations in hand position due to differences in where the participants were standing, we scaled all of the hand coordinates relative to the coordinates for the centre of the participant's body. Figure 3(a) shows the histogram generated for the frontal (X-Y) plane using the right hand coordinates for all data frames. it indicates that right hand motion was predominantly situated in a semi-circular pathway about the centre of the participant, corresponding to outstretched arm movement, pivoting at the shoulder.

When analysing the images for the side-on (Z-Y) plane, we observed little variation in depth, which showed that the movement predominantly occurred in the coronal plane. When comparing the left and right hand histogram images we observed that the spread of motion was much more restricted for the left hand, suggesting that *handedness* influenced how people interacted with the installation. By applying a lower threshold to the histogram values (for both hands), we created a scatter plot of the most common hand positions. We then used a mixture of Gaussian clustering algorithm to outline the overall use of the interaction space and regions where hand motion was most frequent (Fig. 3 (b)).

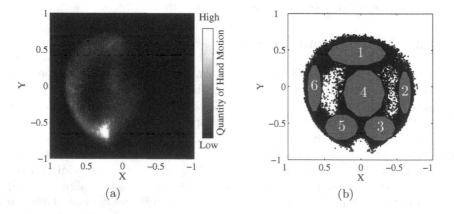

(a)   (b)

Fig. 3. (a) Right-hand X-Y histogram image. (b) Mixture of Gaussian plot showing six regions where hand motion was most prevalent: horizontally outstretched (2 & 6), above the head (1), down by the thighs (3 & 5), and in front of the torso (4)

4.2   Physiological and Kinematic Analysis

From the motion capture data we were able to extract two temporal features of the hand movements, variation in velocity and variation in angle. Velocity was calculated as described in (2) and angle was calculated based on (4) using the X-Y coordinates of each hand relative to the centre of the hip.

Figure 4(a) provides a typical plot of the velocity profile for a single participant's right and left hands, over an eight second window. It shows a high degree of *synchrony* in the timing of the movements of the left hand and the movements of the right hand. Figure 4(b) shows the angle of each hand over the same time window. It reveals that although the movement timing was synchronous, the relative hand positions are either *in phase* or *out of phase*, corresponding to symmetrical and non-symmetrical movement.

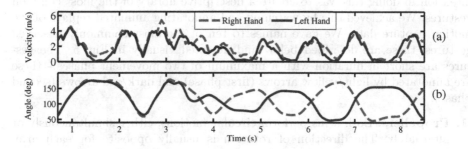

Fig. 4. Plots of right and left hand velocity (a) and angle (b) profiles for a single participant over an eight second window

We were also interested in exploring potential links between participants' behaviour and the content style they were interacting with. We separated the data according to which content style was active when it was recorded, then we compared averaged spatial, kinematic and physiological features of the data sets. The results for hand height (Y position), velocity and average heart rate are shown in Table 2. The hand data sample sizes were 104, 133 and 111 participants for the Wave, Spectrum, and Fire content styles respectively. This is less than the total number of participants because we only selected participants with at least one minute of data, using the first minute (1500 samples) for our analysis. The heart rate data sample sizes were 29, 42 and 34 due to discarding participants with intermittent readings.

These results suggest that participants interacting with the Spectrum content behaved more energetically, indicated by their higher average heart rate and hand velocity. However participants interacting with the Fire content had the highest average hand position. The latter result concurs with our selection criteria, which used hand height as a positive bias towards selection of the Fire content style.

Table 2. Average right hand (RH) motion and heart rate values separated by content style (standard deviation shown in parenthesis)

Content Style	RH height (m)	RH Velocity (m/s)	Heart Rate (bpm)
Wave	-0.09 (0.45)	1.49 (1.67)	94 (13)
Spectrum	-0.08 (0.42)	1.85 (1.83)	102 (13)
Fire	0.01 (0.43)	1.52 (1.50)	97 (17)

4.3   Gestural Analysis

In contrast to the numerically oriented analysis above, we also manually analysed the gestures which participants on the Mood Conductor performed. The intention in doing this was to create a descriptive library of the most common gestures. We achieved this by watching and annotating animated replays of the motion capture data. We gave names to ten of the most commonly observed gestures, these are described below and depicted visually in Fig. 5. The gestures are short in duration with a maximum of two movement phases - these are annotated by light/yellow arrows (first phase) and dark/red arrows (second phase).

1. **Propellers:** Both arms perform circular motions, either simultaneously or alternately. The direction of rotation is usually opposite for each arm, however this may be changeable.
2. **Sway:** Both arms perform a simultaneous left-right/right-left swaying motion above the head.
3. **Flag:** One extended arm performs an up/down flagging motion whilst the other arm is stationary at the participants side. This may also be performed as a single slow movement from the low to high position or vice versa.
4. **Seesaw:** Extended left and right hands move up and down simultaneously but in opposite directions.
5. **Hands Together:** Both hands are held together and circular motions are performed with extended arms.
6. **Angel:** Both extended arms move slowly up and down in synchrony.
7. **270°:** One arm moves through 270° in a circular path from the participants side to a horizontal position across the body. The other arm is stationary.
8. **Traffic Control:** One arm is extended vertically above the head and the other horizontally out to one side. Only one arm moves at a time, either the horizontal arm moves upwards to a vertical position or the vertical arm moves to a horizontal position.
9. **Wave:** Both arms perform a synchronous waving motion above the head, symmetrical about the sagittal plane.
10. **Wheel:** One arm moves in an extended and continuous circular motion, either clockwise or anticlockwise.

Fig. 5. Catalogue of ten of the most commonly observed gestures. Light/yellow and dark/red arrows indicate initial and secondary movement phases respectively.

5 Discussion

How do people formulate an understanding of how to interact, and what gestures do they choose given the unfamiliarity of an interface? From his studies of interactive installations Wei [20] observed that the absence of rules often encourages participants to experiment and invent new meaningful gestures that are given significance by the corresponding changes in the experienced output - a process he termed *neosemy*. Our study attempted a detailed and data-driven investigation of how humans behave when confronted with such novel gesture-based interaction opportunities. By employing various methods of analysis we were able to describe and quantify this behaviour from different perspectives.

The spatial analysis showed that the majority of hand movements occurred along a circular pathway centred on the participants' torsos. It may seem trivial to conclude that this was related to the circular shape of the London Eye. However, it leads us to question the extent to which more complex shapes might influence the perceived interaction space in situations where the gestural interface allows free movement.

By plotting velocity and angle profiles for individual participants we were able to reveal and quantify certain kinematic features of the interaction. In particular we observed highly coordinated phase/anti-phase relationships between participants' left and right hands. This synchronised coupling of hand motion has been observed in previous studies [21]. It also relates to the notion of *movement qualities* - the characterisation of movements according to their temporal features (dynamics), independent of spatial trajectories and shapes [22]. There is certainly scope for further analysis in this area.

When coupling the kinematic results with the heart rate data, our findings suggested that people's average behaviour differed according to the content style they were interacting with. We found that participants interacting with the Spectrum content behaved differently to those interacting with the other two content styles. It is not possible to draw any definite conclusions as to why this was, however the Spectrum content did exhibit more colour variation than the other two content styles. Due to the limitations of collecting data in the wild, we were unable to obtain detailed and in-depth insight into this data, as we did not have access to subjective reports of mood from the participants.

In our analysis of common gestures we were surprised by the frequency at which gestures re-occurred between nights and participants, especially in the absence of any instruction as to how to interact with the installation. There are a number of features that are common to most of these gestures: (i) they tend to be performed in the coronal plane, potentially due to the fact that the main interaction control was also based upon movement in this plane, (ii) they are predominantly performed with extended arms and do not involve much movement of the body, and (iii) each gesture comprises relatively short and repeatable movements that exhibit high degrees of rhythm, synchrony and symmetry.

6   Conclusion

The London Eye Mood Conductor project allowed us to practically explore the intersection of human nonverbal behaviour research and new media art while providing the opportunity to collaborate with artists and design a novel installation which facilitated the collection of data in the *wild*. Consequently, we were able to demonstrate how a varied and quantitative analysis of such data can reveal potentially interesting aspects of human behaviour and affective expression in the context of interactions with new media art. The premise of the installation - to let people represent their mood by controlling the lights on the London Eye - meant that it was particularly amenable to such an investigation. Having said this, it could be argued that a desire to invoke nonverbal behaviour and affective engagement is inherent in the majority of interactive and new media artworks. Given the increasing prevalence of such works, there is a great opportunity for researchers and artists to engage in collaborative studies. For the artist, affective behaviour analysis techniques can facilitate the creation of artworks that are human-centred, where our reaction to the work is juxtaposed with the work's reaction to us. For the researcher, one of main advantages of these studies is the availability of large amounts of naturalistic data, which would be difficult to obtain in laboratory-based experiments. The results of our analysis showed that such data presents new challenges when it comes to the analysis and extraction of meaningful results. Tackling these challenges will be a necessary and important step in affective behaviour understanding *in the wild* for new media art applications.

Acknowledgments. We would like to thank Dominic Harris and Cinimod Studio Ltd for making this project possible. Evan Morgan's work is supported by the Media and Arts Technology Programme, an RCUK Doctoral Training Centre in the Digital Economy. The work of Hatice Gunes is partially supported by the EPSRC MAPTRAITS Project (Grant Ref: EP/K017500/1).

References

1. Tribe, M., Jana, R.: New Media Art. Taschen (2006)
2. Isen, A.M., Daubman, K.A., Nowicki, G.P.: Positive affect facilitates creative problem solving. J. of Personality & Social Psychology 52(6), 1122–1131 (1987)
3. Kim, J., André, E.: Emotion recognition based on physiological changes in music listening. IEEE Transactions on Pattern Analysis and Machine Intelligence 30(12), 2067–2083 (2008)
4. Kim, K.H., Bang, S.W., Kim, S.R.: Emotion recognition system using short-term monitoring of physiological signals. Medical & Biological Engineering & Computing 42(3), 419–427 (2004)
5. Picard, R., Vyzas, E., Healey, J.: Toward machine emotional intelligence: analysis of affective physiological state. IEEE Transactions on Pattern Analysis and Machine Intelligence 23(10), 1175–1191 (2001)
6. Allanson, J., Fairclough, S.H.: A research agenda for physiological computing. Interacting with Computers 16(5), 857–878 (2004)
7. Ravaja, N., Saari, T., Salminen, M., Laarni, J., Kallinen, K.: Phasic emotional reactions to video game events: A psychophysiological investigation. Media Psychology 8(4), 343–367 (2006)
8. Knapp, R.B., Jaimovich, J., Coghlan, N.: Measurement of motion and emotion during musical performance. In: 2009 3rd International Conference on Affective Computing and Intelligent Interaction and Workshops, pp. 1–5. IEEE (September 2009)
9. Anttonen, J., Surakka, V.: Emotions and heart rate while sitting on a chair. In: Proc. CHI, p. 491 (2005)
10. Billinghurst, M.: Gesture based interaction. In: Haptic Input, pp. 1–35 (2011)
11. Sturman, D.J., Zeltzer, D.: A design method for whole-hand human-computer interaction. ACM Tran. on Information Systems 11(3), 219–238 (1993)
12. Castro, B.P., Velho, L., Kosminsky, D.: Integrarte: digital art using body interaction. In: Proc. of the Annual Symposium on Computational Aesthetics in Graphics, Visualization, and Imaging, pp. 11–15 (2012)
13. Visnjic, F., Smith, G.J., Scholz, A.: Creative applications (2013)
14. Scherer, K.R.: Emotion as a Multicomponent Process: A model and some cross-cultural data. Review of Personality and Social Psychology 5, 37–63 (1984)
15. Fox, E.: Emotion Science Cognitive and Neuroscientific Approaches to Understanding Human Emotions. Palgrave Macmillan (September 2008)
16. Pollick, F.E., Paterson, H.M., Bruderlin, A., Sanford, A.J.: Perceiving affect from arm movement. Cognition 82(2), B51–B61 (2001)
17. Russell, J.A.: A circumplex model of affect. J. of Personality & Social Psychology 39(6), 1161–1178 (1980)
18. Castellano, G., Villalba, S.D., Camurri, A.: Recognising human emotions from body movement and gesture dynamics. In: Paiva, A.C.R., Prada, R., Picard, R.W. (eds.) ACII 2007. LNCS, vol. 4738, pp. 71–82. Springer, Heidelberg (2007)
19. Saerbeck, M., Bartneck, C.: Perception of affect elicited by robot motion. In: Proc. of ACM/IEEE Int'l Conf. on Human-Robot Interaction, pp. 53–60 (2010)
20. Wei, S.X.: Resistance is fertile: Gesture and agency in the field of responsive media. Configurations 10(3), 439–472 (2002)
21. Haken, H., Kelso, J.A.S., Bunz, H.: A theoretical model of phase transitions in human hand movements. Biological Cybernetics 51(5), 347–356 (1985)
22. Alaoui, S.F., Caramiaux, B., Serrano, M., Bevilacqua, F.: Movement qualities as interaction modality. In: Proceedings of the Designing Interactive Systems Conference on DIS 2012, pp. 761–769. ACM Press, New York (2012)

Creative Dance: An Approach for Social Interaction between Robots and Children

Raquel Ros and Yiannis Demiris

Imperial College London, SW7 2BT, London, UK
{raquel.ros,y.demiris}@imperial.ac.uk

Abstract. In this paper we discuss the potential of using a dance robot tutor with children in the context of creative dance to study child-robot interaction through several encounters. We have taken part of dance sessions in order to extract strategies and models to inspire and justify the design of a robot dance tutor. Moreover, we present implementation details and preliminary results on a pilot study to extract initial feedback to further improve and test our system with a broader children population.

Keywords: child-robot interaction, creative dance, long-term interaction, edutainment.

1 Introduction

Dance is considered an entertaining activity that allows children to easily engage [14], probably due to the involvement of body movement during the activity which in turn increases enjoyment [2]. But more importantly it *i*) stimulates physical movement, which is essential for the development of fundamental motor skills; *ii*) enhances the development of social skills, such as cooperation, coordination, sharing ideas, sharing physical space, accepting individual differences; *iii*) increases communication skills; and *iv*) promotes the development of creativity and spontaneity [13] [10]. Considered an important educational source, dance is also promoted at schools as part of their curricula (e.g. in England it is part of the Curriculum for England in Physical Education [1]). Dance is not only a good practice for children, but for people in any age range, including elderly people where it has demonstrated to have physical and psychological benefits [7].

In this paper we discuss the potential of using a dance robot tutor with children in the context of creative dance. While our ultimate goal is to study and identify the necessary social skills required to enhance interactions between humans and robots, a more specific one and directly addressed in our current work is to study the impact of creativity in a tutoring setting throughout repeated occasions (at least three different interactions).

Within this context, we believe that in order to engage and sustain interaction between children and robots, besides providing a robotic system with basic social cues (such as head movement, eye-contact, spatial-orientational arrangement, name reference, etc.), it is essential to provide space for the user to explore

A.A. Salah et al. (Eds.) : HBU 2013, LNCS 8212, pp. 40–51, 2013.

and develop its own ideas. Moreover, children are curious and therefore, tend to be more creative than adults by nature. Stimulating and rewarding curiosity is important to enhance the development of creativity [11].

Environments where the pupils are restrained to reproduce the tutor's instructions in a specific way, such as traditional dance classes, may lead pupils to an unsatisfactory state. This risk is higher in environments where the pupil performs the activity without expecting to be an expert (in this case, professional dancers). On the contrary, exploiting creativity leads to feeling more satisfied [5], which in turn, may increase the motivation and engagement in the interaction. From our previous work [12] we have observed that during the first stages of the interaction, children felt motivated and were looking forward to continuing the task. However, as the novelty effect diminished, the task became more tedious and their engagement decreased through time. Limiting the children's spontaneity was a plausible reason for this effect.

An adequate environment can provide stimuli to express ideas and thus, develop creativity [11]. In this work, we propose to use creative dance as a mean to engage the child with the robot in a creative process to explore their own body movement, while linking these ideas to a specific theme.

2   Creative Dance Framework Design

In this work we refer to creative dance as a form of dance where the goal is to explore the body movement based on a set of general guidelines (movement concepts). Thus, on the one hand creative dance provides foundations on elements of dance, movement vocabulary and locomotive skills. And on the other, it promotes creativity motivating pupils to expand and extend movement range at their own rhythm through different stimuli, such as music, emotions, visual resources and observing the creations of others.

Moreover, creative dance can be used as an instrument to convey concepts that children work in their everyday school activities. Some theme examples are the states of water, creation and evolution of volcanoes, painting styles. Since our work is part of the ALIZ-E[1] project, where the targeted children suffer from diabetes or obesity, a candidate knowledge area under investigation is nutrition and healthy diet. Dance concepts are linked to fruits, vegetables, simple/complex carbohydrates and proteins through the sessions. Children have an overview of what they are, how they benefit our body and how often we should eat them to achieve a healthy diet.

To study creative dance and to further design a robot dance tutor we recorded a series of dance sessions. While the global goal is to study interaction strategies used through time between a tutor and pupils, a more specific one within the dance context is to analyze dance methodologies and techniques to teach dance.

A professional dance teacher prepared a 5-days course where the goal was to teach creative dance linked to healthy diet. Fig. 1 depicts a snapshot of one of the sessions. Although the participants in the dance sessions were adults (PhD

---

[1] www.aliz-e.org

Fig. 1. Snapshot of a dance session with a professional dance teacher

students from the department) to allow us to reuse the collected information in our children experiments, the teacher was instructed to perform the sessions as if the they were children between 8 and 10-years-old. This had an special impact on the instructions given, where the dance teacher used simple words and examples that a population of such age would perfectly understand. However, it did not affect neither the methodology nor the movements performed during the sessions. Each participant, of any age, can perform any of the movements within its own capabilities while learning the same foundations.

2.1 Dance Sessions Observations

Sessions were recorded and transcribed to extract task-based and interaction-based features to guide the design of the dance robot. We next summarize them:

- *Domain-specific knowledge*: describing concepts to explore is essential to start creating. If no guideline is given, hardly any new movement can emerge (or quite rarely). Providing a purpose and acquiring domain-specific knowledge is required to produce creative expression [11]. Once pupils understand the concepts, they are able to create movements based on those concepts.
- *Non-verbal and verbal feedback*: While the former corresponds to performing movements (or examples of the motion), the latter corresponds to providing verbal description of the concept. Both are essential to guide the pupils' comprehension and learning. Non-verbal feedback serves as visual input providing most of the information they need to understand the concepts. Verbal feedback is useful to help children recall and name the ideas worked. Analogies are powerful descriptors easy to retain to recall the concepts taught.
- *User specific adaptation*: The teacher constantly observes and evaluates the different capabilities of the pupils. When they manage to perform a movement or sequence of movements (either individually or in small groups) without much difficulty, she immediately asks them to go one step further challenging them. She would usually guide them increasing the complexity of the performance and then let them explore by themselves as much as they can.

- *Learning resources*: Additional visual resources are used to better illustrate the concepts taught. For instance: pictures, objects, videos, board, etc. are shown/used during the sessions. As suggested in [4], using different sources of information (visual, verbal, sound, etc.) promotes the use of different learning strategies, which impacts on the learning effectiveness.
- *Music*: it is an important component used during the sessions. On the one hand it is used to guide the dynamics of the group and their movements (for instance, during warm-up, faster rhythms are used, while during exploration, slow music is played), and on the other hand, it serves as motivational support (specially to start the sessions and breaking the ice). If children like it, they would easily engage in the task and would start moving around along with the teacher. Similar findings were reported in [14].
- *Performance and appreciation*: Pupils like showing the knowledge acquired and their own creations to receive approval from the teacher. Their motivation increases and they feel confident to be challenged with new things. Moreover, it serves as a brainstorming process where their creativity is stimulated by observing others' creations.
- *Motivational feedback*: Fear of failure may restrain creative thinking [11]. The teacher constantly tells the pupils how well they are doing. This encourages to continue the task. When negative feedback should be given, positive words are used while phrasing her comments to avoid disappointment.
- *Activity summary*: At the beginning of each session the teacher would briefly explain the goal and content of the session taking place. If possible, she will also recapitulate what they did in previous sessions to link the concepts worked. During the session, she would briefly describe the next activity to perform so the pupils are aware of what is coming next. At the end of session, before debriefing, she summarizes the lesson they took part of.

2.2 General Methodology

The general methodology distilled from the observations of these sessions is composed of the following stages:

1. *Warm-up*: the teacher starts the session with slow and smooth movements, to stretch and strengthen the body. She gradually increases the dynamics of the movements to completely warm the body.
2. *Exploration*: the teacher explains movement concepts while practicing them with the pupils.
3. *Creation*: individually or in groups, pupils create dance phrases (a sequence of movements) based on the concepts learned in the exploration stage.
4. *Performance and Appreciation*: pupils perform the dance phrases created during the session to show their work to the rest of the classmates. This stage enables them to discuss about the different performances identifying and reinforcing the learned concepts.

Stages 2 through 4 are repeated several times during a session. At each cycle a different concept is explained, explored and performed/observed.

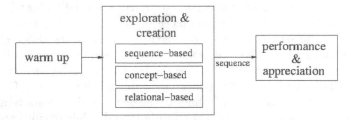

Fig. 2. General methodology for creative dance. The exploration and creation stages are coupled based in three learning models.

Each session tackles different concepts, and therefore, the stages may vary from one session to another one, extending more when required. However, the methodology remains the same. Fig. 2 depicts the overall methodology. We will next go through the different models.

2.3 Learning Models

Through the sessions we took part of, several methods were used to teach dance. While the outcome is the same in all models, i.e. the creation and performance of a sequence, the process through which the pupils learn and create the individual movements of the sequence differ. In this work we focus on three different methodologies to apply in the design of a robot dance tutor.

Sequence-Based Model. This model corresponds to a more traditional one, where the goal is to teach a specific sequence of movements. The sequences is created by the teacher and the pupils reproduce it the in the same way. Fig. 3 depicts the model. Each step (or movement) is shown one at a time to evaluate the performance of the pupils. Once a step is taught, it is added to the sequence. The expanded sequence is practiced every time a new step is added.

This model does not require the use of creativity from the pupils point of view. It is usually used during the warm up stage and in the first session when the teacher and the pupils meet for the first time. However, to introduce creativity in the process, variations on the sequence learned can be applied. The following steps gradually motivate pupils to introduce their own creations:

1. Modify the order of the movements in the predefined sequence.
2. Include repetitions of some movements through the sequence.
3. Modify some movements in terms of dynamics (faster, slower), levels (on the floor), or spatial representation (mirroring).
4. Include as many new movements as they desired.

Thus, although pupils start copying a set of movements, they can end up with a completely different sequence according to their own creativity.

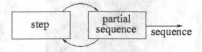

Fig. 3. Diagram for the sequence-based learning model

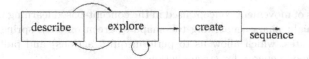

Fig. 4. Diagram for both concept and relational-based models

Concept-Based Model. This model allows the introduction of the foundations of dance, i.e. movement concepts, along with the exploration of the body movement (Fig. 4). First a a concept is described through different means, i.e. performing a movement, showing an image, describing it verbally, through analogies. Next, the pupils explore the new idea using their own body. They are free to create any variation they can think of as long as it corresponds to the concept described. The process is repeated for different concepts until the ideas are well understood. Finally, the pupils are asked to create a sequence with the concepts learned. They can either create their own sequence as they like, or a guideline can be provided (a sequence of concepts), but it is up to the pupils to select the movements used to represent the concepts in the sequence. Fig. 5 shows some of the concepts taught during the dance sessions we took part of.

Relational-Based Model. In Section 2 we stated that creative dance can be used to convey concepts of specific themes linked to movement concepts. Through this model, the pupils not only reinforce their knowledge on the movement concepts seen so far, but also learn and establish links with other ideas. The model can be applied bidirectionally: departing from a theme concept and linking it with movement concepts, or the other way around, i.e. based on a movement concept, link it to theme concepts. Either way, first a description of the movement (or theme concept) is given (*describe* stage in Fig. 4) and the pupils explore different theme concepts (or movements) linked to that description.

For example, to link from a theme concept to a movement concept, the teacher shows an image of a fruit (say a banana) and asks the pupils which (movement) shapes they can see in a banana. A plausible answer would be curved shape. On the other sense, from movement concept to theme concept, the teacher would name a concept (say, spiky shape), and the pupils should think of a fruit which matches that concept and then create a movement with their body to reproduce it (in this case, a valid solution would be a pineapple).

Fig. 5. Examples of movement concept used in the concept-based learning model. From left to right: straight shape (matching the shape of green onions), spring (related to simple carbohydrates, which allow us to perform quick actions) and pull (related to proteins, wich provide energy for strong actions).

To consolidate the concepts linked, the pupils create a sequence as in the previous model, i.e. either on their own or based on a given sequence of theme or movement concepts.

3   Designing a Dance Robot Tutor

The robot's behavior is twofold. On the one hand to perform a dance activity where the robot acts as a tutor guiding the child through the different stages. And on the other hand, to keep the child engaged in the task as much as possible, not only to finish the task, but to repeat the encounter in future occasions.

To this end, the methodology and models described in the previous section have been implemented. Moreover, based on our previous work [12], additional cues for enhancing the social interaction are also included in the design of the robot behavior. This type of behaviors prevent the robot of being too static, being more human-like as suggested in the literature [3] [16] [8] [15]. In this work we make use of the following:

- head movements: the head randomly moves in a smooth way. When the robot addresses a direct question to the child, it faces the child to emphasize that the robot is expecting the child to respond.
- blinking eyes: the robot's eyes are provided with colored LEDs. Turning them on and off simulates natural human eye blinking making the robot appearance more "alive".
- spatial orientation: while interacting with humans, it is important to maintain an appropriate spatial disposition while executing a task (a spatial-orientational arrangement [9]). In this work the robot should be facing the user to show the different motions. Due to the movement of the robot while performing the dance motions, the robot may end up facing some other place in the room instead of facing the user.
- name reference: the robot randomly refers to the child by its name to reinforce the bond between them throughout the session.

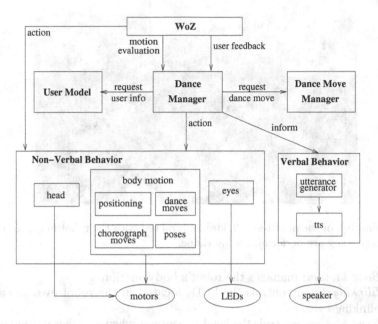

Fig. 6. Diagram of the system architecture. Arrows represent the flow of information between components.

We next briefly describe the system architecture used in this work. An overall description is illustrated in Fig. 6. The implementation of the system has been done using Urbi[2], an open-source software platform to control robots.

- *Dance Manager*: controls the overall robot behavior, implementing both the methodologies described in Sec. 2.3 and the above engaging behaviors.
- *WoZ*: provides external input while the perceptual components are completed. Allows to introduce the child's performance evaluation and answers to questions. Additionally, it allows the operator to re-position the robot.
- *Dance Move Manager*: manages the library of dance movements and provides information to the *Non-Verbal Behavior* for the execution of those.
- *User Model*: in charge of handling the users' interaction history to enable adaptation in the decision process. Besides storing general information about the child (such as Id, name, age and gender), it also keeps track of the dance moves performed
- *Verbal Behavior*: responsible for the verbal output of the robot. The utterances are based on canned text manually created. Variations of each message have been produced to avoid repeated verbalization.
- *Text-To-Speech*: in charge of the speech synthesis, we use the commercial Acapella TTS [6] built-in the robot.
- *Non-Verbal Behavior*: responsible for the non-verbal output of the robot.

---

[2] www.urbiforge.org

Fig. 7. Snapshot of the pilot test. Children interacted with the robot in groups of four. In the image, they are performing a big shape.

- *Body Motion*: manages the robot's body motion.
- *Blinking Eyes*: controls the LEDs located in the robot eyes to emulate blinking eyes.
- *Head Motion*: controls the head movement when no other motion occurs.

4   Preliminary Results

The robot used is the Nao, a humanoid robot from Aldebaran Robotics.[3] The Nao is almost 58cm tall, weights 5.2kg and has a cartoon-like appearance which was considered especially suitable for use with children. It has 25 degrees of freedom, which allow smooth motion specially required for dance movements.

Table 1 describes a trial example of a session. The dance topic corresponds to *shapes* and it is linked to nutrition through fruits and vegetables.

A pilot test of the first prototype has been carried out. In the test, 17 children divided in four groups between 8 and 9-years-old had a chance to interact with the robot (Fig. 7). Although the system is intended to be evaluated later on in one-to-one interactions, we believe that this initial feedback on the proposed framework is valuable to further improve our work.

In general children responded in a very positive way. They liked the robot and the way it moved. They engaged with the robot copying or creating movements and they understood the movement concepts. Creativity easily emerged and they expected the robot to repeat their own creations in turn. They addressed the robot in different ways, verbally (making questions) and non-verbally (waving hands) demonstrating interest in interacting with it.

They reported that sometimes it was difficult to understand what the robot said and that the instructions were not too clear so they felt slightly lost at some points. They also expected the robot to perform some well know dances (e.g. most of them asked for the Gangnam Style).

---

[3] www.aldebaran-robotics.com

Table 1. Trial example of a dance session. (+) and (-) correspond to the evaluation of the child's performance.

stage	input	robot output
greet	Alex Yes	Hi! My name is Nao. I don't know your name yet. Nice to meet you Alex. Would you like to dance with me? Cool, let's try it.
warmup (sequence-based model)		First, we go through a warmup... Ready, and go!
	(+)	Great! ... We now try all the moves we know so far.
exploration & creation (concept-based model)		Alex, We'll now explore about shape. Ok, here we go. Let's learn a new concept, curved.
	(+) (+)	Try another example of curved shape. Go ahead! Nice! ... When I say the name of a shape, a concept, you show it to me. We'll create a dance phrase. Straight.
	(-)	Ok, let's try together.

Table 1. (*continued*)

stage	input	robot output
healthy diet overview		Vegetables and fruits provide vitamins and minerals to our body important to prevent from diseases...
exploration & creation (relational-based model) from theme to movement concept		Let's link the concepts seen so far with the images in the screen. Tell me which shapes can you see.
	(-)	Come on, you can do it! How does banana look like?
	curved	Very good!
exploration & creation (relational-based model) from movement concept to theme	(-)	I'll the name of a shape and you have to show me a fruit or vegetable that has that concept. Spiky Ok, let's try together. Spiky like a pineapple.
farewell		It's been great dancing with you! Thanks.

5 Conclusions

We have proposed an approach for creative dance to study child-robot interaction through several encounters. We took part of dance sessions in order to extract strategies and models to inspire and justify the design of a robot dance tutor.

In the near future we plan to evaluate our system with children in one-to-one interactions during three sessions. Based on our previous work, the evaluation of the interaction will be based on video coding schemes to analyze the level of interaction. Regarding the impact of creativity, we plan to look at the outcomes generated by the children to assess whether creativity emerged through the interactions and how it influenced on the interaction itself. Moreover, we will be able to evaluate whether the interactions have an impact on knowledge gain.

Acknowledgement. This work is supported by the EU FP7 Project ALIZ-E (FP7-ICT-248116).

References

1. Physical Education, The National Curriculum for England (2011)
2. Bianchi-Berthouze, N.: Understanding the role of body movement in player engagement. Human-Computer Interaction 28(1), 42–75 (2013)

3. Bruce, A., Nourbakhsh, I., Simmons, R.: The role of expressiveness and attention in human-robot interaction. In: Int. Conf. on Robotics and Automation, vol. 4, pp. 4138–4142 (2002)
4. Cadopi, M., Chatillon, J.F., Baldy, R.: Representation and performance: Reproduction of form and quality of movement in dance by eight- and 11-year-old novices. British Journal of Psychology 86, 217–225 (1995)
5. Csíkszentmihályi, M.: Creativity: flow and the psychology of discovery and invention. HarperCollins Publishers (1996)
6. Gouaillier, D., Hugel, V., Blazevic, P., Kilner, C., Monceaux, J., Lafourcade, P., Marnier, B., Serre, J., Maisonnier, B.: The nao humanoid: a combination of performance and affordability. CoRR, abs/0807.3223 (2008)
7. Hui, E., Tsan keung Chui, B., Woo, J.: Effects of dance on physical and psychological well-being in older persons. Archives of Gerontology and Geriatrics 49, e45–e50 (2009)
8. Kanda, T., Sato, R., Saiwaki, N., Ishiguro, H.: A two-month field trial in an elementary school for long-term human-robot interaction. Transactions on Robotics 23(5), 962–971 (2007)
9. Kendon, A.: Spacing and orientation in co-present interaction. In: Esposito, A., Campbell, N., Vogel, C., Hussain, A., Nijholt, A. (eds.) COST 2102 Int. Training School 2009. LNCS, vol. 5967, pp. 1–15. Springer, Heidelberg (2010)
10. Michalowski, M., Simmons, R., Kozima, H.: Rhythmic attention in child-robot dance play. In: Int. Symposium on Robot and Human Interactive Communication, pp. 816–821 (2009)
11. Nickerson, R.S.: 20 enhancing creativity. In: Handbook of Creativity, pp. 392 (1999)
12. Ros, R., Baroni, I., Demris, Y.: Adaptive human robot interaction in sensorimotor task instruction: from human to robot dance tutors (submitted, May 2013)
13. Von Rossberg-Gempton, I., Dickinson, J., Poole, G.: Creative dance: Potentiality for enhancing social functioning in frail seniors and young children. The Arts in Psychotherapy 26, 313–327 (1999)
14. Tanaka, F., Movellan, J., Fortenberry, B., Aisaka, K.: Daily HRI evaluation at a classroom environment: reports from dance interaction experiments. In: Conf. on Human-robot Interaction, pp. 3–9 (2006)
15. Tanaka, F., Matsuzoe, S.: Children teach a care-receiving robot to promote their learning: Field experiments at a classroom for vocabulary learning. Journal of Human-Robot Interaction 1(1), 78–95 (2012)
16. Yoshikawa, Y., Shinozawa, K., Ishiguro, H., Hagita, N., Miyamoto, N.: The effects of responsive eye movement and blinking behavior in a communication robot. In: Int. Conf. on Intelligent Robots and Systems, pp. 4564–4569 (2006)

Stylistic Features for Affect-Based Movie Recommendations

Jussi Tarvainen, Stina Westman, and Pirkko Oittinen

Aalto University, Dept. of Media Technology, Espoo, Finland
{jussi.tarvainen,stina.westman,pirkko.oittinen}@aalto.fi

Abstract. In recent years, studies have estimated affective movie content computationally with stylistic features, yet knowledge of the perceptual relation between style and affect remains scarce. Such knowledge would be useful in affect-based movie recommendation systems. To this end, a user study was conducted in which seventy-three participants with varying levels of film expertise rated movie clips according to 13 stylistic features in three modalities (visual, aural and temporal) as well as perceived and felt affect in three dimensions (hedonic tone, energetic arousal and tense arousal). Style-based linear regression models were then constructed for each affect dimension. Visual features contributed the most to hedonic tone and tense arousal, and temporal features to energetic arousal. Also, perceived affect showed greater inter-rater agreement and better modeling performance than felt affect. The results indicate that the influence of specific stylistic features on affect varies by dimension and by whether the affect is perceived or felt.

Keywords: film, style, perceived affect, felt affect.

1 Introduction

Movies are essentially affective in nature: their primary aim is to evoke emotional responses in viewers [14]. According to tenets of formalist film theory, movies do this mainly through their style, which encompasses various techniques of audiovisual expression [23]. Over time, these techniques have become conventions followed by filmmakers and recognized by viewers [2]. In the process, an effective audiovisual shorthand has been developed for the expression of a wide range of affective content. Its power is based on the so-called pre-verbal language of film: the stylistic features of a movie communicate more strongly with the viewer than high-level semantic concepts such as plot or theme [14].

Given the importance of affect in the impression made by a movie, it is likely that an affect-based movie recommendation system would be more useful than the star rating -based systems in use today. Such a system would provide recommendations to viewers based on the affective content of movies as well as viewer preferences. Since affective content is rooted in style, movies could be classified automatically with computational estimates of their stylistic features, eliminating the need for subjective interpretations of the content. Indeed, recent

A.A. Salah et al. (Eds.) : HBU 2013, LNCS 8212, pp. 52–63, 2013.

studies (e.g. [22,25]) have estimated affective movie content with computational stylistic features. Results have, however, been mixed, and two particular shortcomings can be identified: first, a lack of data on the perceptual relation of style to affective content; and second, an assumption that the affective response of different viewers to the same content would be similar.

The purpose of this study is to determine how the stylistic features of a movie influence its affective content, and thereby to provide a perceptual basis for the development of affect-based movie recommendation systems. The study takes into account the distinction between perceived and felt affect; that is, between the affective content expressed by a movie as perceived by the viewer, and the viewer's personal affective response to a movie [11]. Specifically, the study aims to answer two research questions. First, are the perceived and felt affect of a movie rated differently, and if so, which of the two shows more inter-rater agreement? Second, in what ways do various stylistic features contribute to affective content?

The paper is organized as follows. Previous work on models of affect and film style is presented in Section 2. The methodology of the current study is presented in Section 3. Results are presented in Section 4 and their implications discussed in Section 5. Conclusions are drawn in Section 6.

2 Previous Work

2.1 Models of Affect

Affect is a broad category encompassing feelings, emotions and moods [13]. Emotion, in turn, is a conscious affective state marked by cognitive appraisal. However, the two terms are often used interchangeably.

Two emotion theories are prevalent in affective science: categorical and dimensional [17]. Categorical theory sees emotions as discrete states, such as joy, whereas dimensional theory, more popular in recent years, sees them as dimensions of a so-called affective space. The two-dimensional valence–arousal model of affect [18] has proven particularly influential, valence describing the pleasurability of an emotion, from negative to positive, and arousal the degree of alertness associated with the emotion, from calm to aroused. The model has been widely adopted in studies on computational affective content modeling (e.g. [22,28]).

The use of two arousal dimensions, energetic arousal (tired–awake) and tense arousal (calm–tense), has also been proposed [26]. Several studies (e.g. [15,20]) have shown that the two dimensions are independent and that better results can be achieved with two arousal terms than with one. However, despite the benefits involved with using two arousal terms, a single term remains more common.

An important distinction is that between perceived and felt affect; that is, the affect expressed by a stimulus (such as a movie) as perceived by the viewer, and the affective state induced in the viewer as a consequence [11]. The concepts therefore differ by their objects of focus: the former deals with the affective content of the *movie*, and the latter with the affective response of the *viewer*.

This relation has mostly been studied in musicology (e.g. [11]), with the general finding that perceived affect ratings are more objective – and thus more generalizable – than felt affect ratings. In [11] perceived and felt emotion ratings of classical music were found to be mostly similar, although felt emotion was stronger than perceived emotion in connection with valence, and weaker in connection with arousal, and negative perceived emotion corresponded with more positive felt emotion. The standard deviations of the ratings were lower for perceived than felt affect, indicating greater inter-rater agreement for the former. On the other hand, in [12] perceived and felt basic emotion ratings of non-film video clips were found to be highly consistent, with similar standard deviations.

In the context of film, a connotative affective space mixing elements of perceived and felt affect was recently proposed in [1]. However, the relation between the two types of affect in film remains to be systematically studied.

2.2 Film Style

Film style can be split into three modalities: visual, aural and temporal [3]. Visual features are related to the image and include framing, depth of field, lighting, contrast, and color. Aural features are related to the soundtrack and include loudness as well as the use of music, dialogue, and sound effects. Temporal features are related to variations of visual and aural features in time and include, in addition to manipulation of the aforementioned features, shot length, shot motion, and music tempo. Temporal features, especially music tempo [7], have a strong influence on film rhythm [3]. The aforementioned features are given most emphasis in film textbooks (e.g. [3,23]) and can be considered central features of film style.

Whereas much has been written on the relation between film emotion and narrative structure, theme and characters [24,4], there is a notable lack of studies on the influence of specific stylistic features on film affect. Still, similar relations have been shown for other media. For example, valence has been shown to increase with image brightness and saturation [27]; increase with the tempo of music [6]; and also to be affected in various ways by the rhythm and pitch of human speech [16]. Arousal has been shown to decrease with image brightness and increase with saturation [27]; increase with the loudness and rate of speech [16]; increase with the loudness of music (including an increase in tense arousal) [8]; and increase with the intensity of the motion applied to still images [21].

3 Methodology

To study the relation between style and affective content in film, a user test was conducted in which participants rated a series of movie clips according to various metrics. Statistical methods were then employed to determine in which ways stylistic features can be used to model affective movie content.

3.1 Participants

In all, 73 participants took part in the test. Most were university students, from various fields. The average age of the participants was 27.1 years ($SD = 5.4$).

Table 1. The movie clips used in the user test. Timecodes are taken from NTSC DVD releases.

#	Movie title	Year	Timecode [h:mm:ss]	Length [m:ss]
1	*500 Days of Summer*	2009	0:31:20	2:04
2	*Amelie*	2001	2:00:35	1:36
3	*Army of Shadows*	1969	0:38:40	1:54
4	*Before Sunrise*	1995	1:31:57	2:33
5	*Blue Velvet*	1986	1:55:32	2:21
6	*Children of Men*	2006	0:26:00	2:07
7	*Days of Heaven*	1978	0:04:05	1:37
8	*E.T.*	1982	1:47:42	1:10
9	*Punch-Drunk Love*	2002	1:06:30	1:16
10	*Raiders of the Lost Ark*	1981	0:07:45	2:09
11	*The Good, the Bad and the Ugly*	1966	2:45:49	2:17
12	*The Night of the Hunter*	1955	0:56:30	1:58
13	*The Shining*	1980	0:34:59	1:56
14	*Vertigo*	1958	0:26:00	1:45

Sixty percent were female. Thirty-eight percent were experts in film; that is, they had studied film and/or had filmmaking as a hobby. Self-reported fluency in English was required since the movie clips were spoken or subtitled in English.

Data was collected about the participants' age, gender, profession and/or field of study, personality traits, and initial mood. Personality traits were assessed with the Big Five Inventory questionnaire [10] for ratings in five personality factors: agreeableness, conscientiousness, extraversion, neuroticism and openness. Initial mood was assessed with the UWIST Mood Adjective Checklist [15], which is used to evaluate affective states in valence and arousal dimensions.

3.2 Movie Clips

The test sample consisted of 14 movie clips 1–3 minutes in length (Table 1). The clips were selected from a candidate set of 22 clips based on a pilot test whose participants rated each clip by perceived valence and arousal on an affect grid [19]. Due to the large number of participants in the user test, the clips were chosen so that they formed two sets of seven clips with similarly wide valence and arousal distributions, with the sets shown to different participant groups.

The clips were from mainstream movies made between 1955 and 2009 with an average of 180,000 IMDb ratings and an average rating of 8.15/10 [9]. They encompass several genres, such as action, comedy, drama, horror and romance. They also represent various styles in terms of, for example, composition, colors, editing, and sound. Nine clips (3–7, 10, 12–14) contained dialogue or narration; ten (1, 5, 7–14) contained music. All clips were presented in their original language; clip 3 was presented with English subtitles. Each clip contained a complete scene that could be understood without knowledge of the events preceding it.

Table 2. Test sessions, participants and clips

Session	N	Experts [%]	Women [%]	Clips in viewing order
E1	15	67	73	2, 6, 4, 7, 12, 11, 1
N1	19	5	53	
E2	20	75	55	8, 3, 9, 13, 14, 5, 10
N2	19	11	63	

Table 3. Stylistic features by modality

Modality	Features
Visual	*bright, colorful, colorless, dark*
Aural	*dialogue-based, loud, music-based, quiet*
Temporal	*fast, fitful, rhythmic, slow, smooth*

3.3 Procedure

For the test, participants were split into two groups, each viewing a distinct set of seven movie clips. A separate test session was held targeting the expert and naïve participants in either group, resulting in four test sessions in all (Table 2).

The test was conducted in a movie theater with the participants distributed evenly and one seat apart for privacy. Lights were turned off during the presentation of the clips. The test began with a background survey, after which participants watched and rated movie clips according to perceived and felt affect as well as style. Participants rated felt affect before perceived affect to prevent the latter, more objective, rating from influencing the former. They also provided other ratings (various aesthetic features as well as valence and arousal curves) not discussed here. An exit survey was filled out at the end of the test.

3.4 Data and Analysis

Participants used the UWIST Mood Adjective Checklist [15] to produce, for each clip, both a rating of the affective content expressed in a clip (perceived affect), and a rating of their personal affective response to it (felt affect). Using the procedure in [15], the item ratings were transformed into values in three dimensions: hedonic tone (HT), which corresponds to valence; energetic arousal (EA); and tense arousal (TA). These ratings are on a scale of $[-1 \ 1]$, from negative to positive in terms of HT, tired to energetic in terms of EA, and calm to tense in terms of TA [26].

In the clip style assessment, participants rated the applicability of 13 stylistic features (Table 3) to the clip on a scale of $[1 \ 5]$. The features were presented without category or modality labels. The feature set contained features that could be considered semantic opposites, such as *bright* and *dark*. These features were rated separately since they are not necessarily mutually exclusive.

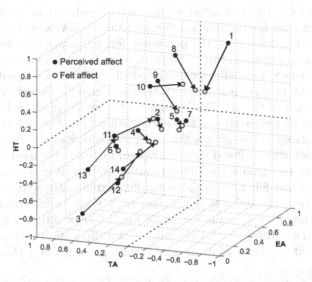

Fig. 1. Clipwise perceived (black) and felt (gray) affect means in HT–EA–TA space

In the exit survey, data was collected about participants' self-reported ease of rating perceived and felt clip affect, on a scale of [1 5] from hard to easy.

Student's t-test and Pearson correlation were used to analyze the relations between perceived and felt affect as well as style and affect. The possible influence of background factors (age, gender, expertise, personality traits, and initial mood) on ratings was tested. Multiple linear regression affect models were constructed using backward stepwise regression with variable removal condition $p < .01$ and checked for linearity, outliers, independence of observations, homoscedasticity, distribution of residuals, and multicollinearity. Models were constructed with four feature sets: all stylistic features; and visual, aural or temporal features. The performances are reported in adjusted R-squared (R^2) units.

A statistical significance limit of $p < .01$ is applied to all results. Correlation limits are $r \geq \pm.10$ for small, $r \geq \pm.30$ for moderate and $r \geq \pm.50$ for large [5].

4 Results

4.1 Perceived and Felt Affect

Mean values for perceived and felt clip affect in the HT–EA–TA affective space are shown in Figure 1. The clips occupied a wide range of values on both the HT and TA dimensions ([−.66 .89] and [−.58 .68], respectively), but a narrower range on the EA dimension ([−.05 .89]).

The arrows in Figure 1 connecting each clip's perceived and felt affect means illustrate that perceived and felt affect were rated differently, with ratings for felt affect closer to zero. Indeed, a statistically significant difference between perceived and felt affect ratings was found for nine of the 14 clips for HT, seven for EA, and ten for TA. Felt affect ratings were greater than perceived affect ratings for eight clips for HT, but smaller for nine for EA, and thirteen for TA. In other words, for most clips, the perceived–felt difference was from negative to positive, from energetic to tired, and from tense to calm. For each dimension, standard deviations were smaller for perceived affect ratings for 12 out of 14 clips, indicating that there was greater inter-rater agreement for perceived affect.

A clip's location in the HT–EA–TA space (Figure 1) was found to influence the similarity of its perceived and felt affect ratings. For each affect dimension, the clips were placed in two groups according to whether or not their ratings for perceived and felt affect differed significantly, and t-tests were used to determine if the clips in the two groups had different affect ratings. It was found that clips whose perceived and felt ratings did not differ significantly were seen as more positive, less energetic and less tense than clips whose affect ratings differed significantly. The effect size was moderate for HT ($r = .43$) and large for EA ($r = .65$) as well as TA ($r = .78$), indicating that a clip's affect ratings influenced the perceived–felt similarity of its arousal ratings more strongly than that of its valence ratings.

Background features had only a weak influence on affect ratings, and their influence can be considered negligible. Also, the participants' self-reported ease of evaluating perceived affect was comparable to that of evaluating felt affect.

4.2 Style

Several stylistic feature pairs produced strong correlations (Table 4). A large positive correlation was found between *bright* and *colorful*, *fast* and *loud* as well as *slow* and *quiet*, indicating that these stylistic means tend to be used together. *Rhythmic* correlated moderately with the temporal features *smooth* and *fast*, the visual feature *colorful*, and the aural feature *music-based*, suggesting that each of the three modalities contributed to an impression of rhythm.

Significant negative correlations were found between all semantically opposite feature pairs (Table 4). The correlations were all large or moderate with the exception of the *smooth–fitful* correlation, suggesting that a clip could be perceived as being both smooth and fitful simultaneously.

All correlations of background features with style ratings were weak. Their influence can therefore be considered negligible.

4.3 Style and Affect

Several stylistic features were found to correlate significantly with perceived affect (Table 5). Having established greater inter-rater agreement for perceived affect ratings (Section 4.1), and given that style–affect correlations were on average stronger for perceived affect, only perceived affect correlations are reported.

Both HT and TA correlated most strongly with visual features, and EA with temporal features. For both HT and TA, the strongest-correlating feature was *dark*, though the correlation was negative for the former and positive for the

Table 4. Significant ($p < .01$) Pearson correlations between stylistic features

Modality	Feature	Visual				Aural				Temporal				
		Bright	Colorful	Colorless	Dark	Dial.-based	Loud	Music-based	Quiet	Fast	Fitful	Rhythmic	Slow	Smooth
Visual	Bright													
	Colorful	.65												
	Colorless	−.30	−.47											
	Dark	−.45	−.34	.31										
Aural	Dial.-based													
	Loud					.26								
	Music-based	.36	.36	−.15	−.20	−.32	.16							
	Quiet		.29				−.49	−.22						
Temporal	Fast		.14		.13		.63		−.41					
	Fitful				.22	.12				.12				
	Rhythmic	.29	.39	−.19			.28	.38	−.17	.31				
	Slow				.23		−.47		.55	−.64		−.23		
	Smooth	.39	.40	−.17	−.18		.25					−.19	.43	

latter. For HT, a large positive correlation was also found with *bright*, and moderate positive correlations with *colorful* and *music-based*. For EA, a large positive correlation was found with *fast*, and moderate positive correlations with *loud*, *rhythmic* and *colorful*. Lastly, for TA, moderate positive correlations were found – in addition to the aforementioned *dark* – with *loud* and *fast*.

A clip's style ratings were found to affect the similarity of its perceived and felt affect ratings. As before, *t* tests were used to determine if clips grouped according to the similarity of their affect ratings had different style ratings. Two stylistic feature pairs were found to influence each affect dimension: *fast–slow* and *loud–quiet*. For each dimension, clips with similar perceived and felt affect ratings were slower and quieter than those with divergent ratings. For *slow*, the effect size was notable for EA ($r = .39$), and for *quiet*, for both EA ($r = .40$) and TA ($r = .33$), suggesting that in terms of perceived–felt similarity, slowness and quietness affected the arousal dimensions more strongly than valence.

4.4 Affective Content Modeling

Affective content models were constructed for each dimension in terms of both perceived and felt affect, with different sets of stylistic features (Table 6). Predictably, models constructed with all features performed the best. TA models had the lowest performance for both perceived and felt affect, suggesting that TA was the most difficult dimension to model. HT and EA models performed better, especially with perceived affect, where both models explained more than half of

Table 5. Significant ($p < .01$) Pearson correlations between stylistic features and perceived affect. The strongest-correlating feature is highlighted for each dimension.

Dimension	Visual				Aural				Temporal				
	Bright	*Colorful*	*Colorless*	*Dark*	*Dial.-based*	*Loud*	*Music-based*	*Quiet*	*Fast*	*Fitful*	*Rhythmic*	*Slow*	*Smooth*
HT	.55	.49	−.35	−.63	−.21		.36			−.15	.18		.29
EA	.29	.35	−.33	−.19		.45	.24	−.46	.60		.40	−.57	.25
TA	−.31	−.25		.45		.39	−.17	−.22	.35			−.29	−.20

Table 6. Perceived and felt affect model performances (adjusted R^2). All models are significant at $p < .01$.

Feature set	HT		EA		TA	
	Perceived	Felt	Perceived	Felt	Perceived	Felt
All	.54	.42	.55	.35	.37	.27
Visual	.50	.32	.16	.19	.21	.21
Aural	.15	.17	.29	.08	.18	.15
Temporal	.08	.22	.48	.29	.22	.12

the variance of the results. For each dimension, better performance was achieved with perceived affect than felt affect. Given this result as well as earlier findings about greater inter-rater agreement for perceived affect, the contributions of individual features (Table 7) are only reported for perceived affect models.

The contributions of different modalities varied by affect dimension. Perceived HT was modeled best by visual features and EA by temporal features, whereas no single modality dominated in the TA model (Table 6). In terms of individual feature contributions (Table 7), *dark* contributed the most to both the HT and TA models, its contribution especially large in the former. It is also notable that *dark* featured in each model, but its semantic opposite *bright* only in the HT model, suggesting that exceptionally dark images could be more important than exceptionally bright ones in terms of affect modeling. In the EA model, the importance of temporal features is reflected by the large contribution of *fast* and *slow*.

Each model contained features that could be considered semantic opposites. However, no multicollinearity was found in any model, suggesting that each of their features provided a unique contribution to the model.

5   Discussion

Perceived and felt affect ratings differed significantly for most clips for each affect dimension, and greater inter-rater agreement was shown for perceived affect

Table 7. Feature contributions (β) in perceived affect models. All contributions are significant at $p < .01$. Each model's strongest-contributing feature is highlighted; adjusted R^2 in parentheses. *Colorless*, which does not contribute to any model, is excluded.

Dim.	(R^2)	Visual			Aural				Temporal			
		Bright	*Colorful*	*Dark*	*Dial.-based*	*Loud*	*Music-based*	*Quiet*	*Fast*	*Fitful*	*Rhythmic*	*Slow*	*Smooth*
HT	(.54)	0.21	0.17	−0.48	−0.17							−0.08	
EA	(.55)		0.17	−0.19		0.14			0.31	−0.11	0.14	−0.27	
TA	(.37)		−0.16	0.29		0.18	−0.12	−0.12	0.16		0.12		−0.14

ratings. Moreover, stylistic features correlated more strongly with perceived affect. These results differ somewhat from those of [11] and [12], where perceived and felt affect ratings were found to be comparable. The results of the current study suggest that for better performance, computational models of affective movie content should focus on perceived affect, which provides a more objective description of a movie's affective content. The compatibility of this content with an individual viewer's preferences can be determined with information about, for example, the viewer's star ratings for other movies with similar affective content.

The similarity of a clip's perceived and felt affect ratings was found to depend on its affect and style ratings. Similarly-rated clips were more positive, less energetic, less tense, as well as slower and quieter than differently-rated clips. The result supports the finding in [11] that negative perceived emotion corresponds to divergent perceived and felt emotion ratings. The influence of the affect and style ratings was greater for EA and TA than for HT, suggesting that they influence the similarity of a movie's perceived and felt arousal ratings more than valence ratings.

Certain stylistic features, such as *bright* and *colorful* and *fast* and *loud*, were found to occur together, suggesting that they are complementary stylistic devices. The first two features correlated most strongly with HT, supporting the result in [27] that brightness and saturation increase valence. They also correlated positively with EA and negatively with TA, suggesting, in light of the results in [27], that brightness affects tense arousal and general arousal similarly, whereas colorfulness affects energetic arousal and general arousal similarly. The last two features contributed positively to both EA and TA, confirming the result in [27] that loudness of music and motion intensity (which can be considered comparable to an impression of fastness) increase arousal, and amending it by the finding about a similar effect for both arousal dimensions.

The results revealed relations between modalities. In particular, positive correlations of *rhythmic* with *colorful* and *music-based*, in addition to the temporal features *fast* and *smooth*, suggest that the impression of rhythm is influenced by the beat of music, as found in [7], and colorfulness, as well as motion intensity and fluidity. Moreover, all of these features correlated significantly with EA, suggesting that it is the most relevant dimension in terms of rhythm.

The strength of the style–affect relation was found to depend on modality, with visual and temporal features on average correlating with affect more strongly than aural features. Furthermore, the influence of different modalities on affect was found to be dimension-specific: both the HT and TA dimensions correlated most strongly with visual features, and EA with temporal features. Similarly, HT was modeled best by visual features, and EA by temporal features. TA was the most difficult dimension to model with any feature set. These results, as well as those concerning the contributions of individual stylistic features in the affect models, illustrate the importance of a multimodal approach to affective movie content modeling, and can be used to aid the selection of features in dimension-specific computational affect models.

6   Conclusions

The results of the study showed that the perceived and felt affect ratings of movie clips differed on each affect dimension, with felt affect ratings on average more positive, less energetic, and less tense. Perceived affect ratings spanned a greater portion of the affective space, indicating better separation of affective contents. They also showed greater inter-rater agreement. Together, these results indicate that computational models of affective movie content should focus on perceived affect.

The study also revealed ways in which stylistic features relate to one another and contribute to various dimensions of affective movie content. In affective content models, hedonic tone was modeled best by visual features such as *dark*, and energetic arousal by temporal features such as *fast*. These findings will be combined with computational estimates of stylistic features in the exploration of affect-based movie recommendation methods.

References

1. Benini, S., Canini, L., Leonardi, R.: A Connotative Space for Supporting Movie Affective Recommendation. IEEE Transactions on Multimedia 13(6), 1356–1370 (2011)
2. Bordwell, D.: The Way Hollywood Tells It. University of California Press (2006)
3. Bordwell, D., Thompson, K.: Film Art: An Introduction. McGraw-Hill, Inc. (1990)
4. Carroll, N.: Film, Emotion, and Genre. In: Plantinga, C., Smith, G.M. (eds.) Passionate Views: Film, Cognition, and Emotion, pp. 21–47. The John Hopkins University Press (1999)
5. Cohen, J.: Statistical Power Analysis for the Behavioral Sciences, 2nd edn. Routledge Academic (1988)
6. Gabrielsson, A., Juslin, P.: Emotional Expression in Music. In: Davidson, R.J., Scherer, K.R., Goldsmith, H.H. (eds.) Handbook of Affective Sciences, pp. 503–534. Oxford University Press (2003)

7. Grahn, J.A., Brett, M.: Rhythm and Beat Perception in Motor Areas of the Brain. Journal of Cognitive Neuroscience 19(5), 893–906 (2007)
8. Ilie, G., Thompson, W.F.: A Comparison of Acoustic Cues in Music and Speech for Three Dimensions of Affect. Music Perception 23(4), 319–330 (2006)
9. IMDb.com, Inc.: IMDb, http://www.imdb.com
10. John, O.P., Naumann, L.P., Soto, C.J.: Paradigm Shift to the Integrative Big Five Trait Taxonomy. In: John, O.P., Robbins, R.W., Pervin, L.A. (eds.) Handbook of Personality, pp. 114–156. Guilford, New York (2008)
11. Kallinen, K., Rajava, N.: Emotion Perceived and Emotion Felt: Same and Different. Musicae Scientiae 10(2), 191–213 (2006)
12. Knautz, K., Stock, W.G.: Collective Indexing of Emotions in Videos. Journal of Documentation 67(6), 975–994 (2011)
13. Lewis, M., Haviland-Jones, J.: Handbook of Emotions, 2nd edn. Guilford (2000)
14. Mackendrick, A.: On Film-Making. Faber & Faber, Ltd. (2006)
15. Matthews, G., Jones, D.M., Chamberlain, A.G.: Refining the Measurement of Mood: The UWIST Mood Adjective Checklist. British Journal of Psychology 81(1), 17–42 (1990)
16. Murray, I.R., Arnott, J.L.: Toward the Simulation of Emotion in Synthetic Speech. Journal of the Acoustical Society of America 93(2), 1097–1108 (1993)
17. Posner, J., Russell, J.A., Peterson, B.S.: The Circumplex Model of Affect: An Integrative Approach to Affective Neuroscience, Cognitive Development, and Psychopathology. Development and Psychopathology 17(3), 715–734 (2005)
18. Russell, J.A.: A Circumplex Model of Affect. Journal of Personality and Social Psychology 39(6), 1161–1178 (1980)
19. Russell, J.A., Weiss, A., Mendelsohn, G.A.: Affect Grid: A Single-item Scale of Pleasure and Arousal. Journal of Personality and Social Psychology 57(3), 493–502 (1989)
20. Schimmack, U., Rainer, R.: Experiencing Activation: Energetic Arousal and Tense Arousal Are Not Mixtures of Valence and Activation. Emotion 2(4), 412–417 (2002)
21. Simons, R.F., Detenber, B.H., Roedema, T.M., Reiss, J.E.: Emotion Processing in Three Systems: The Medium and the Message. Psychophysiology 36(5), 619–627 (1999)
22. Soleymani, M., Kierkels, J.J., Chanel, G., Pun, T.: A Bayesian Framework for Video Affective Representation. In: 3rd IEEE International Conference on Affective Computing and Intelligent Interaction and Workshops, pp. 1–7. IEEE (2009)
23. Spottiswoode, R.: A Grammar of the Film: An Analysis of Film Technique. University of California Press (1950)
24. Tan, E.S.: Emotion and the Structure of Narrative Film. Routledge (1996)
25. Teixeira, R.M., Yamasaki, T., Aizawa, K.: Comparative Analysis of Low-Level Visual Features for Affective Determination of Video Clips. In: 5th IEEE International Conference on Future Information Technology, pp. 1–6. IEEE (2010)
26. Thayer, R.E.: The Biopsychology of Mood and Arousal. Oxford University Press (1989)
27. Valdez, P., Mehrabian, A.: Effects of Color on Emotions. Journal of Experimental Psychology 123(4), 394–409 (1994)
28. Zhang, S., Tian, Q., Huang, Q., Gao, W., Li, S.: Utilizing Affective Analysis for Efficient Movie Browsing. In: 16th IEEE International Conference on Image Processing, pp. 1853–1856. IEEE (2009)

Dynamic Feature Selection for Online Action Recognition

Victoria Bloom, Vasileios Argyriou, and Dimitrios Makris

Kingston University, London, United Kingdom
{Victoria.Bloom,D.Makris,Vasileios.Argyriou}@Kingston.ac.uk

Abstract. The ability to recognize human actions in real-time is fundamental in a wide range of applications from home entertainment to medical systems. Previous work on online action recognition has shown a tradeoff between accuracy and latency. In this paper we present a novel algorithm for online action recognition that combines the discriminative power of Random Forests for feature selection and a new dynamic variation of AdaBoost for online classification.

The proposed method has been evaluated using datasets and performance metrics specifically designed for real time action recognition. Our results show that the presented algorithm is able to improve recognition rates at low latency.

Keywords: feature selection, human action recognition, AdaBoost, Random Forests, RGB-D devices, real-time, online, action points.

1 Introduction

Whole body human computer interaction is a latest development with promising applications in a wide range of domains such as home entertainment, education and healthcare in human computer interaction. A key requirement in many applications is the ability to recognize human actions with low latency to provide an interactive user experience.

Human action recognition is an active area of research in computer vision. Historically, the focus was on improving accuracy using offline action recognition systems. A typical *offline* recognition system processes pre-segmented action sequences of a single action and incorporates information across the entire sequence [5-10]. Recent research has pursued the more complex challenge of *online* recognition systems that run in real-time and process the incoming stream without temporal segmentation. Online recognition systems for different applications may have very different requirements in terms of latency and research has highlighted a tradeoff between accuracy and latency [1-2].

High accuracy and low latency is critical for an interactive system to appear responsive to a user's actions. Latency is dependent on two separate factors which have been defined as observational latency and computational latency. *Observational latency* is the time it takes the system to observe enough frames to make a decision, whereas computational latency is the actual time to perform the computation on a frame. A recognition system runs in real-time if the computation time is less than the frame rate [1].

A.A. Salah et al. (Eds.) : HBU 2013, LNCS 8212, pp. 64–76, 2013.
© Springer International Publishing Switzerland 2013

In this paper we consider both aspects of latency to ensure the approach we develop is applicable for an online recognition system. The danger of focusing on purely the observational latency is that the strategy found may be too complex to implement in real-time. A standard approach to reduce complexity is to choose a subset of features that give us the most information. Specifically, the contribution of this paper is a dynamic feature selection algorithm that consists of novelty in both the feature selection using Random Forests and the online classification using a variant of AdaBoost. The proposed method may be applied to any online recognition problem such as face recognition, sign language recognition and action recognition.

In section 2, we review the state of the art online action recognition systems including feature selection methods for reducing complexity and improving performance. In section 3, we present our feature selection and classification method, and demonstrate how they can be applied to action recognition using pose based features. In section 4, we evaluate the performance of our algorithm using datasets designed specifically for real time action recognition that contain multiple actions in each sequence (see Fig. 1). Experiments show the proposed method improves accuracy at low latency compared to conventional AdaBoost.

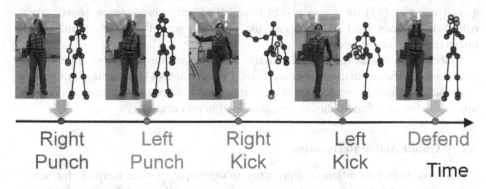

| Right Punch | Left Punch | Right Kick | Left Kick | Defend |

Time

Fig. 1. A fighting sequence from the G3D dataset with "action point" ground truth

2   Related Work

Our work is aimed at interactive systems which require online action recognition. This task is much harder task than offline action recognition as the action has to be detected in real-time based only on a fragment of the action and not the whole action. Traditional algorithms used for offline action recognition [5-10] were not designed to recognize actions with low observational latency so we focus on online approaches.

2.1   Feature Selection

Action classification methods are normally based on applying machine learning approaches on multi-dimensional features. Feature selection reduces the complexity of any classifier and has many benefits including improving prediction performance and reducing training time of classifiers. The aim of feature selection is to find the best subset of features with a minimum number of dimensions that provide satisfactory accuracy. Numerous feature selection methods have been developed which can be divided into wrappers, filters and embedded methods [11].

Filter methods select subsets of variables by ranking individual variables with scoring functions such as correlation coefficients or mutual information criteria. The variable ranking is performed as a preprocessing step independent of the classifier. The benefits of these approaches are their simplicity and computational efficiency. However, wrapper and embedded methods give a better performance improvement over filter methods [11].

Wrapper methods are a simple and powerful way to address the feature selection problem. The wrapper method uses the prediction performance of a given classifier to assess the relative usefulness of subsets of features. The optimal feature subset can be found by testing all possible subsets. However, as there are $(2^d - 1)$ possible combinations of d features, it is computationally unfeasible for large numbers of features as the problem is known to be NP-hard [12]. A wide range of search strategies have been proposed to address this issue, including forward selection, backward selection, best-first, branch-and-bound, simulated annealing and genetic algorithms (see [13] for a review). In pose based action recognition genetic algorithms have been used to determine the optimum set of skeleton joints which improved recognition rates [14].

Embedded methods incorporate variable selection in the process of training and can be more efficient than wrapper methods. Decision trees [15] and Random Forests [16] contain a built-in mechanism to perform variable selection that can estimate the importance of each feature during the classification process.

2.2   Online Action Recognition

There have been two different approaches to developing online methods for action recognition. The first is to extend existing offline approaches and the second is to use direct classification approaches.

Extending successful offline action recognition systems is an obvious approach. Firing Hidden Markov Model (F-HMM) is a variation of HMM with an explicit firing state to detect the action online. The disadvantage is that the complexity of the model is increased by incorporating temporal structure. As expected the accuracy of the online variant is significantly lower than of the original offline method, as the latter incorporates the whole action sequence [2].

Alternatively, direct classification approaches are simpler, faster and have been proved more reliable than F-HMM. Boosting [17] and Random forests classifiers [2], [3] are direct classifiers with state of the art results for online action recognition and they are used commercially for action based game titles. A comparison of Random Forests and AdaBoost in a different field [18] showed that AdaBoost can provide higher classification accuracy at the cost of less efficient computation.

3   Methodology

The main contribution of this paper is a novel method for dynamic feature selection for online recognition. The proposed method combines a wrapper method to improve accuracy with an embedded method to improve computation efficiency. Specifically, Random Forests are used for feature selection, while a novel dynamic variation of AdaBoost is proposed for online classification. Our dynamic feature selection method is independent on the problem domain and type of features. In this section we show how our method can be applied to action recognition using pose based features.

3.1   Pose Based Features

We used pose based features extracted from skeleton data: position difference, position velocity, position velocity magnitude, angle velocity and joint angles similar to those used by [4], [17].

Let $p_{j_i,t} \in \mathbb{R}^3$ be the 3D location $(x_{j_i,t}, y_{j_i,t}, z_{j_i,t})$ and of joint j_i at time t. The position difference features are defined as the difference between each joint $(j_1 - j_{19})$ and the hip center (j_0) in a single pose. For each skeleton there are 57 position difference features as we calculate F^{pdx}, F^{pdy}, and F^{pdz} for 19 joints (all joints except the hip centre).

$$F^{pdx} \left(j_i, j_0; t_1 \right) = x_{j_i,t_1} - x_{j_0,t_1} \tag{1}$$

$$F^{pdy} \left(j_i, j_0; t_1 \right) = y_{j_i,t_1} - y_{j_0,t_1} \tag{2}$$

$$F^{pdz} \left(j_i, j_0; t_1 \right) = z_{j_i,t_1} - z_{j_0,t_1} \tag{3}$$

The position velocity features encode the difference over time of a single joint, where $t_1 \neq t_2$. For each skeleton there are 60 position velocity features as we calculate F^{pvx}, F^{pvy}, and F^{pvz} for all 20 joints.

$$F^{pvx} \left(j_i; t_1, t_2 \right) = x_{j_i,t_1} - x_{j_i,t_2} \tag{4}$$

$$F^{pvy} \left(j_i; t_1, t_2 \right) = y_{j_i,t_1} - y_{j_i,t_2} \tag{5}$$

$$F^{pvz} \left(j_i; t_1, t_2 \right) = z_{j_i,t_1} - z_{j_i,t_2} \tag{6}$$

The position velocity magnitude feature is defined as the Euclidean distance between a single joint separated by time, where $t_1 \neq t_2$. For each skeleton there are 20 position velocity magnitude features as we calculate F^{pvd} for all 20 joints.

$$F^{pvd} \left(j_i; t_1, t_2 \right) = \| p_{j_i,t_1} - p_{j_i,t_2} \| \tag{7}$$

The joint angle features are defined as the quaternions of the angle between three connected joints in a single pose e.g. right wrist, wright elbow and right shoulder. Where features F^{qx}, F^{qy} and F^{qz} define the axis of rotation and feature F^{qw} defines the rotation around that axis at time t. For each skeleton there are 80 joint angle features as we calculate F^{qx}, F^{qy}, F^{qz} and F^{qw} for 20 quaternions.

The angle velocity features are defined as the change in the quaternions of the angle over time, where $t_1 \neq t_2$. For each skeleton there are 80 angle velocity features as we calculate $F^{avx}, F^{avy}, F^{avz}$ and F^{avw} for 20 quaternions.

$$F^{avx}(t_1, t_2) = F^{qx}(t_1) - F^{qx}(t_2) \qquad (8)$$

$$F^{avy}(t_1, t_2) = F^{qy}(t_1) - F^{qy}(t_2) \qquad (9)$$

$$F^{avz}(t_1, t_2) = F^{qz}(t_1) - F^{qz}(t_2) \qquad (10)$$

$$F^{avw}(t_1, t_2) = F^{qw}(t_1) - F^{qw}(t_2) \qquad (11)$$

In total we have a feature vector of 297 features for each skeleton by combining 57 position difference features, 60 position velocity features, 20 position velocity magnitude features, 80 joint angle features and 80 angle velocity features.

3.2   Proposed Feature Selection Method

Random Forests [16] contain a built in mechanism that can estimate the importance of each feature during the training process. A Random Forest consists of a collection of k decision trees:

$$h(x, \Theta_k), k = 1, 2, \ldots K \qquad (12)$$

where the Θ_k are independent identically distributed random vectors and each tree votes for the most popular class at input x. Specifically, Breiman's [16] variable importance algorithm is calculated for each tree by randomizing each variable in turn and measuring the percentage increase in the test set error rate of the "out of bag" permuted variables in comparison to the original variables. The greater the increase in percentage error then the greater the importance of the variable.

Our first technical contribution is Feature Selection by Importance (FSI), which employs a Random Forest to estimate the importance of each feature. Given d features, the Random Forest creates m feature subsets, where $m \leq d$ by thresholding the ranked features from 1 .. d as shown in Fig. 2 and detailed in algorithm 1. As we now have an ordered set of features from most important to least important the search space has been reduced from (2^d - 1) to d and it becomes computationally feasible to exhaustively search for the optimum m.

Algorithm 1. Feature Selection by Importance (FSI)

---

1.   Extract all features from the training dataset.
2.   Train a Random Forest on the training set to obtain the importance of each feature.
3.   The first feature subset is obtained by selecting the feature(s) with the highest importance value.
4.   Add the feature(s) with the next highest importance value to get the next feature subset.
5.   Repeat step 4 until all features have been added to a subset and you have m feature subsets, where $m \leq d$.

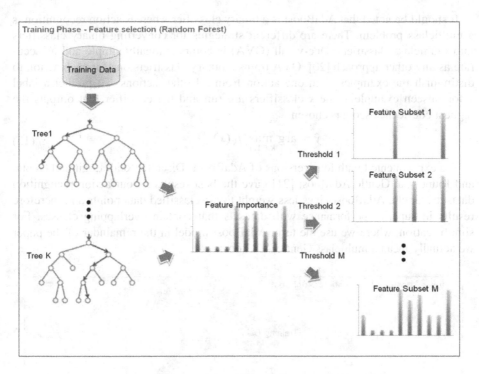

Fig. 2. Feature Selection by Importance (FSI)

3.3   Novel Dynamic Classification Framework

Our second technical contribution is that our method dynamically selects the optimum feature subset at each frame by using multiple AdaBoost [19] models trained with different feature subsets.

The aim of boosting is to combine a group of weak classifiers to produce a strong classifier. A weak classifier has a slightly better chance of obtaining the correct classification than random guessing and can be implemented as simple decision stubs. Each classifier has a weighted vote α_w in the final decision making process. A data point weighted distribution D_w informs the algorithm how much misclassifying a data point will "cost". The key feature of boosting is that, this cost will evolve so that weak classifiers trained later will focus on the data points that were misclassified earlier.

When the training is complete the final strong classifier $H(x)$ takes a new input vector x and classifies it using a weighted sum over the learned weak classifiers h_w calculated as:

$$H(x) = \text{sign} \left(\sum_{w=1}^{W} \alpha_w h_w(x) \right) \qquad (14)$$

where W is the number of weak classifiers and each classifier has a weighted vote α_w.

It should be noted that AdaBoost is a binary classifier whereas action recognition is a multiclass problem. There are different strategies for converting binary classifiers into multiclass classifiers. One-vs-all (OVA) is computationally simple and as accurate as any other approach [20]. OVA trains k binary classifiers one for each action to distinguish the examples from one action from all other actions. To predict a label y for unseen example x, the k classifiers are run and the classifier that outputs the highest confidence score is chosen.

$$\hat{y} = \arg \max_{k \in 1..K} f_k(x) \qquad (15)$$

We experimented with four versions of AdaBoost: Discrete, Real, Logit and Gentle and found that Gentle AdaBoost [21] gave the best results on our action recognition datasets. Gentle AdaBoost gives less weight to misclassified data points and therefore results in superior performance with datasets that contain overlapping classes. For simplification, where we use the term AdaBoost model in the remainder of the paper we actually mean a multiclass Gentle AdaBoost.

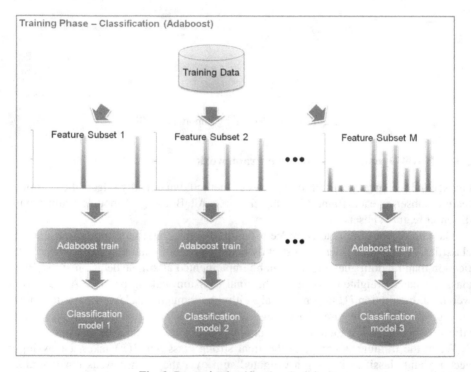

Fig. 3. Dynamic classification (training)

The proposed training for dynamic classification assumes that d features have been grouped into m feature subsets, as described in the section 3.2. Then a set of m AdaBoost models, one for each different feature subsets are learnt (see Fig. 3).

During testing an AdaBoost model is dynamically selected at each frame based on the highest prediction to provide real-time classification (see Fig. 4). Frame based predictions are summed over a sliding window of w frames to smooth results to remove false positives and increase accuracy. The most confident prediction determines the action label for a frame. A change in a frame based action label predicts the action points for the sequence (see algorithm 2).

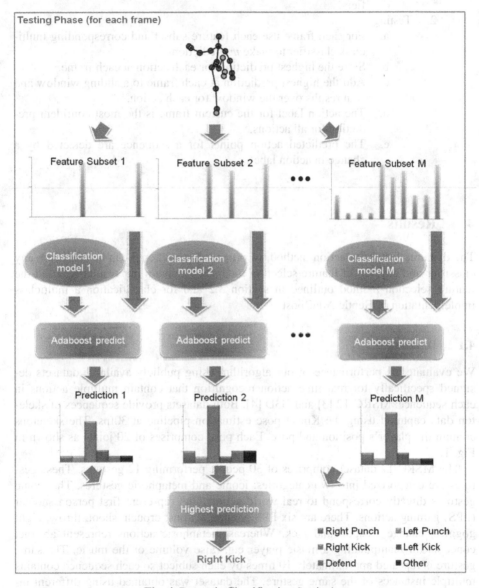

Fig. 4. Dynamic Classification (testing)

Algorithm 2. Dynamic classification

Given d features grouped into m feature subsets:

1. Training
   a. Train the first multiclass classifier using only the features from the first subset.
   b. Repeat step a. for each feature subset to train m multiclass classifiers.
2. Testing
   a. For each frame use each feature subset and corresponding multiclass classifier to make m predictions.
   b. Store the highest prediction for each action at each frame.
   c. Add the highest prediction at each frame to a sliding window and sum results over the window for each action.
   d. The action label for the current frame is the most confident prediction for all actions.
   e. The predicted action points for a sequence are detected by a change in action label.

---

4   Results

The dynamic feature selection method we proposed in section 3 can be used with any classifier and any subset feature selection method. To obtain our results we used the feature selection method outlined in section 3.2 and for classification a multiclass implementation of Gentle AdaBoost.

4.1   Datasets

We evaluate the performance of our algorithm using publicly available datasets designed specifically for real time action recognition that contain multiple actions in each sequence: MSRC-12 [3] and G3D [4]. Both datasets provide sequences of skeleton data captured using the Kinect pose estimation pipeline at 30fps. The skeletons contain the player's position and pose. Each pose comprises of 20 joints as shown in Fig. 1.

The MSRC-12 dataset comprises of 30 people performing 12 gestures. These gestures are categorized into two categories: iconic and metaphoric gestures. The iconic gestures directly correspond to real world actions and represent first person shooter (FPS) gaming actions. There are six FPS gaming actions: crouch, shoot, throw, night goggles, change weapon and kick. Whereas metaphoric actions represent abstract concepts for manipulating a music player e.g. raise volume of the music. The same gesture is repeated approximately 10 times by each subject so each sequence contains multiple instances of the same gesture. The dataset was obtained using different instruction modalities and the modality that produced the most accurate results was video + text so we will use this particular subset of the dataset.

The G3D dataset contains 10 subjects performing 20 gaming actions. These actions are grouped into seven categories: fighting, golf, tennis, bowling, FPS, driving and miscellaneous. Each sequence is repeated three times by each subject. However, in contrast to the MSRC-12 dataset different actions for the same category are mixed together within a sequence and the sequence is repeated three times. Fig. 1 shows example skeleton data for a fighting sequence. The fighting category contains five gaming actions: right punch, left punch, right kick, left kick and defend.

4.2   Ground Truth

To measure the latency of our approach temporal anchors in the ground truth are needed as reference points. An *action point* is defined as a single time instance that an action is clear and can be uniquely identified for all instances of that action [2]. For example, the action point of a punch could be defined as the time at which the hand is maximally extended (see Fig. 1). Action point annotations are available for the MSRC12 dataset and G3D dataset to precisely measure the latency of action recognition methods as well as show the tradeoff between latency and accuracy.

4.3   Performance Evaluation

Following [3] we use a "leave-persons out" protocol. We remove a set of people to obtain the minimum test set that contains instances of all actions. For the MSRC-12 dataset this may be more than one actor as not every actor performs all the actions for the video + text modality. For the G3D dataset this is simply one actor as all actors perform all the actions. The remaining large set is used for the training. This process is repeated 10 times with different subsets to obtain the general performance.

4.4   Real Time Performance Metrics

As our predictions are processed online we need to use a latency-aware performance metric to evaluate our action recognition algorithm. For a specified amount of *latency* (Δms) we need to determine if a prediction made at time t_p for action a is correct in relation to a ground truth action point at time t_g by using the following formula:

$$\Phi(t_p, t_g, \Delta) = \begin{cases} 1 & \text{if} \left(\left| t_g - t_p \right| \le \Delta \right) \\ 0 & \text{otherwise} \end{cases} \tag{16}$$

For a specified amount of *latency* (Δms) we measure the *precision* and *recall* for each action and combine both of these measures to calculate a single F-score [3].

$$F - \text{score}(a, \Delta) = 2 \frac{\text{prec}_a(\Delta) \, \text{rec}_a(\Delta)}{\text{prec}_a(\Delta) + \text{rec}_a(\Delta)} \tag{17}$$

As our system detects multiple actions, we use the mean F-score [3] over all actions, defined as:

$$F - score(A, \Delta) = \frac{1}{|A|} \sum_{a \in A} F - score(a, \Delta) \qquad (18)$$

4.5   Performance Results

The output from our dynamic feature selection method is per frame confidence results for each action (see Fig. 6). Frame based predictions are summed over a sliding window of $s = 10$ frames to smooth the results (see Fig. 7). For each frame the most confident prediction across all the actions determines the action label for that frame. A change in a frame based action label predicts the action points for a sequence (see Fig. 8). The predicted action points were then compared to the ground truth action points (see Fig. 5) using the action point metric described in section 4.4 to obtain a mean F-score at a fixed latency (Δ) of 333ms.

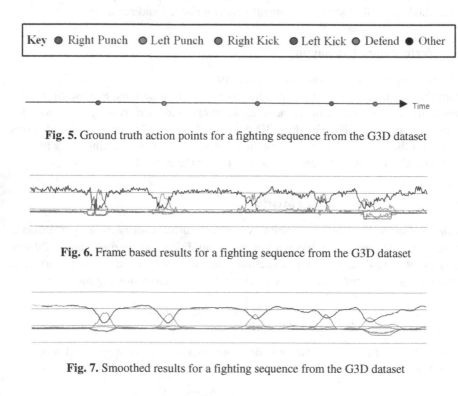

Key ● Right Punch   ● Left Punch   ● Right Kick   ● Left Kick   ● Defend   ● Other

Fig. 5. Ground truth action points for a fighting sequence from the G3D dataset

Fig. 6. Frame based results for a fighting sequence from the G3D dataset

Fig. 7. Smoothed results for a fighting sequence from the G3D dataset

Fig. 8. Predicted action points for a fighting sequence from the G3D dataset

This process was repeated for all sequences in our action recognition datasets. Table 1 shows the mean F-scores (Δ=333ms) for the G3D and MSRC-12 datasets. The results show that our dynamic feature selection method improves accuracy across both datasets in comparison to AdaBoost without any feature selection. For the MSRC-12 and G3D datasets there is a 10% and 2% increase in performance respectively. The smaller increase on the later dataset is because the F-score is already high enough for the AdaBoost method so there is not significant scope for improvement. In our previous work [4] we published results of the standard AdaBoost on the G3D dataset using action timeline performance metrics but for comparison with the state of the art we have reproduced those results here with the action point performance metric. Our results are also very close to state of the art results [3] provided on the MSRC-12 dataset (FPS[1]) using the same latency aware performance metric.

Table 1. Online action recognition results for gaming action datasets

	G3D dataset (Fighting)		MSRC-12 dataset (FPS[1])		
Algorithm	AdaBoost	Dynamic Feature Selection	AdaBoost	Dynamic Feature Selection	Random Forest [3]
Mean F-score	0.896	**0.919**	0.643	0.747	**0.765**

5   Conclusion

This paper proposed a novel method for dynamic feature selection for online recognition that combines the strengths of both embedded and wrapper methods. Specifically, we use the feature selection method built in to Random Forest to determine our feature subsets; then use the reduced feature vectors to train multiple AdaBoost classifiers. Recognition occurs dynamically at each frame inspired by the wrapper approach to select the best model but without the overhead of a cross validation data set.

Our new dynamic feature selection algorithm for real-time action recognition improves the accuracy of baseline Gentle AdaBoost at low-latency, as demonstrated by experiments on publicly available gaming action datasets (G3D, MSRC-12). Future work will include applying our method on other applications, such as such as facial expression and sign language recognition.

References

1. Ellis, C., Masood, S.Z., Tappen, M.F., Laviola Jr., J.J., Sukthankar, R.: Exploring the Trade-off Between Accuracy and Observational Latency in Action Recognition. International Journal of Computer Vision 101, 420–436 (2013)

---

[1] Video + text modality.

2. Nowozin, S., Shotton, J.: Action Points: A Representation for Low-latency Online Human Action Recognition. Technical report (2012)
3. Fothergill, S., Mentis, H., Kohli, P., Nowozin, S.: Instructing people for training gestural interactive systems. In: Proceedings of the SIGCHI Conference on Human Factors in Computing Systems, pp. 1737–1746. ACM, New York (2012)
4. Bloom, V., Makris, D., Argyriou, V.: G3D: A gaming action dataset and real time action recognition evaluation framework. In: 2012 IEEE Computer Society Conference on Computer Vision and Pattern Recognition Workshops, pp. 7–12. IEEE (2012)
5. Bobick, A.F., Davis, J.W.: The recognition of human movement using temporal templates. Pattern Analysis and Machine Intelligence 23, 257–267 (2001)
6. Aggarwal, J.K., Ryoo, M.S.: Human activity analysis: A review. ACM Computing Surveys 43, 16:1–16:43 (2011)
7. Yamato, J., Ohya, J., Ishii, K.: Recognizing human action in time-sequential images using hidden Markov model. In: Computer Vision and Pattern Recognition, pp. 379–385 (1992)
8. Yu, E., Aggarwal, J.K.: Human action recognition with extremities as semantic posture representation. In: Computer Vision and Pattern Recognition Workshops, pp. 1–8 (2009)
9. Schuldt, C., Laptev, I., Caputo, B.: Recognizing human actions: a local SVM approach. In: Proceedings of the 17th International Conference on Pattern Recognition, ICPR 2004, vol. 3, pp. 32–36 (2004)
10. Dollar, P., Rabaud, V., Cottrell, G., Belongie, S.: Behavior recognition via sparse spatio-temporal features. In: Visual Surveillance and Performance Evaluation of Tracking and Surveillance, pp. 65–72 (2005)
11. Guyon, I., Elisseeff, A.: An introduction to variable and feature selection. The Journal of Machine Learning Research 3, 1157–1182 (2003)
12. Amaldi, E., Kann, V.: On the Approximability of Minimizing Nonzero Variables or Unsatisfied Relations in Linear Systems. Theoretical Computer Science 209, 237–260 (1998)
13. Kohavi, R., John, G.H.: Wrappers for Feature Subset Selection. Artificial intelligence 97, 273–324 (1997)
14. Climent-Pérez, P., Chaaraoui, A.A., Padilla-López, J.R., Flórez-Revuelta, F.: Optimal joint selection for skeletal data from RGB-D devices using a genetic algorithm. In: Batyrshin, I., Mendoza, M.G. (eds.) MICAI 2012, Part II. LNCS, vol. 7630, pp. 163–174. Springer, Heidelberg (2013)
15. Olshen, L., Breiman, J., Friedman, R., Stone, C.J.: Classification and Regression Trees. Wadsworth International Group (1984)
16. Breiman, L.: Random Forests. Machine Learning 45, 5–32 (2001)
17. Kinect Gesture Detection using Machine Learning, http://www.microsoft.com/en-us/download/details.aspx?id=28066
18. Miao, X., Heaton, J.S.: A comparison of random forest and Adaboost tree in ecosystem classification in east Mojave Desert. In: 2010 18th Int. Conf. on Geoinformatics, pp. 1–6 (2010)
19. Freund, Y., Schapire, R.E.: Experiments with a New Boosting Algorithm. In: International Conference on Machine Learning, pp. 148–156 (1996)
20. Rifkin, R., Klautau, A.: In Defense of One-Vs-All Classification. The Journal of Machine Learning Research 5, 101–141 (2004)
21. Friedman, J., Hastie, T., Tibshirani, R.: Additive Logistic Regression: a Statistical View of Boosting. Annals of Statistics 28, 2000 (1998)

A Fully Unsupervised Approach to Activity Discovery

Umut Avci and Andrea Passerini

Dipartimento di Ingegneria e Scienza dell'Informazione
Università degli Studi di Trento
Trento, Italy
{avci,passerini}@disi.unitn.it

Abstract. We propose an activity discovery framework that aims at identifying activities within data streams in the absence of data annotation. The process starts with dividing the full sensor stream into segments by identifying differences in sensor activations characterizing potential activity changes. Then, extracted segments are clustered in order to find groups of similar segments each representing a candidate activity. Lastly, parameters of a sequential labeling algorithm are estimated using segment clusters found in the previous step and the learned model is used to smooth the initial segmentation. We present experimental evaluation for two real world datasets. The results obtained show that our segmentation approaches perform almost as good as the true segmentation and that activities are discovered with a high accuracy in most of the cases. We demonstrate the effectiveness of our model by comparing it with a technique using substantial domain knowledge.

Keywords: Activity discovery, sequence segmentation, sequential labeling.

1 Introduction

Activity recognition has long been studied by the machine learning community. Most of the work in the field has focused on supervised approaches in order to train activity models. However, these require the availability of labeled sequences, an expensive and time consuming process. Furthermore, training data are specific to the setting involving the activities to be recognized and the persons involved, as the daily living habits change from an individual to another. Activity discovery aims at identifying activities within data streams in the absence of data annotation. Therefore, it can be used in any possible daily-life scenario. In health monitoring applications, for instance, one of the task is continuously checking the behaviour of a patient in order to determine whether his/her routines are maintained, regardless of the type of activities being performed. Inconsistencies in daily routines, i.e. changes in the structure of performed activities, can suggest problems in patient's health. As many unsupervised learning tasks, activity discovery is a challenging problem: many activities tend to share a similar set of signals (e.g. kitchen sensors for food-related activities), short periods

A.A. Salah et al. (Eds.) : HBU 2013, LNCS 8212, pp. 77–88, 2013.
© Springer International Publishing Switzerland 2013

lacking any signal at all can occur during an activity, to be distinguished from truly "idle" periods where no activity is being performed. Finally the discovery needs to be robust enough to account for variations in the way activities can be performed.

There are few works on activity discovery in the literature. Using sequential patterns in order to represent activities was proposed in [4] and [2]. Both approaches are based on the idea that similar patterns can be used for representing the activities. Following this idea, patterns are first mined from data and then clustered by k-means and LDA respectively. However, these techniques are bound to the quality and coverage of the extracted patterns. Hamid et al. [5] suggests clustering segments instead of patterns extracted from them. For this purpose, segments are represented by histograms each of which then corresponds to a node in an edge-weighted graph. Maximal cliques in the graph are identified as activity candidates. However, the method cannot be used for real activity discovery as segments are assumed to be known in advance. Hong et al. [8] developed an activity discovery approach based on conceptual definitions of activities in terms of Evidential Ontology Networks (EON). A candidate segment that fits an EON best is recognized as the corresponding activity. Since the method works on previously segmented data, the authors later introduced three segmentation approaches [9]. Extracted segments are fed into the EON for determining activities. The method is based on a deep knowledge of the activities being searched, needed to compile the set of rules which are used for the activity discovery phase.

In this paper, we present an activity discovery approach that addresses the abovementioned limitations. The rationale behind the approach is that distinct activities should correspond to separate sets of sensors, e.g. activations of pairs or triplets of sensors, possibly repeated over time, jointly indicating a certain activity. With this reasoning, we assume that transition from one set to another indicates the possible time of an activity change. Following this rationale, we propose two segmentation algorithms looking for the change points in a sensor stream. Extracted segments are then clustered in order to find groups of similar segments each representing a candidate activity. Finally we use segments labeled with cluster identifiers to train the parameters of a sequential labeling algorithm which is then used for smoothing the initial segmentation.

We evaluate our technique in two freely available smart home datasets. The results show that our segmentation approaches perform almost as good as the true segmentation and that activities are discovered with a high accuracy in most of the cases. Comparisons with [8] show that our clustering achieves better results than an ontology network relying on expert-based activity descriptions.

The paper is organized as follows. Section 2 introduces the data representation format and the notion of activity segment. We describe our activity discovery framework in Section 3. An extensive experimental evaluation is reported in Section 4. Finally, conclusions are drawn in Section 5.

2 Data Representation

A dataset $\mathcal{D} = \{\mathbf{x}^{(1)}, \ldots, \mathbf{x}^{(d)}\}$ is a collection of input sequences for a number of days d. An input example $\mathbf{x} = \{\mathbf{x}_1, \ldots, \mathbf{x}_T\}$ consists of a consecutive sequence of observations, each covering a certain time instant t. An observation $\mathbf{x}_t$ is represented by the set of sensors which are active at that time instant (i.e. within its time interval). When feeding input sequences to labeling algorithms (see Section 3.3), observations will be represented as binary vectors rather than sets. Given N sensors, an observation $\mathbf{x}_t$ will thus be encoded as a binary feature vector $\mathbf{x}_t = (x_t^1, \ldots, x_t^N)$, each feature being 1 if the corresponding sensor is active and 0 otherwise.

The labeling task consists of predicting a sequence of activity labels $\mathbf{y} = \{y_1, \ldots, y_T\}$, one for each time instant. Each label $y_t \in [1, L]$ is one of L possible activities, with one indicating no activity. We assume here that activities are not simultaneous, i.e. only a single activity is performed at each time instant. We define an activity segment as a sequence of consecutive time instants labeled with the same activity. A segment $s_u = (b_u, e_u, y_u)$ is represented by its starting and ending time instants $b_u, e_u \in [1, T]$, with $e_u \geq b_u$, and the segment label y_u. A label sequence $\mathbf{y}$ can be split into a sequence $\mathbf{s} = \{s_1, \ldots, s_U\}$ of activity segments such that $b_1 = 1$, $e_U = T$, $b_u = e_{u-1} + 1$ and $y_u \neq y_{u-1}$ for all u. We define as $\mathbf{x}_{b_u:e_u}$ the segment of $\mathbf{x}$ ranging from b_u to e_u included. A collection of $\mathbf{s}$ over all the days forms $\mathcal{S} = \{\mathbf{s}^{(1)}, \ldots, \mathbf{s}^{(d)}\}$ with d being the number of days. Note that in the activity discovery framework we assume no knowledge is available concerning labels, including the number of activities L.

3 Activity Discovery Framework

Our activity discovery process consists of three steps:

1. **Sequence segmentation:** in this step, the full sensor stream is partitioned into segments which represent candidate activities, i.e. each segment should approximately span the whole time horizon in which an activity is continuously conducted. The segmentation procedure scans the stream searching for *changepoints* suggesting a change in the activity being performed.
2. **Segment clustering:** once segments have been identified, a clustering algorithm is employed in order to group together similar segments, each group representing a distinct candidate activity. Designing an appropriate segment similarity measure is crucial here in order to boost performance.
3. **Sequential labeling:** the final step employs the segment clusters produced by the previous step to train the parameters of a sequential labeling algorithm. The learned model is then used to run inference on the full sensor stream obtaining the final segmentation output. The rationale of this component is that the learned probabilistic model should allow to smooth segment borders with respect to the segmentation and clustering output, possibly improving recognition accuracy.

In the following we detail each step of the process.

3.1   Sequence Segmentation

The aim of the segmentation phase is to partition the sensor stream into fragments so that each fragment characterizes the occurrence of an activity. As will be seen in Section 4, activity datasets used for the evaluation differ from each other by the number and the type of the sensors. The fact that the quality of the segmentation is highly depend on the dataset properties necessities a specific handling in algorithm design. For this purpose, we propose two novel approaches, distance-based and context-based segmentation, for each experimental setting.

Distance-based segmentation is based on the idea that an activity is related to the sensor events occurring within a specific range. More specifically, the consecutive activation of two sensors whose distance to each other is less than a threshold (ϕ) is likely to indicate the persistence of the same activity. For example, preparing dinner is typically characterized by activation of kitchen sensors. Any sensor event occurring in the bedroom, however, is probably unrelated to the dinner activity. Selection of the threshold can be done in a number of ways depending on the dataset. One can assume that every activity is bounded with a certain room in the apartment. In this case, the threshold is computed as the distance between the two closest rooms. We used this type of distance in Van Kasteren dataset (see Section 4) as activities are known to be performed in separate rooms.

```
Algorithm 1: Distance-based Segmentation
Input:
  Sequence of observations (D)
  Separation threshold (φ)
  Sensor coordinates (C)
Output:
  Candidate activity borders
begin
  Initialize border candidates (B) to the empty set
  Calculate Manhattan distance matrix (M) of sensor pairings with (C)
  Find active time instants T = (t₁, t₂, ..., tₘ) in D
  for i from 1 to m-1
    Initialize pairwise distances (P) to the empty set
    for all sensor pairing (j,k) ∈ (D(tᵢ), D(tᵢ₊₁))
        P ← P ∪ M(j,k)
    if count(P > φ)/|P| > 0.5
        B ← B ∪ tᵢ
        if tᵢ₊₁ - 1 ∉ T
            B ← B ∪ tᵢ₊₁ - 1
  B ← B ∪ length(D)
  return B
```

Algorithm 1 shows the pseudocode of our distance-based segmentation technique. The algorithm takes as inputs a sequence of observations (D) as sensor activations and the spatial coordinates of all sensors (C), plus a threshold ϕ controlling when to introduce a breakpoint in the sequence. It first computes a matrix M of pairwise distances between sensors using the Manhattan metric, as it provides a natural measure of walking path length. The algorithm then identifies all time instants having at least one sensor activation and iteratively processes each of them. In order to decide whether to introduce a breakpoint at active time instant t_i, the algorithm compares its active sensors with those of the next active time instant t_{i+1}, using the previously computed distance matrix. If more than half of the comparisons have a distance greater than the threshold ϕ, i.e. sensors from the two time instants tend to be far apart, a breakpoint is added at time instant t_i. Note that t_{i+1} is not necessarily the time instant immediately following t_i, as they can be separated by a sequence of time instants lacking any sensor activation, likely indicating an idle "activity". In this case the algorithm introduces an additional breakpoint at time instant $t_{i+1} - 1$, isolating the segment with no activations. Note that conversely, null segments separating two active time instants with spatially close active sensors are merged in the segment containing t_i and t_{i+1}. This can be reasonable as activities often include short periods with no activations, but can miss longer null segments potentially representing idle cases. At the end of this section we introduce a post-processing procedure addressing this problem. Our algorithm resembles the one in [9], and indeed the two produce a very similar segmentation, but the latter requires much more information, concerning the location where specific activities are performed and ad-hoc rules extracted via profound investigation of the sensor stream.

The distance-based segmentation approach is suitable for datasets in which the location information is closely related to the activity being performed. In many cases, on the other hand, information regarding the locations of the sensors is not available, which makes the proposed method inapplicable. Therefore a general approach that does not depend on any kind of knowledge is required. We thus propose the context-based segmentation in which change points in sensor activation patterns are extracted. The rationale behind the approach is that two activities should be related to two distinct patterns of sensor activations, e.g. pairs or triplets of sensors jointly activated in the same time instant. This is implemented by representing each time instant by the set of its up to n-grams, where an n-gram is a set of n sensors jointly active in the time instant. The similarity between two time instants with sets A and B is then computed using the Jaccard index:

$$J(A, B) = \frac{|A \cap B|}{|A \cup B|}$$

We extend this similarity to include the *context* of a time instant by defining a *frame* as a sequence of time instants of a certain length (τ) and considering similarity between frames. The similarity between time instants t_i and t_{i+1} is then computed considering the frames $[t_{i-\tau+1} : t_i]$ and $[t_{i+1} : t_{i+1+\tau}]$, representing each frame by the union of the sets of (up to) n-grams of its time instants, and computing the Jaccard index between the two frames. Algorithm 2 outlines the context-based segmentation approach, where frames exceeding the borders of the sequence are appropriately trimmed.

```
Algorithm 2: Context-based Segmentation
Input:
  Sequence of observations (D)
  Frame size (τ)
  Gram size (n)
Output:
  Candidate activity borders
begin
  Initialize border candidates (B) to the empty set
  L ← length(D)
  for i from 1 to L-1
    if Jaccard(n, D[t_{i-τ+1} : t_i], D[t_{i+1} : t_{i+τ}]) = 0
      B ← B ∪ i
  B ← B ∪ L
  return B
```

The border generation process may result with a number of segments larger than the true one. In order to fix the most obvious cases, we applied a pruning procedure based on a number of simple reasonings. (1) There are a few occasions in which the distance-based algorithm extracts segments of size one when two consecutive time instants have exactly the same active sensors, and these come from two different locations. For instance, toilet activity is interleaved with sleeping, and is characterized by sensor activations from both the bedroom (bedroom door) and the toilet (e.g. toilet flush). If this occurs in a row for a small number of time instants, we merge them together in a single segment. (2) Let a segment without any sensor activation (zero segment) be preceded and followed by two segments whose active sensors either occur in the same location or are similar. These three consecutive segments should be merged into one to represent a single activity or be kept separate as two distinct segments of the same activity separated by an idle segment, depending on the length of the zero segment in the middle. We choose the former option if the resulting segment is smaller than a threshold representing the typical duration of activities, and the latter otherwise. The threshold is computed as the average length of the segments obtained by the segmentation algorithms, after excluding very long segments which likely represent peculiar activities like sleeping or idle. As an example of the merge operation, consider a dinner activity as taking food from the fridge followed by heating food in the microwave and then eating. The time we waited for heating is a zero segment, yet belongs to the same dinner activity. A three minute toilet activity performed two hours after another occurrence of toilet activity, on the other hand, should not be merged with the previous one since it is clear that they are distinct activity occurrences separated by another activity (e.g. sleeping).

3.2 Segment Clustering

The purpose of the clustering step is to determine the intrinsic grouping of the segments extracted in the previous phase so that each group represents an activity. We represent segments in terms of histograms of time instant-based features collected over each segment. Time instant-based features are extracted in the same manner as we did in the context-based segmentation, i.e. up to n-grams of sensors are extracted for each time instant in the input sequence. Found features are then collected over the segments and used for creating histograms as the counts of each feature.

Segment representations are then fed to a clustering algorithm. This has to deal with high-dimensional data, as coming from the up to n-gram feature representation, and automatically identify the number of clusters, which is not known in advance. We rely on the HDDC method [1] which satisfies both requirements. It is based on a modified Gaussian Mixture Model with a dimensionality reduction technique which determines the specific subspace in which each class is located by using eigenvectors of the covariance matrix. Models representing the subspaces are used to choose the number of clusters. To this end, clustering results are computed for different number of clusters and different models and the one maximizing Bayesian Information Criterion is selected. Further details can be found in the original paper [1].

3.3 Sequential Labeling

In principle, our algorithm could end up with the groupings returned by the clustering algorithm, each group representing a candidate activity. However, both segmentation and clustering steps are prone to errors and only provide approximations of actual segments and true groups. We use these approximations to train a sequential labeling algorithm, which assigns a label to each time instant in the sequence. The learned model is then used to run inference on the full sensor stream, providing the final sequential labeling. Each cluster in our setting corresponds to a different label in the sequential model.

We employ a Hidden Semi-Markov model (HSMM) [10] as sequential labeling approach, which is appropriate to label sequences where consecutive time instants tend to share the same label. An HSMM is a variant of HMM which allows for explicit duration distributions for different states, making it especially useful for segmenting sequences into fragments, each characterized by the same label. The joint probability modelled by the HSMM is represented as:

$$p(\mathbf{x}, \mathbf{s}) = \prod_{u=1}^{U} p(y_u|y_{u-1})p(d_u|y_u)p(\mathbf{x}_{b_u:e_u}|y_u) \qquad (1)$$

where $d_u = e_u - b_u + 1$ is the duration of segment s_u. The transition probability $p(y_u|y_{u-1})$ models the probability that activity y_u directly follows y_{u-1}. The duration probability $p(d_u|y_u)$ can be modelled as a histogram distribution (see e.g. [7]), where candidate activity durations are grouped into a certain number of bins (5 in our experiments). The probability of a certain segment of sensor activations given its label is commonly computed as the product of the probabilities of its time instants:

$$p(\mathbf{x}_{b_u:e_u}|y_u) = \prod_{t=b_u}^{e_u} p(\mathbf{x}_t|y_u) \tag{2}$$

where $p(\mathbf{x}_t|y_u)$ is further decomposed as a product of Bernoulli probabilities (active vs inactive) over sensors:

$$p(\mathbf{x}_t|y_u) = \prod_{i=1}^{N} p(x_t^i|y_u) \tag{3}$$

where N is the number of sensors. Given that each label is associated with a cluster from the previous step, parameters of all probabilities can be readily estimated from counts over the cluster segments. The transition probability between labels y_u and y_v, for instance, can be computed as the fraction of times in which a segment from cluster y_v follows one from cluster y_u in the original sequence, with respect to the overall number of segments in cluster y_u.

Once parameters are learned from the clustering results, inference is run on the whole sequence providing the labeled segmentation with maximal probability:

$$s^* = \text{argmax}_s\, p(\mathbf{x}, s) \tag{4}$$

which can be efficiently computed by the well-known Viterbi algorithm [10].

4   Experiments

In this section we first present the experimental setup used for evaluating the proposed approach and then provide results of the experiments.

4.1   Setting

The performance of the proposed framework was evaluated on a collection of freely available[1,2] benchmark datasets. Van Kasteren's dataset was collected over 28 days in a three room apartment occupied by a single resident [6]. The dataset consists of 14 state-change sensors, e.g reed switches and passive infrared. Activities were annotated by recording the start and end time of the corresponding activity either via handwritten diary or bluetooth headset. CASAS dataset differs from the previous one as two residents are simultaneously monitored in an apartment for 46 days, with a sensor network (of 71 nodes) mainly composed of motion and utility usage sensors [3]. Annotators labeled the data using a 3D visualization tool and residents' diaries.

We used the Changepoint feature representation that considers a sensor active (value 1) only in the time instants in which it alters its state [6]. It is robust against noises and is capable of tolerating the dataset specific sensor failures. For example, a door that is left open after completion of an activity causes sensors to be active for

---

[1] https://sites.google.com/site/tim0306/kasterenDataset.zip
[2] http://ailab.wsu.edu/casas/datasets/twor.2009.zip

longer periods than the actual activity duration, which eventually damages the segment information of other activities. Changepoint representation eliminates such activations by only considering activation and deactivation times of the sensors.

The performance of the system was evaluated by using the class accuracy metric proposed in [6]. The measure represents the average percentage of correctly classified timeslices per class and provides a proper model performance when a dataset contains unbalanced classes in terms of appearance frequency. The class accuracy is computed as follows:

$$\text{Class: } \frac{1}{C} \sum_{c=1}^{C} \frac{\sum_{n=1}^{N_c} [inferred_c(n) = true_c(n)]}{N_c} \tag{5}$$

where $[a = b]$ is a binary indicator returning 1 when true and 0 otherwise. C is the number of classes and N_c is the total number of time slices for class c. Precision, recall, and F measure are omitted for space limitations.

4.2 Results

Tables 1, and 2 show confusion matrices computed from the class accuracies for the van Kasteren and the CASAS dataset respectively. As discussed in Section 3.1, we applied the distance-based segmentation to the former and the context-based one to the latter. In all experiments the maximum gram size was set to two as higher values provided similar results while increasing computational complexity. Clustering does not assign names to the detected groups. However, it is clear that if a cluster contains mostly segments corresponding to a certain activity, it can be considered as an approximation of that activity. In order to identify the most likely activity for each cluster, we try all possible distinct activity assignments to clusters and choose the one maximizing class accuracy. If the algorithm identifies more clusters than the true number of activities, the best assignment will assign the clusters in excess to a dummy wrong activity. We do not explicitly report dummy clusters in the Tables, but include their assignments when computing the percentage of correct predictions (i.e. predicted rows do not always sum to one). Note that this best assignment measure is a fair evaluation procedure, as we simply identify for each cluster which is the activity it is most likely representing, forcing each cluster to represent a distinct activity.

The first set of experiments aims at comparing our approach with the evidential ontology network (EON) model proposed in [8] and evaluated on the Van Kasteren dataset. Table 1 shows confusion matrices for the different activities, where rows indicate true activities and columns predicted ones. EON rows report results for the EON model [8], while CLU shows results of our clustering step applied to the true segmentation, the same setting used in [8]. Our approach outperforms the competitor[3] in six out of eight activities and is on par on one.

---

[3] Note that by substantially extending the knowledge concerning activities being searched it is possible to achieve much higher recognition accuracy [8]. However, our aim here is to perform activity detection without any specific knowledge on the activities being performed.

Table 1. Detailed results of van Kastaren Dataset (values as percentages)

		I.	L.	T.	Sh.	Sl.	B.	Din.	Dr.
	EON	72	4	13	3	5	0	3	0
Idle	CLU	100	0	0	0	0	0	0	0
	SEG+CLU+HSMM	74(74)	12(1)	3(4)	0(2)	8(3)	2(2)	1(2)	0(0)
	EON	0	74	11	0	14	1	0	0
Leaving	CLU	0	80	20	0	0	0	0	0
	SEG+CLU+HSMM	4(41)	96(59)	0(0)	0(0)	0(0)	0(0)	0(0)	0(0)
	EON	0	56	27	5	1	11	0	0
Toileting	CLU	9	0	76	6	9	0	0	0
	SEG+CLU+HSMM	4(13)	1(1)	78(32)	5(4)	4(4)	0(1)	0(0)	0(10)
	EON	0	0	0	100	0	0	0	0
Showering	CLU	0	0	0	100	0	0	0	0
	SEG+CLU+HSMM	9(15)	8(0)	1(0)	76(85)	0(0)	0(0)	0(0)	0(0)
	EON	0	0	0	0	100	0	0	0
Sleeping	CLU	62	0	3	7	28	0	0	0
	SEG+CLU+HSMM	35(27)	21(0)	0(1)	0(0)	44(44)	0(0)	0(0)	0(24)
	EON	0	21	14	0	4	44	14	3
Breakfast	CLU	0	0	0	0	0	100	0	0
	SEG+CLU+HSMM	18(31)	0(0)	5(0)	0(0)	9(1)	68(68)	0(0)	0(0)
	EON	0	0	59	0	13	0	28	0
Dinner	CLU	7	0	0	0	0	57	36	0
	SEG+CLU+HSMM	23(12)	2(0)	0(0)	0(0)	0(0)	36(35)	38(53)	0(0)
	EON	37	0	0	0	0	0	0	63
Drink	CLU	14	0	0	0	0	0	0	86
	SEG+CLU+HSMM	9(16)	1(0)	1(5)	0(0)	0(0)	80(64)	8(15)	0(0)

The only case where we get worse results is on Sleeping, which is characterized by a single sensor activation of bedroom door and a long period of no sensor activation. Sleeping is divided into many parts as it is interleaved by the Toilet activity. Segments separating two consecutive Toilet activities do not have any sensor activation, and are thus wrongly clustered in the Idle group[4].

SEG+CLU+HSMM rows report results of our complete approach, while results in brackets show the performance of the segmentation and clustering steps only (SEG+CLU). Clustering generates nine clusters for both true segmentation and predicted one. Activities performed in the kitchen are clustered together in predicted segmentation as they share basically the same sensor activations, explaining the overprediction of Breakfast. Drink, however, is assigned to a distinct cluster in true segmentation which decreased the confusion in prediction of kitchen-oriented activities. Incorporating sequential labeling (SEG+CLU+HSMM rows) provides overall better results, by improving recognition of Leaving and Toileting (while performance for Showering and Dinner are slightly degraded). For Leaving, the improvement is achieved by recovering from incorrect segmentations introducing spurious segments predicted as Idle within a Leaving activity. For Toilet, the clustering algorithm actually spreads segments containing Toilet activities in two different clusters, together with some segments from other

---

[4] [9] Hong et al., Segmenting sensor data for activity monitoring in smart environments.

Table 2. Detailed results of CASAS Dataset (values as percentages)

		I.	B.to.T.	B.	G.	S.	W.at.C.	W.at.D.R.
Idle	CLU	100	0	0	0	0	0	0
	SEG+CLU+HSMM	100(83)	0(7)	0(6)	0(0)	0(0)	0(0)	0(0)
Bed to Toilet	CLU	68	0	0	31	1	0	0
	SEG+CLU+HSMM	28(9)	0(38)	0(1)	70(33)	1(9)	1(3)	0(0)
Breakfast	CLU	7	0	93	0	0	0	0
	SEG+CLU+HSMM	6(29)	0(3)	92(35)	2(7)	0(0)	0(0)	0(0)
Grooming	CLU	12	0	0	88	0	0	0
	SEG+CLU+HSMM	9(6)	0(30)	0(5)	91(41)	0(8)	0(1)	0(0)
Sleeping	CLU	2	0	0	40	58	0	0
	SEG+CLU+HSMM	6(3)	0(3)	0(2)	0(1)	94(51)	0(4)	0(0)
Working at computer	CLU	3	13	0	0	0	82	2
	SEG+CLU+HSMM	12(10)	0(1)	0(6)	0(1)	0(2)	86(36)	2(3)
Working at dining room	CLU	0	0	0	0	0	38	62
	SEG+CLU+HSMM	7(34)	0(0)	0(0)	0(2)	0(0)	8(8)	45(23)

activities, while the HSMM manages to identify most of them as belonging to the same class.

Table 2 reports results of CLU, SEG+CLU+HSMM and (in brackets) SEG+CLU for resident one of the CASAS dataset. A similar behaviour is observed for resident two (results omitted for space limitations). The clustering algorithm generates 10 clusters. The complete model provides significant improvements over SEG+CLU in almost all cases. This is mostly due to recovering portions of segments which were assigned to spurious clusters (clustering detects more clusters than the true number of activities), thanks to the smoothing effect of HSMM and its capacity of correctly modeling duration of activities. This allows the complete model to even slightly improve over the clustering applied to the true segmentation, as shown by comparing rows CLU and SEG+CLU+HSMM. As for the Van Kasteren dataset, a current limitation of the approach is that similar activities tend to be merged into the same cluster. Indeed, both CLU and SEG+CLU+HSMM fail to identify the Bed to Toilet activity, as it is very similar to Grooming in terms of sensor activations involved.

5 Conclusion

In this paper, we presented an activity discovery framework that identifies activities in sensor streams without requiring data annotation. The proposed approach first extracts segments from sequences by identifying candidate activity change-points, clusters extracted segments into groups representing candidate activities, and trains a sequential labeling model with segment clusters, which is then used to provide the final refined segmentation.

The effectiveness and suitability of our approach was evaluated in two smart home datasets. Initial results show that proposed approach succeeds in discovering activities in many situations. Although our technique does not depend on any assumptions on dataset, e.g. type of activities, number of clusters, it outperformed a method using activity definitions as domain knowledge. We observed that our segmentation algorithm produces segments which are quite close to the true ones. The final sequential labeling model succeeds in further refining the results, by smoothing segment borders and recovering part of the segments assigned to spurious clusters.

The proposed framework, however, suffers from a number of limitations. Similar activities tend to be clustered together and are hard to distinguish. In order to prevent this, a better way to represent segments or additional features (e.g. time of the day, duration of the activity etc.) can be defined. Interleaved activities also decrease performance, as when repeatedly going to toilet during the night. Relationships between neighbouring segments could be included in the clustering phase in order to address this problem.

Acknowledgments. This research was partially supported by grant PRIN 2009LNP494 (Statistical Relational Learning: Algorithms and Applications) from Italian Ministry of University and Research.

References

1. Berg, L., Bouveyron, C., Girard, S.: HDclassif: An R Package for Model-Based Clustering and Discriminant Analysis of High-Dimensional Data. Journal of Statistical Software 46(6), 1–29 (2012)
2. Chikhaoui, B., Wang, S., Pigot, H.: ADR-SPLDA: Activity discovery and recognition by combining sequential patterns and latent Dirichlet allocation. Pervasive and Mobile Computing 8(6), 845–862 (2012)
3. Cook, D.J., Schmitter-Edgecombe, M.: Assessing the quality of activities in a smart environment. Methods of Information in Medicine 48(5), 480–485 (2009)
4. Rashidi, P., Cook, D.J., Holder, L.B., Schmitter-Edgecombe, M.: Discovering Activities to Recognize and Track in a Smart Environment. IEEE Transactions on Knowledge and Data Engineering 23, 527–539 (2011)
5. Hamid, R., Maddi, S., Johnson, A., Bobick, A., Essa, I., Isbell, C.: A novel sequence representation for unsupervised analysis of human activities. Artificial Intelligence 173(14), 1221–1244 (2009)
6. van Kasteren, T., Noulas, A., Englebienne, G., Kröse, B.: Accurate activity recognition in a home setting. In: 10th International Conference on Ubiquitous Computing, pp. 1–9 (2008)
7. van Kasteren, T., Englebienne, G., Kröse, B.: Activity Recognition Using Semi-Markov Models on Real World Smart Home Datasets. Ambient Intelligence and Smart Environments Thematic Issue on Smart Homes 2(3), 311–325 (2010)
8. Hong, X., Nugent, C.D.: Implementing evidential activity recognition in sensorised homes. Technology and Health Care 19(1), 37–52 (2011)
9. Hong, X., Nugent, C.D.: Segmenting sensor data for activity monitoring in smart environments. Personal Ubiquitous Computing 17(3), 545–559 (2013)
10. Yu, S.Z.: Hidden semi-Markov models. Artificial Intelligence 174(2), 215–243 (2010)

Transfer Learning of Human Poses for Action Recognition

Mario Rodríguez, Carlos Medrano, Elias Herrero,
and Carlos Orrite*

I3A, University of Zaragoza, Spain

Abstract. In order to increase the success rate of a human action recognition system trained with limited labelled video sequences, we propose an approach which combines an efficient use of the scarce data and a transfer learning improvement. The efficient use of data is implemented using the Fuzzy Observation Hidden Markov Model so as to outperform the constraints of the classical approaches when training with small datasets. Additionally, we use a transfer learning procedure that takes advantage of the fact that some human body poses are shared among actions and then key poses can be trained from external sources. Thanks to this method we have improved the recognition performance in new action classes introduced in the target domain. In order to confirm the usefulness of the approach we have tested the performance using the IXMAS dataset as target domain and the ViHASi dataset as source domain.

Keywords: Human Action Recognition, Transfer Learning, Ubiquitous Computing, Computer Vision, Video Analysis.

1 Introduction

The ubiquitous presence of human activities video recordings and its increasing importance in real-world applications such as surveillance or ambient intelligent application (e.g. visual monitoring of elderly and disabled people at home) has stimulated much research in computer vision, especially in the areas related to human motion analysis, see a recent survey by [1]. The hope of most systems is that an automatic video understanding system would enable a minimum human participation in the process of monitoring wide areas in a reliable manner.

However, in most of the real scenarios the amount of labelled footage is not enough for training a robust human action recognition system. As depicted in Figure 1a, composed by images of human activities in real scenarios, human activities take place in a wide spectrum of scenarios performed by different actors and recorded from random viewpoints. These variabilities produce that for a newly installed activity recognition system is impossible to collect sufficient amount of "clean" and "precisely" labelled training videos in a short period.

* This work is partially supported by Spanish Grant TIN2010-20177 (MICINN) and FEDER and by regional government DGA-FSE. Mario Rodriguez has got a FPI grant from the MICINN.

A.A. Salah et al. (Eds.) : HBU 2013, LNCS 8212, pp. 89–101, 2013.
© Springer International Publishing Switzerland 2013

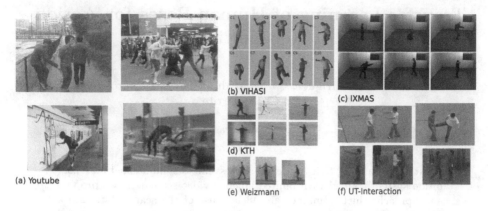

Fig. 1. Samples from real world scenarios and public human action databases

Therefore, we propose a machine learning system which deals with this problem from two sides. First, we use a discrete Hidden Markov Model (dHMM) recognition system, proved to be adequate for sequences, but using the modified version Fuzzy Observation HMM (FO-HMM) [2] suitable for limited training examples. From the original method we replace the Motion History Image features by the raw silhouettes as pose descriptors. Second, we include a transfer learning stage where information from external human recordings, nowadays available elsewhere, is introduced in the system in order to produce a more representative codebook. Currently the availability of video sequences containing human activities is enormous, and as depicted in Figure 1 many of them provided by public dataset or even virtually created.

We can notice in the images the high variability involving human activities footage which inevitably affects to the recognition system. An in-depth analysis allows us to summarize the sources of this variability thanks to what it is possible to develop a right strategy and minimize its effects. In Figure 2 we divide the sources of variability into three groups:

1. Actor. Actions are performed by subjects with various shapes, clothes, and no action is exactly repeated in the same way even if the actor is the same.
2. Scenario. The videos can be recorded in different places or in different times which implies changes in the background, in the illumination or in the viewpoint
3. Camera Settings. The use of several devices involves a freedom in the camera resolution, lenses and so on.

Almost all the features used in human action recognition systems are independent of the camera settings and can be considered independent of the scenario, although the actor behaviour can be somehow affected by its surrounding. However, these variabilities affect the working of the features extractor because the image quality is a direct modifier of the features quality. The most used features in the state of the art methods try to find key points in the images, or

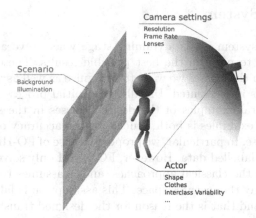

Fig. 2. Sources of variability in a human action recognition system based on computer vision

the sequences, in order to characterize the human poses (static) or combine information of human poses and short movements (dynamic) surrounding these points. Some of the most common examples are the static information of HoGs or dynamic HoFs [3], or the static Sift and its dynamic counterpart 3D-Sift [4]. Although all of them can be used in the study carried out in this paper, for the sake of simplicity we have chosen the silhouettes already provided in the used databases IXMAS [5] and ViHASi [6]. Although there is not a feature extractor able to obtain clean silhouettes in an uncontrolled environment, silhouettes describe well human poses and adapt properly to our study. It is worth noting that we use a single fixed camera as recorder and then we just obtain 2-dimensional information, what implies a 2-d poses characterization high dependent on the camera viewpoint.

Our study deals with an environment where we install a new camera recording human activities we want to recognize. In a initial short period we are able to record few actions of a limited number of action classes with which we can train the recognition system. However, in the future we want to introduce new action classes for recognizing, and then train the system again. Our goal is to train the whole system just once, when the very first actions are available, and then train only a new FO-HMM for the new classes. We have proved how the transfer learning stage improves the recognition rates when including new action classes in the system.

The rest of the paper is organized as follows. In Section 2 we describe the proposed approach, explaining the principles of FO-HMM, analysing the used transfer learning and defining the Fuzzy Observation finally used. In Section 3 we present the experiments carried out in order to evaluate the approach. Finally, in Section 4 we explain the conclusions and propose some discussion.

2   Proposed System

Every recognition system needs a training stage where several parameters are estimated in order to perform the best possible results. These parameters are mainly related with the classes we want to recognize as well as with the scenario where the system is implemented. Usually, this initial process is carried out by learning from several examples of the desired classes in the specific scenario, and the number of examples is both, crucial for the accuracy of the results and expensive to increase. In particular, we propose the use of FO-HMM [2], designed to cope with scant labelled data. However, FO-HMM only solves problems with incomplete data in the classical approaches, and it assumes that the codebook characterize properly the features space. This assumption is false when training with limited data and that is the reason for the designed transfer learning stage that improves the features space characterization.

2.1   Fuzzy Observation-HMM

We assume a task where the goal is to predict a label ω^* from an input O. Each ω^* is a member of a set of possible labels and each vector O is a vector of local observations $O = \{o_1, o_2, \ldots, o_T\}$. The training set consists of labelled examples (O_i, ω_i) for $i = 1 \ldots M$, where each $\omega_i \in \Omega$, and each $O_i = \{o_{i,1}, o_{i,2}, \ldots, o_{i,T}\}$. This task can be achieved by training a HMM model per class respectively, as depicted in the right of Figure 3. Thus, for a given unknown sequence, the class label is assigned via Maximum Likelihood (ML) after evaluating the sequence in every HMM.

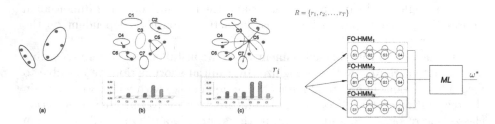

Fig. 3. Observation probability distribution parametrization in the different HMM approaches. (a) Continuous-HMM (b) Discrete-HMM (c) FO-HMM. Included Fuzzy Observation HMM framework for action recognition.

HMM is a widely used tool in sequences recognition systems [7]. A HMM is a probabilistic model in which the process modelled is assumed to be a Markov Chain composed by a finite set of states. The states are not observable (they are hidden) but every observation of the sequence generated by the HMM obeys a probability distribution associated to a specific state. Formally, the parameters of the Markov model are $\lambda = \{N, A, B, \pi\}$. N is the number of states, i.e., $S = \{S_1, \ldots S_N\}$. $A = \{a_{ij}\}$ is the state transition matrix where the transition probability a_{ij} represents the frequency of transiting from state i to state j. B is the observation probability distribution. Finally, $\pi = \{\pi_i\}$ is the initial state probability distribution where $\pi_i = Pr(q_1 = S_i)$, $1 \leq i \leq N$ being q_t the state at time t. With the aid of several sequences of observations and with a fixed topology of the HMM it is possible to estimate the model parameters using the Baum-Welch optimization.

In relation to the observation probability distribution B, the classical approaches can be divided into two: (i) discrete-HMM where the possible observations in a state belong to a codebook being $b_j(v_k) = Pr(o_t = v_k \mid q_t = S_j)$, o_t the observation at time t and $V = \{v_1, v_2, ..., v_K\}$ the symbols of a codebook of size K, and (ii) continuous-HMM where the possible observations are n-dimensional real vectors and their probability distribution is usually modelled with a Mixture of Gaussians (MoG). Taking into account that we are working with sequences of real vectors codifying human poses, it seems reasonable the use of the cHMM, however both cases suffer from incomplete data when training with limited number of labelled sequences. Looking the continuous example in Figure 3a we see red dots representing the training observations and two ellipses surrounding them representing the MoG that model the probability distribution of the observations. With an adequate number of observations it is possible to train a reliable MoG representing the probability distribution but, as we dispose of sparse information, the obtained model is unreliable. Human motion has a high variability and the probability of new actions in positions out of the model is too high for a robust system. The discrete-HMM, on the other hand, constraints the freedom of a real vector to a specified codebook. In Figure 3b we see the same red dots in the same data space represented in the continuous example, but in this case we force the observation to belong to a specific codeword of a designed codebook. This codebook is trained with the examples available quantizing the data space and again, a higher number of training examples will produce a more suitable codebook. Moreover, the scarce training examples can lead to zero probability of some codewords, and then the likelihood estimation be zero because of just one outlier. Usually, in order to avoid this effect some kind of regularization is implemented, but without any intelligence.

Finally, in Figure 3c we can see a modification in the use of the observations for training and testing the HMMs that we call Fuzzy Observations (FO). In this approach, we use the same codebook of dHMM but applying it in a different way. We know that we are working with n-dimensional real vectors but the winner takes all rule removes much of the position information, so we replace this rule with a fuzzy assignation. Every observation has a probability of belonging to every codeword depending on the distance to the specific codeword. With this modification we solve the problem of zero probability but also we assign a more reliable probability in the codewords because some examples may land in a unclear place that the winner takes all rule force to a specific codeword but the FO distribute among every codeword. Formally, a FO is a vector $\mathbf{r}$ that we normalize in order to represent probabilities in a Dirichlet distribution, producing a simplex $\Delta = \{\mathbf{r} \in \mathbb{R}^n : r \geq 0 : \mathbf{e}^T \mathbf{r} = 1\}$ where $\mathbf{e}$ is a vector of unit components. Moreover, we can define each component of a FO as $p(v_k|o_t)$, probability that observation o_t belongs to codeword v_k, then $\mathbf{r}_t = \{p(v_k|o_t)\}_{k=1}^{K}$. However, the use of FO implies a modification on the Baum-Welch algorithm used to estimate the parameters, described in [2].

2.2 Codebook Creation with Transfer Learning

Transfer learning applied in human action recognition has experimented a great increase of researches as we can realize in recent surveys [8] [9]. It is based in the use of external information from a source domain that complements the limited data available in a target domain where the recognition task is implemented. We can find several strategies in the literature that the previous surveys try to organize. In [10] the authors use an inter-lingua in order to merge data from source domains and target domain, considering labelled data available only in the source domain, which classifies their method as uninformed supervised (US). In [11] a similar approach is implemented by creating a cross domain codebook where labelled actions from both domains are modelled with Bag of Words (BoW), being an informed supervised (IS) transfer learning method. Authors in [12] create a codebook with unlabelled data from the source domain and train the recognition with labelled data from the target domain, being an informed unsupervised (IU) transfer learning method. The literature is really extensive, but most of the methods use similar approaches [13] [14].

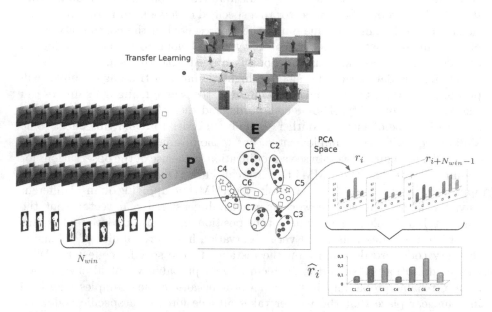

Fig. 4. Sketch of the Fuzzy Observation extraction from a codebook created with Transfer Learning and a window merge

Our proposal uses unlabelled data from the source domain, and "translates" it into the target domain using a dimensionality reduction PCA trained with the available target domain data. The target domain data available for training is labelled so we are doing an IU transfer learning. Attending to the definitions of transfer learning in [8], our method is an inductive transfer learning because the source task models just poses whereas the target task uses sequences of poses.

In Figure 4 we observe the diagram of the FO creation where the codebook is trained using transfer learning. Initially we suppose the availability of few labelled sequences in the objective scenario. Every frame of these sequences is projected into the PCA space obtaining a vector of points, $\mathbf{P} = \{p_t\} \ni p_t \in \mathbb{R}^d$. This vector $\mathbf{P}$ produces a sparse point cloud representing the human poses recorded in the target domain sequences, in Figure 4 this points are represented by squares, stars and pentagons. However, a reliable codebook should represent the whole spectrum of possible poses in the actions to be recognized. In addition, there are multiple public databases composed of frames with subjects performing different actions that we can project into the same space $\mathbf{E} = \{e_t\} \ni e_t \in \mathbb{R}^d$. The combination of both sources of data allows us to dispose of a point cloud doing a better representation of the different poses humans acquire $\{\mathbf{P}, \mathbf{E}\}$, in Figure 4 we see the addition of red circles. Finally, we use the K-means algorithm in order to obtain the $V = \{v_1, v_2, ..., v_K\}$ clusters representing the symbols of the codebook by minimizing the objective function which includes the complete point cloud.

$$\arg\min_{V} \sum_{i=1}^{K} \sum_{x_j \in S_i} \|x_j - \mu_i\|^2 \tag{1}$$

where μ_i is the mean of points in v_i. $\forall x_j \in \{\mathbf{P}, \mathbf{E}\}$.

The usefulness of this approach lies in the assumption that different actions can share some of their posses, even if they belong to different datasets. Suppose we have a kick sequence in the source domain, and this sequence shares some initial poses with a punch sequence. On the other hand, we have trained a recognition system without punch nor kick sequences in the target domain, but we now dispose of a punch sequence to introduce in the recognition system. The codebook has been trained with the source kick sequence and thanks to it the codebook models better the punch sequence and can allow us to train a new FO-HMM without retraining the codebook and retraining all the previous FO-HMMs. Moreover, the Transfer Learning can fill some gaps in the labelled sequences and avoid overfitting when the codebook represents just the limited labelled poses.

As we have mentioned before, the used features are dependent of the camera viewpoint, and is clear that shared poses are available when using close camera viewpoints in source and target datasets.

Once clusters are obtained we model the codebook as a set of Gaussians with mean and covariance matrix empirically calculated using the samples of the specific cluster. Then, the sequence of FO is obtained by evaluating every observed pose o_t in the Gaussians representing symbols. Even if it does not represent a mathematically correct similarity measure, the values obtained are equally valuables for our purpose.

$$r_{t,k} = p(v_k|o_t) = \frac{\mathcal{N}_k(o_t; \mu_k, \Sigma_k)}{\sum_{i=1}^{K} \mathcal{N}_i(o_t; \mu_i, \Sigma_i)} \tag{2}$$

where the denominator is a normalization factor.

2.3 Merge of Poses in a Time Window

When obtaining the FOs from single frames there is a high probability of producing outliers in the sequences. In order to minimize this problem we propose the modification of the FOs by doing a simple average of the fuzzy values as shown in Figure 4. First, a window size is fixed N_{win} and later the average fuzzy vector is computed.

$$\widehat{r}_{i,k} = \frac{\sum_{j=i}^{i+N_{win}-1} r_{i,k}}{N_{win}} \tag{3}$$

where $\widehat{r}_{i,k}$ is the k component of the fuzzy observation $\widehat{r}_i$ and the denominator N_{win} is the window size. Then, the components $p(v_k|o_t)$ are replaced with the new components $\widehat{r}_{i,k}$ obtaining the vector of local observations used in the FO-HMM, $\widehat{R} = \{\widehat{r}_1, \widehat{r}_2, \ldots, \widehat{r}_{\widehat{T}}\}$

3 Approach Evaluation

In this section we evaluate the proposed framework in a scenario with limited labelled data available. The validity of FO-HMM have been already proven so we check the performance of the proposed FO improvements. In this purpose we select the IXMAS database [5] as target domain and the virtual human action database ViHASi [6] as source domain for transfer learning. We call success rate the rate of correctly classified actions.

The IXMAS dataset, Figure 1c, is composed by 13 actions performed each 3 times by 11 actors. The recording has been made from 5 viewpoints. As we consider the new scenario with fixed viewpoint we use only one camera, and following the authors of the database suggestion we discard two of the actors due to their irregular performance, so we dispose of 27 repetitions per action. Additionally, we discard 2 classes suggested as well by the authors so we dispose of 11 actions. The initial experiments are carried out over 5 diverse classes of IXMAS (sit down, walk, wave, punch and kick) so as to recreate a scenario with few initial training classes and then allows to introduce 6 new classes not used in the codebook and PCA training. The training is carried out using only 1 sequence per class, and using a leave one sequence out process we test every action sequence from the target dataset. Once a sequence test has been selected we randomly select an action per class from the remaining sequences in order to train the system. The poses of these five actions are used to train a PCA projection with a variability of 80%, and their projections are clustered, creating the codebook of 50 symbols.

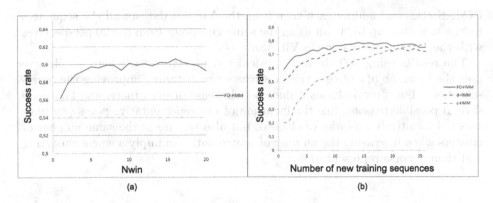

Fig. 5. Success rate increasing the window size (a). Comparison of cHMM, dHMM and FO-HMM increasing the training sequences (b).

The results shown in Figure 5a are used for select the window size. We can observe how the use of the window improve the results, and the size reaches an stationary state after 5 frames. Although FO-HMM has been already proved as a good method for training limited labelled datasets, we carried out a new experiment, shown in Figure 5b, comparing its results with cHMM and dHMM. In this comparison FO-HMM and dHMM use the same codebook, and all three cases reduce the dimensionality with the same PCA model. The interest of this experiment lies in the large number of training sequences available in IXMAS. We obtain that FO-HMM improves both methods when training with few sequences and as expected cHMM overtakes it when using a lot of them (over 24 for this experiment). On the other hand, dHMM appears to maintain an offset with respect to FO-HMM even if we increase the number of training sequences.

We continue the experiments evaluating the transfer learning improvement using the source domain. The ViHASi dataset, Figure 1b, has been virtually created with 20 action classes, 9 different actors and 40 perspective camera views. The interest for a virtual dataset in contrast to a real world scenario lies in the easiness of the implementation of new examples.

The usefulness of the transfer learning lies in the better representation of the poses space it allows. We evaluate how good is the representation through the following distance. Consider the pose vector $\mathbf{x}_t$ represented with the Fuzzy Observation $\mathbf{r}_t$ (column vector). If μ is a matrix which columns represents the clusters centroids we can estimate the original pose vector with Equation 4, which is a linear combination of the cluster means.

$$\widehat{\mathbf{x}}_t = \mu \mathbf{r}_t \tag{4}$$

Now the euclidean distance between the estimated pose vector $\widehat{\mathbf{x}}_t$ and the actual pose vector $\mathbf{x}_t$ represents how good the codebook is. We have carried out an experiment evaluating the average distance in all the IXMAS pose vectors but those from the 5 initial IXMAS sequences, with which we have trained the PCA and the codebook. The codebook has been trained with one random sequence per

IXMAS class and adding each time from the ViHASi dataset all the sequences from a new class up to 20, all using the same viewpoint from the 20 perspectives with the same vertical angle in ViHASi.

The results using 300 clusters are depicted in Figure 6a, where we observe how the inclusion of source actions decreases the distance (improving the representation), but after 5 classes it does not decrease or even increases. There are several possible reasons, like the inclusion of not representative poses (we have selected intuitively an order of classes), but also the use of the same number of clusters when increasing the number of source data can imply a worse clustering and then a worse representation.

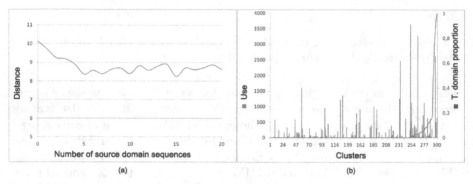

(a)   (b)

Fig. 6. Distance between estimated and actual pose vectors (a) Use of clusters ordered by theirs domain proportion (b)

In Figure 6b we show how the clustering is conformed and used. From the previous experiment we select the case with 7 actions from ViHASi (collapse, grenade, hero door slam, jump kick, punch, walk and walk turn 180). In the graph we observe the result of obtaining the Fuzzy Observation from the 6 actions remaining unused in IXMAS, which are composed by 43728 poses. The bars graph shows how each cluster is used to compose the FOs of those poses, and we have ordered them attending their proportion of target and source domain composition. We can observe how the most used clusters are found along all proportions being almost insignificant the target and source domain proportions.

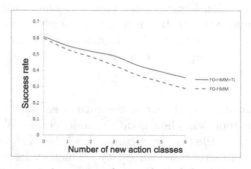

Fig. 7. Average success rate increasing the number of classes not used in the codebook

Finally we want to compare the recognition rate between the use of Transfer Learning and the original FO-HMM, where the only difference is the codebook. Comparing both cases when recognizing the 5 target sequences of IXMAS we obtain a slight difference between the use of Transfer Learning (FO-HMM+TL) and the direct use of FO-HMM. In the first case we obtain a 61% of recognition, and with FO-HMM a 59%. From this results we might conclude that the transfer learning only complicates the process without any benefit. But the strongest point of the method is the availability of train new sequences using the original codebook. Using the remaining 6 actions in IXMAS, we include one by one and we test the results in both method, shown in Figure 7. Although the starting point of both methods is really close, when the number of actions increase we detect how the lines separate, obtaining FO-HMM+TL the best results.

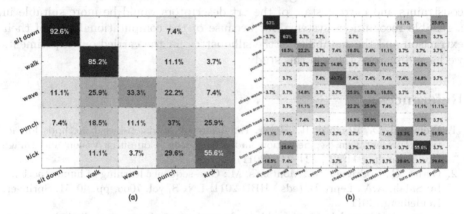

(a)   (b)

Fig. 8. Confusion Matrix with (a) 5 classes and (b) 11 classes

In Figure 8 we show the Confusion Matrix using Transfer Learning in two cases, when 5 and 11 IXMAS classes are classified. We can see how the initial classes are worse recognized when including new classes as expected, but in Figure 8b we can observe as well how the initial five classes keeps a better recognition rate in comparison with the new ones. So, the average recognition rate of the initial 5 classes shown in the (b) confusion matrix is a 42% while the overall recognition rate is close to 35%. This is explained considering that the codebook includes points from those initial classes.

4 Conclusions

As the number of cameras deployed for surveillance and safety in urban environments has increased considerably in the recent years, it becomes necessary to develop video-based recognition systems to automatically monitor such scenarios. However, in many practical scenarios, the amount of available videos is insufficient to train a robust model for recognition. In this regard, we have provided a novel approach for creating Fuzzy Observations in order to run a

FO-HMM algorithm. The simple use of a window for filtering outliers in the sequences is a first improvement. On the other hand, the main addition is the transfer learning stage thanks to which it will be possible to create a set of pre-trained clusters covering many features so that the set-up of the system in a new scenario will just imply the selection of the right clustering and a short training stage.

The major problem of the transfer learning presented lies in the manually selected source domain. In the future, an automatic selection looks necessary and it will make possible a fast adaptation to new scenarios. A quantitative measure of the codebook quality, allowing an automatic selection of source and target domain inputs, clustering process and clustering size will be a clear improvement of the process.

Moreover, it is worth noting that the silhouette as pose descriptor have several constraints and current state of the art descriptors would be more suitable in a reliable recognitions system. But because of the computational cost of their extraction and the suitability of the silhouettes for the carried out experiments we have discarded them in this study.

References

1. Weinland, D., Ronfard, R., Boyer, E.: A survey of vision-based methods for action representation, segmentation and recognition. Computer Vision and Image Understanding 115(2), 224–241 (2011)
2. Orrite, C., Rodríguez, M., Montañés, M.: One-sequence learning of human actions. In: Salah, A.A., Lepri, B. (eds.) HBU 2011. LNCS, vol. 7065, pp. 40–51. Springer, Heidelberg (2011)
3. Laptev, I., Marszałek, M., Schmid, C., Rozenfeld, B.: Learning realistic human actions from movies. In: IEEE Conference on Computer Vision and Pattern Recognition (CVPR) (June 2008)
4. Scovanner, P., Ali, S., Shah, M.: A 3-dimensional sift descriptor and its application to action recognition. In: Proceedings of the 15th International Conference on Multimedia, MULTIMEDIA 2007, pp. 357–360. ACM, New York (2007)
5. Weinland, D., Ronfard, R., Boyer, E.: Free viewpoint action recognition using motion history volumes. Computer Vision and Image Understanding 104(2-3), 249–257 (2006)
6. Ragheb, H., Velastin, S., Remagnino, P., Ellis, T.: ViHASi: virtual human action silhouette data for the performance evaluation of silhouette-based action recognition methods. In: Proceedings of the 1st ACM Workshop on Vision Networks for Behavior Analysis, VNBA 2008, pp. 77–84. ACM, New York (2008)
7. Rabiner, L.R.: A tutorial on hidden markov models and selected applications in speech recognition. Proceedings of the IEEE 77(2), 257–286 (1989)
8. Pan, S.J., Yang, Q.: A survey on transfer learning. IEEE Transactions on Knowledge and Data Engineering 22(10), 1345–1359 (2010)
9. Cook, D., Feuz, K.D., Krishnan, N.C.: Transfer learning for activity recognition: a survey. In: Knowledge and Information Systems, pp. 1–20 (2013)
10. Liu, J., Shah, M., Kuipers, B., Savarese, S.: Cross-view action recognition via view knowledge transfer. In: IEEE Conference on Computer Vision and Pattern Recognition (CVPR), pp. 3209–3216. IEEE (2011)

11. Bian, W., Tao, D., Rui, Y.: Cross-domain human action recognition. IEEE Transactions on Systems, Man, and Cybernetics. B Cybernetics 42(2), 298–307 (2012)
12. Zhu, Y., Zhao, X., Fu, Y., Liu, Y.: Sparse coding on local spatial-temporal volumes for human action recognition. In: Kimmel, R., Klette, R., Sugimoto, A. (eds.) ACCV 2010, Part II. LNCS, vol. 6493, pp. 660–671. Springer, Heidelberg (2011)
13. Hu, D.H., Zheng, V.W., Yang, Q.: Cross-domain activity recognition via transfer learning. Pervasive and Mobile Computing 7, 344–358 (2011)
14. Fei-Fei, L., Fergus, R., Perona, P.: One-shot learning of object categories. IEEE Transactions on Pattern Analysis and Machine Intelligence 28, 594–611 (2006)

ATTENTO: ATTENTion Observed
for Automated Spectator Crowd Analysis

Davide Conigliaro[1,2], Francesco Setti[2], Chiara Bassetti[2], Roberta Ferrario[2],
and Marco Cristani[1,3]

[1] Verona University
[2] Institute of Cognitive Sciences and Technologies, CNR
[3] Italian Institute of Technology, IIT

Abstract. We propose a new type of crowd analysis, focused on the *spectator crowd*, that is, people "interested in watching something specific that they came to see" [1]. This scenario applies on stadiums, amphitheaters etc., and shares some aspects with classical crowd monitoring: actually, many people are simultaneously observed, so that per-person analysis is hard; however, here the dynamics of humans is more constrained, due to the architectural environment in which they are situated; specifically, people are expected to stay in a fixed location most of the time, limiting their activities to applaud, support/heckle the players or discuss with the neighbors. In this paper, we start facing this challenge by considering hockey matches, locating a videocamera 25-30 meters far from the bleachers, pointing at the crowd: in this scenario, aggregations of spectators that exhibit similar behavior are detected, and the behavior is classified into a set of predefined classes, highlighting the overall excitement. To these aims, in a first step we focus on individual frames, clustering local flow measures into spatial regions. The clustering is then extended by adding the temporal axis into the analysis, looking for non-random spatio-temporal clusters; for this purpose, the Lempel-Ziv complexity is considered. This way, choral activities can emerge, indicating for example fan groups belonging to different teams. After this, with the adoption of entropic measures, the degree of excitement of such groups can be quantified.

Keywords: spectator crowd, Lempel-Ziv complexity, spatio-temporal clustering.

1 Introduction

Crowd analysis is a videosurveillance topic that focuses on large masses of people, where the single person cannot be finely characterized, due to the small visual resolution, the frequent total occlusions and the complex dynamics. As a consequence, crowd analysis has grown with its own set of peculiar techniques, most of them avoiding to perform standard surveillance operations (for example, people detection, tracking, gesture recognition); instead, motion flow information [2, 3] is usually exploited as ingredient of higher level descriptors (as multiresolution

A.A. Salah et al. (Eds.) : HBU 2013, LNCS 8212, pp. 102–111, 2013.

histograms [4], spatiotemporal cuboids [5], appearance or motion descriptors [6], spatiotemporal volumes [7], dynamic textures [8]), which eventually are fed into standard classifiers.

In this paper, we focus on a novel applicative field for crowd analysis, centered on the modeling of the so called *spectator crowd* [1]. The idea is to observe people while they are watching a public show, as in a sport arena, a movie theater, a classroom, a court, and recording and analyzing their activities. This scenario differs substantially from those analyzed by the typical crowd modeling techniques: due to *territoriality* principles, people are assumed to stay near a fixed location for most of the time, i.e., their seat [9, 10], while what is mainly being monitored in the crowd analysis literature are moving people. In addition, people here are assumed to have a strong relation with the event or contest they are watching, that becomes a kind of reference point, where the focus of attention [11] of the crowd is located, and around which the space is structured. In classical crowd modeling no such clear reference point is present.

In this new scenario, diverse techniques and applications can be developed, generalizing the videosurveillance context to the multimedia realms of the entertainment and the edutainment:

– **Spectators segmentation**: finding diverse groups of people among the spectators, for example the fans of the opposite teams in a sport match; attentive VS distracted students in a classroom; enthusiastic VS annoyed spectators at a theater play; in the entertainment and edutainment fields, detecting when the audience is bored may trigger reactive mechanisms that for example inform the speaker/teacher that something should be done for rekindle the observers;
– **Excitement calculation**: in a given time interval, quantizing the level of excitement of some parts or of the entire crowd; this could be beneficial for example for marketing purposes.
– **Event segmentation**: segmenting diverse activities of the crowd (clapping hands, making a wave, heckling), and studying how these activities are related with the observed event (i.e. some people clap their hands when the favorite team scores a goal, or get excited when a foul is or is not signaled by the referee);
– **Augmented video summarization**: the spectator feedback, automatically recognized, may help in highlighting exciting or crucial events that should be included in a video summarization of the show;
– **Comparative analysis of spectators**: various factors can be compared, like fans of different teams in the same sport [12], or fans of different sports [13], where spectators are arranged differently etc.;
– **Interpretation of crowd's intentions**: discriminating whether a display of crowd excitement is determined by a rejoicing VS aggressive attitude, to foresee the subsequent crowd's behavior.

In the following, we will show how the first two aspects discussed above, i.e., spectators segmentation and excitement calculation, can be faced using Social Signal Processing methods [14–16], where Social Psychology and sociological notions are incorporated into Computer Vision and Pattern Recognition algorithms[1]. In particular, we will focus on a sport scenario, where people watch hockey matches. In this scenario, assuming a single camera capturing the whole crowd, located at 25-30 meters from the bleachers, we divide the acquired scene into squared patches, extracting from each patch local flow information (position, flow intensity and direction). These features are then fed into a per-frame Gaussian clustering framework [17], that groups together patches with similar dynamics. These instantaneous associations are then summed along the temporal axis, creating a spatio-temporal similarity matrix; such matrix is weighted by a factor (the Lempel-Ziv complexity [18]) which indicates how randomic the instantaneous associations have been during the entire sequence. Finally, the weighted spatio-temporal similarity matrix becomes the input of a single-link hierarchical clustering, whose dendrogram models the different fan groups, even when they are spatially merged.

Concerning the excitement calculation, entropic measures based on the optical flow are exploited, to indicate how much lively the fan groups are. The rationale is that the excitement for a group of people is high when we have a strong, various and coordinated dynamic activity.

The remaining of the paper is organized as follows: Sec. 2 explores the related literature, showing how the proposed problem has interesting connections with some studies in sociology that could constitute a foundation for the visual analysis of behavior. Our framework is presented in Sec. 3, followed by preliminary results in Sec. 4; Sec. 5 draws some conclusions and future perspectives.

2   Related Literature

Under a computer vision perspective, not many approaches modeling spectator crowds watching sports are present in the literature. Conversely, the sociological realm exhibits some relevant studies. Schweingruber and McPheil in [19] has built a model for characterizing "collective actions-in-common", i.e., actions performed spontaneously by several people in coordination. This study, though not specifically centered on viewers, but rather on various forms of crowd, singles out seven dimensions for the analysis of crowd behavior: orientation (facing), vocalization (producing sounds other than words with mouth), verbalization (uttering words), vertical locomotion (movement of the body over the same point on the ground), horizontal locomotion (movement of the body from one point on the ground to another), gesticulation (meaningful bodily configuration based on fingers, hands, and arms movements mainly), and manipulation (using hands to applaud or to strike, carry, throw, pull, etc.). Such study is interesting from our point of view as it includes most of the behaviors we intended to observe in spectators crowds. Other studies, as [20], have challenged the idea that a

---

[1] The last two aspects, in order to be studied seriously, imply the availability of a background behavioral model, which is not the case here; we thus leave such analyses to future studies. Finally, the augmented video summarization application implies multimedia aspects that cannot be dealt with here.

crowd can be seen as an undistinguished collection of individuals, highlighting how crowds can rather be segmented in subgroups of different size, composition and organization, based on their previous acquaintance, on common goals etc. Starting from this idea, one of the aims of this paper is exactly that of trying to identify how the crowd may be segmented with automatic means. Turning to spectator crowds, some scholars have discussed how collective behavior, like applauding, is generated in contexts where a crowd is attending to a public event, for example in public speeches, as is the case for [21]. Regarding the sociology of sport, many works have been produced, but most of them deal with violence in sport, as shown in [22], where the motivations that bring people to watch sports alive are also discussed. Finally, few works have specifically considered fans of hockey teams (for instance [23]), analyzing how their support can influence the players. In this work we have taken inspiration from the analyses displayed in the works mentioned above and focused on extracting *locomotion* and *gesticulation* features from the video recordings of the spectators.

3   Our Framework

In the following, we will detail the methodologies adopted for solving the *spectators segmentation* and the *excitement calculation* issues (see Sec. 1).

3.1   Spectators Segmentation and Excitement Calculation

As a first step, standard motion flow is computed on the image plane, extracting at each pixel direction and intensity. Then, assuming people as static [9, 10] and considering the size of people, flow information can be re-arranged into a grid of N squared patches $\{x\}$. On each patch x, at each time frame, we extract four measures: the first is the flow intensity $I(x)$, obtained by averaging over the flow intensity values of the patches' pixels; intuitively, this cue encodes how much movement characterizes a patch. The second cue is the flow direction entropy $E_{dir}(x)$, calculated over the related flow direction values (opportunely quantized); $E_{dir}(x)$ describes the kind of movement in the patch: high entropy values mean random directions, while low values address homogeneous movement in the patch. The last two measures are the x, y patch centroid coordinates. In other words, at each time step, each patch is described as a 4D point.

The segmentation occurs in two steps: first, a Gaussian clustering with automatic model selection [17] is applied on the values of all the patches in a given time frame. This way, an instantaneous grouping is inferred. This process is replicated for all the T frames. We define then the $N \times N \times T$ matrix M: at time t, $M(i, j, t) = 1$ if patches i and j are in the same cluster, 0 otherwise. At this point, we want to check the non-randomness of the associations of two given patches i, j: the rationale is that non random associations are more plausibly indicating a strong relation among the patches. Therefore, for each couple of patches, we calculate the Lempel-Ziv complexity [18]: high complexity indicates a randomic aspect in the temporal evolution of the association between i and *j.* After this, we compute the summation over t of the matrix M, obtaining the $N \times N$ matrix M_T. As final spatio-temporal similarity among patches, we thus take

$$S = M_T \bullet \frac{1}{LZ} \qquad (1)$$

where LZ indicates the $N \times N$ matrix containing the Lempel-Ziv complexity scores, and "$\bullet$" indicates point to point multiplication. The rationale is that we want to highlight associations that are strong in time (several instantaneous associations) which are also non random. Making the similarity matrix S as a distance (computing the point-to-point reciprocal), it is possible to perform single link hierarchical clustering, and to obtain the spectator segmentation, which partitions the scene in regions where the behavior of the crowd is similar (in terms of the measures quoted above).

For each region r, a *local* level of excitement is estimated by computing the value:

$$Exc(r) = \frac{I(r) \times E_{\text{dir}}(r)}{E_{\text{int}}(r)^2} \qquad (2)$$

over a short time interval (in the order of seconds); here, $E_{\text{int}}(r)$ is the entropy of the motion flow *intensities* at a given time step. The rationale of this measure is that we consider as an high excitement for a group of people an intense (high $I(r)$) movement with diverse directions (high $E_{\text{dir}}(r)$), computed in a coordinated fashion for all people belonging to that region (low E_{int}).

Finally, the average of $Exc(r)$ over all frames is considered as the excitement cue in a given interval for the region r.

4   Experiments

In order to test our framework, we built a novel repository which consists of videos taken during the 2013 IIHF Ice Hockey U18 World Championship, played in Asiago from the 7th to the 13th of April 2013. In particular, two entire matches were recorded (Italy VS Norway, Italy VS Slovenia), each by two cameras, mounted frontally at a distance of about 25 meters from the spectators' stand. Each camera was pointing at an half of the whole stand, the zoom being fixed. Therefore, for each match we have two sequences, further divided in 3 as the times of the hockey play. This resulted in 12 videos at 30 fps, with a resolution of 640x480 pixels for a total duration of about 6 hours.

From this dataset, we extracted 6 videos, each lasting three minutes, and we focused on the spectators segmentation and the excitement calculation (see Sec. 1). The ground truth labels have been manually set for each frame of the videos, by assigning to the patches one among these classes: background (patches with no people); quiet spectators (patches with people who don't exult); excited spectators (patches with standing up and exulting people).

The videos have been analyzed considering a grid of rectangular patches of size 40×80, with the patches overlapping for half of their size, in both dimensions. Flow has been computed on the entire scene every 10 frames, so we have 3 processed frames per second; after that, the flow direction has been quantized in five values (up, down, left, right, none) where the fifth value corresponds to all those flow vectors whose intensity is inferior to a given threshold $I = 0.8$.

4.1 Spectators Segmentation and Excitement Calculation

For each video, we first computed the frame-based Gaussian clustering and subsequently the temporal hierarchical clustering considering separately the two matrices M'_T and S', which are the distance matrices (computing the point-to-point reciprocal) of M_T and S, respectively. We considered the matrix M'_T without the Lempev-Ziv complexity to investigate how important it is to take into account randomness in the processing. This way, for each window we get interesting spectators segmentations, clearly explaining the occurred events; for longer windows, the segmentation tends to discriminate solely the presence of the crowd against the background. The clustering results obtained by operating directly on M'_T and S' were compared, in order to determine which distance matrix is the most informative.

In order to measure the agreement between the ground truth labels and the two clustering procedures, we computed four different indices of external validity, that is: Rand index, adjusted Rand index, Jaccard index, Fowlkes-Mallows index [24]; furthermore, we calculated an error rate, which is the percentage of error class labels of the clustering solution compared with true labels, adopting the figure of merits suggested in [25]. The results are shown in Fig. 1. All the boxplots of the four indices show that Lempel-Ziv complexity improves the segmentation/clustering results; also the error rate is lower using S'.

The picture on the left in Fig. 2 shows an example of ground truth labels assigned to the patches. The three different colors are a measure of the excitement of each class. Here the background region includes 196 patches which have been assigned the blue color. The spectators are divided into two classes: the *quiet spectators* region (light blue) includes 102 patches, while the region of major excitement (dark red) includes 43 patches with cheering and clapping people.

A first interesting result is that the excitement level, automatically computed for each region by eq. 2, is consistent with what the expert has indicated in the ground truth. In particular, the three clusters corresponding to background, quite spectators and excited spectators generate excitement levels of 0.0033, 0.0075 and 0.0217, respectively.

In Fig. 2, the center and right images show the segmentation obtained by considering the methods with M'_T and S'. At a glance, the colors and the regions' sizes of the last image suggest that the method which uses S' is closer to the ground truth. This is confirmed by the results shown in the row V_1 of Table 1, where the error rates for the excitement level computation are shown, calculated as:

$$Err(r) = \frac{|Exc_{\text{gt}}(r) - Exc_{\text{x}}(r)|}{Exc_{\text{gt}}(r)} \tag{3}$$

where $Exc_{\text{gt}}(r)$ is the average excitement level computed for the ground truth region r over all the video and $Exc_{\text{x}}(r)$ is the same value computed for the region

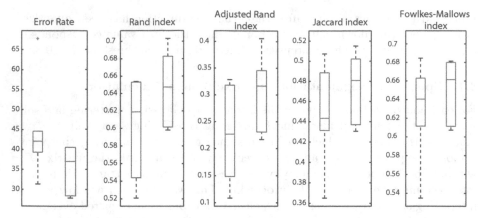

Fig. 1. Boxplots of the five different external validity indices computed by considering all 6 videos. In each plot the first box refers to the clustering results obtained by operating directly on M'_T an the second on S'. On each box, the central mark is the median, the edges of the box are the 25th and 75th percentiles, respectively; the whiskers extend to the most extreme data points not considered outliers, and outliers are plotted individually as red crosses. Low values in error rate and high values in other indexes indicate better segmentation performance.

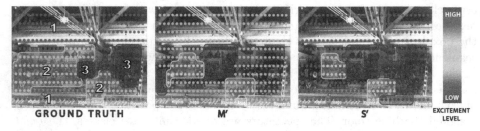

Fig. 2. Spectators segmentation and excitement calculation obtained from the first video (best viewed in colors). The image on the left shows the ground truth segmentation. The numbers indicate the excitement (in ascending order) estimated by the expert who made the ground truth. Region 1 is the background, region 2 includes quite people and region 3 comprises more excited spectators. The center and right images refer to the segmentation obtained by using M'_T and S', respectively. Each dot in the images is plotted at the center of the respective patch, and its color depends on the mean excitement level of the region to which it belongs.

r obtained with our two methods of segmentation, by using M'_T and S'. The mean error rate for each video and region, highlighted in the last row of the table, shows that the regions obtained by the segmentation on the matrix S' achieve an excitement level more similar to the ground truth, than the method that exploits M'_T.

Table 1. Error rates $Err(r)$ for excitement level estimation. M'_T and S' indicate the two different methods of segmentation, ignoring or considering the randomness value given by the Lempev-Ziv complexity, respectively. R_1, R_2 and R_3 are the background and the regions of quite and excited spectators, respectively. $V_1 \ldots V_6$ indicate each tested video. The last row shows the average value of each column.

	M'_T			S'		
	R_1	R_2	R_3	R_1	R_2	R_3
V_1	0.578	0.138	0.263	0.122	0.024	0.172
V_2	0.339	0.167	0.119	0.394	0.119	0.038
V_3	0.646	0.372	0.451	0.646	0.650	0.270
V_4	1	0.371	0.543	0.620	0.193	0.354
V_5	0.174	0.113	0.228	0.167	0.201	0.039
V_6	0.527	0.940	0.065	0.331	0.830	0.302
Average	**0.544**	**0.350**	**0.278**	**0.380**	**0.336**	**0.195**

5   Conclusions

The study of spectators crowd dynamics offers new perspectives in the crowd modeling field. In this paper we have performed a preliminary study, first of all reasoning on the possible applications that can be developed in such a scenario, and presenting effective implementations for some of them; in particular, we have shown how spectators can be segmented on the basis of their behavior, and how their excitement level can be inferred by looking exclusively at the crowd activity. Much more can be done, by employing more sophisticated models: dynamic Bayesian networks may embed spatial and temporal reasoning in a unique model; gesture recognition, face detection and expression recognition may provide detailed cues to better understand the nature of the spectators activities, allowing the discrimination between supporting, heckling or just watching, absent in the present work. Further developments may be achieved by adopting different sensors, like infrared and pan-tilt-zoom cameras. Audio analysis can also be fruitful, especially in the case of sport events: in absence of facial information, capturing whistles instead of shouts of joy may be crucial to perform sentiment analysis of the crowd. From a sociological point of view, proxemics principles can be taken into account [26], in order to assess if social relations can be discovered by analyzing interpersonal distances among seated people, following the same idea of [27].

An important theme to be inquired is the establishment of the ground truth for such kinds of scenarios. In this paper we have adopted a sort of "expert-based ground truth", in that we have compared our findings with what had been explained in sociological theories. Alternatively, a more complete approach of this kind (expert) would be based on an ethnographic study: in that case the ground truth would be built on the basis of participant observation carried out by several ethnographers (team ethnography), doing fieldwork on the stands of an arena, stadium, amphitheater, etc. This, moreover, could be complemented with ethnomethodologically oriented videoanalysis (see [28]). A completely different approach to ground truth would be to found it in a more "bottom-up" way, by asking directly to those belonging to the crowd, either exactly the crowd that was attending the recorded event, or, more generically, people that can report about an experience of participation to a public event as a viewer. Even in this case, there are various ways to implement such approach, ranging from structured questionnaires to in-depth interviews. Notwithstanding all that have already been mentioned, of course privacy and ethical issues should also be taken more seriously into account in the nearest future developments of this study.

Acknowledgments Davide Conigliaro, Francesco Setti, Chiara Bassetti and Roberta Ferrario are supported by the VisCoSo project grant, financed by the Autonomous Province of Trento through the Team 2011 funding programme.

References

1. Berlonghi, A.: Undestanding and planning for different spectator crowds. Safety Science 18, 239–247 (1995)
2. Mehran, R., Oyama, A., Shah, M.: Abnormal crowd behavior detection using social force model. In: IEEE Conference on Computer Vision and Pattern Recognition (CVPR), pp. 935–942 (2009)
3. Raghavendra, R., Del Bue, A., Cristani, M., Murino, V.: Abnormal crowd behavior detection by social force optimization. In: Salah, A.A., Lepri, B. (eds.) HBU 2011. LNCS, vol. 7065, pp. 134–145. Springer, Heidelberg (2011)
4. Zhong, H., Shi, J., Visontai, M.: Detecting unusual activity in video. In: IEEE Conference on Computer Vision and Pattern Recognition (CVPR), pp. 819–826 (2004)
5. Kratz, L., Nishino, K.: Anomaly detection in extremely crowded scenes using spatio-temporal motion pattern models. In: IEEE Conference on Computer Vision and Pattern Recognition (CVPR), pp. 1446–1453 (2009)
6. Andrade, E.L., Blunsden, S., Fisher, R.B.: Modelling crowd scenes for event detection. In: Proceedings of the 18th International Conference on Pattern Recognition (ICPR), vol. 1, pp. 175–178. IEEE Computer Society, Washington, DC (2006)
7. Laptev, I.: On space-time interest points. International Journal of Computer Vision (IJCV) 64(2-3), 107–123 (2005)
8. Mahadevan, V., Li, W., Bhalodia, V., Vasconcelos, N.: Anomaly detection in crowded scenes. In: IEEE Conference on Computer Vision and Pattern Recognition (CVPR), pp. 1975–1981 (2010)
9. Guyot, G.W., Byrd, G.R., Caudle, R.: Classroom setting: An expression of situational territoriality in humans. Small Group Research 11, 120–128 (1980)
10. Kaya, N., Burgess, B.: Territoriality. seat preferences in different types of classroom arrangements. Environment and Behavior (EAB) 39(6), 859–876 (2007)
11. Goffman, E.: Behaviour in Public Places. Notes on the Social Organization of Gatherings. Free Press of Glencloe., New York (1963)
12. Roadburg, A.: Factors precipitating fan violence: a comparison of professional soccer in britain and north america. The British Journal of Sociology (BJS) 31(2), 265–276 (1980)

13. Goldstein, J.H., Arms, R.L.: Effects of observing athletic contests on ostility. Sociometry 34(1), 83–90 (1971)
14. Vinciarelli, A., Pantic, M., Bourlard, H.: Social Signal Processing: Survey of an emerging domain. Image and Vision Computing 27(12), 1743–1759 (2009)
15. Cristani, M., Murino, V., Vinciarelli, A.: Socially intelligent surveillance and monitoring: Analysing social dimensions of physical space. In: IEEE Computer Society Conference on Computer Vision and Pattern Recognition Workshops (CVPRW), pp. 51–58 (2010)
16. Cristani, M., Raghavendra, R., Del Bue, A., Murino, V.: Human behavior analysis in video surveillance: A social signal processing perspective. Neurocomputing 100, 86–97 (2013)
17. Figueiredo, M.A.T., Jain, A.: Unsupervised learning of finite mixture models. IEEE Transactions on Pattern Analysis and Machine Intelligence (PAMI) 24(3), 381–396 (2002)
18. Kaspar, F., Schuster, H.G.: Easily calculable measure for the complexity of spatiotemporal patterns. Physical Review A 36, 842–848 (1987)
19. Schweingruber, D., MacPheil, C.: A method for systematically observing and recording collective action. Sociological Methods Research (SMR) 27(4), 451–498 (1999)
20. McPhail, C.: From clusters to arcs and rings: Elementary forms of sociation in temporary gatherings. Research in Community Sociology (suppl. 1), 35–57 (1994)
21. Atkinson, J.M.: Public speaking and audience responses: some techniques for inviting audience applause. In: Maxwell Atkinson, J., J.H., (eds.) Structures of Social Action: Studies in Conversation Analysis, pp. 370–407. Cambridge University Press, Cambridge (1984)
22. McDonald, M.A., Milne, G.R., Hong, J.: Motivational factors for evaluating sport spectator and participant markets. Sport Marketing Quarterly (SMQ) 11(2), 100–113 (2002)
23. Bowker, A., Boekhoven, B., Nolan, A., Bauhaus, S., Glover, P., Powell, T., Taylor, S.: Naturalistic observations of spectator behavior at youth hockey games. The Sport Psychologist (TSP) 23, 301–316 (2009)
24. Halkidi, M., Batistakis, Y., Vazirgiannis, M.: On clustering validation techniques. Journal of Intelligent Information Systems (JIIS) 17(2-3), 107–145 (2001)
25. Wang, K., Wang, B., Peng, L.: Cvap: Validation for cluster analyses. Data Science Journal 8, 88–93 (2009)
26. Hall, E.T.: Handbook for proxemic research. Anthropology News 36(2), 40–40 (1995)
27. Cristani, M., Paggetti, G., Vinciarelli, A., Bazzani, L., Menegaz, G., Murino, V.: Towards computational proxemics: Inferring social relations from interpersonal distances. In: SocialCom/PASSAT, pp. 290–297 (2011)
28. Heath, C., Hindmarsh, J., Luff, P.: Video in Qualitative Research. Analysing Social Interaction in Everyday Life. Sage, London (2010)

Human Behavior Understanding
with Wide Area Sensing Floors

Martino Lombardi, Augusto Pieracci, Paolo Santinelli,
Roberto Vezzani, and Rita Cucchiara

Softech-ICT, University of Modena and Reggio Emilia
Via Vignolese, 905 - 41125 Modena - Italy
{martino.lombardi,augusto.pieracci,paolo.santinelli
roberto.vezzani,rita.cucchiara}@unimore.it
http://imagelab.ing.unimore.it

Abstract. The research on innovative and natural interfaces aims at developing devices able to capture and understand the human behavior without the need of a direct interaction. In this paper we propose and describe a framework based on a sensing floor device. The pressure field generated by people or objects standing on the floor is captured and analyzed. Local and global features are computed by a low level processing unit and sent to high level interfaces. The framework can be used in different applications, such as entertainment, education or surveillance. A detailed description of the sensing element and the processing architectures is provided, together with some sample applications developed to test the device capabilities.

Keywords: Sensing floor, human behavior understanding, OSC, natural interfaces.

1 Introduction

The creation of sensing environments constitutes one of the major trends in interfacing humans with virtual worlds, computers and cyberspaces. Natural and new human computer interfaces overcome now standard interfaces: for instance, human actions and events can be automatically captured and decoded by distributed sensors, without the need of direct interaction with input devices such as pads, mouses, keyboards, and so on. Entertainment and edutainment applications, for example, got a great benefit from hands-free visual devices, such as the well known Microsoft Kinect, webcams or smart cameras.

Vision based devices are suitable for behavior recognition of single users, capturing their details and body parts with a suitable resolution. However, they have some drawbacks for monitoring multiple people or covering wide areas. This last case, in fact, requires a network of sensors. In addition, the placement constraints and the handling of occlusions due to furniture, objects and other people usually impose the adoption of multiple views, especially in indoor environments. Furthermore, privacy issues strongly limited the usability and also the user acceptability in some cases.

Following the same objective of hands-free devices, we propose an innovative sensing floor called "Florimage device", that is able to capture and measure the pressure

A.A. Salah et al. (Eds.) : HBU 2013, LNCS 8212, pp. 112–123, 2013.

field exerted by people or objects on the tiles. Instead of optical images, the floor is able to generate a "pressure image", where each pixel corresponds to a spatial portion of the floor and the pixel value is related to the pressure applied by people or object onto the floor itself. The technology we developed is modular and scalable (See Figure 1(a)). This result is obtained adding a sensing layer below the ceramic tiles. The solution proposed is cheap enough to allow the coverage of wide areas and the sensing elements do not change the design or the appearance of the floor.

The proposed sensing floor allows a plethora of applications, spanning from entertainment to surveillance, from multimedia content access to medical rehabilitation. In this paper, and in particular in Section 4, we will describe some sample applications we developed to test the system capabilities.

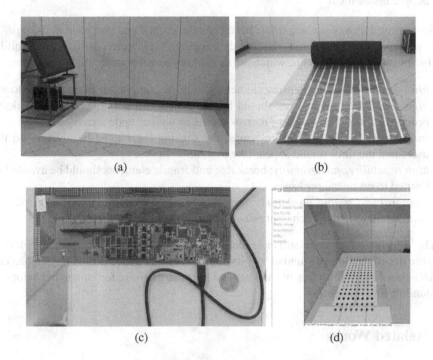

(a)   (b)

(c)   (d)

Fig. 1. Pictures of the installed prototype. a) the prototype floor, b) the contact stripes, c) the capturing board and d) a virtual reconstruction of the environment.

Some preliminary experiments have been described in [1], where an initial prototype of the "Florimage device" was exploited to monitor indoor environments for surveillance applications. In this paper we provided a detailed characterization of the sensor response (the *floor image*), the description of the data processing system and the methodology to understand the human behavior by pressure images. In particular, two processing layers have been defined, working at a low and high level respectively. The two layers communicate through the Open Sound Control (OSC) protocol [2,3], that spreads data and events detected from the low level processing to each client application.

In Section 4 we will present the following five sample applications:

- *Human Media Player*: the person location on the floor controls a media player setting the current position in the media item;
- *Memory game*: the player can turn the cards of the well known memory game by jumping on the corresponding tile;
- *Music edutainment*: the floor is divided in small portions that emulate a piano key, allowing several edutainment games in the music field;
- *Foot painting*: the user paints original artworks or allow to reveal a hidden painting by changing his position on the floor;
- *Intrusion detection*: safe regions could be defined and the sensing floor will detect people inside them.

Some prototypes of sensing floors have been developed and proposed in the past. A representative subset of them is described in Section 2. However, none of them fulfills all the following requirements, which are mandatory to generate a reliable solution:

- *low cost*: the cost of the sensing elements should be comparable to traditional floors;
- *high scalability*: the sensors should be integrated into a hierarchical network, in order to allow the coverage of narrow rooms as well as wide areas;
- *transparent design*: for design issues, the sensing layer must be invisible to the users and the floor should appear like traditional floors;
- *high reliability and durability*: breakable and fragile elements should be avoided or limited to protected packages;
- *temporal and spatial resolutions*: they should be high enough to allow people detection and tracking, even in presence of multiple targets.

The "Florimage device" is still under developing within the long-term project "Florimage: the floor is an Image" funded by Florim S.p.A and Regione Emilia Romagna. The project aims at creating a flexible and general purpose platform for human behavior understanding and interaction.

2 Related Works

Several prototypes of sensing floors for human-based action detection and identification have been presented in the past. The adopted sensors exploited different physical characteristics; among the others, the pressure as measurable quantity, and the proximity effect related with the electrical properties of a human body are the mainly used.

Lee Middleton et al. [4] developed a prototype of a floor sensor mat as a gait recognition system. The sensor consists of individual switches arranged in a separated pair of wires by foam a deformable material. The design shows simplicity and scalability even if switches do not provide a response commensurate with the strength of the applied force. Chen-Rong Yu et al. [5] proposed a localization system to accurately estimate human position. It performs single person and multiple people tracking in a home environment. The Condensation algorithm is exploited to locate residents' position via multi-camera and sensory floor approaches. Domnic Savio et al [6] developed a smart carpet that can be laid on the floor. The sensor set forms a self-organizing sensor network. To identify the footstep, clustering algorithms based on Maximum Likelihood Estimate and Rank Regression have been applied. The proposed approach is scalable and commercially viable even if the binary nature of the embedded nodes does not provide a response commensurate with the applied weight. Miika Valtonen et al [7] described an unobtrusive two-dimensional human positioning and tracking system based on a low-frequency electric field. The capacitance between multiple floor tiles and a receiving electrode is measured. The method is based on the fact that humans well conducts a low-frequency signal. The proposed method does not provide any information related with the human weight; it is not possible to detect any kind of non conductive objects, regardless of the weight; also the conditioning circuits are very complex. In the work by Prashant Srinivasan et al. [8] a portable high-resolution pressure sensing floor prototype able to detect pressure information about the human interaction with the system is described. The pressure sensing floor consists of several sensor mats; each of them is composed of a 42x48 grid of pressure sensors with size of 48.8 cm x 42.7 cm. The sensor elements of the mat are made using a pressure sensitive polymer between conductive teaks on sheets of Mylar. The sensor elements change the resistance with the applied pressure. Jan Anlauff et al. [9] presented a prototype of a floor surface based on sensing elements made out of conductive black art paper. The sensing elements are grouped into modules forming a grid of resistors able to measure quasi-static forces. The proposed approach is a low cost alternative for spatially resolved tactile sensing. The employed signal conditioning system is based on the matrix arrangements of the sensing elements but the proposed solution suffers of mutual interference between different sensors in the matrix. Finally, in the work by Rishi Rajalingham et al. [10] a probabilistic approach to the tracking and estimation of the lower body posture is presented. Their sensing floor has limited sizes, it is not easily scalable and commercially viable. It employes off the shelf resistive force sensors. It consists of a 66 array of rigid tiles, 30 cm on each side. Tiles are equipped with four resistive force sensors, which are located at the corners. An array of six small-form-factor computers is used for data processing.

3   Hardware Architecture

The modularity of the system is one of the key aspect of the proposed sensing floor. As depicted in Figure 2, the system is composed of five main items: the sensors, the capturing boards, the communication network, the processing unit, and the client applications.

The sensors are obtained by introducing a sensing layer below a commercial floating floor. The sensing stratum replaces the polymeric layer which is usually adopted to cobble surfaces using floating floors. Each element is located in the crosses of a regular grid. A board equipped with micro controllers is connected to each matrix of sensors (Base Node). The sensed values are sampled and digitized at a constant frame rate and sent via Blue-tooth to a processing unit for their analysis. A hierarchical communication network is also proposed for scalability reasons and it can be used when the number of BNs exceeds the capabilities of a single processing unit. A low-level data processing

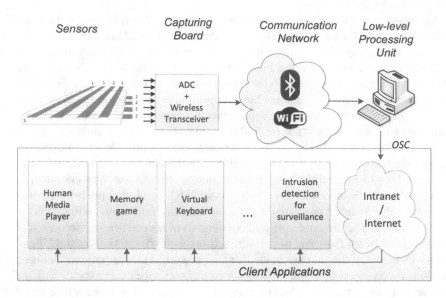

Fig. 2. The five main components of the Florimage architecture

analyzes the data, filters noise and errors, detects actions and events. The obtained information are sent to client applications using the Open Sound Control (OSC) protocol [2], as detailed in Section 4.

Differently from other solutions which have been proposed in the past [11,8,12], each sensing element looks like a normal floating tile. Thus, it inherits some key advantages: low cost, easy tile replacement, high resilience, high stability, feasible relocation of the floor. The proposed approach allows to make wide sensing areas at affordable costs. Some pictures of the prototype floor and the embedded board used to capture and transmit the data are reported in Figure 1.

3.1   Sensing Elements

The key element of the proposed sensors is represented by a commercial paving technology, called floating floors. A floating floor does not need to be nailed or glued to the sublayer and thus it might be constructed over a sub-floor or even over an existing floor. It consist of a polymeric, felt or cork layer holding up a laminate floor. Drowning commercial pressure sensors such as FSR or piezoelectric elements into the padding layer allows to reach very high performances in terms of measurement precision and reliability. However, the solution becomes too expensive and thus unfeasible in wide areas.

We propose to replace the traditional polymeric layer with a sensing element made using a sandwich structure. A conductive polymer (3) is put between aluminum stripe electrodes, lengthwise (1) and crosswise (2) (see Figure 2), generating a grid of sensors, one on each cross. When a pressure is applied on the top of the tiles, the rough surface of the conductive rubber is compressed onto the electrodes surface [13]. As a result, the contacting area between rubbers and electrodes is increased whilst the resistance between them is proportionally reduced. The resistance at each cross is acquired using the board shown in Figure 4(b). We exploited very slim ceramic tiles for the higher layer. The tiles are 600mmx600mm large and thin enough (4.5 mm) to allow the sensing elements below them to capture the presence of walking people.

The sensor response has been characterized placing objects with an increasing weight on a tile and measuring the resistance of the sensor located below the object. Figure 3 plots the sensor response as a function of the applied weight. Even if the response is not linear, it can be reasonably approximated with a polynomial expression of the second order. The polynomial coefficients can be calibrated given the specific floor. However, in the described applications we are interested in founding reasonable thresholds only, which is guaranteed by the monotonic behavior of the response shown in the graph.

In addition to esthetic and design reasons, the ceramic tiles play an important role in the sensor device, since they act as a blurring filter, spreading the pressure of the objects on a wide area. As a consequence, each sensor captures the weights applied on a neighborhood of its position. To test and measure this behavior of the tiles, we have placed the weights at different positions with respect to the sensing node. A picture of the tile used for the experiment is reported in Figure 4(a). The object positions have been marked on the tile and the sensing node has been placed in the middle of the tile. Figure 3(b) plots the sensor response as a function of the sensor-to-object distance.

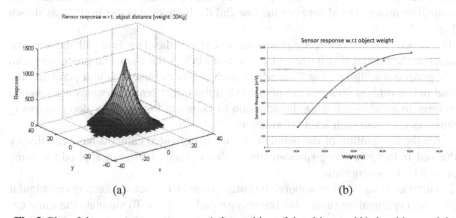

(a)   (b)

Fig. 3. Plot of the sensor response w.r.t. a) the position of the object and b) the object weight

Each Base Node is equipped with a capturing board which measures the electric resistance at each grid cross, digitizes and transmits the values to the processing unit. In Figure 4(b) the block diagram of the electronic part is shown. The frames are sent to the processing unit which runs the system application through a wireless communication interface. More details on the capturing board and the communication network can be found in [1].

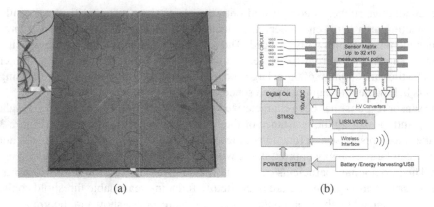

(a)   (b)

Fig. 4. a) the portion of floor and b) the schema of the electronic device used to characterize the sensor response

4   From Pressure to Human Behavior Understanding

The software part of the framework has been split into two different layers. A low-level pre-processing step collects the data coming from different sensor nodes, filters the noise, computes feature vectors and detect some simple events as described in [1]. Filtered data as well as the detected events are sent to the high-level applications. The intermediate protocol used between the low and the high level layers is OSC, as shown in Figure 2.

The processing unit collects, processes and stores the data from all the sensors. Thanks to the regular distribution of the sensors below the floor, the processing unit firstly generates a "floor image", in which each sensor corresponds to a pixel and the spatial neighborhood relations are preserved. Subsequent sensor samples are handled as frames in a video, allowing the adoption of common image and video processing techniques to extract high level information.

Since the recognition of the people behavior using video cameras has been deeply addressed in the past using spatio-temporal descriptors[14,15], we applied the same approach to the sensor data.

In video analysis, spatio-temporal 3D patches can be extracted selecting rectangular regions and aggregating successive frames cropped on them. To simulate the same approach, we selected a single tile of the floor and we collected the NxM values of the sensors below it during a short time interval (2 seconds, corresponding to 20 frames). The obtained matrix $I(x, y, t)$ is processed in order to generate a feature vector for the classification step. We adopted a feature vector composed by aggregated measures which do not depend on the spatial and temporal position of the selected event within the analyzed block. In other words, the feature vector does not depend on the absolute position of a person within the analyzed floor tile. Let $M(t)$ be the mean value of I at time t, $x(t) = \sum_{x=1}^{M} \sum_{y=1}^{N} (x \cdot I(x, y, t))$ and $y(t) = \sum_{x=1}^{M} \sum_{y=1}^{N} (y \cdot I(x, y, t))$ the coordinates of the barycenter $b(t) = (x(t), y(t))$. $C(t)$ is the covariance matrix of the vectors $\{x, y, I(x, y, t)\}$. Let be $\{e_1(t), e_2(t), e_3(t)\}$ the three eigenvalue of the matrix $C(t)$. The features $\Phi = \{\phi_1, \ldots, \phi_{15}\}$ are extracted as average, min or max of the previous defined values as follows:

$$
\begin{aligned}
\phi_1 &= \tfrac{1}{n} \cdot \sum_{t=1}^{n} M(t) \\
\phi_2 &= \tfrac{1}{n} \cdot \sum_{t=1}^{n} \left(M(t) - \phi_1\right)^2 \\
\phi_3 &= \tfrac{1}{n} \cdot \sum_{t=2}^{n} |M(t) - M(t-1)| \\
\phi_4 &= \tfrac{1}{n} \cdot \sum_{t=2}^{n} \left(|M(t) - M(t-1)| - \phi_3\right)^2 \\
\phi_5 &= \tfrac{1}{n} \cdot \sum_{t=2}^{n} \|b(t) - b(t-1)\| \\
\phi_6 &= \tfrac{1}{n} \cdot \sum_{t=1}^{n} (\|b(t) - b(t-1)\| - \phi_5)^2 \\
\{\phi_7 \ldots \phi_9\} &= \tfrac{1}{n} \cdot \sum_{t=1}^{n} \{e_1(t) \ldots e_3(t)\} \\
\{\phi_{10} \ldots \phi_{12}\} &= \min_t \{e_1(t) \ldots e_3(t)\} \\
\{\phi_{13} \ldots \phi_{15}\} &= \max_t \{e_1(t) \ldots e_3(t)\}
\end{aligned}
\tag{1}
$$

where ϕ_1 and ϕ_2 are the mean and variance of $M(t)$ over the temporal interval; ϕ_3 and ϕ_4 are the mean and variance of the $M(t)$ variations. ϕ_5 and ϕ_6 take into account the movement of the barycenter. Finally, ϕ_7 to ϕ_{15} evaluate the average, the minimum and the maximum three eigenvalues of the covariance matrix.

The obtained feature vector has been provided as input to a set of supervised classifiers trained to detect the presence of a person or a fixed object on top of the tiles. If a person is detected, the same feature vector is evaluated to further classify its posture or actions. We developed a collection of Randomized Trees classifiers for both the tasks. A qualitative and quantitative analysis is reported in [1], that shows the very high accuracy of the approach. For example, the *jumping event* is detected with an accuracy close to 96%.

4.1 OSC Communication Protocol

The low level processing unit communicates with the client applications using the Open Sound Control protocol (OSC) [2] over UDP. Open Sound Control (OSC) is a digital media content format for streams of real-time audio control messages. It can be considered as a sort of evolution of the MIDI protocol. Although its origin, OSC had a lot of applications outside of audio technology, founding use in domains such as control and robotics [3].

Each application client starts with a request to the floor device, indicating its IP address and port. As a result, the floor device will send an acknowledgment as well as some useful details about the sensor (spatial extension, number of nodes and sensors, sampling frequency, and so on). After that, the client can ask the floor to receive the processed data or the original sensor values. Each type of required information can be enabled or disabled by the client through specific OSC commands.

A list of the implement OSC messages is reported in Table 1. Among the others, the following server-to-client messages have been used in the described applications. The *baricenter* message is sent after each frame capture and it indicates the baricenter of the response field. If a single person is walking on the floor, the baricenter will provide an estimation of his position.

Table 1. List of the main OSC commands for the communication between the sensing floor and the client applications

Client to Server	
/florimage/request/register [ip] [port]	register the client [ip],[port] to the server
/florimage/request/datastream/baricenter	
/florimage/request/alive	The client should periodically send this command to keep the communication alive
/florimage/request/getconfig	The server will answer to this command by sending the configuration parameters
Server to Client	
/florimage/datastream/sensors [data]	Stream of the sensor data
/florimage/datastream/baricenter [x] [y]	Baricenter of the pressure field
/florimage/datastream/featurevector [data]	Stream of feature vectors ϕ_i
/florimage/event/person [x] [y]	Person detected at the position (x, y)
/florimage/event/jump [x] [y]	Jumping person detected at the position (x, y)

5   Interactive Applications

We have developed some interactive applications in order to test the system capabilities and to show the wide range of uses allowed by the platform. The five demo applications have been introduced in Section 1. All of them are based on the OSC messages generated by the low level processing unit. In this section we provide some additional details on the application logic and potential target.

Human Media Player. The core of this application is a multimedia content. In the case of a video, the position of a user on the floor controls the media position. To this aim, we exploited only one coordinate of the *baricenter* OSC command filtered with a smoothing function to obtain a fluid playback.

$$mediapos(t) = mediapos(t - 1) \cdot \lambda + medialength \cdot \frac{baricenter.x}{floor.length} \cdot (1 - \lambda) \quad (2)$$

where the coefficient λ is the smoothing ratio. A screenshot of the media player application is reported in Figure 5(a).

Memory game. This application is under development within a children education project. The well known *memory game* is controlled by the floor. The children should jump on a tile to flip the corresponding card. As a edutainment game, the drawing reported on the cards are collected from famous historical, television or political couples. A screenshot of the memory game application is reported in Figure 5(b).

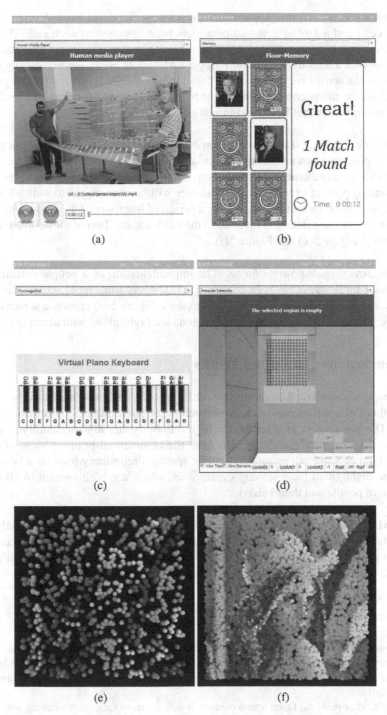

Fig. 5. Screen shots of the four sample applications described in the paper: a) human media player, b) memory game, c) music edutainment, d) intrusion detection, e-f) foot painting

Music edutainment. In this application, the sensing floor has been divided into 81 squared cells and a key of a virtual piano has been assigned to each cell. The complete *datastream* has been used to compute the mean sensor response within each cell. The values over a sensitivity threshold trigger a Midi note event, whose velocity is proportional to the sensor response and the duration is fixed. Walking and jumping on the floor will allow the user to play songs or to simply generate a music feedback. The corresponding screenshot is shown in Figure 5(c).

Foot Painting. This application will be probably located in a showroom of out project partner. A pixelated famous painting is initially hidden. Each part of the painting is associated to a sensing element. The detection of a stimulus over the sensor will reveal the corresponding portion of the painting. The user will be encouraged to walk all around the floor to recover the entire image. After a period of inactivity of the sensor, the corresponding part of the painting is reverted to the hidden state. Two of the adopted images are shown in Figure 5(e) and Figure 5(f).

Intrusion detection and Surveillance. The implementation of a people detection for surveillance applications has been described in [1], where some basic actions were classified in addition to the detection of the intruders. Figure 5(d) reports a screenshot of the surveillance dashboard, where the intrusions are highlighted with alarm events.

6 Conclusions and Future Works

In this paper we described an innovative sensing floor that can be used as input device in a plethora of applications, such as entertainment, surveillance, multimedia content access. The low cost of production, the high reliability and high scalability make the proposed solution very promising also from the commercial point of view, allowing wide installments in both private and public spaces. Preliminary tests on a laboratory prototype highlighted their sensing capabilities, which are high enough to allow the detection of people and their behavior.

Acknowledgements. This work was supported by Florim Ceramiche S.p.A. (Italy) and within the Regional Operational Programme POR FESR 2007-2013 of Softech-ICT. The foot painting and the edutainment applications are under developing in collaboration with the Italian Company Vision-e s.r.l.

References

1. Vezzani, R., Lombardi, M., Pieracci, A., Santinelli, P., Cucchiara, R.: Sensing floors for privacy-compliant surveillance of wide areas. In: Proceedings of the 10th IEEE International Conference on Advanced Video and Signal-Based Surveillance, Krakw, Poland (August 2013)
2. Wright, M., Freed, A.: Open sound control: A new protocol for communicating with sound synthesizers. In: International Computer Music Conference, pp. 101–104. International Computer Music Association, Thessaloniki (1997)

3. Schmeder, A., Freed, A., Wessel, D.: Best practices for open sound control. In: Linux Audio Conference, Utrecht, NL (May 1, 2010)
4. Middleton, L., Buss, A., Bazin, A., Nixon, M.: A floor sensor system for gait recognition. In: Fourth IEEE Workshop on Automatic Identification Advanced Technologies, pp. 171–176 (2005)
5. Yu, C.R., Wu, C.L., Lu, C.H., Fu, L.C.: Human localization via multi-cameras and floor sensors in smart home. In: IEEE International Conference on Systems, Man and Cybernetics, vol. 5, pp. 3822–3827 (2006)
6. Savio, D., Ludwig, T.: Smart carpet: A footstep tracking interface. In: Int'l Conf. on Advanced Information Networking and Applications Workshops, vol. 2, pp. 754–760 (May 2007)
7. Valtonen, M., Maentausta, J., Vanhala, J.: Tiletrack: Capacitive human tracking using floor tiles. In: IEEE International Conference on Pervasive Computing and Communications, pp. 1–10 (March 2009)
8. Srinivasan, P., Birchfield, D., Qian, G., Kidané, A.: A pressure sensing floor for interactive media applications. In: Proc. of the Int'l Conf. on Advances in Computer Entertainment Technology, pp. 278–281 (2005)
9. Anlauff, J., Großhauser, T., Hermann, T.: Tactiles: a low-cost modular tactile sensing system for floor interactions. In: Proc. of the 6th Nordic Conf. on Human-Computer Interaction: Extending Boundaries, pp. 591–594. ACM (2010)
10. Rajalingham, R., Visell, Y., Cooperstock, J.: Probabilistic tracking of pedestrian movements via in-floor force sensing. In: Canadian Conference on Computer and Robot Vision, May 31-June 2, pp. 143–150 (2010)
11. Paradiso, J., Abler, C., Hsiao, K.Y., Reynolds, M.: The magic carpet: physical sensing for immersive environments. In: Extended Abstracts on Human Factors in Computing Systems, pp. 277–278 (1997)
12. Rangarajan, S., Kidane, A., Qian, G., Rajko, S., Birchfield, D.: The design of a pressure sensing floor for movement-based human computer interaction. In: Kortuem, G., Finney, J., Lea, R., Sundramoorthy, V. (eds.) EuroSSC 2007. LNCS, vol. 4793, pp. 46–61. Springer, Heidelberg (2007)
13. Weiss, K., Worn, H.: The working principle of resistive tactile sensor cells. In: Proc. of IEEE International Conference on Mechatronics and Automation, vol. 1, pp. 471–476 (2005)
14. Laptev, I.: On space-time interest points. Int. J. Comput. Vision 64(2-3), 107–123 (2005)
15. Gorelick, L., Blank, M., Shechtman, E., Irani, M., Basri, R.: Actions as space-time shapes. IEEE Trans. Pattern Anal. Mach. Intell. 29(12), 2247–2253 (2007)

Efficient Graph Construction for Label Propagation Based Multi-observation Face Recognition

Fadi Dornaika[1,2], Alireza Bosaghzadeh[1], and Bogdan Raducanu[3]

[1] University of the Basque Country UPV/EHU, San Sebastian, Spain
[2] IKERBASQUE, Basque Foundation for Science, Bilbao, Spain
[3] Computer Vision Center, 08193 Bellaterra, Barcelona, Spain

Abstract. Human-machine interaction is a hot topic nowadays in the communities of multimedia and computer vision. In this context, face recognition algorithms (used as primary cue for a person's identity assessment) work well under controlled conditions but degrade significantly when tested in real-world environments. Recently, graph-based label propagation for multi-observation face recognition was proposed. However, the associated graphs were constructed in an ad-hoc manner (e.g., using the KNN graph) that cannot adapt optimally to the data. In this paper, we propose a novel approach for efficient and adaptive graph construction that can be used for multi-observation face recognition as well as for other recognition problems. Experimental results performed on Honda video face database, show a distinct advantage of the proposed method over the standard graph construction methods.

1 Introduction

In the field of human-machine interaction, faces play a major role. For instance, socially oriented robots are specifically designed to support richer forms of interactions with humans. Their primary mission is to detect human presence, engage in an interaction and behave in a personalized manner. State-of-the-art face recognition techniques can achieve very high accuracy rates under controlled conditions. However, most of current face recognition systems lack robustness in uncontrolled environments (e.g., outdoor scenarios, homes, offices, etc.), since they are pretty sensitive to pose, lighting, occlusions and other variations (such as the presence of natural or artificial structures: beards, moustaches, glasses, etc.). Hence, the challenge is two-fold: to discriminate between different persons and at the same time to be able to recognize the same person affected by one or several of the aforementioned transformations. In particular, head pose problem has been one of the bottlenecks for most current face recognition techniques, because it changes significantly a person's appearance. In order to generalize the face recognition tools, it is mandatory to increase the robustness of the face recognition approach.

In Multimedia and Human Machine Interaction context, the system must continuously deal with an incoming flow of face images and has to guarantee a temporal coherence of a person's identity during the whole duration of the interaction process. In many cases, the difficulty arises from the fact that there is only a small time frame to capture a face with a high probability that the grabbed images do not contain the required frontal

A.A. Salah et al. (Eds.) : HBU 2013, LNCS 8212, pp. 124–135, 2013.

face images. On the other hand, videos very often provide non-frontal faces. To this end two categories of approaches were proposed. The first category uses manifold learning paradigms [4,21] in which the face subspace is constructed using many examples depicting subjects in different poses. The second category generates frontal face from the input image and then apply classic face recognition methods on the reconstructed frontal face image. The second category can be split into two main kinds of approaches: i) 3D morphable models [3], and ii) View-based methods [7]. View-based methods train a set of 2D models, each of which is designed to cope with shape or texture variation within a small range of viewpoints.

In [5], the authors propose a Local Linear regression method for pose invariant face recognition. The proposed method can generate the virtual frontal view from a given non-frontal face image. The whole non-frontal face image is partitioned into multiple local patches and then linear regression is applied to each patch for the prediction of its virtual frontal patch. The method requires the pose of the non-frontal pose as input in order to predict the frontal face. Following the approach of Active Appearance Models, [20] develops a face model and a rotation model which can be used to interpret facial features and synthesize realistic frontal face images when given a single novel face image. In [2], the authors address the non-frontal face recognition using morphable models.

As can be seen, 3D based and view based methods have many limitations. For instance, the 3D morphable models require 3D scans and have high computational load. The view-based methods very often require very tedious learning that require that the images are annotated by their face poses. In order to overcome the above limitations, multi-observation face recognition can offer an alternative [15,26,11,18]. In this case, the observations can be either a temporal sequence of face images (video sequence) or just a subset of images. Obviously, recognizing persons by using more than one face image can improve the performance of recognition systems since the test images contain more information that may include more views and more lighting variations that help reducing ambiguities that affect one single snapshot based recognition systems. Most of video-based face recognition methods use complicated training schemes in order to classify the multiple observations (e.g., [16]). In the context of semi-supervised learning, graph-based label propagation can be seen as a powerful tool that solves the multi-observation recognition problem. In [8], the authors proposed a graph-based label propagation method that can infer the labels of unknown observations by optimizing a penalty function based on label consistency. In [12], the authors extended the work of [8] by including the constraint that multiple observations have the same label. However, in both works the graph was constructed in a ad-hoc way, that is, it uses a KNN graph. In this paper, we propose a graph construction method that is based on efficient and adaptive coding scheme. We use the obtained graph in order to infer the label of multi-observation. The results are obtained with the public Honda face database.

The remainder of the paper is structured as follows: in Section 2, we provide some backgrounds about graph construction methods. Section 3 describes our proposed graph construction that is based on Weighted Regularized Least Square coding. Section 4 presents the recognition procedure. The experimental results on face recognition are presented in Section 5. Section 6 concludes the paper.

2   Background

The data graph is a powerful tool that encodes pairwise similarities among data samples. To this end, a weighted graph $G = (V; E; \mathbf{W})$ is constructed, where V denotes the set of N nodes of the graph corresponding to N data samples and $E \subseteq V \times V$ denotes the set of edges between nodes. For undirected graphs, $\mathbf{W}$ is a symmetric non-negative similarity matrix representing the weights of the edges, i.e., node i is connected to node j by an edge whose weight is equal to w_{ij}. An ideal similarity matrix, hence an ideal similarity graph G, is one in which nodes that correspond to points from the same subspace are connected to each other and there are no edges between nodes that correspond to points in different subspaces. Figure 1 illustrates a fully connected graph depicting the pairwise similarities among 6 face images.

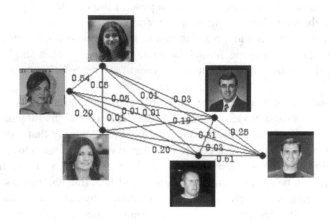

Fig. 1. A fully connected graph that encodes pairwise similarities among 6 face images

2.1   KNN graph

The KNN graph is a well known scheme for constructing data graphs. Given N data points $\mathbf{x}_1, \mathbf{x}_2, \ldots, \mathbf{x}_N \in \mathbb{R}^D$, one can build a nearest neighbor graph G to model the local geometrical structure. For each data point $\mathbf{x}_i$, we find its k nearest neighbors and put an edge between $\mathbf{x}_i$ and its neighbors. Let $N(\mathbf{x}_i) = \{\mathbf{x}_1, \mathbf{x}_2, \ldots, \mathbf{x}_k\}$ be the set of its k nearest neighbors. Thus, the weight matrix of G can be defined as follows:

$$W_{ij} = \begin{cases} sim(\mathbf{x}_i, \mathbf{x}_j) & \text{if } \mathbf{x}_j \in N(\mathbf{x}_i) \text{ or } \mathbf{x}_i \in N(\mathbf{x}_j) \\ 0, & otherwise \end{cases} \qquad (1)$$

where $sim(\mathbf{x}_i, \mathbf{x}_k)$ is a real value that encodes the similarity between $\mathbf{x}_i$ and $\mathbf{x}_k$. Simple choices for this function are the Kernel heat and the cosine.

2.2 ϵ-ball Graph

The ϵ-ball graph is similar to the KNN graph. However, instead of linking pairs according to the KNN rule, the neighbors of a given $\mathbf{x}_i$ are set to the data samples that belong to a sphere centered at $\mathbf{x}_i$ and having ϵ as radius.

2.3 ℓ_1 Graph

In traditional graph construction process, the graph adjacency structure and the graph weights are derived separately (previous sections). In [23], the authors argue that the graph adjacency structure and the graph weights are interrelated and should not be separated. Thus it is desired to develop a procedure which can simultaneously completes these two tasks within one step. Instead of building a graph in two different processes of adjacency construction and graph weight calculation, [23] tried to unify them in one single process. This has the advantage that both relationship and degree of similarity can be simultaneously estimated. In their work, every sample is coded as a sparse linear combination of the rest of the training samples. If $\mathbf{y} \in \mathbb{R}^D$ denotes an input sample (test or training sample) and matrix $\mathbf{X} \in \mathbb{R}^{D,N}$ a database with N training samples, then the goal is to represent input $\mathbf{y}$ as a sparse linear combination of matrix X. Thus, it can be written as

$$\min \|\mathbf{a}\|_1 \ s.t \ \ \mathbf{y} = \mathbf{X}\mathbf{a} \tag{2}$$

where $\mathbf{a} \in \mathbb{R}^N$ is the coefficient vector. Due to the presence of noise, Eq (2) will become:

$$\min \|\mathbf{a}\|_1 \ s.t \ \ \|\mathbf{y} - \mathbf{X}\mathbf{a}\|_2 < \xi \tag{3}$$

which ξ represents a given tolerance error. After solving the above minimization problem, the components of the sparse vector $\mathbf{a}$ shows the contribution of each sample in reconstructing the input signal $\mathbf{y}$. The more similar a signal in the database to the sample, the bigger it's coefficient (absolute value). The samples in the database which are far from the input signal will have very small or zero coefficients. In this way the neighbors and their weights are calculated simultaneously. Therefore, by using the above coding for every training sample $\mathbf{x}_i$ with respect to the rest of the set, one can compute N sparse vector $\mathbf{a}_i$. From these coefficients, one can set the graph matrix $\mathbf{W}$ (w_{ij} is set to $|\mathbf{a}_i(j)|$).

There are different methods that can solve the above ℓ_1 minimization problem like gradient projection [9], homotopy [17], iterative shrinkage-thresholding [6], proximal gradient, and alternating direction [25]. In [24] the authors reviewed those five representative ℓ_1 minimization methods and compared them in speed and accuracy. The main focus was on the face recognition application. The conclusion shows that none of the above methods were able to outperform in all aspects of speed, accuracy and resistance of noise.

3   Proposed Graph Construction

As explained in the previous section there are many different methods to build a graph. Our objective is to provide an efficient tool for graph construction that has the same advantages of ℓ_1 graphs. In our proposed method, we construct the graph of a database by directly using the coding of any training image with respect to the rest of the set. We were inspired by recent advances in collaborative coding, namely the Weighted Regularized Least Square minimization method (WRLS) proposed in [22]. In this work, the authors proposed a linear coding scheme in order to classify samples according to the collaborative reconstruction error. Their proposed criterion is based on the sum of three parts: (i) L_2 norm of the reconstruction error, (ii) a regularization term set to the L_2 norm of the coefficients vector, (iii) a weighted sum of the squared coefficients. Since the weights are set to the distances between the test sample and the training samples, a kind of sparsity is included in the global criterion.

3.1 Weighted Regularized Least Square (WRLS) Coding

In our work we use the following coding scheme in order to automatically generate the data graph:

$$\min_{\mathbf{a}} \left(\|\mathbf{y} - \mathbf{X}\mathbf{a}\|^2 + \sigma \sum_{i=1}^{N} p_i \, a_i^2 \right) \tag{4}$$

where σ is a regularization parameter having small positive value and the p_i's are non-negative weights. The above optimization problem has the following closed form solution:

$$\mathbf{a}^\star = (\mathbf{X}^T \mathbf{X} + \sigma \mathbf{P})^{-1} \mathbf{X}^T \mathbf{y} \tag{5}$$

where $\mathbf{P}$ is $N \times N$ diagonal matrix whose diagonal elements P_{ii} are set to p_i. In our work, we use the following formula for the weights:

$$P_{ii} = p_i = 1 - \exp(-\|\mathbf{y} - \mathbf{x}_i\|^2)$$

If the test sample $\mathbf{y}$ is far from the sample $\mathbf{x}_i$ then the weight of the unknown coefficient a_i tends to 1 so that the program in (4) attempt to get a small a_i. On the other hand, if the test sample is very close to the sample $\mathbf{x}_i$, the constraint on a_i is released.

3.2 WRLS Graph

The detailed procedure for the WRLS graph construction is listed in Algorithm 1. Note that the constructed WRLS graph is a directed graph, i.e., the weight matrix $\mathbf{W}$ is asymmetric.

4 Multi-observation Recognition Based on Label Propagation

Label propagation is very often linked to the case of semi-supervised learning where the goal is to infer the unknown labels from the known ones using a given criterion [8]. Let C denotes the total number of classes. Let $\mathbf{X}_u$ (a $D \times r$ matrix) denote the r unknown observations. Let $\mathbf{X}_l$ (a $D \times N$ matrix) denote the N known observations (i.e., the training samples). The union of both data sets provides the data matrix $\mathbf{X} = (\mathbf{X}_l, \mathbf{X}_u)$. The corresponding label matrix is denoted by $\mathbf{Y} = (\mathbf{Y}_l, \mathbf{Y}_u)$ (a $C \times (N + r)$ matrix).

Data: A given training sample set $\mathbf{X}$
Result: A weight matrix $\mathbf{W}$

Set the diagonal elements of $\mathbf{W}$ to zero ;
for $i = 1, \ldots, N$ **do**
  Pick the sample $\mathbf{x}_i$ from $\mathbf{X}$;
  $\mathbf{X}' = \mathbf{X} - \{\mathbf{x}_i\}$;
  Compute the $(N-1) \times (N-1)$ diagonal matrix $\mathbf{P}$;
  Calculate the $N-1$ vector $\mathbf{a}$ as $\mathbf{a} = (\mathbf{X}'^T \mathbf{X}' + \sigma \mathbf{P})^{-1} \mathbf{X}'^T \mathbf{x}_i$;
  for $j = 1, \ldots, N$ **do**
    if $i < j$ then
    | Set $W_{ij} = |a_j|$
    else
    | Set $W_{ij} = |a_{j-1}|$
    end
  end
end

Algorithm 1. WRLS graph construction

Each column vector $\mathbf{y}_i$ of $\mathbf{Y}$ is a vector characterizing the probabilities of the sample $\mathbf{x}_i$ belonging to different classes, namely,

$$y_i(c) = p(c|\mathbf{x}_i); c = 1, 2, \ldots, C$$

where $p(c|\mathbf{x}_i)$ is the posterior probability of the class c for the given sample $\mathbf{x}_i$. For a labeled sample $\mathbf{x}_i$, $y_i(c) = 1$ if $\mathbf{x}_i$ belongs to the cth class; $y_i(c) = 0$, otherwise.

The problem of label propagation is to infer the label matrix $\mathbf{Y}_u$ given the whole data $\mathbf{X} = (\mathbf{X}_l, \mathbf{X}_u)$ and the known label matrix $\mathbf{Y}_l$. This can be achieved by minimizing the following criterion:

$$\min E(\mathbf{Y}) = \sum_{i,j} \|\mathbf{y}_i - \mathbf{y}_j\|^2 W_{ij} \tag{6}$$

An explanation of this objective is as follows. When the samples $\mathbf{x}_i$ and $\mathbf{x}_j$ are similar, namely, the graph weight W_{ij} is large, the distance between $\mathbf{y}_i$ and $\mathbf{y}_j$ should be small in order to minimize the objective, namely the class information of the sample $\mathbf{x}_i$ and $\mathbf{x}_j$ should be similar.

The objective can be further rewritten as

$$\min E(\mathbf{Y}) = \sum_{i,j} \|\mathbf{y}_i - \mathbf{y}_j\|^2 W_{ij} \tag{7}$$

$$= trace(\mathbf{Y} \mathbf{D}_{row} \mathbf{Y}^T + \mathbf{Y} \mathbf{D}_{col} \mathbf{Y}^T - \mathbf{Y} \mathbf{W} \mathbf{Y}^T - \mathbf{Y} \mathbf{W} \mathbf{Y}^T) \tag{8}$$

$$= trace(\mathbf{Y} \mathbf{L} \mathbf{Y}^T) \tag{9}$$

where $\mathbf{D}_{row}$ is a diagonal matrix whose diagonal elements are the row sums of the corresponding rows of $\mathbf{W}$, and $\mathbf{D}_{col}$ is a diagonal matrix whose diagonal elements are the column sums of the corresponding columns of $\mathbf{W}$. $\mathbf{D}_{row} - \mathbf{W}$ and $\mathbf{D}_{col} - \mathbf{W}^T$ are the row and column Graph Laplacian matrices respectively. It is obvious that the matrix $\mathbf{L} = \mathbf{D}_{row} + \mathbf{D}_{col} - (\mathbf{W} + \mathbf{W}^T)$ is symmetric.

Since the r observations have the same unknown label, the unknown label matrix $\mathbf{Y}_u$ will have C configurations $(\mathbf{Y}_u(1), \ldots, \mathbf{Y}_u(C)$ where $\mathbf{Y}_u(c)$ has only the cth row equal to ones and the the rest of the rows are zeros. Therefore, the whole label matrix $\mathbf{Y} = (\mathbf{Y}_l, \mathbf{Y}_u)$ can be written as $\mathbf{Y} = (\mathbf{Y}_l, \mathbf{Y}_u(c))$ where $\mathbf{Y}_l$ is constant. To infer the label of the unknown observations $\mathbf{X}_u$, the following formula can be used:

$$c^\star = \arg\min E(\mathbf{Y}_c) \tag{10}$$

where $\mathbf{Y}(c) = (\mathbf{Y}_l, \mathbf{Y}_u(c))$. Thus, the optimal label is inferred using C evaluations of the term $E(\mathbf{Y}_c)$. The procedure for the multi-observation recognition based on the WRLS graph is illustrated in Algorithm 2.

Data: A set of multiple observations $\mathbf{X}_u$, a training set $\mathbf{X}_l$ and their labels $\mathbf{Y}_l$
Result: The label of the unknown observations $c*$

Compute the WRLS graph over the data $\mathbf{X} = (\mathbf{X}_l, \mathbf{X}_u)$ (Algo 1) ;
Estimate the label c^* using Eq. (10)

Algorithm 2. Multi-observation recognition via WRLS graph based label propagation

5 Experimental Results

Data Preparation. Our approach has been tested on the Honda video database (HVDB) [13,14]. HVDB has been acquired for the purpose of face tracking and recognition. It depicts persons sitting in front of a camera in a totally uncontrolled environment and performing unconstrained in-plane and out-of-plane head motion. Some samples are depicted in figure 2. The resolution of the images is 640x480 pixels and the videos were recorded at 15 frames per second. We selected from this database a subset of 22 video clips belonging to 22 different persons.

The used dataset contains 2317 images organized in 22 classes, with an average of 100 images per class. The cropped images were resized to 50×50 pixels. The cropped images are normalized using the zero-mean unit-variance. A sample gallery is depicted in figure 3.

We conducted two groups of experiments. In the first group, we use single snapshots in order to recognize faces using a manifold representation followed by the Nearest Neighbor classifier. In the second group of experiments we use the label propagation theory in order to recognize faces based on several observations. In the latter group, we consider two cases: the KNN graph and the proposed method for automatic graph building.

Single Image Face Recognition. For single snapshot face recognition evaluation, we applied a manifold representation approach. This implies that the original, high-dimensional data, are embedded into a low-dimensional subspace, without any relevant

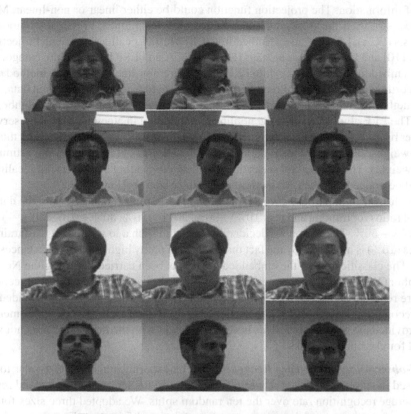

Fig. 2. Some samples from the Honda Video database

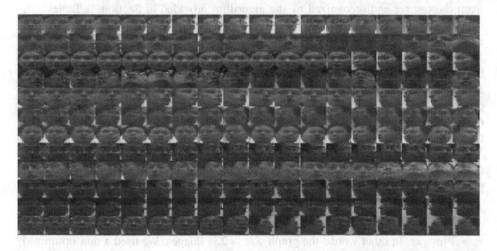

Fig. 3. Some samples of cropped face images from the Honda Video database

loss of information. The projection function could be either linear or non-linear. More concrete, we used the following manifold learning techniques: Principal Component Analysis (PCA), Locally Linear Embedding (LLE) [19], Locality Preserving Projections (LPP) [10] and Laplacian Eigenmaps (LE) [1]. PCA and LPP belong to the category of linear embedding techniques, while LLE and LE are non-linear. The PCA method estimates orthogonal projection directions that maximize the variance of original data. The LPP method searches a linear projection that preserve the locality of the neighboring data. The LLE algorithm seeks the nonlinear embedding in a neighborhood preserving manner by exploiting the local symmetries of linear reconstructions, and seeking the optimal weights for local reconstruction. The embedding is obtained using the estimated local weights. The LE method seeks the nonlinear embedding by preserving locality. It should be noticed that the LPP method is the linearized version of LE.

For classification purposes, we adopted 10 random splits of data. We split the data in several ratios for training and test: $10\% - 90\%$, $20\% - 80\%$, $30\% - 70\%$, $40\% - 60\%$ and $50\% - 50\%$. The reason we decided to start with such a low percentage of training images (10%) is motivated by the fact that we have a pretty high number of instances per class. The classification in the embedded space has been carried out using the Nearest Neighbor (NN) approach. The recognition rates for the case of single snapshot recognition are reported in table 1. We can observe that (i) the PCA technique has provided the best recognition results for both the cropped and rectified faces; (ii) the LLE method has provided the worst results. This is very consistent with the fact that LLE is not very suited for classification tasks.

Multi-observation Image Face Recognition. The experimental setup is similar to the one used in single image face scenario. We again use the ten random splits and report the average recognition rate over the ten random splits. We adopted three sizes for the number of test images of the same person: $r = 3$, 4 and 5 images. For every training percentage and for every value of r, several hundreds of subsets are picked at random from the test set and recognized by the algorithm provided in Section 4. Tables 2,3, and 4 summarize the performance for the training/test ratios $10\% - 90\%$, $20\% - 80\%$, and $30\% - 70\%$, respectively. In each of these tables, we compare two methods: (1) the KNN graph based label propagation and (2) our proposed graph-based label propagation (Section 4). For the KNN graph based method, several values for K were tested and the best performance were reported in these Tables. As can be seen the use of our proposed graph construction method has improved the recognition performance. Furthermore, this improvement is more obvious when the training size and/or the size of the multiple observation becomes very small.

Table 5 summarizes the performance of the single image face recognition scheme (PCA) and the Multi-observation face recognition scheme (proposed graph-based label propagation). For the latter scheme, the number of test images is kept fixed to 3 ($r = 3$).

Algorithms' Complexity. We have measured the computing time of the proposed graph construction method. To this end, we used the training percentage of 10% together with $r = 3$ images. In other words, the graph size is 234 images. We used a non-optimized MATLAB code running on a PC equipped with an Intel Core i7 CPU at 2.93 Ghz.

Table 6 summarizes the performance of three methods for graph construction: (i) the KNN graph, (ii) the ℓ_1 graph, and (iii) our proposed method. The first column depicts the CPU time associated with the graph construction stage, the second column depicts the CPU time associated with the recognition step (label propagation), and the third column depicts the recognition rate. Although the ℓ_1 provided more accurate recognition rate, our proposed graph construction method was 43.3 times faster. This makes the online face recognition based on ℓ_1 graph method unfeasible whereas this is still feasible with our proposed graph construction.

Table 1. Best average recognition accuracy using manifold representation and the NN classifier

Train	10%	20%	30%	40%	50%
PCA	**74.73%**	**85.86%**	**91.67%**	**94.24%**	**95.85%**
LLE	34.18%	42.71%	47.84%	53.99%	64.53%
LPP	67.54%	80.40%	86.36%	89.62%	91.64%
LE	68.82%	77.48%	82.34%	85.52%	87.62%

Table 2. Method comparison for multi-observation recognition. The size of training is 10%.

Number of observations (Images)	3	4	5
KNN graph	80.92	85.37	88.21
Proposed graph	**84.28**	**87.06**	**88.81**

Table 3. Method comparison for multi-observation recognition. The size of training is 20%.

Number of observations (Images)	3	4	5
KNN graph	92.53	95.64	96.67
Proposed graph	**95.52**	**97.33**	**97.98**

Table 4. Method comparison for multi-observation recognition. The size of training is 30%.

Number of observations (Images)	3	4	5
KNN graph	96.21	97.95	98.65
Proposed graph	**97.75**	**98.74**	**99.67**

Table 5. Method comparison. Second row: Recognition rates for singe snapshot recognition (PCA followed by NN classifier), Third row: Proposed method for multi-observation recognition using three face images. For the latter scheme, the number of test images is kept fixed to 3 ($r = 3$).

Training data set	10%	20%	30%
Single snapshot (PCA space)	74.73	85.86	91.67
Proposed scheme	**84.28**	**95.52**	**97.75**

Table 6. CPU time associated with three graph construction methods. The size of the graph is 234 images. The number of unlabeled images is 3.

	Graph construction (CPU time)	Recognition (CPU time)	Recognition rate
KNN graph	0.0035 (seconds)	0.004 (seconds)	80.92 %
ℓ_1 graph	24.06 (seconds)	0.004 (seconds)	85.46 %
Proposed WRLS graph	0.498 (seconds)	0.004 (seconds)	84.43 %

6   Conclusions

In this paper, we proposed a novel approach for efficient and adaptive graph construction that can be used for multi-observation face recognition as well as for other recognition problems. Experimental results performed on Honda video face database, show a distinct advantage of the proposed method over the standard graph construction methods.

Acknowledgment. This work was supported by the Spanish Government under the projects TIN2010-18856 and TIN2009-14404-C02-00.

References

1. Belkin, M., Niyogi, P.: Laplacian eigenmaps for dimensionality reduction and data representation. Neural Computation 15(6), 1373–1396 (2003)
2. Blanz, V., Grother, P., Phillips, P.J., Vetter, T.: Face recognition based on frontal views generated from non-frontal images. In: IEEE International Conference on Computer Vision and Pattern Recognition (2004)
3. Blanz, V., Vetter, T.: Face recognition based on fitting a 3D morphable model. IEEE Transactions on PAMI (2003)
4. Cai, D., He, X., Zhou, K., Han, J., Bao, H.: Locality sensitive discriminant analysis. In: International Joint Conference on Artificial Intelligence (2007)
5. Chai, X., Shan, S., Chen, X., Gao, W.: Locally linear regression for pose-invariant face recognition. IEEE Trans. on Image Processing 16(7) (2007)
6. Combettes, P., Wajs, V.: Signal recovery by proximal forward-backward splitting. Multiscale Modeling and Simulation 4(4), 1168–1200 (2005)
7. Cootes, T.F., Wheeler, G.V., Walker, K.N., Taylor, C.J.: View-based active appearance models. Image and Vision Computing (2002)
8. Zhou, D., Bousquet, O., Lal, T.N., Weston., J., Schölkopf, B.: Adv. neural inf. process. syst. In: Learning with Local and Global Consistency (2004)
9. Figueiredo, M.A.T., Nowak, R., Wright, S.: Gradient projection for sparse reconstruction: Application to compressed sensing and other inverse problems. IEEE Journal of Selected Topics in Signal Processing 1(4), 586–597 (2007)
10. He, X., Niyogi, P.: Locality preserving projections. In: Conference on Advances in Neural Information Processing Systems (2003)
11. Hewitt, R., Belongie, S.: Active learning in face recognition: Using tracking to build a face model. In: V4HCI, New York City (2006)
12. Kokiopoulou, E., Frossard, P.: Graph-based classification of multiple observation sets. Pattern Recognition 43(12), 3988–3997 (2010)

13. Lee, K.C., Ho, J., Yang, M.H., Kriegman, D.: Visual tracking and recognition using probabilistic appearance manifolds. Computer Vision and Image Understanding 99, 303–331 (2005)
14. Lee, K.C., Kriegman, D.: Online learning of probabilistic appearance manifolds for video-based recognition and tracking. In: IEEE International Conference on Computer Vision and Pattern Recognition (2005)
15. Lee, K., Ho, J., Yang, M.H., Kriegman, D.: Video-based face recognition using probabilistic appearance manifolds. In: CVPR, pp. 313–320 (2003)
16. Liu, X., Chen, T.: Video-based face recognition using adaptive hidden markov models, pp. 340–345 (2003)
17. Malioutov, D., Cetin, M., Willsky, A.: Homotopy continuation for sparse signal representation. In: Proceedings of the IEEE International Conference on Acoustics, Speech, and Signal Processing (ICASSP 2005), vol. 5, pp. v/733–v/736 (2005)
18. Manyam, O.K., Kumar, N., Belhumeur, P., Kriegman, D.: Two faces are better than one: Face recognition in group photographs. In: International Joint Conference on Biometrics (IJCB), Washington, DC (October 2011)
19. Roweis, S., Saul, L.: Nonlinear dimensionality reduction by locally linear embedding. Science 290(5500), 2323–2326 (2000)
20. Shan, T., Lovell, B.C., Chen, S.: Face recognition robust to head pose from one sample image. In: IEEE International Conference on Face and Gesture Recognition (2006)
21. Tenenbaum, J.B., de Silva, V., Langford, J.C.: A global geometric framework for nonlinear dimensionality reduction. Science 290(5500), 2319–2323 (2000)
22. Waqas, J., Yi, Z., Zhang, L.: Collaborative neighbor representation based classification using l2-minimization approach. Pattern Recognition Letters 34, 201–208 (2013)
23. Yan, S., Wang, H.: Semi-supervised learning by sparse representation. In: SIAM Conference on Data Mining, pp. 792–801 (2009)
24. Yang, A.Y., Sastry, S.S., Ganesh, A., Ma, Y.: Fast l1-minimization algorithms and an application in robust face recognition: a review. Tech. rep. (2010)
25. Yang, J., Zhang, Y.: Alternating direction algorithms for l1-problems in compressive sensing. Tech. rep. (2009)
26. Zhou, S., Krueger, V., Chellappa, R.: Probabilistic recognition of human faces from video. Computer Vision and Image Understanding 91(1-2), 214–245 (2003)

Multiple Local Curvature Gabor Binary Patterns for Facial Action Recognition

Anıl Yüce, Nuri Murat Arar, and Jean-Philippe Thiran

Signal Processing Laboratory (LTS5),
École Polytechnique Fédérale de Lausanne, Switzerland
{anil.yuce,murat.arar,jean-philippe.thiran}@epfl.ch

Abstract. Curvature Gabor features have recently been shown to be powerful facial texture descriptors with applications on face recognition. In this paper we introduce their use in facial action unit (AU) detection within a novel framework that combines multiple Local Curvature Gabor Binary Patterns (LCGBP) on different filter sizes and curvature degrees. The proposed system uses the distances of LCGBP histograms between neutral faces and AU containing faces combined with an AU-specific feature selection and classification process. We achieve 98.6% overall accuracy in our tests with the extended Cohn-Kanade database, which is higher than achieved previously by any state-of-the-art method.

1 Introduction

Being the most important non-verbal means of human communication, facial expressions have gained extreme importance for computer vision especially with the ease of access of recent technological developments. Besides the various applications of basic emotion recognition, recognizing facial actions now serves much more in areas such as intelligent human computer interaction or diagnosis and treatment of certain pathological conditions.

The recent interesting work, such as [11], which investigates the detection of expressions of pain, or [17], which presents a method for the detection of asymmetric lip movements, for instance, all point out to the need for increased facial action recognition accuracy to capture more subtle muscle movements in both intensity and time. To this end, we introduce a framework with a novel set of features for action unit (AU) detection that achieves much higher accuracy than previously presented state-of-the-art methods.

The AUs are the basic units of facial movement, that are defined by the Facial Action Coding System (FACS) [7]. FACS serves as a method to objectively define every independent motion on the face. For an overview of recent advances and the state-of-the-art in AU and facial expression detection, the reader is referred to [19], which is the meta-analysis of the first facial expression recognition challenge and includes the summary of up to date work using shape and appearance based methods.

In this work we propose the variation among frames of a combination of Local Curvature Gabor Binary Patterns (LCGBP) as descriptors of facial action. LCGBP is an extension to the Local Gabor Binary Patterns (LGBP) which have been used extensively for face recognition and AU detection (e.g. [22], [16]), since they have proven

A.A. Salah et al. (Eds.) : HBU 2013, LNCS 8212, pp. 136–147, 2013.

to be quite robust against variations of conditions such as illumination. By adding the effect of curved formations, which exist commonly in the facial texture, the curvature Gabors provide a more efficient way of representing the facial components [8] and it was previously shown in our recent work that they are successful in recognizing facial identity [2]. Here, we apply this idea by using the change in LCGBP histograms between neutral and expressive images for detecting the AUs. Using this variation of histograms between frames has shown to be more efficient than using the histograms themselves directly ([16], [21]). The main contribution of our work is introducing a unique way of extracting Gabor features, which includes the curvature information and proves by the very high accuracy results to be very powerful descriptors for facial actions, combined with a feature selection and classification phase that was proven in our previous work [21] to be efficient with such features.

The rest of the paper is formed as follows: In Section 2 we explain the formulation of LCGBP, in Section 3 we describe the framework that we propose for AU detection and detail the parameter selection. Section 4 presents the test settings and results obtained by several experiments on the CK+ database and comparisons with other types of features and recent existing methods in the literature. Finally, we report our conclusions and possible future directions for further improving the system in Section 5.

2 Local Curvature Gabor Binary Patterns

2.1 Curvature Gabor (CG) Wavelets

Gabor wavelets have been recognized as one of the most successful feature extraction methods for face representation. They form a well-established image decomposition because of their spatial locality and orientation selectivity characteristics. Therefore, they are optimally localized in the space and frequency domains, and can be used successfully in facial image processing for face and facial expression recognition and analysis.

The conventional Gabor wavelet definition is as follows:

$$\psi(\boldsymbol{x}; \nu, \mu) = \frac{k_{\nu,\mu}^2}{\sigma^2} e^{(-\frac{k_{\nu,\mu}^2 ||\boldsymbol{x}||^2}{2\sigma^2})} [e^{(ik_{\nu,\mu}\boldsymbol{x})} - e^{(-\frac{\sigma^2}{2})}] \tag{1}$$

where $\boldsymbol{x} = \begin{pmatrix} \hat{x} \\ \hat{y} \end{pmatrix} = \begin{pmatrix} x\cos(\frac{\mu\pi}{M}) + y\sin(\frac{\mu\pi}{M}) \\ -x\sin(\frac{\mu\pi}{M}) + y\cos(\frac{\mu\pi}{M}) \end{pmatrix}$ and $e^{(ik_{\nu,\mu}\boldsymbol{x})}$ is the oscillatory wave function, whose real and imaginary parts are respectively the cosine and sine functions. μ controls the orientation of the filters, with M being the total number of different orientations, and ν scales the center of the filter in the frequency domain [6].

A typical neutral face image contains curve-like features because it contains permanent facial components (e.g. eyebrows, lips) as well as straight features. Since facial expressions are generated by the movement of groups of muscles in any orientation and transient features like wrinkles and furrows, images with expressions contain even more curvature characteristics than straight ones. Therefore, to model these curve-like features, we include CG wavelets for face representation in addition to the conventional Gabor wavelets.

Peters et al. [14] obtained CG wavelets by adding a curvature parameter to the conventional Gabor formulation as follows:

$$\psi(\boldsymbol{x}; \nu, \mu) = \frac{k_{\nu,\mu}^2}{\sigma^2} e^{\left(-\frac{k_{\nu,\mu}^2 ||\boldsymbol{x}||^2}{2\sigma^2}\right)} [e^{(ik_{\nu,\mu}\hat{x})} - e^{(-\frac{\sigma^2}{2})}] \qquad (2)$$

$$\boldsymbol{x} = \begin{pmatrix} \hat{x} \\ \hat{y} \end{pmatrix} = \begin{pmatrix} xcos(\frac{\mu\pi}{M}) + ysin(\frac{\mu\pi}{M}) + c(-xsin(\frac{\mu\pi}{M}) + ycos(\frac{\mu\pi}{M}))^2) \\ -xsin(\frac{\mu\pi}{M}) + ycos(\frac{\mu\pi}{M}) \end{pmatrix} \qquad (3)$$

where c corresponds to the curvature ratio.

CG wavelets do not have the orientation symmetry as in conventional Gabor wavelet as shown in Fig. 1 ([2]). For the conventional Gabor wavelet setting, it is usually sufficient to have 8 orientations ($M = 8$). However, this number should be increased to 16 to obtain the same orientation utilization in case of CG wavelets.

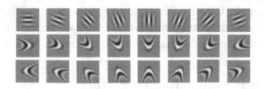

Fig. 1. Illustration of orientation asymmetry in CG wavelets with $c = 0.1$ (middle and bottom row) in comparison with the conventional Gabor wavelet (top row) (Image courtesy of [2])

In CG wavelets, one can use different curvature degrees, i.e., $c = \{0.05, 0.1, 0.2\}$, and Gaussian sizes, i.e., $\sigma \in \{0.5\pi, \pi, 2\pi\}$, for multi-curvature utilization as well as scale space utilization. In this way, a more powerful representation of facial structures is obtained by extracting both fine and coarse features with straight and curved filters.

2.2   Local Binary Patterns

The local binary pattern (LBP) transformation has been proposed as a texture description method [12] and has proven to be very effective in representing facial texture and been widely used for both face and facial action recognition [1][18]. It maps the texture variation around each pixel to a binary pattern and the histogram of these patterns in a local window can be used directly as a descriptor for that certain region of interest. The computation of the pattern for a pixel at position x of an image I is as follows:

$$LBP_P(x) = \sum_{p=0}^{P-1} t(I(x_p) - I(x)).2^p \qquad (4)$$

In this representation, each $I(x_p)$ is a neighboring pixel of the center pixel $I(x)$ on a neighborhood defined by the number of pixels P as well as the shape (e.g. rectangular or circular) and the distance to the central pixel which determines the resolution of the transformation. The function $t(x)$ is the simple thresholding function which returns 1 if the input pixel difference is positive and 0 if it is negative. In this way we obtain a $P - bit$ binary value, or an integer between 0 and $2^P - 1$ to represent each pixel.

In this work we use an 8-pixel circular neighborhood with the radius 1, giving 256 possible patterns. It has been shown, however, that only 58 of these patterns, called the uniform patterns, are sufficient to describe the majority of the texture information [13]. So we can reduce the size of the descriptor to 59 bins by assigning all the non-uniform patterns into a single bin.

Applying the LBP on top of Gabor magnitude images with various scales and orientations results in obtaining a richer representation and finer description of the facial texture [22]. In our work we extend this variation of descriptors by also including multiple curvature degrees and Gaussian sizes, obtaining the Local Curvature Gabor Binary Patterns (LCGBP) representation. Of course, this extension substantially increases the number of features obtained, and introduces more redundancy between features and possibly noise for the final classification task. Therefore, whether using directly the LCGBP histogram bins as features or, as we perform in this particular work, using a dissimilarity measure for the histograms between frames, a feature selection or dimension reduction technique is essential to be able to perform a meaningful classification using these features. The details on how we compute the histogram dissimilarity as well as the feature selection technique and the types of selected features are explained in more detail in the following sections.

3   Facial Action Recognition Framework

This section describes in detail each step in our automated facial action unit detection system using LCGBP as seen in Fig. 2.

3.1   Face Localization

To be able to perform an effective feature extraction among all images in the dataset, we first need to locate our region of interest, which is the face, as accurately and consistently as possible. Face detection systems which output a rectangular region around the face are generally not reliable enough to extract appearance features because of the variety across subjects, expressions and head poses. Therefore, we choose to use a facial point tracking system instead, which provides more stable boundaries for the face region.

In this paper, we localize 66 facial landmarks as seen in Fig. 2, using a publicly available automatic face tracking system proposed by Saragih et al. [15]. The face tracker is based on constrained local models (CLM) [5] with regularized landmark mean-shift as the fitting strategy [15]. The CLM, similar to the Active Appearance Model (AAM) [4], uses a combined model for the shape and texture, but the model in CLM consists of templates of appearance around each facial landmark point which allows accurately tracking facial points even under extreme head poses, intensive facial expressions and presence of occlusions.

Once we locate the facial landmarks using the face tracker, we crop the image using the most extreme landmarks on the horizontal and vertical directions of the facial mask

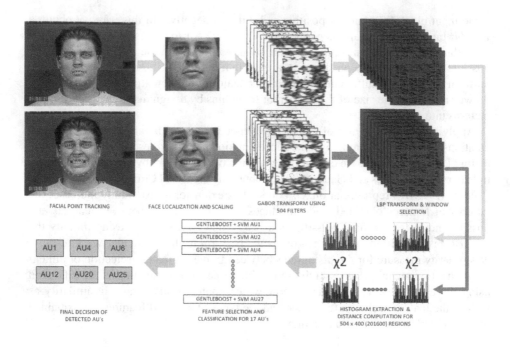

FACIAL POINT TRACKING   FACE LOCALIZATION AND SCALING   GABOR TRANSFORM USING 504 FILTERS   LBP TRANSFORM & WINDOW SELECTION

GENTLEBOOST + SVM AU1
GENTLEBOOST + SVM AU2
GENTLEBOOST + SVM AU4

χ^2 χ^2

GENTLEBOOST + SVM AU27

AU1   AU4   AU6

AU12   AU20   AU25

FINAL DECISION OF DETECTED AU's   FEATURE SELECTION AND CLASSIFICATION FOR 17 AU's   HISTOGRAM EXTRACTION & DISTANCE COMPUTATION FOR 504 x 400 (201600) REGIONS

Fig. 2. Complete flowchart of the proposed framework for an input video

obtained, with a certain safety margin (Fig. 2). No rotation or texture warping is performed, since the databases that we use to train and test our system were recorded in quite constrained situations with respect to head pose and since the types of features we use have proven to be robust against misalignments. In this paper we only aim to show the strength of LCGBP as features for facial action recognition compared to other types of features. As future work registration of facial texture will be added to the system to gain more robustness against cases of unconstrained head pose. In our system we only scale each detected face region to a fixed size of 120 by 120 pixels.

3.2 Feature Extraction

After locating and scaling the face region we extract the appearance features using a combination of LCGBP transforms, which is the LBP transform applied on top of the image filtered by various curvature Gabor wavelets, as explained previously in Section 2 and as represented in Fig. 2. For our training and testing purposes we apply this filtering to the frame with a neutral expression and the frame with the peak of the posed expression separately for each sample video, since we utilize the comparison between those frames. For the CK+ database [10] these frames correspond to the first and last frames respectively. At this point the system requires that a frame is marked as neutral expression, then the method can be applied to any other frame of the same subject to detect action units at different intensities. This automatization problem can be solved by projecting the subject face with any expression to the PCA space created by examples of expressionless faces, as proposed in [16]. However, this method was not tested in the scope of this paper.

The first step of feature extraction is applying the Gabor transforms to the input images. The classic method for generating Gabor representations of images is to apply wavelets in different scales and orientations with a fixed Gaussian size. In addition to adding the curvature component in various degrees we also include wavelets with different Gaussian sizes, similar to [2]. This is expected to result in a richer representation of finer details of facial texture components, which are crucial for high accuracy action recognition, compared to a single Gaussian size, and so is proven with our test results (presented in the following section). To be more precise we use Gabor wavelets of 3 different scales ($\nu \in \{0, 1, 2\}$), 8 (or 16 in case of curvature, see Fig. 1) orientations ($\mu \in \{0, \cdots, 7\}$), 3 Gaussian sizes ($\sigma \in \{\pi/2, \pi, 2\pi\}$) and 4 curvature degrees ($c \in \{0, 0.05, 0.1, 0.2\}$). This results in a total of 504 separate filters ($1 \times 3 \times 3 \times 8 + 3 \times 3 \times 3 \times 16$).

Next we apply the uniform LBP transform on each of the magnitude images of the outputs of these 504 filters for both the neutral and peak expression frame. Then to obtain the local texture information we calculate the histograms on 400 overlapping windows of sizes 20 by 20, 20 by 40, 40 by 20 and 40 by 40 with an overlap size of 10, all units in pixels. The conventional tendency in the literature for LBP histogram extraction has been to use non-overlapping windows of a fixed size, but as shown recently in our previous work [21], varying the size and performing a more extensive search using overlaps, combined with a powerful feature selection step, results in a more informative feature set. Then we compute for each of these windows the χ^2 distance of corresponding histograms in the neutral and peak expression frames, and obtain our full set of features of size 201600 (400×504). Using these alterations from the neutral face as features not only eliminates the variation caused by identity ([16], [21]) but also allows tracking the relative intensity of the movement between frames.

3.3 Relevant Feature Selection and AU Detection

The extensive representation and search strategy chosen in the feature extraction technique results in a huge number of features which causes two main problems. First problem is that most of these features are correlated with each other so using them in combination in a classification task introduces an unnecessary computational burden. Secondly, only a portion of them are relevant to the task, i.e. detecting a specific action unit. The irrelevant features cause only noise and a decrease in accuracy in classification. Therefore we need to use a feature selection method that addresses both of these problems and that is specific to each action unit. Boosting techniques allow both reducing the dimensionality of the feature vector and eliminating the irrelevant features, since they are trained in a manner that maximizes the classification rate.

We adopt in this work the GentleBoost technique, since it has already been shown in the literature to be effective when used in combination with Support Vector Machines (SVM) ([20],[21]), which is the classification method that we utilize. For 17 AUs, which have a reasonable number of examples in our training database (CK+), we select 1000 features out of 201600 using GentleBoost separately, so we obtain the most relevant features in terms of Gabor parameters and the location in the 2D space. Then we train,

once again for each AU, an SVM, for which the two output classes are whether the
AU is present or not. The details of the various tests and results are presented in the
following section.

4   Action Unit Detection Results

In this section we report the results of our experiments performed on the Extended
Cohn-Kanade database of facial expressions (CK+) [10]. The database consists of 593
videos of 123 subjects performing a facial expression formed by a single or multiple
AUs, manually coded by trained FACS coders. Each sample video starts with a neutral
expression and ends with the peak of the expression. We train and test our system using
only this final frame of each sequence. All presented results are those obtained by a
leave-one-subject-out test, i.e. training the SVM classifier on samples of 122 subjects
and testing it on the remaining subject. We perform the tests for each AU using 100,
200, 300, 400, 500, 750 and 1000 features in the SVM and at each case choose the
number of features giving the highest overall accuracy rate. Using the publicly available LibSVM implementation [3] we have tested both linear-SVMs and RBF kernels
(parameters optimized using a 5-fold cross validation). Here, however, we only report
results using the RBF kernels, since they result in better accuracy compared to the linear SVM in every AU, but there is no substantial difference when comparing different
types of features.

4.1   Comparing Types and Combinations of Gabor Features

We first compare the test results obtained by various parameter settings for the LCGBP
and also using only LBP as a baseline comparison method. All settings are kept the
same for this comparison, except only for the LBP the maximum number of features
tested in the training phase of SVM is kept at the highest possible, i.e. 400.

   We have tested 14 configurations in addition to the standard LBP features; namely
12 settings for LCGBP with 3 scales and 8 (or 16) orientations and a fixed Gaussian
size (σ) chosen from 0.5π, π or 2π and fixed curvature degree (c) from $0, 0.05, 0.1, 0.2$
(0 meaning standard LGBP with 9600 total features, each of the rest yields 19200), one
setting combining all proposed σ choices with $c = 0$ (28800 features) and one setting
combining all possible σ and c choices (201600 features), which is the setting for the
main proposed system. The comparison in three types of accuracy measures (overall
accuracy, F1 and area under Receiver-Operator-Characteristics (ROC) curve (AUC))
averaged over 17 AUs (Upper face AUs 1, 2, 4, 5, 6, 7, 9 and lower face AUs 11, 12, 15,
17, 20, 23, 24, 25, 26, 27) can be seen in Fig. 3. The ROC curve was obtained by alternating the SVM decision threshold. The first observation, other than the definite superiority of LGBP to standard LBP, is that for all the single σ settings the curvature Gabors
perform significantly better than the non-curvature standard Gabor setting, which is the
first indication of the effectiveness of curvature features for facial action recognition.
Another important comparison is the one between the 4 non-curvature LGBP settings.
Using different sizes of Gaussians in the Gabor formulation in combination with each

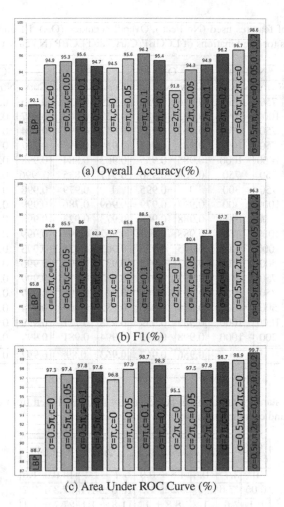

Fig. 3. Comparison of three different accuracy measures for different LCGBP feature settings & LBP

other results in a substantial increase in accuracy with respect to any fixed σ configuration. This indicates the necessity of alternating the Gaussian size along with the scale and orientation in any Gabor setting, which contradicts with the usual tendency in the literature for selecting Gabor wavelets for facial expression or AU detection.

The proposed setting, which is combining 3 different σ values and 4 different curvature degrees gives the highest classification accuracy for all action units, as expected. The results for each AU tested can be seen in Table 1 in comparison with the non-curvature case combining different σ's. The superiority is clearly not because of the greater number of features extracted (201600 vs. 28000), but because the various curvature degrees and filter sizes allow extracting those that are relevant to each action unit. We observe that

Table 1. Number of features used (No Feat.), Overall accuracy (OA), F1 and area under ROC curve (AUC) values for combinations of LCGBP(Curv.) and LGBP (No curv.) for 17 AUs

AU	No Feat.		OA		F1		AUC	
	Curv.	No curv.	Curv.	No curv.	Curv.	No curv.	Curv.	No curv.
AU1	750	750	0.976	0.958	0.959	0.928	0.995	0.983
AU2	1000	1000	0.992	0.987	0.978	0.965	0.997	0.998
AU4	750	750	0.963	0.935	0.942	0.897	0.994	0.976
AU5	750	1000	0.985	0.965	0.956	0.895	0.997	0.992
AU6	1000	1000	0.985	0.955	0.963	0.884	0.998	0.991
AU7	750	750	0.968	0.936	0.917	0.835	0. 996	0.969
AU9	750	300	1	0.995	1	0.979	0.998	0.994
AU11	1000	300	0.997	0.979	0.969	0.786	0.999	0.984
AU12	1000	1000	0.988	0.968	0.973	0.923	0.998	0.994
AU15	1000	750	0.988	0.969	0.962	0.897	0.999	0.993
AU17	1000	1000	0.975	0.956	0.963	0.935	0.993	0.989
AU20	500	1000	0.983	0.975	0.937	0.905	0.996	0.991
AU23	750	500	0.993	0.971	0.967	0.838	0.999	0.993
AU24	750	1000	0.993	0.965	0.964	0.796	0.999	0.989
AU25	500	1000	0.979	0.966	0.982	0.969	0.994	0.994
AU26	1000	1000	0.989	0.959	0.938	0.721	0.999	0.987
AU27	200	1000	0.998	0.995	0.994	0.981	0.999	0.999
Avg.			**0.986**	0.967	**0.963**	0.89	**0.997**	0.989

Table 2. Mean and standard deviation of percentage of features chosen from different Gaussian sizes defined by σ and curvature values (c).

c \ σ	0.5π	π	2π	Total
0	3.7 ± 0.6	4.8 ± 0.9	5.4 ± 1.4	13.9 ± 1.6
0.05	7.6 ± 1	9.2 ± 1.2	10.6 ± 1.4	27.3 ± 2.2
0.1	7.6 ± 1.2	8.8 ± 1	11.3 ± 1.1	27.7 ± 1.1
0.2	8.2 ± 1	9.7 ± 0.8	13.3 ± 2.6	31.1 ± 2.3
Total	27 ± 2.6	32.5 ± 1.8	40.5 ± 2.7	

for some AUs the difference between the two cases is less significant than others, and this can be explained by the variation of amount of curvature that shapes the deviation from the resting state for each action unit. However, observing Table 2, which shows the ratio of features chosen by the GentleBoost with respect to σ and c values and the deviation among action units, we can say that none of the types of features show a too powerful dominance over others in none of the AUs, although the non-curvature features are selected significantly less frequently than the rest. This suggests that every type of feature chosen is of similar importance to the detection task and their combination is essential for such a high classification accuracy.

4.2   Comparison with Existing Work

We compare our results, as shown in Table 3, with 3 recently conducted works ([20], [16] and [21]) which have reported results on the Cohn-Kanade database and have used similar techniques either in the feature extraction or the classification phase, in addition to the baseline system proposed in [10]. Valstar et al. [20] have used the evolution of certain facial landmarks throughout the video sequence as features and utilized the Gentleboost and SVM as the feature selection and classification methods. In our recently published work [21], we have also used Gentleboost and SVM with a combination of shape features similar to [20] and LBP features that are improved with the help of three filters. The work in [16] uses as features directly the bins of histogram difference of LGBP magnitude images extracted from 16 non-overlapping windows with a fixed Gaussian size and no curvature, and as classification adopts SVM with a specially trained kernel. In [10] the database was validated using 68 geometrically normalized facial point locations and canonical normalized appearance vectors as features for an SVM classification.

Table 3. Accuracy comparison with 4 other methods; No of AUs represents the number of common AUs taken into consideration

Type of acc.	F1(%)		AUC(%)		AUC(%)		AUC(%)	
No of AUs	14		17		16		14	
Method	[20]	Our Met.	[10]	Our Met.	[16]	Our Met.	[21]	Our Met.
	61.86	**96.09**	94.5	**99.7**	96.45	**99.69**	96.9	**99.65**

As seen in Table 3, our method certainly outperforms all the other state-of-the-art methods on the CK+ database in AU detection accuracy. The comparison with the two methods ([20] and [21]) using the same type of feature selection and classification, and the database validation system [10] which also uses SVM, shows the efficiency of the type of features utilized in our system. Although it is only fair to say that the comparison with [20] is not exactly straightforward since the authors have used many frames from each sequence, instead of using only the peak expression one, which naturally causes a decrease in the classification accuracy. Also, they have used the CK database [9] instead of the CK+, which is a previous version that includes less subjects and sequences. The comparison with [16], which uses a rather complicated classification scheme, also proves the utility of using curvature based features in addition to combining different sizes of Gabor wavelets.

These initial results obtained on the CK+ database demonstrates a great potential of the proposed features, but additional tests certainly need to be performed on larger databases to show the generalizability of the system, which remains as principal future work.

5   Conclusions

We have presented a novel framework for facial action unit detection in videos. The proposed system consists of extracting a combination of curvature Gabor features at different filter sizes, applying the LBP on top and computing the difference in histograms for neutral and peak frames. Then the obtained features are used in an AU specific feature selection and classification process to detect the present AUs. We achieve 98.6% accuracy, 96.3% F1 and 99.7% AUC scores in average for the leave-one-out test performed on the CK+ database, which is to our knowledge the highest reported to date. To assess the generalizability of the system, further tests should be performed with a dataset containing a larger variability among expressions. However, the extremely high accuracy presented in this work already shows the representation and discriminative power of the proposed features, which we believe will constitute an important position in future facial action recognition and expression analysis research.

Acknowledgements. This work has been partially supported by the Swiss National Science Foundation through the National Centre for Competence in Research (NCCR) on Interactive Multimodal Information Management (IM2) and partially through the project number 13594.1 PFFLR-ES funded by the Swiss Commision for Technology and Innovation (CTI). The authors would also like to thank Dr. Hua Gao for the helpful discussions and suggestions.

References

[1] Ahonen, T., Hadid, A., Pietikainen, M.: Face description with local binary patterns: Application to face recognition. IEEE Transactions on Pattern Analysis and Machine Intelligence 28(12), 2037–2041 (2006)

[2] Arar, N.M., Gao, H., Ekenel, H.K., Akarun, L.: Selection and combination of local gabor classifiers for robust face verification. In: IEEE 5th International Conference on Biometrics: Theory, Applications and Systems (BTAS), pp. 297–302 (2012)

[3] Chang, C.C., Lin, C.J.: Libsvm: A library for support vector machines. ACM Transactions on Intelligent Systems and Technology 2(3), 1–27 (2011)

[4] Cootes, T.F., Edwards, G.J., Taylor, C.J.: Active appearance models. IEEE Transactions on Pattern Analysis and Machine Intelligence 23(6), 681–685 (2001)

[5] Cristinacce, D., Cootes, T.: Feature detection and tracking with constrained local models. In: Proceedings of the British Machine Vision Conference 2006, pp. 929–938 (2006)

[6] Daugman, J.: Uncertainty relation for resolution in space, spatial frequency and orientation optimized by two-dimensional visual cortex filters. Journal of Opt. Soc. Amer. 2(7), 1160–1169 (1985)

[7] Ekman, P., Friesen, W.: The facial action coding system: A technique for the measurement of facial movement. Consulting Psychologists Press, Inc., San Francisco (1978)

[8] Hwang, W., Huang, X., Noh, K., Kim, J.: Face recognition system using extended curvature gabor classifier bunch for low-resolution face image. In: IEEE International Conference on Computer Vision and Pattern Recognition Workshops (CVPRW), pp. 15–22 (2011)

[9] Kanade, T., Cohn, J., Tian, Y.: Comprehensive database for facial expression analysis. In: Proceedings of the Fourth IEEE International Conference on Automatic Face and Gesture Recognition, pp. 46–53 (2000)

[10] Lucey, P., Cohn, J.F., Kanade, T., Saragih, J., Ambadar, Z., Matthews, I.: The extended cohn-kanade dataset (ck+): A complete dataset for action unit and emotion-specified expression. In: IEEE International Conference on Computer Vision and Pattern Recognition Workshops (CVPRW), pp. 94–101 (2010)

[11] Lucey, P., Cohn, J., Matthews, I., Lucey, S., Sridharan, S., Howlett, J., Prkachin, K.: Automatically detecting pain in video through facial action units. IEEE Transactions on Systems, Man, and Cybernetics, Part B: Cybernetics 41(3), 664–674 (2011)

[12] Ojala, T., Pietikainen, M., Harwood, D.: A comparative study of texture measures with classification based on featured distributions. Pattern Recognition 29(1), 51–59 (1996)

[13] Ojala, T., Pietikainen, M., Maenpaa, T.: Multiresolution gray-scale and rotation invariant texture classification with local binary patterns. IEEE Transactions on Pattern Analysis and Machine Intelligence 24(7), 971–987 (2002)

[14] Peters, G., Kruger, N., von der Malsburg, C.: Learning object representations by clustering banana wavelet responses. In: 1st International Workshop on Statistical Techniques in Pattern Recognition, pp. 113–118 (1997)

[15] Saragih, J.M., Lucey, S., Cohn, J.F.: Deformable model fitting by regularized landmark mean-shift. Int. J. Comput. Vision 91(2) (January 2011)

[16] Senechal, T., Bailly, K., Prevost, L.: Automatic facial action detection using histogram variation between emotional states. In: 20th International Conference on Pattern Recognition (ICPR), pp. 3752–3755 (2010)

[17] Senechal, T., Turcot, J., el Kaliouby, R.: Smile or smirk? automatic detection of spontaneous asymmetric smiles to understand viewer experience. In: IEEE International Conference on Automatic Face and Gesture Recognition (2013)

[18] Shan, C., Gong, S., McOwan, P.W.: Facial expression recognition based on Local Binary Patterns: A comprehensive study. Image and Vision Computing 27(6), 803–816 (2009)

[19] Valstar, M.F., Mehu, M., Jiang, B., Pantic, M., Scherer, K.: Meta analysis of the first facial expression recognition challenge. IEEE Transactions on Systems, Man, Cybernetics, Part B: Cybernetics 42(4), 966–979 (2012)

[20] Valstar, M.F., Pantic, M.: Fully automatic recognition of the temporal phases of facial actions. IEEE Transactions on Systems, Man, Cybernetics, Part B: Cybernetics 42(1), 28–43 (2012)

[21] Yuce, A., Sorci, M., Thiran, J.P.: Improved local binary pattern based action unit detection using morphological and bilateral filters. In: IEEE International Conference on Automatic Face and Gesture Recognition (FG) (2013)

[22] Zhang, W., Shan, S., Gao, W., Chen, X., Zhang, H.: Local gabor binary pattern histogram sequence (lgbphs): a novel non-statistical model for face representation and recognition. In: 10th IEEE International Conference on Computer Vision, vol. 1, pp. 786–791 (2005)

A Dense Deformation Field for Facial Expression Analysis in Dynamic Sequences of 3D Scans*

Hassen Drira[1], Boulbaba Ben Amor[1], Mohamed Daoudi[1],
and Stefano Berretti[2]

[1] Institut TELECOM, TELECOM Lille 1, LIFL (UMR 8022), Lille, France
{mohamed.daoudi,boulbaba.benamor,hassen.drira}@telecom-lille.fr
[2] Department of Information Engineering, University of Florence, Florence, Italy
{stefano.berretti}@unifi.it

Abstract. In this paper, we present a fully automatic approach for identity-independent facial expression recognition from 3D video sequences. Towards this goal, we propose a novel approach to extract a dense scalar field that represents the deformations between faces conveying different expressions. We extract relevant features from this deformation field using LDA and then train a dynamic model on these features using HMM. Experiments conducted on BU-4DFE dataset following state-of-the-art settings show the effectiveness of the proposed approach.

1   Introduction

Automatic recognition of facial expressions has emerged as an active research field with applications in several different areas, such as human-machine interaction, psychology, computer graphics, facial animation of 3D avatars, etc. The first systematic studies on facial expressions date back to the late 70s with the pioneering work of Ekman [1]. In these studies, it is evidenced that, apart the *neutral* expression, the *prototypical* facial expressions can be categorized into six classes, representing *anger, disgust, fear, happiness, sadness* and *surprise*.

This categorization of facial expressions has been proved to be consistent across different ethnicities and cultures, so that these expressions are in some sense "universally" recognized. In his studies, Ekman also evidenced that facial expressions can be coded through the movement of face points as described by a set of *action units*. These results inspired many researchers to analyze facial expressions in videos by tracking facial features and measuring the amount of facial movements in subsequent frames [2]. In fact, there is the awareness that facial expressions are highly dynamical processes and looking at sequences of face instances, rather than to still images, can help to improve the recognition performance. More properly, facial expressions can be seen as dynamical processes that involve the 3D space and the temporal dimension (3D plus time, referred to

---

* This work is supported by the French Research Agency (ANR) through the 3D Face Analyzer project under the contract ANR 2010 INTB 0301 01.

A.A. Salah et al. (Eds.) : HBU 2013, LNCS 8212, pp. 148–159, 2013.

as 4D), rather than being just a static or dynamic 2D behavior. In addition, 3D face scans are expected to feature less sensitivity to lighting conditions and pose variations. These considerations motivated a progressive shift from 2D to 3D in performing facial shape analysis, with the research on 3D facial expression recognition gaining a great impulse thanks to the recent availability of new databases, like the *Binghamton University* BU-3DFE [3], and the *Bosphorus* database [4].

Now, the introduction of appropriate data sets, such as the BU-4DFE developed at *Binghamton University* [5], makes also possible the study and recognition of facial expressions from 4D data. This trend is also inspired by the revolution of inexpensive acquisition devices, such as the consumer 3D cameras. In such conditions, the extension of traditional methods developed for expression recognition from 2D videos or from 3D static models can be not effective or even possible and new solutions are required. Indeed, the use of 4D data for face analysis is still at the beginning, with just few works performing face recognition from sequences of 3D face scans [6,7,8], and some works focussing on facial expression recognition. Recent literature which addresses this last topic is revised in the following.

In [9], a spatio-temporal expression analysis approach based on 3D dynamic geometric facial model sequences is proposed. The approach integrates a 3D facial surface descriptor and Hidden Markov Models (HMMs) to recognize facial expressions. Experiments were performed on the BU-4DFE. The main limit of this solution resides in the use of 83 manually annotated landmarks of the BU-4DFE. In [10], a method that exploits 3D motion-based features between frames of 3D facial geometry sequences for dynamic facial expression recognition is proposed. An expressive sequence is modeled to contain an onset followed by an apex and an offset. Feature selection methods are applied in order to extract features for each of the onset and offset segments of the expression. These features are then used to train an HMM in order to model the full temporal dynamics of the expression. The system was tested on a subset of the BU-4DFE for the recognition of *happiness, anger* and *surprise*. 3D facial shapes are compared using facial level curves in [11]. The pair- and segment-wise distances between the level curves comprise the spatiotemporal features for expression recognition from 3D dynamic faces. High recognition accuracy on the *happiness, sad* and *surprise* expressions of the BU-4DFE are reported. From this analysis, it emerges that solutions specifically tailored for 4D expression recognition from dynamic sequences of facial scans are still preliminary, being semi-automatic or capable of discriminating between only a subset of expressions.

In this paper, we propose a fully automatic facial expression recognition approach that exploits the motion extracted from 3D facial videos. An overview of the proposed approach is given in Fig. 1. In the preprocessing stage, the 3D mesh in each frame is aligned to the previous one and cropped. The 3D motion is then captured based on a dense scalar field, which represents the 3D deformation between two successive frames. A Linear Discriminant Analysis (LDA) is then used to transform the derived feature space to an optimal compact space, which better separates different expressions. Given the optimized features, the second stage is to learn one HMM for each expression. Temporal modeling of the full expression is performed via neutral-onset-apex-offset HMMs, in an unsupervised fashion. Expression classification is finally performed by using HMMs trained with the time variations of the extracted features. Experimental results show that the proposed approach is capable to improve state of the art performance on the BU-4DFE.

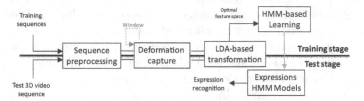

Fig. 1. Overview of the proposed approach in training and test stages, including preprocessing, 3D deformation capture, dimension reduction, and HMM-based classification

The present work includes the following main contributions:

- A novel Dense Deformation Field (DDF) defined on radial curves of 3D faces, which grounds on Riemannian shape analysis and is capable to accurately capture the deformations occurring between 3D faces;
- A new approach for facial expression recognition from 3D dynamic sequences, which combines the high descriptiveness of DDF extracted from successive 3D faces of a sequence with the temporal modeling and classification provided by HMMs;
- A thorough experimental evaluation that compares the proposed solution with state of the art methods using a common dataset and setting; Results shows that our approach is capable to achieve state of the art results.

Finally, to the best of our knowledge, this is the first fully automatic approach for dynamic 3D facial expressions recognition.

The rest of the paper is organized as follows: In Sect. 2, a face representation model is proposed that captures facial features relevant to categorize expression variations in 3D dynamic sequences. In Sect. 3, the HMM based classification of the selected features is addressed. Experimental results and comparative evaluation obtained on the BU-4DFE are reported and discussed in Sect. 4. Finally, conclusions and future research directions are outlined in Sect. 5.

2   Modeling 3D Facial Deformations

One basic idea to capture facial deformation across 3D video sequences is to track densely meshes' vertices along successive 3D frames. To do so, as the meshes resolutions vary across 3D video frames, establishing a dense matching on consecutive frames is necessary. Sun et al. [9] proposed to adapt a generic model (a tracking model) to each 3D frame. However, a set of 83 predefined landmarks is required to control the adaptation based on radial basis function. The main limitation is that the 83 points are manually annotated in the first frame of each sequence. A second solution has been presented by Sandbach et al. [10], where the authors used an existing non-rigid registration algorithm (FFD) based on B-splines interpolation between a lattice of control points. The dense matching is a step of the preprocessing stage which is used to estimate a motion vector field between frames t and t-1. However, the results provided by the authors are limited to three facial expressions: *happy*, *angry* and *surprise*.

To address the problem of densely model 3D facial deformations, we propose to represent facial surfaces by a set of parameterized radial curves emanating from the tip of the nose. Such an approximation of facial surfaces by an indexed collection of curves can be seen as a solution to facial surface parameterizations, which captures locally their shapes (see Fig. 2(b)). We will discuss more the benefits of such representation later in Sect. 2.1. A parameterized curve on the face, $\beta : I \rightarrow \mathbb{R}^3$, where $I = [0,1]$, is represented mathematically using the *square-root velocity function* [12], denoted by $q(t)$, according to: $q(t) = \dfrac{\dot{\beta}(t)}{\sqrt{\|\dot{\beta}(t)\|}}$.
This specific parametrization has the advantage of capturing the shape of the curve and provides simple computation. Let define the space of such functions: $\mathcal{C} = \{q : I \rightarrow \mathbb{R}^3, \|q\| = 1\} \subset \mathbb{L}^2(I, \mathbb{R}^3)$, where $\| \cdot \|$ implies the $\mathbb{L}^2$ norm. With the $\mathbb{L}^2$ metric on its tangent spaces, $\mathcal{C}$ becomes a Riemannian manifold. The shortest path ψ^* on the manifold $\mathcal{C}$ between the two curves q_1 and q_2 (called geodesic path) is a critical point of the following energy:

$$E = \frac{1}{2} \int < \dot{\psi}(t), \dot{\psi}(t) > dt \, , \tag{1}$$

where ψ denotes a path on the manifold $\mathcal{C}$ between q_1 and q_2, $\dot{\psi} \in T_\psi(\mathcal{C})$ is a tangent vector field on the curve $\psi \in \mathcal{C}$ and $< . >$ denotes the $\mathbb{L}^2$ inner product on the tangent space. In our case, as the elements of $\mathcal{C}$ have a unit $\mathbb{L}^2$ norm, $\mathcal{C}$ is a Hypersphere in the Hilbert space $\mathbb{L}^2(I, \mathbb{R}^3)$. The geodesic path between any two points $q_1, q_2 \in \mathcal{C}$ is simply given by the minor arc of the great circle connecting them on this Hypersphere, $\psi^* : [0,1] \rightarrow \mathcal{C}$, given by the following expression:

$$\psi^*(\tau) = \frac{1}{\sin(\theta)} \left(\sin((1 - \tau)\theta)q_1 + \sin(\theta\tau)q_2 \right) \, , \tag{2}$$

and $\theta = d_{\mathcal{C}}(q_1, q_2) = cos^{-1}(\langle q_1, q_2 \rangle)$. We point out that $sin(\theta) = 0$ if the distance between the two curves is null, in other words $q_1 = q_2$. In this case, for each τ, $\psi^*(\tau) = q_1 = q_2$. The tangent vector field on this geodesic is then given as $\frac{d\psi^*}{d\tau} : [0,1] \rightarrow T_\psi(\mathcal{C})$:

$$\frac{d\psi^*}{d\tau} = \frac{-\theta}{\sin(\theta)} \left(\cos((1 - \tau)\theta)q_1 - \cos(\theta\tau)q_2 \right) \, . \tag{3}$$

Knowing that on geodesic path, the covariant derivative of its tangent vector field is equal to 0, $\frac{d\psi^*}{d\tau}$ is parallel along the geodesic ψ^* and we shall represent it with $\frac{d\psi^*}{d\tau}|_{\tau=0}$. Accordingly, Eq. (3) becomes:

$$\frac{d\psi^*}{d\tau}\Big|_{\tau=0} = \frac{\theta}{\sin(\theta)}\left(q_2 - \cos(\theta)q_1\right)\ ,\tag{4}$$

with $\theta \neq 0$. We illustrate a geodesic path between two elements of the sphere in Fig. 2(g), the covariant derivative of this vector field corresponds to the tangential component of the tangent vector. Thus, $\frac{d\psi^*}{d\tau}\big|_{\tau=0}$ is sufficient to represent this vector field, the remaining vectors can be obtained by parallel transport of $\frac{d\psi^*}{d\tau}\big|_{\tau=0}$ along the geodesic ψ^*.

In the practice, the first step to capture the deformation between two given 3D faces F_1 and F_2 is to extract the radial curves. Let β_α^1 and β_α^2 denote the radial curves that make an angle α with a reference radial curve on faces F_1 and F_2, respectively. The reference curve is chosen to be the vertical curve as the faces have been rotated to the upright position during the preprocessing step. The tangent vector field $\dot{\psi}_\alpha{}^*$ that represents the energy E given in Eq. (1) needed to deform β_α^1 to β_α^2 is then computed for each index α. We consider the magnitude of this vector field at each point k of the curve for building a Dense Deformation Field (DDF) on the facial surface $V_\alpha^k = ||\dot{\psi}^*|_{(\tau=0)}(k)||$, where α denotes the angle to the vertical radial curve and k denotes a point on this curve. This DDF quantifies the local deformation between the faces F_1 and F_2 (100 curves with 50 points each have been considered).

Figure 2(a) illustrates the proposed idea. A neutral mesh is reported on the left. The vector field is computed between the neutral face and apex frames of each expression. Values of the vector field are reported using range of colors (i.e., black colors represent the highest deformations, whereas the lower values of the

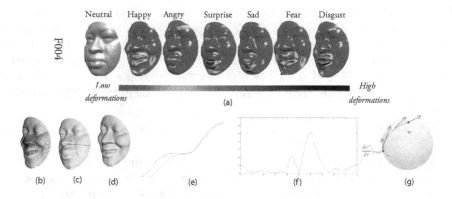

Fig. 2. (a) The first row reports deformation maps computed by the proposed method for the six emotional states computed from a neutral face. In the second row, we illustrate: (b) The extracted radial curves; (c) A radial curve on a neutral face, and (d) The correspondent radial curve on the face with happy expression; (e) The two curves are reported together. The plot of the trade-off between points on the curve and values of magnitude of $\frac{d\psi^*}{d\tau}\big|_{\tau=0}(k)$ is reported in (f) and an illustration of this parallel vector field across the geodesic between q_1 and q_2 in the space of curves $\mathcal{C}$ is reported in (g).

vector field are represented in blue). It can be observed, as the regions with high deformation lie in different parts of the face for different expressions. For example, as intuitively expected, the corners of the mouth and the cheeks are mainly deformed for happiness expression. In Fig. 2(b), we illustrate the face conveying happy expression with extracted radial curves. Figure 2(c) and Fig. 2(d) illustrate two correspondent radial curves on neutral and happy faces respectively. These curves are reported together in Fig. 2(e), where the deformation between them can be observed though they lie at the same angle and belong to the same person. The amount of the deformation between the two curves is computed using Eq. (4) and the plot of the magnitude of this vector at each point of the curve is reported in Fig. 2(f).

2.1   Motion Features Extraction

In this paper, we aim at learning facial deformations due to expressions across a 3D video sequence. Such deformations are known to be characterized by subtle variations induced mainly by the motion of facial feature points. These subtle changes are important and present difficult issues for analyzing facial motions. The deformation between two faces is obtained by a pairwise comparison of correspondent curves. Based on this comparison, we calculate a DDF V_α^k between two given 3D faces, which measures the motions of feature points and thus captures the changes in facial surface geometry. Fig. 3 illustrates a direct application of the V_α^k and its effectiveness in capturing deformations from one facial surface to another belonging to two consecutive frames in a video sequence. This figure shows two subsequences extracted from videos in the BU-4DFE database for a female subject while conveying happy and surprise expressions. For each sequence, texture and 3D scans of sample frames are shown. In both the cases, the DDF V_α^k computed between consecutive frames (i.e., the current frame and the previous one) in the subsequence is reported using a chromatic scale. Two colors are used to this end: Red is associated with high V_α^k values and corresponds to facial regions affected by high deformations; Blue color is associated with regions that remain stable from one frame to another.

The feature extraction process begins with a first step which characterizes each 3D frame by a scalar field computed between the current frame and the previous one in a given video sequence. In this way, we obtain as many fields as the number of frames in the sequence, where each field contains as many scalar values as the number of points composing the collection of radial curves representing the

Fig. 3. Examples of DDF extraction from 3D video sequences: Happy expression (left); Surprise (right)

facial surface. In practice, the size of V_α^i is 1×5000 considering 5000 points on the face. The second step consists of applying dimensionality reduction, using Linear Discriminant Analysis (LDA), in order to reduce the dimension of our feature space. We use LDA to project the scalar values to an optimal feature space, which is sensitive to deformations due to different expressions. This step allows us to enhance the discriminative power of our feature relatively to the six prototypic expressions, and transforms the n-dimensional feature space to an optimal d-dimensional space. In our approach, we deal with six expressions, so n is reduced to $d = 5$. The individual 5-dimensional feature vector extracted for the 3D frame at instant t of a sequence is indicated as f^t in the following. Once extracted, the feature vectors are used to train HMMs and to learn deformations due to expressions along a temporal sequence of frames.

3   Expression Classification Based on HMMs

Let $\lambda = \{A, B, \pi\}$ denote an HMM to be trained, and N be the number of hidden states in the model. We indicate the states as $S = \{S_1, S_2, ..., S_N\}$, and the state at instant time t is q_t. The state transition probability distribution is indicated as $A = \{a_{ij}\}$, where $a_{ij} = P(q_{t+1} = S_j | q_t = S_i)$, with $1 \leq i, j \leq N$. In a discrete domain, states of the model can emit symbols from a discrete alphabet derived from the physical output of the system being modeled. In the case the inputs of the model are multidimensional feature vectors with values in a continuous domain, the alphabet of symbols can be derived using clustering techniques. In this way, feature vectors are clustered around a number of cluster centers that are used as *codebook* of the input vectors. The individual symbols are indicated as $W = \{w_1, w_2, \ldots, w_M\}$, being M the number of distinct cluster centers. Given an observation w_k, $B = \{b_j(k)\} = P(w_k \text{ at } t | q_t = S_j)$ is the observation probability distribution in state j, that is the probability that the observation k being produced from state j, independent of t. Finally, with $\pi = \{\pi_i\}$ is denoted the initial probability array, being $\pi_i = P(q_1 = S_i)$.

In our case, sequences of 3D frames constitute the temporal dynamics to be classified, and each prototypical expression is modeled by an HMM (a total of 6 HMMs λ^{expr} is required, with $expr \in \{an, di, fe, ha, sa, su\}$). Four states per HMM (N=4) are used to represent the temporal behavior of each expression. This corresponds to the idea that each sequence starts and ends with a neutral expression (state S_1); The frames that belong to the temporal intervals where the face changes from neutral to expressive and back from expressive to neutral are modeled by the *onset* (S_2) and *offset* (S_4) states, respectively; Finally, the frames corresponding to the highest intensity of the expression are captured by the apex state (S_3). Fig. 4 exemplifies the structure of the HMMs in our framework.

The training procedure of each HMM is summarized as follows:

- Feature vectors f^t of the training sequences are first clustered to identify a *codebook* of symbols using the standard LBG algorithm. This provides the required mapping between multidimensional feature vectors, taking values in a continuous domain, and the alphabet of symbols emitted by the HMM states;

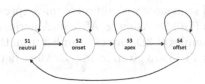

Fig. 4. Structure of the HMMs modeling a 3D facial sequence using four states: *neutral*, *onset*, *apex* and *offset*. As shown, from each state a transition is possible to the state itself or to the next one (*Bakis* or left-right HMM).

- Expression sequences are considered as observation sequences $O = \{O^1, O^2, \ldots, O^T\}$, where each observation O^t at time t is given by the feature vector f^t;
- Each HMM λ^{expr} is initialized with random values and the *Baum-Welch* algorithm is used to train the model using a set of training sequences. This estimates the model parameters while maximizing the conditional probability $P(O|\lambda^{expr})$.

Given a 3D sequence to be classified, it is processed as in Sect. 2, so that each feature vectors f^t corresponds to a *query* observation $O = \{O^1 \equiv f^1, \ldots, O^T \equiv f^T\}$. Then, the query observation O is presented to the six HMMs λ^{expr} that model different expressions, and the *Viterbi* algorithm is used to determine the best *path* $\bar{Q} = \{\bar{q}^1, \ldots, \bar{q}^T\}$, which corresponds to the state sequence giving a maximum of likelihood to the observation sequence O. The likelihood along the best path, $p^{expr}(O, \bar{Q}|\lambda^{expr}) = \bar{p}^{expr}(O|\lambda^{expr})$, is considered as a good approximation of the true likelihood given by the more expensive *forward* procedure, where all the possible paths are considered instead of the best one. Finally, the sequence is classified as belonging to the class corresponding to the HMM whose log-likelihood along the best path is the greatest one.

4   Experimental Results

The proposed framework for facial expression recognition from dynamic sequences of 3D face scans has been experimented using the BU-4DFE database, which has been recently created at *Binghamton University* [5]. The 3D scans have been generated by capturing a sequence of stereo images of subjects exhibiting facial expressions and producing a depth map for each frame according to a passive stereo-photogrammetry approach. The range maps are then combined to produce a temporally varying sequence of 3D scans. Subjects were requested to perform the six prototypic expressions separately, in such a way that each expression sequence contains neutral expressions in the beginning and the end. In particular, each expression was performed gradually from neutral appearance, low intensity, high intensity, and back to low intensity and neutral. Each 3D sequence captures one expression at a rate of 25 frames per second and each 3D sequence lasts approximately 4 seconds with about 35,000 vertices per scan (i.e., 3D *frame*). The database consists of 101 subjects (58 female and 43 male) including 606 3D model sequences with 6 prototypic expressions and a variety of ethnic/racial ancestries (i.e., 28 Asian, 8 African-American, 3 Hispanic/Latino, and 62 Caucasian). Examples of 3D frames sampled from the *happy* and *surprise* 4D sequences of subject F045 are given in Fig. 3. More details on the BU-4DFE can be found in [5].

4.1 Expression Classification Performance

4D expression sequences of the BU-4DFE are affected by large outliers, mainly acquired in the hair, neck and shoulders regions. In order to remove these uninformative parts from each 3D frame, a preprocessing step is performed. In this way, the nose tip of the face is automatically detected in the first frame of the sequence then, using a sphere centered on this point, the facial region is cropped. The same operation is applied to all the subsequent frames using a region based technique to track the nose tip along the sequence. Finally, Iterative Closest Point (ICP) alignment is applied to the cropped faces in the sequence in order to obtain 3D scans with frontal pose.

After these preprocessing operations, data of 60 subjects have been selected to perform recognition experiments, following the setting used in other works [9]. The 60 subjects are randomly partitioned into 10 sets, each containing 6 subjects, and 10-fold cross validation has been used for test, where at each round 9 of the 10 folds (54 subjects) are used for training while the remaining (6 subjects) are used for test. The recognition results of 10 rounds are then averaged to give a statistically significant performance measure of the proposed solution.

The proposed approach is able to correctly classify all the sequences with an accuracy of 100%. Indeed, the classification model is capable to correctly identify 3D dynamic expression sequences. This provides a measure of the overall capability to classify 3D frames sequences composed of around hundred frames and with a typical behavioral pattern.

In some contexts the classification of individual 3D frames is also relevant in that can permit an online analysis of a 3D video. Following the experimental protocol proposed in [9], this is obtained by the definition of a large set of very short subsequences extracted using a sliding window on the original expression sequences. The subsequences have been defined in [9] with a length of 6 frames with a sliding step of one frame from one subsequence to the following one. For example, with this approach, a sequence of 100 frames originates a set of $6 \times 95 = 570$ subsequences, each subsequences differing from one frame from the previous one. This accounts for the fact that, in general, the subjects can enter the system not necessarily starting with a neutral expression, but with a generic expression. Classification of these very short sequences is regarded as an indication of the capability of the expression recognition framework to identify individual expressions. According to this, for this experiment we retrained the HMMs on 6 frame subsequences constructed as discussed above. The 4-state structure of the HMMs still resulted adequate to model the subsequences. Also in this experiment, we performed 10-folds cross validation on the overall set of subsequences derived from the 60×6 sequences (31970 in total).

The results obtained by classifying individual 6-frames subsequences of the expression sequences (*frame-by-frame* experiment) are reported in the confusion matrix of Tab. 1. Values in the table have been obtained by using 6-frames subsequences as input to the 6 HMMs and using the maximum emission probability criterion as decision rule. It is evident that the proposed approach is capable to accurately classify very short sequences containing very different 3D frames, with an average accuracy of 93.83%. It can be noted that the lower recognition is obtained for the *disgust* expression (91.54%), which is mainly confused with the *angry* and *fear* expression. Interestingly, these three expressions capture negative emotive states of the subjects, so that similar facial muscles can be activated.

Table 1. Average confusion matrix for 6-frames subsequences (percentage values)

	Angry	Disgust	Fear	Happy	Sad	Surprise
Angry	**93.95**	1.44	1.79	0.28	2.0	0.54
Disgust	3.10	**91.54**	3.40	0.54	1.27	0.15
Fear	1.05	1.42	**94.55**	0.69	1.67	0.62
Happy	0.51	0.93	1.65	**94.58**	1.93	0.40
Sad	1.77	0.48	1.99	0.32	**94.84**	0.60
Surprise	0.57	0.38	3.25	0.38	1.85	**93.57**

4.2   Discussion and Comparative Evaluation

To the best of our knowledge, the only three works reporting results on expression recognition from dynamic sequences of 3D scans are [9], [10] and [11]. These works have been verified on the BU-4DFE dataset, but the testing protocols used in the experiments are quite different, so that a direct comparison of the results reported in these papers is not possible.

The approach in [9] is not completely automatic and also presents high computational cost. In fact, a generic model is adapted to each depth scan of a 3D sequence. The adaptation is controlled by a set of 83 pre-defined keypoints that are manually identified and tracked in 2D. The expression recognition experiments were performed on 60 selected subjects out of the 101 subjects of the BU-4DFE database, by generating a set of 6-frame subsequences from each expression sequence to construct the training and testing sets. The process was repeated by shifting the starting index of the subsequence every one frame till the end of the sequence. The rationale used by the authors for this shifting was that a subject could enter the recognition system at any time, thus requiring the recognition process to start from any frame. Following a 10-fold cross-validation, an average recognition rate of 90.44% was reported.

The method proposed in [10] is fully automatic with respect to the processing of facial frames in the temporal sequences, but uses *supervised* learning to train a set of HMMs. Though performed offline, supervised learning requires manual annotation and counting on a consistent number of training sequences that can be a time consuming operation. In addition, a drawback of this solution is the computational cost due to Free-Form Deformations based on B-spline interpolation between a lattice of control points for nonrigid registration and motion capturing between frames. This hinders the possibility of the method to adhere to a real time protocol of use. Preliminary tests were reported on three expressions: *angry*, *happiness* and *surprise*. However, these experiments were carried out on a subset of subjects accurately selected as acting out the required expression. Verification of the classification system was performed using a 10-fold cross-validation testing. On this subset of expressions and subjects, an average expression recognition rate of 81.93% is reported.

In [11] a fully automatic method is also proposed, that uses an *unsupervised* learning solution to train a set of HMMs. In this solution, preprocessing is very important in that an accurate alignment of the 3D mesh of each frame is required in order to extract the level set curves that are used for face representation. This increases the computational cost of the approach making questionable its use where a real time constraint is required. Expression recognition is performed on 60 subjects from the BU-4DFE database for the expressions of *happiness*, *sadness* and *surprise*. Results of 10-fold cross-validation show an overall recognition accuracy of 92.22%, with the highest performance of 95% obtained for the happiness expression.

Table 2 summarizes the results scored by the above methods compared to those presented in our work. Considering the classification of the entire 4D sequences, our solution clearly outperforms those in [10] and [11], even working on six expressions instead of just three, evidencing the capability of the proposed face representation to capture salient features to discriminate between different expressions. With respect to the *frame-by-frame* classification experiment, our results are more than 3% better than those in [9], with the advantage of using a completely automatic approach and a simpler classification model using temporal HMMs with fewer states.

Table 2. Comparison to earlier work

Average RR	[9] *(T-HMM)*	[9] *(R2D-HMM)*	[10][1]	[11][2]	**This work**
Frame-by-frame	80.04 %	90.44 %	73.61 %	-	**93.83 %**
Sequence	-	-	81.93 %	92.22 %	**100 %**

[1] Performances provided for *happiness*, *anger* and *surprise* expressions.
[2] Performances provides for *happiness*, *sadness* and *surprise* expressions.

5   Conclusions

In this paper, we presented a fully automatic approach for identity-independent facial expression recognition from 3D video sequences. Starting from a facial shape representation based on collections of radial curves, a Riemannian shape analysis was applied to quantify dense deformations and extract motion from successive 3D frames. The resulting features are then used to train a HMM after LDA-based feature space transformation. The proposed approach outperforms previous ones; It is capable to accurately classify very short sequences containing very different 3D frames, with an average accuracy of 93.83% following state-of-the-art settings on the BU-4DFE dataset. A limitation of the approach is the nose tip detection in case of non frontal views and/or occlusion. The BU-4D contains frontal 3D faces without occlusion, however, in realistic scenario, more elaborated techniques should be applied to detect the nose tip.

References

1. Ekman, P.: Universals and cultural differences in facial expressions of emotion. In: Proc. Nebraska Symposium on Motivation, Lincoln, NE, vol. 19, pp. 207–283 (1972)
2. Zeng, Z., Pantic, M., Roisman, G., Huang, T.: A survey of affect recognition methods: Audio, visual, and spontaneous expressions. IEEE Transactions on Pattern Analysis and Machine Intelligence 31, 39–58 (2009)
3. Yin, L., Wei, X., Sun, Y., Wang, J., Rosato, M.: A 3D facial expression database for facial behavior research. In: Proc. IEEE Int. Conf. on Automatic Face and Gesture Recognition, Southampton, UK, pp. 211–216 (2006)
4. Savran, A., Alyüz, N., Dibeklioğlu, H., Çeliktutan, O., Gökberk, B., Sankur, B., Akarun, L.: Bosphorus database for 3D face analysis. In: Schouten, B., Juul, N.C., Drygajlo, A., Tistarelli, M. (eds.) BIOID 2008. LNCS, vol. 5372, pp. 47–56. Springer, Heidelberg (2008)
5. Yin, L., Chen, X., Sun, Y., Worm, T., Reale, M.: A high-resolution 3D dynamic facial expression database. In: Int. Conf. on Automatic Face and Gesture Recognition (FGR 2008), Amsterdam, The Netherlands, pp. 1–6 (2008)
6. Li, Y., Mian, A., Lu, W., Krishna, A.: Using kinect for face recognition under varying poses, expressions, illumination and disguise. In: Proc. IEEE Workshop on Applications of Computer Vision, Tampa, FL, pp. 186–192 (2013)
7. Benedikt, L., Kajic, V., Cosker, D., Rosin, P., Marshall, D.: Facial dynamics in biometric identification. In: Proc. British Machine Vision Conference, Leeds, UK, pp. 1–10 (2008)
8. Benedikt, L., Cosker, D., Rosin, P.L., Marshall, D.: Assessing the uniqueness and permanence of facial actions for use in biometric applications. IEEE Transactions on Systems, Man and Cybernetics - Part A 40, 449–460 (2010)
9. Sun, Y., Yin, L.: Facial expression recognition based on 3D dynamic range model sequences. In: Proc. Eur. Conf. on Computer Vision, Marseille, France, pp. 58–71 (2008)
10. Sandbach, G., Zafeiriou, S., Pantic, M., Rueckert, D.: A dynamic approach to the recognition of 3D facial expressions and their temporal models. In: IEEE Conf. on Automatic Face and Gesture Recognition, Santa Barbara, CA, pp. 406–413 (2011)
11. Le, V., Tang, H., Huang, T.S.: Expression recognition from 3D dynamic faces using robust spatio-temporal shape features. In: IEEE Conference on Automatic Face and Gesture Recognition, Santa Barbara, CA, pp. 414–421 (2011)
12. Srivastava, A., Klassen, E., Joshi, S.H., Jermyn, I.H.: Shape analysis of elastic curves in euclidean spaces. IEEE Transactions on Pattern Analysis and Machine Intelligence 33, 1415–1428 (2011)

NovA: Automated Analysis of Nonverbal Signals in Social Interactions

Tobias Baur, Ionut Damian, Florian Lingenfelser, Johannes Wagner,
and Elisabeth André

Human Centered Multimedia, Augsburg University,
Universitätsstr. 6a, 86159 Augsburg, Germany
{baur,damian,lingenfelser,wagner,andre}@hcm-lab.de
http://www.hcm-lab.de

Abstract. Previous studies have shown that the success of interpersonal interaction depends not only on the contents we communicate explicitly, but also on the social signals that are conveyed implicitly. In this paper, we present NovA (NOnVerbal behavior Analyzer), a system that analyzes and facilitates the interpretation of social signals conveyed by gestures, facial expressions and others automatically as a basis for computer-enhanced social coaching. NovA records data of human interactions, automatically detects relevant behavioral cues as a measurement for the quality of an interaction and creates descriptive statistics for the recorded data. This enables us to give a user online generated feedback on strengths and weaknesses concerning his social behavior, as well as elaborate tools for offline analysis and annotation.

1 Introduction

In a conversation between humans, information is not only shared in an explicit manner. On the contrary, a myriad of implicit social signals is communicated that may even have a deeper influence on the outcome of a conversation than the word meanings themselves. There is empirical evidence that our impact on others is shaped less by the contents of an utterance, but rather by the accompanying social signals. According to studies by Albert Mehrabian [1], the contents of an utterance only contribute with 7% to its success while the impact of the vocal signals (conveyed by the nuances of voice) and the non-verbal signals (including body language and facial expressions) is much higher with 38% and 55% respectively.

In our research, we present NovA (NOnVerbal behavior Analyzer), a system that analyzes and interprets these signals automatically as a starting point for social coaching in human-human settings. NovA does not only allow us to record data of social interactions in a systematic manner, but it also enables the learners to inspect previous interactions and provides them with an objective report of the social interactions.

Automated behavior analysis is not only of benefit in the context of social training. It may also support researchers of multidisciplinary areas in their daily

A.A. Salah et al. (Eds.) : HBU 2013, LNCS 8212, pp. 160–171, 2013.

work. Scientific disciplines, such as psychology, ethnology, anthropology and others, have been concerned with the systematic exploration of human behavior for a long time. Thereby, an important component of a regular work flow is the annotation of audiovisual recordings of human behavior. The annotation of such recordings requires several iterations and is very time-consuming. With our analysis tool NovA, we aim to accomplish most of these iterations in a fully automated manner by creating a variety of diagrams including bar charts, heat maps, timeline diagrams with automated labeling that help to point out characteristics encountered in interpersonal interaction.

2 Related Work

To get insight into human social behavior, researchers have to rely on a large variety of information, e.g. video recordings of face-to-face meetings and acceleration sensor-based data of the user's daily activities [2]. Progress in the field has been boosted by a variety of annotation tools that facilitate the labeling of corpora at different levels of granularity following a pre-defined coding scheme. Examples include Elan, [3] Anvil [4] and Exmeralda [5]. However, since the manual annotation of data is rather time-consuming, methods to automate the coding process are highly desirable.

Techniques for the automated analysis of social behaviors patterns were pioneered by Pentland and his group at MIT Media Lab with the development of wearable devices, so-called sociometers, to capture the people's verbal and non-verbal signals. They investigated not only the social behaviors of people engaged in face-to-face conversations [6], but also analyzed interaction patterns from larger groups of people using smartphones with dedicated sensors [7]. Social constructs that have been investigated by Pentland and others include internal user states, such as interest [8], engagement [9] and emotions [10], and personality traits [11], such as dominance and extraversion.

To analyze social behaviors, a large variety of verbal and non-verbal cues has been taken into account. Dong and colleagues [12] analyze speech activity and fidgeting, i.e. the amount of movement in a person's hands and body, to detect functional roles in a group. Hung and Gatica-Perez [13] studied audio cues (such as overlapping speech), video cues (such as motion energy), and audio-visual cues (such as the amount of movement during speech) to determine the level of group cohesion in meetings. Methods have been developed to detect a user's emotions from various modalities including facial expressions [14], gestures [15], speech [16], postures [17] and physiological measurements [18]. Also, multimodal approaches to improve emotion recognition accuracy are reported, mostly by exploiting audiovisual combinations [19] [20]. Results suggest that integrated information from audio and video leads to improved classification reliability compared to a single modality - even with fairly simple fusion methods.

NovA combines work on annotation tools with technologies to automatically analyze human behavior. The user interface of NovA has been inspired by existing annotation tools and makes use of multiple tracks to code relevant social features. However, unlike conventional annotation tools, NovA performs the segmentation and labeling of the data completely automatically. Most tools for automated behavior analysis rely on an offline classification of the recorded data, where relevant features are extracted from the data and mapped onto given social constructs. A problem with this approach results from the subjectivity of data interpretation. NovA distinguishes from earlier work on automated behavior analysis by combining a descriptive with interpretative coding approaches. Not only does it present the user with an interpretation of the data in terms of higher-level social constructs, but also visualizes statistics of the descriptive features on which the interpretation of the data is based. In addition, it is able to provide verbalized explanations. The motivation behind this approach is to increase the transparency of the system for the social coaches and their trainees.

3   Foundations of the NovA Approach

Compared to natural language, the capabilities of social cues to convey meaning are strongly limited. Their strength lies, however, in the communication of implicit information, such as the engagement of people in a conversation and the self efficacy they convey when presenting themselves. Based on interviews with job counselors we decided to focus on four user states that are implicitly conveyed in interviews by body postures and gestures *Social Attraction, Engagement, Self Efficacy* and *Attitude*.

Social Attraction refers to the amount of appreciation a person evokes in others [21]. The relation of body language and social attraction has been investigated in various studies in social sciences. McGinley et al. [22] conclude that open body positions are usually received as more positive than positions with arms or legs crossed. According to Schouwstra and Hoogstraten [23] upright postures with the head up receive more positive judgments than the opposite.

Sidner and colleagues define [24] *Engagement* as "the process by which two (or more) participants establish, maintain and end their perceived connection during interactions they jointly undertake". Pease [25] demonstrates how engagement is portrayed by an orientation of the body and face towards the interlocutor. Another aspect of engagement is the overall amount of movements. Here it is necessary to distinguish whether the user is speaking or listening. While speakers tend to show their engagement using a high amount of overall activity, in the role of a listener, interlocutors should show less overall activity because such a behavior is usually interpreted as a sign of distraction.

People with a high amount of *Self Efficacy* are "confident that they will be able to master difficult situations" [26]. Self efficacy is usually conveyed by calm, fluid and high energy movements while quick and jerky movements tend to make a person appear nervous. In addition, a high amount of self manipulations, such as scratching one's head, reveals the anxiety of people in a social situation. Pease [25] provides various examples of body postures that signal a high amount of self efficacy, such as placing both feet apart or both hands behind the head with the elbows facing outward.

In psychology, the term *Attitude* refers to the expression of favor or disfavor towards a particular person or theme [27]. Usually, open body postures, such as opened arms, are interpreted as a sign of willingness to cooperate while closed body postures, such as crossing one's arms, rather communicate the opposite [25].

4   Social Cue Recognition

For recording and preprocessing human behavior data, NovA relies on our previously developed Social Signal Interpretation framework (SSI) [28] which supports both frame-by-frame and event-based annotations. In the case of frame-by-frame annotations, a value referring to a particular attribute, such as the distance between the two hands of a person, is computed at each point in time. For event-based annotations, we implemented a mechanism that triggers an event each time the beginning or the end of a social cue, such as a particular arm configuration, is detected.

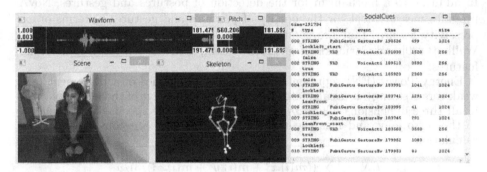

Fig. 1. The recording process with skeleton and face tracking, audio graph, audio pitch information, as well as the event board that shows detected social cues, such as gestures, head poses, voice activity detection etc

The detected events are saved in an XML-based structure including a synchronized timestamp and the event's duration. Figure 1 shows the interface for the recording of data. It illustrates the Kinect skeleton and facial tracking, as well as online recognized social cues, waveform graph and audio pitch. In the following subsections we present social cues that are recognizable by NovA.

4.1   Gesture and Posture Detection

For event-based gesture analysis, NovA makes use of our Full Body Interaction framework (FUBI) [29]. In FUBI postures and gestures are defined in an XML-based definition language and are detected by a motion tracking device, such as the Microsoft Kinect. For NovA we defined a set of behavioral primitives, which includes relations between hands, elbows, and feet to each other and to other body parts. Further we investigate the torso and head orientation. Based on the behavioral primitives, we implemented the following recognizers:

1. Typical hand positions: hands together at a particular height of the body, neck touch with left/right hand, head touch with left/right hand, head touch with both hands

2. Characteristic Leg Configurations: standing or sitting with legs apart, closed or crossed

3. Characteristic Arm Configurations: standing or sitting with spread arms at a particular height of the body, arms close to body at a particular height, arms stemmed in hips and arms behind the head with elbows facing outward

4. Common Postures for the Upper Trunk: leaning forward and leaning backward

5. Typical head postures & gestures: looking away, head shakes, head nods, head tilts

4.2 Movement Expressivity

In addition to a mechanism for the detection of postures and gestures, NovA provides measurement for the quality of postures and gestures in terms of expressivity features that are computed frame-by-frame. Based on the work by Wallbott [30] and Caridakis et al. [15], we computed the following expressivity features:

Energy/Power (EN) represents the dynamic properties of a movement (e.g. weak versus strong). It is calculated from the first derivative of the motion vectors in all three dimensions where $m()$ is the motion of the specified joint relative to the torso joint and n is the number of frames that are considered for the calculation.

$$EN = \sqrt{\sum_{i=0}^{n}((m(i).x^2 + m(i).y^2 + m(i).z^2)/3)/n}$$

Fluidity (FL) differentiates smooth movements from jerky ones. This feature aims to capture the continuity between movements. It is calculated as the sum of the variance of both hands' motion vectors' norms (l, r) (respectively feet for leg postures).

$$FL = Var(\sum_{i=0}^{n} l(i)/n) + Var(\sum_{i=0}^{n} r(i)/n)$$

Spatial extent (SE) is modeled as the space that is used for gesturing in front of the recorded person. It is calculated as the maximum Euclidean distance of the position of the two hands (l ,r) (respectively feet for leg postures).

$$SE = max(d(|\, r(i) - l(i)\, |))$$

Overall activation (OA) represents the quantity of the movement (passive versus active). It is calculated as the sum of the motion vectors' norm of both hands (respectively feet for leg postures):

$$OA = \sum_{i=0}^{n} |\, r(i)\, | + |\, l(i)\, |$$

Temporal extent (TP) represents the duration of a gesture (short vs sustained). The duration of each gesture is computed from the starting and end points synchronized with the recording time in the SSI framework.

4.3 Facial Expressions

For detecting facial expressions, we make use of Fraunhofer Institute's SHORE [31] as well as the Kinect Facial Tracking SDK[1] which are also integrated in our system. Various occurrences of facial expressions, such as smiles, are computed using a threshold based approach.

5 Mapping Social Cues to User States

To determine the user states described in Section 3 NovA supports the use of Bayesian networks. These networks can be assigned directly to the SSI framework for frame-wise updating with probabilities and evidences in real time. A typical network designed to recognize the user states of *Social Attraction*, *Engagement*, *Self Efficacy* and *Attitude* consists of several unconditional, observed nodes that describe the evidences and probabilities monitored by social cue recognition and expressivity calculations and are updated every frame by the framework. These evidence nodes feed into conditional nodes that estimate a higher level statement based on the recognized cues. Observed as well as conditional nodes lead to the final child node, which models a user state. The Bayesian networks can be modeled with existing tools, such as GeNIe[2].

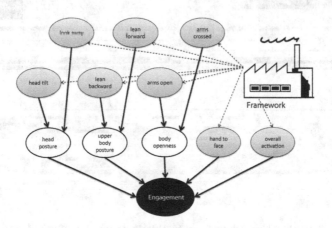

Fig. 2. A simplified Bayesian network to determine Engagement

---

[1] http://msdn.microsoft.com/en-us/library/jj130970.aspx
[2] http://genie.sis.pitt.edu/

As an example, Figure 2 shows the diagram of a simplified Bayesian network, meant to recognize *Engagement*. The structure of the network has been defined in accordance to social theories, extracted from relevant literature (See Section 3). Eight observed, unconditional parent nodes (head tilt, look away, lean backward, lean forward, arms open, arms crossed, hand to face and overall activation) are constantly updated by the framework with evidences from gesture recognizers and calculation values from expressivity calculation. Six of these parent nodes influence interconnected conditional nodes (head posture, upper body posture and body openness), the other two directly feed into the final *Engagement* node. We want to point out that in Figure 2 we demonstrate a simplified version of a predefined Bayesian network to determine *Engagement*. Besides predefined BNs, starting probabilities as well as probability tables and related social cues can also be defined by users of the system themselves.

6   The User Interface of NovA

6.1   Graphical Interface

The user interface of NovA has been developed following the requirements of tools for annotating human social interactions. Like other tools, it offers annotation on multiple tracks based on a user-defined coding scheme that has been, in our case, adapted to the situation of human-human or human-agent dialogue.

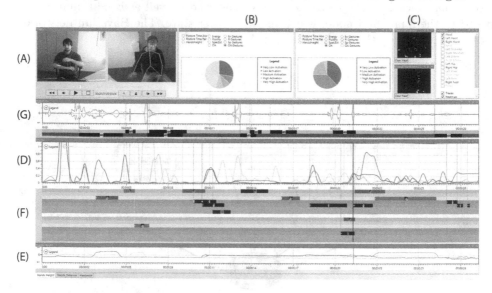

Fig. 3. NovA's graphical user interface. In this instance data for two users has been loaded. It shows both videos (with and without skeleton, (Figure 3 A)), pie charts for expressivity features (Figure 3 B), heatmaps (Figure 3 C), a waveform graph with voice activity detection events (Figure 3 G), the timeline graph showing automatically created annotations (Figure 3 F) and the hands height graph (Figure 3 E).

Annotations are automatically added corresponding to social cues recognized by the system by placing boxes along a horizontal timeline. Typically, different kinds of behaviors are coded on different parallel tracks so that their temporal relationships are clearly visible.

Figure 3 shows the graphical user interface of NovA. The GUI includes the video recordings of up to two recorded people (Figure 3 A) in addition to diagrams with descriptive statistics (Figure 3 B), Heatmaps (Figure 3 C) as well as timeline diagrams showing the temporal dynamics of their behaviors.

Timeline diagrams contain:

1. Tracks that correspond to behavioral characteristics collected frame by frame, such as motion energy (Figure 3 D) or the height of the hands (Figure 3 E) and

2. Tracks that correspond to events, such as the occurrence of particular social cues (Figure 3 F).

The screenshot shown in Figure 3 only depicts a particular instantiation of the graphical user interface of NovA which can be dynamically adapted depending on the tasks to be conducted. For example, all windows are customizable in size and position and can also be removed or hidden.

Another example of a frame-by-frame annotation is the representation of the waveform corresponding to the audio signal (Figure 3 G). Phases with high peaks indicate high intensity (e.g. a loud voice) while phases with tiny peaks represent silent phases.

Each annotation includes additional information that may be displayed on demand. It includes a reference picture, the exact duration, calculated expressivity parameters and a description of a possible interpretation. For the case of detection errors or the need of adding annotations that could not be detected automatically, NovA also offers the possibility to manually add or delete event-based annotations or to edit their temporal position and duration. In addition, annotation schemes are fully customizable and can contain both automated and manual annotations.

6.2 Illustrating Example

In the following, we present an example to illustrate behavior analysis in NovA. Figure 4 illustrates how the system tries to determine the level of engagement of an interviewee. On the left picture (a) the participant has an open body posture, while looking towards the interlocutor and orientating his body in the same direction. In the center picture (b), nothing specific is detected, and the right picture (c) demonstrates the outcome when the participant uses body language regarded as indicator of a low amount of engagement (see Section 3), such as leaning back, looking away and crossing the arms. Bar charts are representing the outcome of the user state recognition for each calculation, which is performed every second.

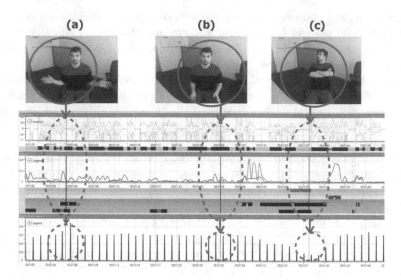

Fig. 4. Comparison of detected cues for high (a), medium (b) and low engagement (c)

7   Applications

NovA was originally developed for the EU-funded project TARDIS[3]. TARDIS attempts to support young adults in job interviews by developing a scenario-based game with virtual agents acting as recruiters. One large issue Europe faces is the rising number of young people who are out of employment, education or training (NEETs). NEETs often have underdeveloped socio-emotional and interaction skills [32], such as a lack of self-confidence, lack of sense of their own strengths or social anxiety [33]. This can cause problems in various critical situations such as job interviews where they need to convince the recruiter of their fit in a company. To address this issue, many European countries have specialized inclusion centers meant to aid young people secure employment through coaching by professional practitioners. One problem of this approach is that it is very expensive and time-consuming. Considering this, technology-enhanced solutions, such as digital games, present themselves as viable and advantageous alternatives to the existing human-to-human coaching practices.

Within TARDIS, NovA serves to analyze the learner's social cues when interacting with a virtual recruiter during a job interview simulation. Providing such an environment is highly desirable from the point of view of improving practice, since it enables a repeatable experience that can be modulated to suit the individual needs of the learner. It may also mitigate negative side effects resulting from real-life settings, in particular, the stress associated with engaging in unfamiliar interactions with others. In this context, the recognition rate of our social cue detection for body language and voice activity detection has been

---

[3] Training young Adult's Regulation of emotions and Development of social Interaction Skills - http://tardis.lip6.fr

Fig. 5. NovA serves to analyze the learner's social cues when interacting with a virtual recruiter during a job interview simulation in the TARDIS project

evaluated and achieved a mean recognition rate of 88% [34]. Various knowledge elicitation studies have been conducted using real job seeking youngsters and trainer practitioners [35]. Ongoing user experience evaluations have shown so far that user's self reports about their behavior characteristics correspond to NovA's calculated results. The data of mentioned studies has been used to shape the design of NovA, the choice in social cues and our preliminary Bayesian networks (BNs) for detecting user states.

8   Conclusion

In this paper we presented NovA, a system that processes data from state of the art sensor technology for automated recognition and analysis of human behavior. NovA offers an online component for recording and processing data in real time and a user interface to visualize and analyze data. The user interface's primary use is the debriefing and post-hoc analysis of social interactions. It allows users to reflect on their behavior, and thus learn to perform better in social situations.

NovA is able to automatically recognize various social cues, such as gestures, postures, expressivity features or facial expressions. Additionally NovA provides support for feeding such social cues to specially designed Bayesian Networks to compute higher level user states.

The possibility to automatically detect human behavior can help researchers from various disciplinary areas. On the one hand engineers might use higher-level information on the user's behavior to improve assistant robots, virtual agents or other user assistant software such as the job-interview training game developed in the TARDIS project. On the other hand automated behavioral analysis- and coding can help psychological researchers by reducing their workload. To maximize our contribution to the research community we made NovA available for download at http://openssi.net/nova.

As part of our future work we plan to further validate the performance of the system's user state detection. Additionally, we plan to investigate the use of physiological sensor devices and eye-trackers that promise more detailed information on a user's affective and emotional state.

Acknowledgments. This work was partially funded by the European Commission within FP7-ICT-2011-7 (Project TARDIS, grant agreement no. 288578).

References

1. Mehrabian, A.: Silent messages: Implicit Communication of Emotions and Attitudes. Wadsworth Publishing Co Inc., Belmont (1981)
2. Eagle, N., Pentland, A.: Reality mining: Sensing complex social signales. J. of Personal and Ubiquitous Computing 10(4), 255–268 (2006)
3. Wittenburg, P., Brugman, H., Russel, A., Klassmann, A., Sloetjes, H.: Elan: A professional framework for multimodality research. In: Proc. of the Fifth International Conference on Language Resources and Evaluation (LREC), pp. 879–896 (2006)
4. Kipp, M.: Anvil: The video annotation research tool. In: Handbook of Corpus Phonology. Oxford University Press, Oxford (2013)
5. Schmidt, T.: Transcribing and annotating spoken language with exmaralda. In: Proc. of the LREC-Workshop on XML Based Richly Annotated Corpora, Lisbon 2004, pp. 879–896. ELRA, Paris (2004)
6. Curhan, J., Pentland, A.: Thin slices of negotiation: predicting outcomes from conversational dynamics withing the first 5 minutes. J. of Applied Psychology 92(3), 802–811 (2007)
7. Pentland, A.: Automatic mapping and modelling of human networks. Physica A(378), 59–67 (2007)
8. Schuller, B., Müller, R., Eyben, F., Gast, J., Hörnler, B., Wöllmer, M., Rigoll, G., Höthker, A., Konosu, H.: Being bored? recognising natural interest by extensive audiovisual integration for real-life application. Image Vision Comput. 27(12), 1760–1774 (2009)
9. Rich, C., Ponsleur, B., Holroyd, A., Sidner, C.L.: Recognizing engagement in human-robot interaction. In: Proc. of the 5th ACM/IEEE Intl. Conf. on Human-Robot Interaction, HRI 2010, pp. 375–382. IEEE Press, Piscataway (2010)
10. Zeng, Z., Pantic, M., Roisman, G.I., Huang, T.S.: A survey of affect recognition methods: Audio, visual, and spontaneous expressions. IEEE Trans. Pattern Anal. Mach. Intell. 31(1), 39–58 (2009)
11. Pianesi, F., Mana, N., Cappelletti, A., Lepri, B., Zancanaro, M.: Multimodal recognition of personality traits in social interactions. In: Proc. of the 10th International Conference on Multimodal Interfaces, ICMI 2008, pp. 53–60. ACM, NY (2008)
12. Dong, W., Lepri, B., Cappelletti, A., Pentland, A.S., Pianesi, F., Zancanaro, M.: Using the influence model to recognize functional roles in meetings. In: Proc. of the 9th International Conference on Multimodal Interfaces, ICMI 2007, pp. 271–278. ACM, New York (2007)
13. Hung, H., Gatica-Perez, D.: Estimating cohesion in small groups using audio-visual nonverbal behavior. Trans. Multi. 12(6), 563–575 (2010)
14. Sandbach, G., Zafeiriou, S., Pantic, M., Yin, L.: Static and dynamic 3d facial expression recognition: A comprehensive survey. Image Vision Comput. 30(10), 683–697 (2012)
15. Caridakis, G., Raouzaiou, A., Karpouzis, K., Kollias, S.: Synthesizing gesture expressivity based on real sequences. In: Workshop on Multimodal Corpora: from Multimodal Behaviour Theories to Usable Models. LREC, Genoa (2006)
16. Vogt, T., André, E., Bee, N.: Emovoice - a framework for online recognition of emotions from voice. In: André, E., Dybkjær, L., Minker, W., Neumann, H., Pieraccini, R., Weber, M. (eds.) PIT 2008. LNCS (LNAI), vol. 5078, pp. 188–199. Springer, Heidelberg (2008)

17. Kleinsmith, A., Bianchi-Berthouze, N.: Form as a cue in the automatic recognition of non-acted affective body expressions. In: D'Mello, S., Graesser, A., Schuller, B., Martin, J.-C. (eds.) ACII 2011, Part I. LNCS, vol. 6974, pp. 155–164. Springer, Heidelberg (2011)
18. Kim, J., André, E.: Emotion recognition based on physiological changes in music listening. IEEE Trans. Pattern Anal. Mach. Intell. 30(12), 2067–2083 (2008)
19. Camurri, A., Volpe, G., De Poli, G., Leman, M.: Communicating expressiveness and affect in multimodal interactive systems. IEEE MultiMedia 12(1) (2005)
20. Scherer, S., Marsella, S., Stratou, G., Xu, Y., Morbini, F., Egan, A., Rizzo, A(S.), Morency, L.-P.: Perception markup language: Towards a standardized representation of perceived nonverbal behaviors. In: Nakano, Y., Neff, M., Paiva, A., Walker, M. (eds.) IVA 2012. LNCS, vol. 7502, pp. 455–463. Springer, Heidelberg (2012)
21. Simpson, J.A., Harris, B.A.: Interpersonal attraction. In: Weber, A.L., Harvey, J.H. (eds.) Perspectives on Close Relationships, pp. 45–66. Prentice Hall (1994)
22. McGinley, H., LeFevre, R., McGinley, P.: The influence of a communicator's body position on opinion. J. of Personality and Social Psychology 31(4), 686–690 (1975)
23. Schouwstra, S., Hoogstraten, J.: Head position and spinal position as determinants of perceived emotional state. Perceptual and Motor Skills 81, 673–674 (1995)
24. Sidner, C.L., Kidd, C.D., Lee, C., Lesh, N.: Where to look: a study of human-robot engagement. In: IUI 2004: Proc. of the 9th International Conference on Intelligent User Interfaces, pp. 78–84. ACM Press, New York (2004)
25. Pease, A.: Body Language. Sheldon Press, London (1988)
26. Bandura, A.: Self Efficacy: The Exercise of Control. Palgrave Macmillan, New York (1997)
27. Forgas, J.P., Cooper, J., Crano, W.D.: The Psychology of Attitudes and Attitude Change. Taylor & Francis Group, New York (2010)
28. Wagner, J., Lingenfelser, F., Baur, T., Damian, I., Kistler, F., André, E.: The social signal interpretation (ssi) framework - multimodal signal processing and recognition in real-time. In: Proceedings of the 21st ACM International Conference on Multimedia, Barcelona, Spain (2013)
29. Kistler, F., Endrass, B., Damian, I., Dang, C., André, E.: Natural interaction with culturally adaptive virtual characters. Germany Journal on Multimodal User Interfaces Heidelberg/Berlin (2012)
30. Wallbott, H.: Bodily expression of emotion. European Jrl. of Social Psychology (28), 879–896 (1998)
31. Ruf, T., Ernst, A., Küblbeck, C.: Face detection with the sophisticated high-speed object recognition engine (shore). In: Microelectronic Systems, pp. 243–252. Springer (2011)
32. Hammer, T.: Mental health and social exclusion among unemployed youth in scandinavia. a comparative study. Intl. Jrnl. of Social Welfare 9(1), 53–63 (2000)
33. Pan, X., Gillies, M., Barker, C., Clark, D.M., Slater, M.: Socially anxious and confident men interact with a forward virtual woman: An experiment study. PLoS ONE 7(4) (2012) e32931
34. Damian, I., Baur, T., André, E.: Investigating social cue-based interaction in digital learning games. In: Proc. of the 8th International Conference on the Foundations of Digital Games, SASDG (2013)
35. Porayska-Pomsta, K., Anderson, K., Damian, I., Baur, T., André, E., Bernardini, S., Rizzo, P.: Modelling users' affect in job interviews: Technological demo. In: Carberry, S., Weibelzahl, S., Micarelli, A., Semeraro, G. (eds.) UMAP 2013. LNCS, vol. 7899, pp. 353–355. Springer, Heidelberg (2013)

Social Behavior Modeling Based on Incremental Discrete Hidden Markov Models

Alaeddine Mihoub[1, 2], Gérard Bailly[1], and Christian Wolf[2]

[1] GIPSA-Lab, Speech & Cognition department, Grenoble, France
[2] LIRIS, Lyon, France

Abstract. Modeling multimodal face-to-face interaction is a crucial step in the process of building social robots or users-aware Embodied Conversational Agents (ECA). In this context, we present a novel approach for human behavior analysis and generation based on what we called "Incremental Discrete Hidden Markov Model" (IDHMM). Joint multimodal activities of interlocutors are first modeled by a set of DHMMs that are specific to supposed joint cognitive states of the interlocutors. Respecting a task-specific syntax, the IDHMM is then built from these DHMMs and split into i) a *recognition model* that will determine the most likely sequence of cognitive states given the multimodal activity of the interlocutor, and ii) a *generative model* that will compute the most likely activity of the speaker given this estimated sequence of cognitive states. Short-Term Viterbi (STV) decoding is used to incrementally recognize and generate behavior. The proposed model is applied to parallel speech and gaze data of interacting dyads.

Keywords: Face to face interaction, behavior model, action-perception loops, cognitive state recognition, gaze generation, HMMs, Online Viterbi decoding, latency.

1 Introduction

Face to face interaction is one of the most basic forms of communication for the human being in daily life [1]. Nevertheless, it remains a complex bi-directional multimodal phenomenon in which interlocutors continually convey, perceive and interpret the other person's verbal and nonverbal messages and signals [2]. Indeed, co-verbal cues [3] – such as body posture, arm/hand gestures (e.g. beat, deictic and iconic), head movement (e.g. node and tilt), facial expressions (e.g. frowning), eye gaze, eyebrow movement, blinks, as well as nose wrinkling and lips moistening – are largely involved in the decoding and encoding of linguistic and non-linguistic information. Several authors have notably claimed that these cues strongly participate in maintaining mutual attention and social glue [4][5].

Hence, social robots or conversational agents capable of ensuring a natural and multimodal communication should cope with complex perception-action loops that should mimic complex human behavior. In other terms, the social robot must be able to accomplish two main functionalities: (1) interaction analysis and (2) multimodal

A.A. Salah et al. (Eds.) : HBU 2013, LNCS 8212, pp. 172–183, 2013.

behavior synthesis. In this context, we present a statistical modeling framework for capturing regularities of multimodal joint actions during face-to-face interaction, which allows us to achieve both interaction analysis and behavior synthesis. More precisely, this framework is based on the assumption that reactions to other's actions are ruled by the estimation of the underlying chaining of the cognitive states of the interlocutors.

The paper is organized as follows: The next section reviews state-of-the art of face to face interaction nonverbal analysis and then the behavior generation systems. Our modeling framework and its current implementation are introduced in section 3. Section 4 illustrates its modeling performance using speech and gaze data collected in a previous experiment [6] and shows the results. Finally, discussions and our conclusion are presented in section 5.

2   Related Work

Face to face interaction analysis represents an emerging research area due to the increasing awareness of the scientific challenge and the diversity of applications. Actually automatic analysis treats many issues [7], among which can be mentioned: addressing, turn taking, activity recognition, roles, degree of interest or engagement, state of mind (e.g. neutral, curious, confused, amused) and dominance. A large number of models were proposed to cope with these problems. For instance, Otsuka et al [8] estimate turn taking ("who responds to whom and when?") with a Dynamic Bayesian Network consisting of three layers: (1) at the bottom, the behavior layer (contains head gestures and utterances); (2) in the middle, the interaction layer (contains gaze patterns); (3) at the top, the regime layer (contains conversations regimes). Only the first layer is observable, the others are latent and need to be estimated. To recognize group actions, Zhang et al [9] proposed a two layered HMM, where the first layer estimates individual actions from raw audio-visual data. The second one estimates group actions taking in consideration the results of the first layer. Conditional Random Fields are used in [10] for automatic role recognition in multiparty conversations. First, speaker diarization is applied to list turns; second, acoustic features are extracted from turns and finally, features vectors are mapped into a sequence of roles. More complete reviews on issues and models related to nonverbal analysis of social interaction can be found in [11][7].

In the context of multimodal behavior generation, several platforms have been proposed for humanoid robots and virtual agents. Cassel et al. [12] notably developed the BEAT ("Behavior Expression Animation Toolkit") system which allows from textual input to synthesize appropriate and synchronized behaviors with speech such as iconic gestures, eye gaze and intonation. The nonverbal behavior is assigned on the basis of linguistic and contextual analysis relying on a set of rules extracted from research on human conversational behavior. Krenn [13] introduced the NECA ("Net Environment for Embodied Emotional Conversational Agents") project which aims to develop a platform for the implementation of emotional conversational agents for Web-based applications. This system controls a complete scene generator and provides an ECA with communicative (e.g eye brow raising, head nodes) as well as non communicative behavior (e.g physiological breathing, walking/moving from one location to another). Another major contribution of the NECA project is Gesticon [14] which consists of a repository of predefined co-verbal gestures and animations that can be accessed via functional descriptors. Gesticon is based on a general specification that may drive both physical and virtual agents. Another interesting system called "MAX", the "Multimodal Assembly eXpert", has been developed by Kopp [15]. The system allows interacting, in virtual reality environment, with a virtual agent and doing collaborative tasks. MAX is able to generate reactive and deliberative action using synthetic speech, gaze, facial expression, and gestures.

These different systems have many similarities: multimodal actions are selected, scheduled and combined according to rules that describe a sort of grammar of behaviors. The SAIBA framework [16] is an international effort to establish a unique platform and therefore speed up advancements in the field. It is organized into three main components: "Intent planning", "Behavior planning" and "Behavior realization". SAIBA adopted the Gesticon from the NECA platform and introduced two novel Markup Languages, the Behavior Markup Language (BML) [17] and the Functional Markup Language (FML) [18]. It is important to notice that SAIBA offers a general framework for building behavioral models. In fact, the processing within each component and its internal structure is treated as a "black box" and it is the researchers' responsibility to fill the boxes with their specific transducers. Through FML and BML, SAIBA aims at normalizing data types and information flows between different levels of representation of the behavior and bridge the gap between different modules: FML represents the output of the "Intent planning" component and BML the output of the "Behavior planning" one. Many systems have adopted the SAIBA framework, notably SmartBody [19] and the GRETA platform [20].

Human interactions are paced by multi-level perception-action loops [21] and one major missing aspect of the SAIBA was the perception dimension. The Perception Markup Language (PML) [2] has been recently introduced to fill this gap. It is the first step towards a standardized representation of perceived nonverbal behaviors. PML was inspired by the previous efforts in the field of non verbal behavior generation (FML and BML) and was designed in synergy with these standards. If PML has been equipped with the capability to carry uncertainty but the link between the uncertain perceptual representations and actions remains an open question. In the next section we will present our general behavior model which combines PML, FML and BML levels into a joint multimodal representation of task-specific human behavior. But unlike pre-mentioned rule-based models (BEAT, NECA, etc), this model relies on machine learning to organize sequences of percepts and actions into so-called joint behavioral states using Hidden Markov Models (HMMs).

3   General Behavior Model

This section presents a probabilistic/statistical approach for designing a dynamic model for the generation of pertinent multimodal behavior for a humanoid robot or an

ECA engaged in a collaborative task with a human partner. This model should thus be able to perceive and understand the partner's actions on their joint environment and generate adequate actions that should reflect its current understanding of the evolution of the joint plan.

A complete interaction can be seen as a sequence of discrete tasks, sub-tasks or activities [11]. In the following, we will consider a situated conversation as a sequence of cognitive states that structure the joint behaviors of the conversation partners. In our model, we dispose of P cognitive states; each cognitive state is modeled by a single Discrete Hidden Markov Model $(\lambda_p = (A_p, B_p, \Pi_p)_{p=1..P})$ whose n hidden states model the co-variations of the partners' behaviors. The proper chaining of these HMMs obeys to a task-specific syntax and results from lawful mutual attention and collaborative actions. Hence, the whole interaction is modeled by a global Discrete HMM $(\lambda = (A, B, \Pi))$ that concatenates the different single models. Thus the global DHMM λ is composed of N hidden states ($N=nP$). As a matter of fact, the selection and sequencing of these HMMs is equivalent to the ordering of instructions in the FML level within the SAIBA framework. Consequently, the problem of 'intent planning' is solved by the process of HMM states decoding [22], usually performed by the Viterbi algorithm.

As mentioned before, HMM states are associated with homogenous joint sensory-motor behaviors: the observation vector $O = (o_t)_{t=1..T}$ is in fact composed of two streams: (1) the sensory stream (o_t^p) collects perceptual cues and roughly correspond to the low-level PML level in the SAIBA framework; (2) the motor stream (o_t^a) is responsible for initiating actions and roughly corresponds to the BML level in the SAIBA framework. The observation vector is then defined as follows:

$$o_t = (o_t^p, o_t^a) \tag{1}$$

Note that the sensory stream may include sensory consequences of actions. These may be of different natures: efferent copies of actions, accompanying proprioceptive or exteroceptive signals. Compared to the Gesticon, our sensory-motor states (Fig. 1) intrinsically associate actions and percepts and do not differentiate between the perceptual responses of an action and motor responses for a perceived event that are appropriate to the current joint cognitive state.

3.1   Training, Sensory-Motor State Alignment, Cognitive State Recognition, and Action Generation

The training process is as follow: Each individual model is trained separately; then from single HMMs we get local emission Matrices $(B_p)_{p=1..P}$ and simply concatenate them to build the global emission matrix B. Like-wise, The global transition matrix A is built from the different trained intra-HMM transitions matrices $((A_p)_{p=1..P})$. In addition the inter-HMMs transition probabilities are trained in order to complete this matrix A. Note that more sophisticated syntactic models such as n-grams can be used. In practice, at an instant t, only perceptual information is available and actions are emitted according to these input cues. For that reason, once we get the global trained HMM, two models are extracted: a recognition model λ_R and a generative model λ_G with a modified structure for the emission matrix B. For λ_R only perception observations are selected (i.e. $o_t = o_t^p$) and for λ_G only action observations are selected (i.e. $o_t = o_t^a$). The perception for action loop combines recognition and synthesis: λ_R decodes percepts and performs the sensory-motor states alignment while λ_G further generates the adequate actions.

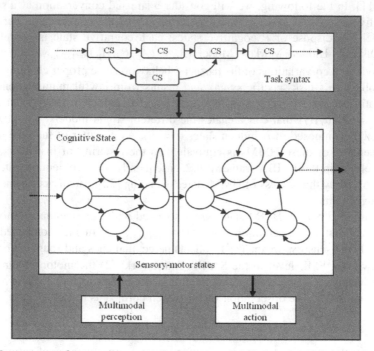

Fig. 1. Management of perception-action loops in a probabilistic scheme linking observation, states and task syntax (sequence of cognitive states)

3.2   Incremental Discrete Hidden Markov Model

The Viterbi algorithm allows estimating of the most likely state sequence S^* according to an observed sensory stream O and a HMM model λ:

$$S^* = arg\max_S(S|O,\lambda) \tag{2}$$

This alignment between observations and states is usually performed in two steps:

1. A forward step computes the partial likelihoods δ_t and stores the best predecessor for each state at each time frame in a matrix of backtracking pointers ψ_t.
2. A backtracking step on ψ_t builds the optimal path from the end of the observation sequence.

In order to exploit partial backtracking for on-line decoding, several solutions have been proposed that use a fixed sliding or overlapping window [23] [24] [25] [26]. It consists of dividing the sequence into fixed-size inputs and then decodes them independently. An alternative approach consists of using an expending window and comparing partial paths until convergence to the same trajectory [27] [28] [29]. The central idea of the Short-Time Viterbi (STV) algorithm [28] and its variants is that the window is continuously expending forward until a convergence/fusion point is found. When this is the case, it shrinks from behind. The main advantage of this method is that the solution is strictly equivalent to the full Viterbi algorithm. The major draw-back is that the fusion point can be very far ahead.

In this paper, we adopted a bounded version of the STV (BSTV): we set up a thre-shold beyond which the path with maximum likelihood up to a given number of frames ahead of the current frame is retained when there is no fusion point within that horizon. The BSTV algorithm is described briefly as follow:

```
 1:  initiate δ₁; ψ₁; a=1;
 2:  for each new frame b
 3:     for each state j=1:N
 4:        calculate δb(j) and ψb(j);
 5:        backtracking: S*t-1 = ψt(j) with t=b:a+1;
 6:        save the local path;
 7:     end
 8:     given all local paths find fusion point f;
 9:     if (b-a<threshold and f exists)
10:        local path for t=a:f is selected; a=f+1;
11:     else if (b-a>=threshold)
12:        path with max likelihood is selected;
13:        f=b;a=b;
14:        b=b+1;
15:     else b=b+1;
16: end
```

Although, the optimal solution is not always selected, the latency is fully con-trolled. We will show that short latencies obtained in practice do not degrade signifi-cantly the performance of the decoder.

In the next section, we apply this Incremental Discrete Hidden Markov Model (IDHMM) to multimodal experimental speech and gaze data of computer-mediated dyadic conversations.

4   Experimental Results

We used the dataset of Bailly et al. [6], who collected speech and gaze data from dyads playing a speech game via a computer-mediated communication system that enabled eye contact and dual eye tracking. The experimental setting is shown in Fig. 2: the gaze fixations of each subject over 5 regions of interest (ROI: face, left & right eye, mouth, elsewhere) are estimated by positioning dispersion ellipsis on fixa-tion points gathered for each experiment after compensating for head movements. The speech game involved an instructor who read and utter a sentence that the other subject (respondent) should repeat immediately in a single attempt. The quality of the repetition is rated by the instructor. Dyads exchange Semantically Unpredictable Sentences (SUS) that force the respondent to be highly attentive to the audiovisual signal.

The experiment was designed to study adaptation: one female speaker HL interacted with ten subjects (6 female colleagues, 3 female students and one male student), both as an instructor for ten sentences and as a respondent for another ten sentences.

Fig. 2. Mediated face-to-face conversation [6]. Top: People sit in two different rooms and dialog through couples of cameras, screens, microphones and loudspeakers. Gaze of both interlocutors are monitored by two eye-trackers embedded in the TFT screens. Note that pinhole cameras and seats are positioned at the beginning of the interaction so that the cameras coincide with the top of the nose of each partner's face. Bottom: four regions of fixation are tracked on each speaker's face: left and right eye, mouth and face (mainly the nose ridge).

4.1   Data

The observation sensory streams consist here of discrete observations: the voice activity (cardinality 2: on/off) and ROI (cardinality 5) of the two speakers. The cognitive states (CS) have been labelled semi-automatically and corrected by hand. We distinguish between seven CS: reading, preparing to speak, speaking , waiting, listening, thinking and else (laughing, etc). These CS may occur for each speaker in three different roles: initiator, respondent or none (free interaction before, after and when exchanging roles).

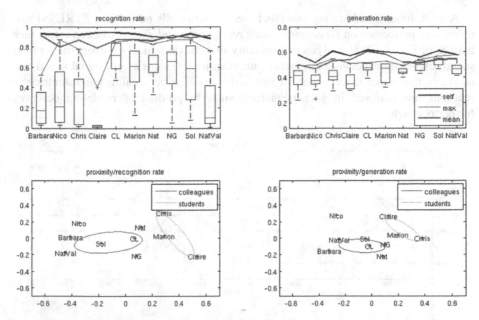

Fig. 3. Recognition (left) and generation (right) performance. Top: the performances of interlocutor-independent (II: dark red), interlocutor-dependent (ID: boxplots and maximum with light red) and self DHMMs (dark blue) are displayed for each interlocutor. Bottom, a MDS projection of the performances of the ID models cue proximities between interlocutor-specific behaviors: note its coherence with the a priori clustering of their social relations with HL.

4.2   Behavioral Models

We tested the ability of DHMMs and IDHMM to estimate the cognitive state of the main subject "LN" given her voice activity ($v1$), gaze ($g2$) and voice activity of her conversational partner ($v2$), and predict her gaze behavior ($g1$). Consequently, we use the recognition model λ_R to decode $o_t = (v1, v2, g2)$ and next λ_G to generate the gaze ($g1$). Before presenting results, it is important to mention that decision trees and Support Vector Machines have been used. For both classifiers, correct classification rate of the cognitive state and the gaze were respectively 81% and 43%. Next we will show that our HMMs outperform these classifiers.

4.3   Results Using DHMMs

We build and test different models in an offline mode using HTK [30]: for interlocutor-dependent (ID) vs. interlocutor-independent (II) models. For each interlocutor, the corresponding II model is trained on the other 9 interactions. In addition, a set of 9 ID models is also built using data from the each other interlocutor. II and ID models are thus all trained on data from other interlocutors. Results are illustrated in Fig. 3: the mean recognition and correct generation rate of II models are respectively 93% and 56% (compared to a random assignment at 23% taking into account a priori distributions of ROI). The II models result in better performances comparing with ID models, which explains that the mean behavior outperforms the individual ones.

A multidimensional scaling analysis based on Kruskal's normalised STRESS1 criterion was performed on ID cognitive state recognition and gaze prediction errors (see bottom of Fig. 3). This analysis of proximity of behaviors nicely mirrors the a priori social relationships between HL and her interlocutors. Gaze is a very social signal and no doubt that social determinants of interaction such as personalities and dominance relations are mirrored in gaze behaviors: such by-product of modeling deserves further research.

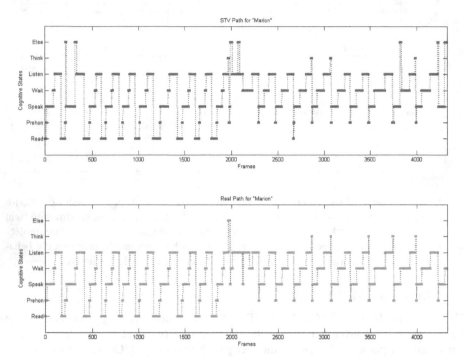

Fig. 4. Recognition path (for a specific interlocutor "Marion") using the incremental model (top) vs. ground truth (bottom)

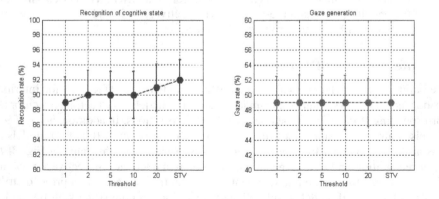

Fig. 5. Recognition and generation results using the incremental model

4.4   Results Using IDHMM

HMMs are trained with HTK, then the BSTV algorithm and the global HMM are implemented in Matlab using PMTK3 toolkit [31]. The mean recognition rate of 92% shows that STV is able to capture the structure of the interaction (see Fig. 4 and Fig. 5). It confirms also that STV performance is as good as an offline processing. However, the problem with STV is mastering the output delay. We observe that ~80% of latencies are fewer than 5 frames. However, maximum values could be very important. In our case, for the all subjects, the maximum latency was 259 frames which represent an unsuitable delay for real-time application. BSTV is used to control these delays. Theoretically, an optimal trade-off ought to be sought because of the inverse relationship between performance and latency. In our case, results (Fig. 5) have shown that our IDHMM is able to estimate the Viterbi path with low thresholds/latencies as well as for a long term processing (e.g. 90% for a threshold equal to 2). Moreover the mean generation performance (49%) is not affected and remains practically the same at all thresholds. While the full connectivity of the state transition matrix explains why almost 80% of latencies are fewer than 5 frames (i.e. deviations of the local path to the global path may be rapidly reconnect when robust cues are encountered), another important factor is the syntax of the task: the chaining of sub-tasks is very regular and highly constraints the alignment of cognitive states.

5   Conclusions

We have proposed a modeling framework for the recognition and the generation of joint multimodal behavior. Sub-task sensory-motor HHM are trained and split into sensory HMM for sub-task recognition and motor HMM for motor generation. Short-term Viterbi with a limited horizon is used to perform incremental recognition and generation. We showed that even with low thresholds, performances of the model were not significantly degraded. This first model will be extended to the joint modeling of discrete and continuous observations, notably taking into account the strengths of trajectory HMM.

A noteworthy property of these statistical behavior models is the estimation of behavioral proximities/distances between subjects. This could be exploited for social evaluation but also to organize and select behavior models most adapted to an unknown interlocutor.

Due to lack of space, many technical details such as the initialization and training of Markov models for discrete observations and fully-connected states deserve in-depth analysis and require more research effort. In particular, performance would largely benefit from the modeling of state durations (here related to gaze fixations).

Acknowledgments. This research is financed by the Rhône-Alpes ARC6 research council.

References

[1] Otsuka, K.: Multimodal Conversation Scene Analysis for Understanding People's Communicative Behaviors in Face-to-Face Meetings, pp. 171–179 (2011)

[2] Scherer, S., Marsella, S., Stratou, G., Xu, Y., Morbini, F., Egan, A., Morency, L.-P.: Perception markup language: towards a standardized representation of perceived nonverbal behaviors. In: Intelligent Virtual Agents, pp. 455–463 (2012)

[3] Argyle, M.: Bodily Communication. Taylor & Francis (1975)

[4] Lakin, J.L., Jefferis, V.E., Cheng, C.M., Chartrand, T.L.: The Chameleon Effect as Social Glue: Evidence for the Evolutionary Significance of Nonconscious Mimicry. Journal of Nonverbal Behavior 27(3), 145–162 (2003)

[5] Kopp, S.: Social resonance and embodied coordination in face-to-face conversation with artificial interlocutors. Speech Commun. 52(6), 587–597 (2010)

[6] Bailly, G., Raidt, S., Elisei, F.: Gaze, conversational agents and face-to-face communication. Speech Communication 52(6), 598–612 (2010)

[7] Gatica-Perez, D.: Automatic nonverbal analysis of social interaction in small groups: A review. Image and Vision Computing 27(12), 1775–1787 (2009)

[8] Otsuka, K., Sawada, H., Yamato, J.: Automatic inference of cross-modal nonverbal interactions in multiparty conversations: 'who responds to whom, when, and how?' from gaze, head gestures, and utterances. In: Proceedings of the 9th International Conference on Multimodal Interfaces, New York, NY, USA, pp. 255–262 (2007)

[9] Zhang, D., Gatica-Perez, D., Bengio, S., McCowan, I.: Modeling individual and group actions in meetings with layered HMMs. IEEE Transactions on Multimedia 8(3), 509–520 (2006)

[10] Salamin, H., Vinciarelli, A.: Automatic Role Recognition in Multiparty Conversations: An Approach Based on Turn Organization, Prosody, and Conditional Random Fields. IEEE Transactions on Multimedia 14(2), 338–345 (2012)

[11] Gatica-Perez, D.: Analyzing group interactions in conversations: a review. In: 2006 IEEE International Conference on Multisensor Fusion and Integration for Intelligent Systems, pp. 41–46 (2006)

[12] Cassell, J., Vilhjalmsson, H., Bickmore, T.: BEAT: the Behavior Expression Animation Toolkit (2001)

[13] Krenn, B.: The NECA project: Net environments for embodied emotional conversational agents. In: Proc. of Workshop on Emotionally Rich Virtual Worlds with Emotion Synthesis at the 8th International Conference on 3D Web Technology (Web3D)., vol. 35. St. Malo, France (2003)

[14] Krenn, B., Pirker, H.: Defining the gesticon: Language and gesture coordination for interacting embodied agents. In: Proc. of the AISB-2004 Symposium on Language, Speech and Gesture for Expressive Characters, pp. 107–115 (2004)

[15] Kopp, S., Jung, B., Lessmann, N., Wachsmuth, I.: Max - A Multimodal Assistant in Virtual Reality Construction. KI 17(4), 11 (2003)

[16] Kopp, S., Krenn, B., Marsella, S.C., Marshall, A.N., Pelachaud, C., Pirker, H., Thórisson, K.R., Vilhjálmsson, H.H.: Towards a Common Framework for Multimodal Generation: The Behavior Markup Language. In: Gratch, J., Young, M., Aylett, R.S., Ballin, D., Olivier, P. (eds.) IVA 2006. LNCS (LNAI), vol. 4133, pp. 205–217. Springer, Heidelberg (2006)

[17] Vilhjálmsson, H., Cantelmo, N., Cassell, J., Chafai, N.E., Kipp, M., Kopp, S., Mancini, M., Marsella, S., Marshall, A., Pelachaud, C.: The behavior markup language: Recent developments and challenges. In: Intelligent Virtual Agents, pp. 99–111 (2007)

[18] Heylen, D., Kopp, S., Marsella, S.C., Pelachaud, C., Vilhjálmsson, H.H.: The Next Step towards a Function Markup Language. In: Prendinger, H., Lester, J.C., Ishizuka, M. (eds.) IVA 2008. LNCS (LNAI), vol. 5208, pp. 270–280. Springer, Heidelberg (2008)

[19] Thiebaux, M., Marsella, S., Marshall, A.N., Kallmann, M.: Smartbody: Behavior realization for embodied conversational agents. In: Proceedings of the 7th International Joint Conference on Autonomous Agents and Multiagent Systems, vol. 1, pp. 151–158 (2008)

[20] Le, Q.A., Pelachaud, C.: Generating Co-speech Gestures for the Humanoid Robot NAO through BML. In: Efthimiou, E., Kouroupetroglou, G., Fotinea, S.-E. (eds.) GW 2011. LNCS, vol. 7206, pp. 228–237. Springer, Heidelberg (2012)

[21] Bailly, G.: Boucles de perception-action et interaction face-à-face. Revue Fran\ccaise De Linguistique Appliquée 13(2), 121–131 (2009)

[22] Rabiner, L.R.: A tutorial on hidden markov models and selected applications in speech recognition. In: Proceedings of the IEEE, pp. 257–286 (1989)

[23] Seward, A.: Low-Latency Incremental Speech Transcription in the Synface Project

[24] Ryynänen, M., Klapuri, A.: Automatic Bass Line Transcription from Streaming Polyphonic Audio. In: Proceedings of the 2007 IEEE International Conference on Acoustics, Speech, and Signal Processing, pp. 1437–1440 (2007)

[25] Lou, Y., Zhang, C., Zheng, Y., Xie, X., Wang, W., Huang, Y.: Map-matching for low-sampling-rate GPS trajectories. In: Proceedings of the 17th ACM SIGSPATIAL International Conference on Advances in Geographic Information Systems, New York, NY, USA, pp. 352–361 (2009)

[26] Yuan, J., Zheng, Y., Zhang, C., Xie, X., Sun, G.-Z.: An Interactive-Voting Based Map Matching Algorithm, pp. 43–52 (2010)

[27] Šrámek, R., Brejová, B., Vinař, T.: On-line Viterbi Algorithm and Its Relationship to Random Walks. arXiv:0704.0062 (March 2007)

[28] Bloit, J., Rodet, X.: Short-time Viterbi for online HMM decoding: Evaluation on a real-time phone recognition task. In: IEEE International Conference on Acoustics, Speech and Signal Processing, ICASSP 2008, pp. 2121–2124 (2008)

[29] Goh, C.Y., Dauwels, J., Mitrovic, N., Asif, M.T., Oran, A., Jaillet, P.: Online map-matching based on Hidden Markov model for real-time traffic sensing applications. In: 2012 15th International IEEE Conference on Intelligent Transportation Systems (ITSC), pp. 776–781 (2012)

[30] HTK, The Hidden Markov Model Toolkit, http://htk.eng.cam.ac.uk/

[31] Dunham, M., Murphy, K.: PMTK3: Probabilistic modeling toolkit for Matlab/Octave, http://code.google.com/p/pmtk3/

MMLI: Multimodal Multiperson Corpus of Laughter in Interaction

Radoslaw Niewiadomski[1], Maurizio Mancini[1], Tobias Baur[2], Giovanna Varni[1], Harry Griffin[3], and Min S.H. Aung[3]

[1] Università degli Studi di Genova, Viale Francesco Causa, 13, 16145 Genova, Italy
{radek,giovanna}@infomus.org, maurizio.mancini@unige.it
[2] Augsburg University, Universitätsstr. 6a, 86159 Augsburg, Germany
baur@hcm-lab.de
[3] University College London, Gower Street, London, WC1E 6BT, United Kingdom
{harry.griffin,m.aung}@ucl.ac.uk

Abstract. The aim of the Multimodal and Multiperson Corpus of Laughter in Interaction (MMLI) was to collect multimodal data of laughter with the focus on full body movements and different laughter types. It contains both induced and interactive laughs from human triads. In total we collected 500 laugh episodes of 16 participants. The data consists of 3D body position information, facial tracking, multiple audio and video channels as well as physiological data.

In this paper we discuss methodological and technical issues related to this data collection including techniques for laughter elicitation and synchronization between different independent sources of data. We also present the enhanced visualization and segmentation tool used to segment captured data. Finally we present data annotation as well as preliminary results of the analysis of the nonverbal behavior patterns in laughter.

1 Introduction

Laughter is one of the most commonly appearing human communicative signals [1]. Despite its high incidence, knowledge about the multimodal expressive pattern of laughter is rather limited. Laughter is a very complex behavior that includes the majority of expressive modalities. Most research to date has focused on acoustic and facial cues of laughter. However, they are often accompanied by body movements and changes in posture[2] including, among others, head backwards movements and trunk/shoulders vibrations caused by forced exhalations. We argue that special attention should be paid to these body movements, as they are important in both laughter detection and synthesis. Laughter synthesis, for example, may benefit from the analysis of laughter episodes' body movements, as realistic body movements are crucial in distinguishing between laughter and smile visual patterns.

It was shown that many different types of laughter e.g. happy, embarrassed, contemptuous or schadenfreude laughter can be differentiated on a linguistic basis [3]. However it is still not clear if these laughter types also exhibit distinctive

A.A. Salah et al. (Eds.) : HBU 2013, LNCS 8212, pp. 184–195, 2013.

expressive patterns. Existence of distinct expressive patterns for two laughter types i.e. *Duchenne laughter* (i.e. a sign of enjoyment) and *social laughter* was shown (see [4]). It is also suggested that voluntary down/up regulation of laughter can be detected from acoustic and facial cues [2].

Building a multimodal laughter corpus is a challenging task because laughter mainly occurs during social interaction. This important aspect of laughter is often neglected and existing corpora usually contain data captured in induced, non-interactive setups e.g. data of people watching a video containing funny stimuli (e.g., [5,6]). Another approach consists of capturing the behaviors of the participants of multi-party meetings (e.g., [7,8]). These corpora allow one to capture the dynamics of the whole interaction but often contain only audio modality, and to our knowledge there is no database that focuses on capturing body movements.

In this paper we describe a new corpus - Multimodal and Multiperson Corpus of Laughter in Interaction[1] (MMLI). Capturing this data we focus on laughter full body movements in different contexts, and for different laughter types. The MMLI corpus will be made freely available for research purposes on the ILHAIRE database website: http://qub.ac.uk/ilhairelaughter.

2   State of the Art

Only a few corpora exist that were explicitly created with the purpose of studying laughter. More often the data collected for other aims e.g. multi-participants meetings analysis (such as AMI Corpus [8] or ICSI Meeting corpus [7]) is used. For instance, Truong and Leeuwen [9] selected audible laugh episodes from the ICSI corpus to build an acoustic laughter detector. Existing corpora often focus on one modality only. They are created ad-hoc with a concrete aim e.g. acoustic or visual laughter detection. Aiming at emotion differentiation in laughter Szameitat et al. [10] recorded 8 actors performing four types of laughter i.e., joyous, tickling, schadenfreude, and taunting. The actors were instructed to put themselves into emotional states with the help of self-induction techniques. The database contains 429 audio episodes and it was used to investigate the acoustical correlates of laughter expressing four emotions. Scherer et al. [11] collected the FreeTalk corpus consisting of 90 minutes of multiparty conversations of four participants. The corpus includes audio and video recordings (with 360 degree camera) of about 300 laugh episodes and was used for audio visual laughter detection.

The AudioVisualLaughterCycle corpus [5] contains multimodal data of about 1000 spontaneous laughter episodes recorded from 24 subjects. Each subject was recorded while watching a 10-minute comedy video. Each episode was captured with one motion capture system (either Optitrack or Zigntrack) and synchronized with the corresponding audiovisual sample. The material was manually segmented

---

[1] The research leading to the results presented in this paper has received funding from the European Union Seventh Framework Programme (FP7/2007-2013) under grant agreement no. 270780 (ILHAIRE project).

into single laugh episodes. The number of episodes for a subject ranges from 4 to 82.

Aiming to collect multimodal data for automatic audiovisual laughter detection Petridis et al. created the MAHNOB database [6]. It contains nearly 4 hours of recordings with the participation of 22 subjects who were recorded while watching funny video clips. The collected data is publicly available and consists of audio, the upper body video, as well as recordings of a thermal camera. It mostly contains induced laughter of enjoyment (563 episodes) but also posed smiles and laughs as well as speech. The database was primarily used for laughter vs. speech discrimination showing the advantage of a multimodal approach over audio-only detection in noisy environments.

Suarez et al. [12] created the PinoyLaughter audiovisual laughter corpus containing about 500 spontaneous and acted laugh episodes. The aim was to display various emotions that can be transmitted with laughter such as happiness, giddiness, excitement, embarrassment and hurtful laughter. While professional actors acted emotions, spontaneous laughter was collected from volunteers. Both acted and spontaneous data was pre-processed, manually segmented, and then annotated both with discrete and dimensional labels of emotions. Different emotional states were recognized mainly from the audio modality and the context.

With the aim of collecting samples of different laughter types such as conversational laughter McKeown et al. [13] reviewed existing six databases and built the ILHAIRE laughter database. This corpus contains audio and video of more than 1000 laugh episodes in various contexts: laughter induced by watching funny clips; laughter in conversations or when performing some engaging tasks.

Table 1. Comparison of main laughter corpora

Name	Modality			Interaction type			Laughter type (e.g., social)
	Audio	Face/Head	Body	Posed	Induced	Interactive	
MAHNOB	yes	yes	no	yes	yes	no	enjoyment, posed
AVLC	yes	yes	no	no	yes	no	enjoyment
PinoyLaughter	yes	yes	no	yes	yes	no	different emotions
Szameitat	yes	no	no	yes	no	no	different types
FreeTalk	yes	yes	no	no	no	yes	enjoyment
ILHAIRE	yes	yes	no	yes	yes	yes	enjoyment, social/conversational

As shown in Table 1 most of the existing corpora consist of audio and eventually facial cues of laughter. They often contain only posed or induced (i.e. non interactive) laughter. Finally, none of them offer high quality data of full body movements.

3   MMLI Data Collection

By capturing data for the MMLI corpus of laughter we mainly aimed at:

- capturing full body movements with special attention to shoulders, torso and respiration,

- capturing laughter in different contexts, and in particular, during unsupervised "free" interactions,
- capturing different types of laughter.

To collect multimodal data we built a complex setup that allowed us to collect the information from different sources. First of all, three high precision inertial motion capture systems were used to collect high quality data of body movements. These systems were complemented by Microsoft Kinect sensors, high frame rate cameras and a respiration sensor. All the data is synchronized through a freely available software called SSI (see Section 4). This allows one to analyze not only synchronization between different modalities in a laughter episode but also intra-subject synchronization.

To capture laughter in different contexts and various laughter types we invited groups of friends and asked them to perform six enjoyable tasks (T1 - T6). Beside classical laughter inducing tasks such as watching funny clips we proposed participants to play several "simple" social games, i.e. games regulated by one simple general rule in which participants are free to improvise. We supposed that a lack of detailed rules could encourage easy-going spontaneous behaviors that may include reactions such as commenting, joking, irony, or even embarrassment or schadenfreude. Additionally, some tasks were expected to cause down or up regulation of laughter. Thus, we expected that the resulting data could consist not only of enjoyment laughter, but also of some other laughter categories.

3.1   Techical Setup

In the data collection we captured the behavior of up to three interacting participants at the same time. For this purpose, as shown in Figure 1, we used 2 types of different inertial mocap systems:

- (XS1, XS2) 2 out of 3 participants were captured using Xsens MVN Biomech system[2] that is composed of 17 inertial sensors placed on Velcro straps. Data is captured at 120 frames per second; each frame consists of 22 joints' location and rotation in a 3D reference space. Data can be exported to common formats like C3D or BVH,
- (AZ) the third participant was recorded with the Animazoo IGS-190 system, equipped with 19 inertial sensors. Recorded data consists of 3D body joints' rotation in BVH format.

Additionally audio and video were recorded:

- 2 (M1 - M2) personal wireless microphones (Mono, 16 kHz) placed close to the participants' mouth,
- 1 (A1) microphone (Mono, 16 kHz) placed in between the participants to record the room ambient sound,
- 4 (W1 - W4) webcams Logitech Webcam Pro 9000 (640x480, 30fps),

---

[2] www.xsens.com

- 2 (C1, C2) high-frame rate cameras Philips PC webcam SPZ5000 (640x480, 60fps),
- 2 (K1, K2) Kinect cameras. Kinect cameras were used to collect video (640x480, 30fps) as well as additional data of face, head and body movements. The Kinect SDK allows tracking and extraction of 100 facial points, 20 body points, as well as 6 high-level facial actions such as: smiling or frowning; all these data are extracted with the frequency of 30Hz,
- 1 (RS) Respiration sensor (ProComp Infiniti, Thought Technology) to capture thoracic and abdominal circumference of one participant at 256 samples/second.

Two different setups (S1 and S2) were used. In the main setup, S1, used for tasks T1, T2, T5 and T6 (see Section 3.2) the cameras were placed as in Figure 1.

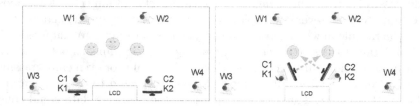

Fig. 1. a) Setup S1; b) Setup S2 - Tasks T3 and T4

Tasks T3 and T4 consist of two social games expected to trigger different types of laughter (see Section 3.2). According to the literature (e.g. [2]) face allows one distinguish between different laughter types, so we decided to record close-ups of the participants' faces. For this reason, setup S2 with cameras C1-C2 and K1-K2 placed closely to the participants faces was used for these task (see Figure 1).

3.2   Scenarios

In order to record spontaneous as well as controlled laugh reactions we asked participants to perform the following tasks: T1 - watching funny videos together, T2 - watching funny videos separately, T3 - "Yes/no" game, T4 - "Barbichette" game, T5 - pictionary game, and T6 - tongue twisters.

T1 and T2 consist of classic laughter inducing task, i.e., watching funny videos selected by experimenters and participants. Differently to other laughter corpora (e.g. [5]) in our data collection participants were not left alone; they could talk freely (e.g. comment videos) and hear each other. In more details, in task T1, all the participants, as well as a part of the technical stuff watched a 9 minute video. In T2 one participant was separated from everyone else by a curtain, which completely obscured her view of the others participants while still allowing her to hear (see Figure 2).

T3 and T4 are two social games that were expected to trigger different laughter types such as enjoyment or social laughter as well as down and up regulation.

Fig. 2. The views from cameras W3 and W4 in task T2

These were carried out in turns with all participants taking each role or competing against every other participant in the triad. In T3 one of the participants must respond quickly to questions from the other participants without saying "yes", "no" or any variation of these. The role of the other two participants is to ask questions and distract him in an attempt to provoke the use of the prohibited words. T4 is a classic French children's game that we included in order to elicit down-regulated laughter. Two participants face each other, make eye contact and hold the other's chin. The aim of the game is to avoid laughing; the one who laughs first is the one who loses. Players may do anything (talk, move, pull faces etc.) but must maintain physical and eye contact. In this scenario the third person acts as a judge and plays against the winner in the next round.

In T5 one participant drew words printed on a piece of paper extracted from an envelope. His task was to convey the word to the other participants by drawing on a large board. Each participant had 2 minutes to convey as many words as possible, each correct answer worth one point. The groups of participants competed against each other with the promise of the highest scoring group receiving a special prize.

T6 involved participants in pronouncing tongue twisters in four different languages (French, Polish, Italian, and English). One participant read the tongue twisters which were printed on a piece of paper held by another participant. The other two participants were encouraged to distract and ridicule the speaker e.g. by using a fake laughter, in order to make him laugh.

3.3   Protocol

For the purpose of the data collection it was important that participants knew each other well, so we recruited groups of friends.

Data collection consisted of recording all inter-subject interactions. Thus, there was no clear start and end of recordings between tasks. In particular we also recorded the participants between tasks. Experimenters were present most of the time in the recording room, they talked with participants and commented the events; they even participated in some of the tasks. This procedure was chosen because much of the laughter interaction occurs between the tasks, i.e. when participants comment on the previous events, or they discuss freely. We did not wanted to interrupt these spontaneous interactions.

Each person could participate only in one session. One session consisted of six tasks T1 - T6. It lasted about 2 hours and included from 31 to 51 minutes of recording. The participants were first asked to complete additional questionnaires. Next, they were fitted with mocap sensors and microphones. Additionally, three small green markers were placed on the shoulder and chest of each participant to track body movements with vision processing algorithms. The fully equipped participants can be seen in Figure 2. The session usually started with a task T1. The order of the remaining tasks was variable. At the end participants were debriefed and given small gifts.

We recorded 6 sessions with 16 participants: 4 triads & 2 dyads (groups G3 and G5), age 20 - 35; 3 females; 8 French, 2 Polish, 2 Vietnamese, 1 German, 1 Austrian, 1 Chinese and 1 Tunisian. Participants were not obliged to speak French during the sessions. They could use the language they usually speak with each other. The instructions were given in one of 3 languages: English, French or Polish.

4 Data Synchronization

For collecting, processing and synchronizing multimodal data between different signals we used the open-source Social Signal Interpretation framework[3] (SSI) [14]. SSI allows synchronization of data from different sensor devices in real time. For our extended scenario with a high number of sensor devices SSI was extended to support not only local synchronization on a single computer, but also on multiple machines. As SSI guarantees local synchronization, the multi-computer approach is realized by a host-client architecture where multiple clients wait for a host to send a start command. To ensure all network delays can be detected at a later point we first processed a clock synchronization between all machines. For our data set we found a negligible maximum delay of only a few milliseconds.

We ran up to 8 computers simultaneously. Each of the two most powerful machines, that is, machines 1 and 2, performed the recording of an Xsens motion capture suit, a Kinect sensor, an additional webcam, as well as high quality audio recordings (XS1, M1, W1, K1 and XS2, M2, W2, K2 resp.). Machine 3 performed the recording of the Animazoo motion capture suit (AZ) and machine 4 recorded both rear cameras: W3 and W4, as well as ambient audio of the room (A1). Machines 5 and 6 ran two instances of the EyesWeb platform (see Section 5.1 for further details) used to record high frequency cameras (C1,C2, 60Hz). These two instances were synchronized to start recording when the start command, sent by the host, was received. Machine 7 was attached in some of the sessions involving video playback, to also ensure that the playback position of the video watched by participants was synced with all the other data. Finally, for some of the sessions, we also recorded respiration data (RS) on machine 8, which had to

---

[3] http://openssi.net

be synchronized by hand as the used sensor device was not yet integrated in the framework.

5 Data Playback, Annotation, Segmentation and Processing

The EyesWeb XMI platform[4] is a modular system that allows both expert (e.g., researchers in computer engineering) and non-expert users (e.g., artists) to create multimodal installations in a visual way [15]. We developed some EyesWeb tools to play back, annotate, segment, and process the corpus data.

5.1 Playback

The playback tool, illustrated in Figure 3, allows one to select a recording session and play back the multimodal data in a synchronized way. A synchronization counter/clock signal is generated at $120Hz$. This signal provides two different information: (i) it encodes a *frame number* that is increased by 1 each time the signal is generated; (ii) it is a clock, that is, when the signal is received, the receiving module generates its output. Separate file reading modules are associated with each recorded stream: Xsens, Animazoo, cameras, respiration. In the current version of the playback tool audio is not yet supported. Each reading module receives the same number of synchronization signals but the encoded number is scaled depending on the original frame rate of the recorded stream. For example, the Animazoo data stream is recorded at $60Hz$, so the value encoded in the synchronization signal is divided by 2; the webcam video is recorded at $30Hz$, so the synchronization signal value is divided by 4.

The stream data and video frames corresponding to the synchronization signal are then read from the stream and video files and the result is a multimodal synchronized output consisting of a 3D visualization of the participants' bodies, videos corresponding to the setup camera and the respiration sensor's graph.

5.2 Annotation and Segmentation

Another tool, based on the playback tool, for annotating and segmenting the recorded sessions has been developed using EyesWeb XMI.

The annotation phase (label A in Figure 4) consists of determining the start and end frame of each laughter event in which a particular participants' behavior can be observed (e.g., at least one of the participants laughs). During this phase, the user sets up starting and ending frame number via a GUI. Each time these numbers are modified a synchronization signal is generated (as described in Section 5.1) and the corresponding video frames coming from the recorded video streams are shown, providing a feedback to the user. Once the segment's frame interval is decided by the user, the pair ($startframe, endframe$) is stored into the session's annotation file.

---

[4] http://www.eyesweb.infomus.org

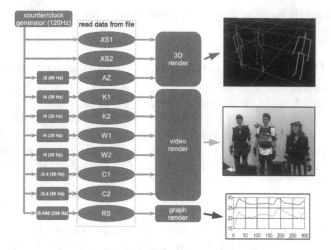

Fig. 3. The EyesWeb XMI playback tool

In the segmentation phase (label S in Figure 4), the annotation file is read and the starting and ending frame of each segment are provided as input to the counter/clock generator: that is, a sequence of consecutive frame numbers in the interval $[startframe, endframe]$ is provided as input to the playback tool. Then, the corresponding video and 3D frames coming from the recorded video and 3D streams are written to separate files.

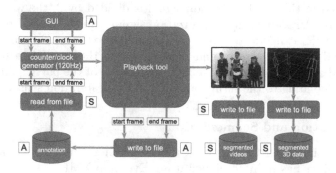

Fig. 4. The EyesWeb XMI annotation and segmentation tool

6 Results

During 6 sessions we collected nearly 4 hours and 16 minutes of data. Due to some technical problems we were not able to record 4 tasks: namely task T2 for group G1, G2 and task T6 for group G1, G3. We annotated *laughter events* and *laughter episodes*. A *laughter event* is a time interval in which at least one of the participants laughs. Annotation of laughter events is useful to analyze the overall laughter dynamics and to measure how successful respective task was in producing the laugh. A *laughter episode* corresponds to a single laugh generated by one participant. Thus one laughter event can be composed of several laughter episodes that correspond to different people that laugh at the same time. The annotation contains the following information: participants' task (T1-T6), start and end time of laughter event and camera (W1, W4, C1, C2, K1, K2) that captured the event.

We annotated 439 laughter events[5] , corresponding to 31 minutes of laughter, that is, 12% of total recording time (4 hours and 16 minutes). The rates obtained in other laughter data collections are not much different: 5−8% in meeting recordings (FreeTalk, [11]), 18% in laughter inducing study (AVLC, [5]). We observed variability in the laughter frequency between the tasks (6% - 22%) and between groups (4% - 16%). The details are reported in Tables 2 and 3, and in Figure 5. Interactive games based tasks appear to elicit more laughter than laughter inducing tasks with the highest rate of laughter events in barbichette game (T4). Results of Tasks T1 and T2 cannot be compared as different videos were shown to the participants in T1 and T2. One out of two dyads, group G5, was laughing particularly rarely. The quantity of laughter in other groups is comparable.

Table 2. Laughter per group

Group	Task duration	Laughter events			Laughter episodes		
		Number of events	Duration	Percentage of laughter	Number episodes	Average duration	Std
G1	00:37:35	74	00:03:37	9.62%	91	3.09s	2.29s
G2	00:48:40	47	00:07:55	16.27%	49	8.02s	6.52s
G3	00:31:40	68	00:04:22	13.79%	76	3.03s	3.36s
G4	00:51:31	99	00.08.16	16.05%	137	4.90s	4.64s
G5	00:42:00	59	00:01:43	4.09%	58	1.89s	1.04s
G6	00:44:55	92	00:04:58	11.06%	109	3.28s	2.16s

Table 3. Laughter per task

Task	Task duration	Laughter events			Laughter episodes		
		Number of events	Duration	Peecentage of laughter	Number episodes	Average duration	Std
T1	00:56:24	83	00:05:31	9.78%	101	4.23s	5.09s
T2	00:13:45	24	00:01:48	13.09%	29	4.93s	2.88s
T3	00:43:05	86	00:04:54	11.37%	98	4.05s	3.16s
T4	00:46:52	94	00:10:21	22.08%	110	3.86s	5.79s
T5	00:58:05	64	00:03:30	6.03%	71	4.67s	3.37s
T6	00:38:10	88	00:04:47	12.53%	111	2.99s	3.22s

---

[5] We consider only laughs occurred when certain task was performed. Laughs between tasks were not included.

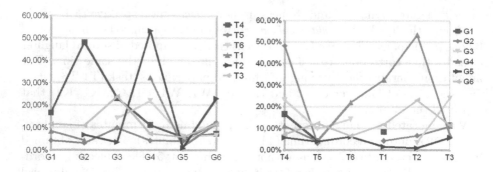

Fig. 5. Percentage of laughter events per task and group

7   Conclusion

We presented collection and analysis of the MMLI corpus. To our knowledge, this is the first corpus of this richness, dedicated to different laughter contexts, containing various data sources (mocap, audio, video, physiological), a large spectrum of captured modalities and that is synchronized across multiple participants. We proposed different scenarios that were successful in eliciting the laughter in our participants. We presented tools to synchronize and visualize the multimodal data from many cameras, various inertial mocap systems as well as Kinects. In the future, we will conclude the annotation work. Through FACS coding and perceptive studies we aim to validate whether our corpus does contain different laughter types. We will work on laughter detection from body cues as well as fusion algorithms that take into account more than one modality. We also plan to build a model of laughter mimicry and contagion in the interaction. Our corpus will be made freely available for research purposes on the ILHAIRE database website: http://qub.ac.uk/ilhairelaughter.

Acknowledgment. The research leading to the results presented in this paper has received funding from the European Union Seventh Framework Programme (FP7/2007-2013)under grant agreement no. 270780 (ILHAIRE project).

References

1. Chapman, A.: Humor and laughter in social interaction and some implications for humor research. In: McGhee, P., Goldstein, J. (eds.) Handbook of Humor Research, vol. 1, pp. 135–157 (1983)
2. Ruch, W., Ekman, P.: The expressive pattern of laughter. In: Kaszniak, A. (ed.) Emotion, Qualia and Consciousness, pp. 426–443. World Scientific Pub., Tokyo (2001)
3. Huber, T., Ruch, W.: Laughter as a uniform category? a historic analysis of different types of laughter. In: 10th Congress of the Swiss Society of Psychology, University of Zurich, Switzerland (2007)

4. Huber, T., Drack, P., Ruch, W.: Sulky and angry laughter: The search for distinct facial displays. In: Banninger-Huber, E., Peham, D. (eds.) Current and Future Perspectives in Facial Expression Research: Topics and Methodical Questions, Universitat Innsbruck, pp. 38–44 (2009)

5. Urbain, J., Niewiadomski, R., Bevacqua, E., Dutoit, T., Moinet, A., Pelachaud, C., Picart, B., Tilmanne, J., Wagner, J.: AVLaughterCycle: Enabling a virtual agent to join in laughing with a conversational partner using a similarity-driven audiovisual laughter animation. Journal on Multimodal User Interfaces 4(1), 47–58 (2010)

6. Petridis, S., Martinez, B., Pantic, M.: The mahnob laughter database. Image Vision Comput. 31(2), 186–202 (2013)

7. Janin, A., Baron, D., Edwards, J., Ellis, D., Gelbart, D., Morgan, N., Peskin, B., Pfau, T., Shriberg, E., Stolcke, A., Wooters, C.: The ICSI Meeting Corpus. In: Proceedings of the 2003 IEEE International Conference on Acoustics, Speech, and Signal Processing (ICASSP 2003), vol. 1, pp. 364–367 (2003)

8. Carletta, J.: Unleashing the killer corpus: experiences in creating the multi-everything AMI Meeting Corpus. Language Resources and Evaluation 41(2), 181–190 (2007)

9. Truong, K.P., van Leeuwen, D.A.: Automatic discrimination between laughter and speech. Speech Communication 49(2), 144–158 (2007)

10. Szameitat, D.P., Alter, K., Szameitat, A.J., Wildgruber, D., Sterr, A., Darwin, C.J.: Acoustic profiles of distinct emotional expressions in laughter. Journal of The Acoustical Society of America 126 (2009)

11. Scherer, S., Schwenker, F., Campbell, N., Palm, G.: Multimodal laughter detection in natural discourses. In: Ritter, H., Sagerer, G., Dillmann, R., Buss, M. (eds.) Human Centered Robot Systems. Cognitive Systems Monographs, vol. 6, pp. 111–120. Springer, Heidelberg (2009)

12. Suarez, M.T., Cu, J., Maria, M.S.: Building a multimodal laughter database for emotion recognition. In: Calzolari, N. (ed.) Proceedings of the Eight International Conference on Language Resources and Evaluation (LREC 2012). European Language Resources Association (ELRA), Istanbul (2012)

13. McKeown, G., Cowie, R., Curran, W., Ruch, W., Douglas-Cowie, E.: ILHAIRE laughter database. In: Proceedings of the LREC Workshop on Corpora for Research on Emotion Sentiment and Social Signals (ES 2012). European Language Resources Association (ELRA), Istanbul (2012)

14. Wagner, J., Lingenfelser, F., Baur, T., Damian, I., Kistler, F., André, E.: The Social Signal Interpretation (SSI) Framework - Multimodal Signal Processing and Recognition in Real-Time. In: Proceedings of The 21st ACM International Conference on Multimedia, Spain (2013)

15. Camurri, A., Coletta, P., Varni, G., Ghisio, S.: Developing multimodal interactive systems with EyesWeb XMI. In: Proceedings of the 2007 Conference on New Interfaces for Musical Expression (NIME 2007), pp. 302–305 (2007)

Real-Time Comprehensive Sociometrics for Two-Person Dialogs

Umer Rasheed[1], Yasir Tahir[3], Shoko Dauwels[2], Justin Dauwels[1], Daniel Thalmann[1], and Nadia Magnenat-Thalmann[3]

[1] School of Electrical and Electronic Engineering (EEE)
[2] CIRCQL, Nanyang Business School
[3] Institute for Media Innovation (IMI), Nanyang Technological University, Singapore

Abstract. A real-time system is proposed to quantitatively assess speaking mannerisms and social behavior from audio recordings of two-person dialogs. Speaking mannerisms are quantitatively assessed by low-level speech metrics such as volume, rate, and pitch of speech. The social behavior is quantified by sociometrics including level of interest, agreement, and dominance. Such quantitative measures can be used to provide real-time feedback to the speakers, for instance, to alarm to speaker when the voice is too strong (speaking mannerism), or when the conversation is not proceeding well due to disagreements or numerous interruptions (social behavior). In the proposed approach, machine learning algorithms are designed to compute the sociometrics (level of interest, agreement, and dominance) in real-time from combinations of low-level speech metrics. To this end, a corpus of 150 brief two-person dialogs in English was collected. Several experts assessed the sociometrics for each of those dialogs. Next, the resulting annotated dialogs are used to train the machine learning algorithms in a supervised manner. Through this training procedure, the algorithms learn how the sociometrics depend on the low-level speech metrics, and consequently, are able to compute the sociometrics from speech recordings in an automated fashion, without further help of experts. Numerical tests through leave-one-out cross-validation indicate that the accuracy of the algorithms for inferring the sociometrics is in the range of 80-90%. In future, those reliable predictions can be the key to real-time sociofeedback, where speakers will be provided feedback in real-time about their behavior in an ongoing discussion. Such technology may be helpful in many contexts, for instance in group meetings, counseling, or executive training.

1 Introduction

In recent years, human behavior has gained much attention in the information sciences community. Specifically, automatic analysis of human behavior has become a major research topic, because of its important potential applications and its scientific challenges. Human behavior involves various patterns of actions and activities, attitudes, affective states, social signals, semantic descriptions, and contextual properties [1]. A promising approach to human behavior understanding is to apply pattern recognition and modeling techniques to automatically and objectively deduce various aspects human behavior from different kinds of recordings and measurements, e.g., audio and video recordings [2].

A.A. Salah et al. (Eds.) : HBU 2013, LNCS 8212, pp. 196–208, 2013.

Speech analysis is one of the most common ways to analyze human behavior. Speaking mannerisms are a direct manifestation of human behavior, and play a vital role for the meetings to be pleasant, productive, and efficient [3]. If speaking mannerisms become mutually compatible and aligned, the meetings are more likely to be productive [4]. Appropriate feedback on speaking mannerisms and behavior during conversations may help to improve communications skills. This is especially true for real-time feedback, which allows the speaker to adjust on the fly.

In this paper, we aim to develop real-time algorithms to automatically quantify a variety of speaking mannerisms and social behavior in two-person dialogs for real-time sociofeedback (see Fig.1). Quantitative measures can provide a comprehensive picture of the behavior of participants in dialogs. In the following, we will briefly review related studies, and will highlight the novelties and contributions of this paper.

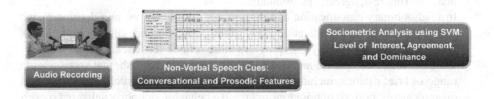

Fig. 1. System Overview. The system records audio data, computes several conversational and prosodic features, and from those features, computes levels of interest, agreement and dominance via SVM.

Several recent studies consider modeling and automatic detection of personality traits, social relations and social roles etc from speech recordings [5-14]. In [12-13], several efforts have been made in automatic detection of speaker traits, social signals, conflict, emotions etc from short clips. Also automatic detection of interest or activity levels in multi-party dialogs has recently been explored [15-16]. The concept of hotspots is introduced in [16] to identify periods of high interest in meeting recordings. In [17], emphasis and interest in conversations is inferred from speech pitch. Furthermore, in [18] a PDA-based system is proposed to extract interest levels in conversations. Interest level has also been investigated in computer-assisted learning [19]. Similarly, detection of agreement has been investigated in meeting scenarios such as broadcast conversations [20-23]. In most of those studies, the proposed algorithms are evaluated on the annotations from the ICSI corpus [22]. Dominance and similar concepts like emerging leader have been investigated in a similar manner. In social psychology, dominance is usually interpreted either as a personality characteristic or in relation to the hierarchical position of an individual within a group [24]. In [25-26], methods are proposed that detect dominance in multi-party dialogs in an automated fashion from non-verbal audio and visual cues.

The current studies on automated behavioral analysis of dialogs have the following limitations:

- In most studies, only one aspect of social behavior in dialogs is considered, e.g., dominance or activity level [15-25].

- Most of the recent literature only considers two levels of social behavior, e.g., active vs. non-active, or dominant vs. non-dominant [15, 19, 25, 26]. However, there have been studies that perform multi-level classification of personality traits, interest, conflict etc from short clips of 10-30s using lexical features [11-13].
- Typically, the speech corpus used for analysis and testing purposes is limited in scope, and mostly contains a specific kind of dialog, e.g. broadcast shows [9-11, 15-23, 26]. In most dialogs analyzed so far, the speakers tend to cooperate and the conversations proceed smoothly. Problematic scenarios such as conflicts, disagreements and boredom have received little attention [12].

In this paper, we introduce the following contributions and novelties:

- We consider multiple aspects of behavior in dialogs simultaneously, including a variety of speaking mannerisms (e.g., volume, pitch, and rate of speech) and social behavior (interest, agreement, dominance).
- Instead of binary classification of behavior (e.g., dominant vs. non-dominant), we consider multi-level classification (low, slightly low, normal, slightly high, high). As a result, the proposed system provides more refined feedback.
- We have collected a novel annotated speech corpus, in English, that spans a wide range of brief dialogs, including also problematic situations such as conflicts and disagreements, periods of boredom, aggressive behavior, or poorly delivered speech (e.g., low voice or fast pace). Each dialog in the corpus has been assessed by at least 5 people with regard to speaking mannerisms and social behavior (interest, agreement, dominance).
- The proposed automated algorithms have low computational complexity and can readily be used in real-time. Therefore, they can provide feedback while the dialog is still ongoing. Sociofeedback can be provided via many platforms, for example, smartphones, voice over IP (e.g., Skype), or humanoid robots (e.g., Nao robot).
- Our objective in the long term is to provide real-time feedback on social behavior in dialogs, for training purposes and also for therapy of psychiatric patients with deficits in social behavior.

Specifically, we propose the following approach. First, low-level speech cues are extracted from the audio recordings, e.g., volume, rate, and pitch of speech. We apply feature selection methods such as Information Gain (IG) and Correlation-based Feature Selection (CFS) to determine the most relevant low-level speech cues for quantifying social behavior [27-28]. We then train machine learning algorithms such as support vector machines (SVM) [29] with those features as inputs, to quantify certain aspects behaviors, i.e., level of interest, agreement, and dominance. We collected and annotated a new speech corpus to train the machine learning algorithms. Through this training procedure, the algorithms learn how the three sociometrics (level of interest, agreement, and dominance) depend on the low-level speech metrics, and consequently, are able to compute the sociometrics from speech recordings in an automated fashion in real-time, without further help of experts. The real-time sociometrics can be helpful to provide feedback to participants in dialogs.

In this paper, we limit ourselves to behavior detection of face-to-face two-person conversations. In the future, we intend to scale our system towards small-group interactions. We also plan to incorporate visual cues alongside, in order to attain more detailed sociometrics. The ultimate goal is not limited to feature selection/pattern recognition/classicification but development of a system that can provide sociofeedback for different types of social interactions, e.g. job interviews, business meetings, or group discussions [30].

The paper is structured as follows. In Section 2, we describe the collected speech corpus and our experimental setup. In Section 3, we elaborate on the low-level speech metrics. In Section 4, we specify the sociometrics, and explain our machine learning approach to automated prediction of sociometrics. In Section 5 we offer concluding remarks, and suggest several topics for future research.

2   Speech Corpus

The newly collected speech corpus contains 150 two-person conversations, each at least 2.5-3 minutes long. Consequently, the dataset consists of 300 individual audio recordings in total. The total number of individuals participating in the corpus is 22, of which 17 are males and 5 are females. The participants are students of Nanyang Technological University (NTU). The age of the students is from 18 to 30 (M=25, SD=1.20). The topics of conversations ranged from discussion of assignments, projects of students, to social and political views. In some of the dialogs, there are problematic situations such as conflicts and disagreements, periods of boredom, aggressive behavior, or poorly delivered speech (e.g., low voice or fast pace). The length of each recording is relatively long (2-3 minutes) as compared to other corpora [13-14, 22]. The 2-3 minute conversations provide overall sense of sociometrics and hence are useful in studying the design of appropriate sociofeedback. In the following, we discuss how we recorded the corpus, and how it has been annotated.

2.1   Experimental Procedure

The following section explains the procedure of experiment in detail:

1. First, we setup the recording system properly. We adopt easy-to-use portable equipment for recording conversations; it consists of lapel microphones for each of the two speakers and an audio H4N recorder that allows multiple microphones to be interfaced with the computer. The audio data is recorded in brief consecutive segments and sent to a central server running MATLAB. The speech is saved in a 2-channel audio .wav file in order to allow precise computation of overlap-related features such as interruptions.
2. The two participants sit about 1.5m apart so that each microphone only records the voice of the respective participant, and there is no interference from the other participant.
3. We attach the microphones to the participants in proper manner, in order to obtain a high-quality recording.
4. We brief the participants about the experiment. We provide them a list of topics that they can choose from. The two participants are asked to agree on a topic for the subsequent discussion. The topics of discussion range from small talk to heated debates on sports, politics, etc. We selected the topics of discussion carefully in order to evoke a variety of behaviors.

5. Only the two participants remain in the meeting room. The recording system is controlled remotely through a wireless connection.
6. We start the recording via a laptop remotely connected to the server.
7. We monitor the conversation remotely for about 2.5-3 minutes at least, without any interruption. Participants are allowed to talk as long as they wish. As the participants do not need to keep track of time, they can freely engage in the conversation.

2.2 Manual Annotation

Each audio recording in the corpus is annotated by a pool of at least 5 people ("judges"). There were 14 judges in total, each assessing a subset of the corpus. For each audio recording, the judges completed a questionnaire (see Table 1) related to speaking mannerisms and behavioral aspects of each participant. The responses range from 1 (low) to 5 (high). For example, if a participant seems bored, his interest level is annotated as "low"; in contrast, if the participant seems excited, then the interest level is assessed as "high". Table 2 shows the standard deviation of the annotations for the different values

Table 1. Questionnaire for sociometric assessment

Assessment of Speech Mannerism
This person was too loud.
This person was not audible.
This person screamed at other participants.
This person spoke too fast.
This person spoke too slow.
This person stuttered while speaking.
The speech clarity was satisfactory.
This person spoke in a monotonic way.
This person is not responsive.
This person interrupted the other participant(s).
Assessment of Social Behavior
This person seemed to be actively engaged in the conversation.
This person seemed to agree with what other person has to say.
This person seemed to be the dominant of the two.

Table 2. Standard deviation of manual annotation by multiple judges, for each level of interest, agreement, and dominance. "Low" corresponds to an average score below 1.5, "slighly low" is associated with an average score between 1.5 and 2.5, and so on.

Category	Low	Slightly Low	Normal	Slightly High	High
Interest	0.71	0.96	1.10	1.15	0.63
Agreement	0.63	0.84	0.74	0.92	0.64
Dominance	0.54	1.03	0.51	0.67	0.57

of each metric. As can be seen from that table, the standard deviation remains low for most of the classes, suggesting there is no large disparity among the judges. However, for certain classes the standard deviation is a little high.

3   Inferring Speech Mannerisms from Speech Cues

We consider two types of low-level speech metrics: conversational and prosody related cues. The conversational cues account for *who* is speaking, *when* and *how much*, while the prosodic cues quantify *how* people talk during their conversations. Non-verbal speech cues play a significant role in group conversations [9-11]. In the following, we briefly review the conversational and prosodic cues that we consider in this study. Then we explain how we infer speaking mannerisms from those cues.

3.1   Conversational Cues

In order to compute the conversational features, we first perform speech detection by means of a hidden Markov model (HMM) that uses energy-independent features [31]. This approach to speech detection is robust to low sampling rates, significant levels of noise, and variations in the distance between speaker and microphone. The speech detection algorithm works in real-time. The time taken for 2-3 min dialog takes 5-8 seconds on a laptop with 2GHz dual-core processor and 2GB RAM. Once the audio signals have been segmented in periods of speech and without speech, we compute the following conversational cues: the number of natural turns, speaking percentage, mutual silence percentage, turn duration, interjections, interruptions, failed interruptions, and response time (see Fig.2).

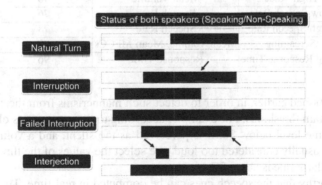

Fig. 2. Illustration of turn-taking, interruption, failed interruption, and interjection. Those conversational cues are derived from the binary speaking status (speaking vs. non-speaking). Periods of speaking and non-speaking are indicated in black and white respectively [30].

3.2   Prosodic Cues

We consider the following prosodic cues: amplitude, larynx frequency (F0), formants (F1, F2, F3), and mel-frequency cepstral coefficients (MFCCs); those cues are extracted from 30ms segments at a fixed interval of 10ms. Those cues fluctuate rapidly in time. Therefore, we compute various statistics of those cues over a time period of several seconds, including minimum, maximum, mean and entropy, in order to assess speaking mannerisms.

3.3 Speech Mannerism

From the speech cues, we assess a variety of speech mannerisms in real-time. This quantitative information can be provided to the speaker as feedback about an ongoing dialog. Specifically, we aim to detect the following speech mannerisms: the speech volume is too low/high, the speaker is screaming, the speech rate is too low/high, and the speaker is taking too much time to respond. The system monitors relevant speech cues for each speech mannerism (see Table 3), and checks whether any cue is abnormally low or high. For instance, low (high) speech volume is detected when the speech signal volume is below (above) a certain threshold. Likewise, fast speaking is detected when the speech rates is above a certain threshold. In order to set those thresholds, we analyze short clips of speech of approximately 10s each. From the scores provided by the judges, we can define speech mannerisms. For instance, when the average score for "This person was too loud" is 4.5 or higher, the speaker is considered to be speaking too loud. Similarly, when the average score for "This person spoke too slow" is 4.5 or higher, the speaker is considered to be speaking too slow.

Table 3. Prediction level for speech mannerisms

Speech Mannerism	Corresponding Feature(s)	Detection Rate(%)
Low Voice	Mean Volume	88
High Voice	Mean Volume	90
Low Speech Rate	Speech Rate	76
High Speech Rate	Speech Rate	78
Screaming	Mean Volume, Mean MFCCs	92
Long Response Time	Response Time	96

As we mentioned earlier, in order to detect such mannerisms from the speech cues, we choose certain thresholds. For example, according to the annotations of the speech corpus, a volume level below 30dB is perceived as too silent, and a volume level of above 80dB is usually considered too loud. We select the values of the thresholds such that the false-alarm rate is about 5%.

It is noteworthy that the speech cues can be computed in real-time. That also holds for detecting speech mannerism from those cues. Therefore, if any of these speech cues fall above or below a certain threshold, then the system can provide feedback in real-time to the participant. For instance, if the speech volume is too high, the system can inform the participant to lower the voice and vice versa.

Our results are summarized in Table 3-5. In Table 3, we list the sensitivity (detection rate) of the threshold-based detector for different speech mannerisms. Tables 4-5 show the confusion matrices for the classification of speech mannerisms. Overall, the results suggest that basic speech mannerisms can be detected accurately from speech cues.

Table 4. Confusion matrix for speech mannerisms: speech volume and rate

Speech Mannerism	Low	Normal	High	Classified as
	22	2	0	Low
Volume	3	36	2	Normal
	0	2	18	High
	19	1	0	Low
Speech Rate	6	23	3	Normal
	0	1	17	High

Table 5. Confusion matrix for speech mannerisms: screaming and long response time

Speech Mannerism	True	False	Classified as
Screaming	23	2	True
	2	48	False
Long Response Time	19	2	True
	1	48	False

4 Sociometrics

In this section, we describe how we quantify social behavior in dialogs. Specifically, we compute three sociometrics: level of interest, agreement, and dominance. Those sociometrics are inferred from combinations of speech cues. First we discuss how we can assess the relevance of the different speech cues for the three sociometrics. Next we explain how we infer the sociometrics in an automated fashion from selected speech cues.

4.1 Feature Selection

The speech cues tend to be highly correlated with some sociometrics, and totally uncorrelated with others. Consequently, it is crucial to select appropriate speech cues in order to predict the sociometrics. We apply two feature selection algorithms, viz. Information Gain (IG) and Correlation-based Feature Selection (CFS) [27-28], to determine the most relevant features for inferring each of the three sociometrics. In the following, we briefly review these two methods.

Information gain is one of the simplest of the attribute ranking algorithms. If A is a particular feature and C is the class (one of the 5 values of the sociometric), then the entropy $H(C)$ and $H(C|A)$ of the class before and after observing the feature respectively can be written as:

$$H(C) = - \sum_{c \in C} p(c) \log_2 (p(c)), \tag{1}$$

$$H(C|A) = - \sum_{a \in A} p(a) \sum_{c \in C} p(c) \log_2 (p(c)). \tag{2}$$

The amount by which the entropy of a particular class decreases is a measure of to the amount of information about the class provided by the feature, and is referred as

Table 6. Information gain and CFS subset merit of the features used for optimal classification

Category	Feature	Info Gain	CFS Subset Merit
Interest	Speaking %	1.130	0.718
	Turn Duration	0.564	0.540
	Mutual Silence	0.468	0.392
	Volume	0.420	0.312
	Response Time	0.392	0.192
Agreement	Interruptions	0.888	0.605
	Total Overlap	0.508	0.400
	Mutual Silence	0.227	0.191
	Larynx Frequency (F0)	0.212	0.166
	Volume	0.167	0.218
Dominance	Speaking % Difference	1.079	0.783
	Turns Difference	0.695	0.540

information gain. Hence each feature A_i can be scored by means of its information gain [23]:

$$IG_i = H(C) - H(C|A_i) = H(A_i) - H(A_i|C) = H(A_i) + H(C) - H(A_i, C). \qquad (3)$$

Correlation feature selection (CFS), on the other hand, evaluates subsets of features rather than individual features. This method accounts for the usefulness of individual features for predicting the class along with the level of inter-correlation between them. The CFS subset merit is high when the features in the subset are highly correlated with the class, and have low inter-correlation with each other. CFS subset merit is calculated as:

$$\text{Merit}_S = \frac{k\bar{r}_{cf}}{\sqrt{k + k(k-1)\bar{r}_{ff}}}, \qquad (4)$$

where Merit_S is the heuristic merit of a feature subset S containing k features, $\bar{r}_{cf}$ is the average feature-class correlation whereas $\bar{r}_{ff}$ is the average feature-feature inter-correlation [27].

Table 6 shows the results the Information Gain and CFS subset Merit for feature sets that yield best classification results. Usually the feature-sets include many features [32]. However, in such approach it becomes unclear what the key factors are, as the classifiers have many features as input. In this work, the feature-set for classification is kept small so that in future the system could be implemented for real-time sociofeedback on smartphones and humanoid robots etc. The table indicates that speaking percentage, turn duration, mutual silence percentage, volume, and response time are useful features for inferring the interest level; difference of turns and speaking percentage are good features for quantifying dominance; whereas interruptions, overlap, mutual silence percentage, volume, and F0 are relevant for quantifying agreement.

4.2 Multi-Class Classification

The sociometrics, including level of interest, agreement, and dominance, can take five values (1, 2, ..., 5). That value is estimated from relevant speech cues (cf. Table 6). Specifically, we view this problem as multi-class classification, where the number of class equal five.

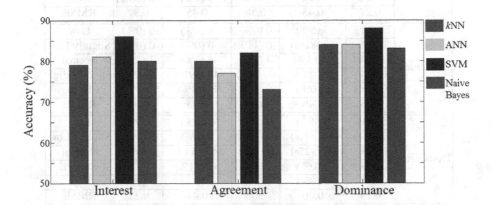

Fig. 3. 5-class classification performance for kNN, ANN, SVM, and naive Bayes

We train multi-class classifiers in a supervised manner using the newly collected speech corpus. The (rounded) average score provided by the judges serve as label for supervised learning. We consider four kinds of multi-class classifiers: k-nearest neighbor, Artificial Neural Network (ANN), Naive Bayes, and SVM [29, 33-35]. The 5-class classification performance of these four algorithms for each sociometric is summarized in Fig.3. The classification performance is computed by leave-one-out crossvalidation i.e. each sample n is classified by all of the instances in the training set N other than n itself, so that almost all of the data is available for each classification attempt. As can be seen from Fig.3, the SVM performs better than the three other classifiers for all three sociometrics. The confusion matrices obtained by SVM for level of interest, agreement and dominance are displayed in Table 7. As can be seen from Fig.3 and Table 7, the values of the sociometrics can be inferred reliable from the speech cues by SVM.

Now we will briefly address the computational complexity of our approach. It takes approximately 5 seconds to train each SVM, 5-10 seconds to compute the speech detection and speech cues from 2-3 min dialogs, and less than a second to perform multi-class classification by SVM. In order to infer sociometrics, the speech cues need to be calculated, followed by classification. The total time required for inferring the sociometrics from a 2-3 min dialog is therefore about 5-10 seconds using 2GB dual-core processor and 2GB RAM. Consequently, the sociometrics can be inferred in real-time, and as a result, they maybe used to provide feedback to the speakers in real-time, while the dialog is ongoing.

Table 7. Confusion matrix for level of interest, agreement, and dominance

Behavior	Low	Slightly Low	Normal	Slightly High	High	Classified as
	32 (91%)	7 (9%)	0 (0%)	0 (0%)	0 (0%)	Low
	3 (9%)	60 (80%)	7 (7%)	0 (0%)	0 (0%)	Slightly Low
Interest	0 (0%)	8 (11%)	88(87%)	6 (13%)	0 (0%)	Normal
	0 (0%)	0 (0%)	6 (6%)	36 (80%)	6 (14%)	Slightly High
	0 (0%)	0 (0%)	0 (0%)	3 (7%)	38 (86%)	High
	0.27	0.45	0.36	0.45	0.37	RMSE
	22 (78%)	3 (5%)	0 (0%)	0 (0%)	0 (0%)	Low
	5 (18%)	49 (82%)	10 (11%)	0 (0%)	0 (0%)	Slightly Low
Agreement	1 (4%)	8 (13%)	74 (79%)	4 (7%)	2 (3%)	Normal
	0 (0%)	0 (0%)	9 (10%)	45 (79%)	5 (8%)	Slightly High
	0 (0%)	0 (0%)	0 (0%)	8 (14%)	55 (89%)	High
	0.38	0.46	0.45	0.43	0.50	RMSE
	45 (93%)	3 (4%)	0 (0%)	0 (0%)	0 (0%)	Low
	3 (7%)	67 (84%)	4 (5%)	0 (0%)	0 (0%)	Slightly Low
Dominance	0 (0%)	10 (12%)	74 (87%)	6 (13%)	0 (0%)	Normal
	0 (0%)	0 (0%)	7 (8%)	39 (81%)	4 (10%)	Slightly High
	0 (0%)	0 (0%)	0 (0%)	3 (6%)	35 (90%)	High
	0.25	0.40	0.36	0.44	0.32	RMSE

5   Discussion and Conclusion

In this paper, we presented a novel approach towards comprehensive real-time analysis of speech mannerism and social behavior. Using low-level speech metrics, we quantified speech mannerisms and sociometrics, i.e., interest, agreement and dominance of the speaker. We collected a diverse speech corpus of two-person conversations; it allowed us to train machine learning algorithms for reliable 5-level classification of the sociometrics with speech cues as input features.

The combined metrics for speech mannerisms and social behavior provide a clear picture of human behavior in dialogs. For instance, high volume, high dominance coupled with low agreement level may suggest that the participant is upset and behaving aggressively. Similarly, low volume, low interest and low dominance may suggest that the participant is bored. More research is required to interpret the interplay between the three sociometrics.

Although preliminary, the results are encouraging: the sociometrics can be computed fast and reliably, enabling real-time sociofeedback. In current work, we are exploring applications of sociofeedback. In the future, we will include video recordings in conjunction with audio recordings. Our current speech corpus contains 150 conversations only. We intend to collect a much larger, diverse dataset, in order to generalize the findings. Also, the current work is limited to two-person face-to-face dialogs. In the future, we will scale the system to multi-party dialogs. The ultimate aim in this line of research is to develop template-based sociofeedback system for various types of social interactions, e.g., interviews, coaching sessions, group discussions.

Acknowledgements. This research project is supported in part by the Institute for Media Innovation (Seed Grant M4080824) Nanyang Technological University (NTU).

References

1. Salah, A.A., Gevers, T., Sebe, N., Vinciarelli, A. (eds.): HBU 2010. LNCS, vol. 6219. Springer, Heidelberg (2010)
2. Salah, A.A., Gevers, T., Sebe, N., Vinciarelli, A.: Challenges of human behavior understanding. In: Salah, A.A., Gevers, T., Sebe, N., Vinciarelli, A. (eds.) HBU 2010. LNCS, vol. 6219, pp. 1–12. Springer, Heidelberg (2010)
3. Pentland, A.S.: Honest Signals: How They Shape Our World. MIT Press (2008)
4. Pentland, A.S.: Socially aware, computation and communication. Computer 38(3), 33–40 (2005)
5. Barzilay, R., Collins, M., Hirschberg, J., Whittaker, S.: The rules behind roles: Identifying speaker role in radio broadcasts. In: Proceedings of Association for the Advancement of Artificial Intelligence (AAAI), pp. 679–684 (2000)
6. Liu, Y.: Initial study on automatic identification of speaker role in broadcast news speech. In: Proceedings of HLT/NAACL, pp. 81–84 (2000)
7. Hutchinson, B., Zhang, B., Ostendorf, M.: Unsupervised broadcast conversation speaker role labeling. In: Proceedings of International Conference on Acoustics, Speech and Signal Processing (ICASSP), pp. 5322–5325 (2010)
8. Salah, A.A., Lepri, B., Pianesi, F., Pentland, A.: Human Behavior Understanding for Inducing Behavioral Change: Application Perspectives. In: Salah, A.A., Lepri, B. (eds.) HBU 2011. LNCS, vol. 7065, pp. 1–15. Springer, Heidelberg (2011)
9. Vinciarelli, A., Salamin, H., Polychroniou, A., Mohammadi, G., Origlia, A.: From Nonverbal Cues to Perception: Personality and Social Attractiveness, pp. 60–72. COST 2102 Training School (2011)
10. Pianesi, F., Zancanaro, M., Not, E., Leonardi, C., Falcon, V., Lepri, B.: Multimodal support to group dynamics. In: Proceedings of Personal and Ubiquitous Computing, vol. 12(3), pp. 181–195 (2008)
11. Mohammadi, G., Mortillaro, M., Vinciarelli, A.: The Voice of Personality: Mapping Nonverbal Vocal Behavior into Trait Attributions. In: Proceedings of the International Workshop on Social Signal Processing, pp. 17–20 (2010)
12. Schuller, B., Steidl, S., Batliner, A., Vinciarelli, A., Sherer, K., Ringeval, F., Chetouani, M., Weninger, F., Eyben, F., Marchi, E., Mortillaro, M., Salamin, H., Polychroniou, A., Valente, F., Kim, S.: The INTERSPEECH 2013 Computational Paralinguistics Challenge: Social Signals, Conflict, Emotion, Autism. Interspeech (2013)
13. Schuller, B., Steidl, S., Batliner, A., Noth, E., Vinciarelli, A., Burkhardi, F., Son, R.V., Weninger, F., Eyben, F., Bocklet, T., Mohammadi, G., Weiss, B.: The INTERSPEECH 2012 Speaker Trait Challenge. Interspeech (2012)
14. Nishimura, R., Kitaoka, N., Nakagawa, S.: Analysis of relationship between impression of human-to-human conversations and prosodic change and its modeling, pp. 534–537. Interspeech (2008)
15. Gatica-Perez, D., McCowan, I., Zhang, D., Bengio, S.: Detecting Group Interest-Level in Meetings. In: Proceedings of International Conference on Acoustics, Speech and Signal Processing (ICASSP), vol. 1, pp. 489–492 (2005)
16. Hornler, B., Rigoll, G.: Multi-modal activity and dominance detection in smart meeting rooms. In: Proceedings of International Conference on Acoustics, Speech and Signal Processing (ICASSP), pp. 1777–1780 (2009)
17. Kennedy, L., Ellis, D.: Pitch-based emphasis detection for characterization of meeting recordings. In: Proceedings of IEEE Workshop on Automatic Speech Recognition and Understanding (ASRU), pp. 243–248 (2003)

18. Eagle, N., Pentland, A.: Social network computing. In: Proceedings of UBICOMP, pp. 289–296 (2003)
19. Germesin, S., Wilson, T.: Agreement detection in multiparty conversation. In: Proceedings of the 2009 International Conference on Multimodal Interfaces (ICMI), pp. 7–14 (2009)
20. Wang, W., Yaman, S., Precoda, K., Richey, C.: Automatic identification of speaker role and agreement/disagreement in broadcast conversation. In: Proceedings of International Conference on Acoustics, Speech and Signal Processing (ICASSP), pp. 5556–5559 (2011)
21. Kim, S., Valente, F., Vinciarelli, A.: Automatic detection of conflicts in spoken conversations: Ratings and analysis of broadcast political debates. In: Proceedings of International Conference on Acoustics, Speech and Signal Processing (ICASSP), pp. 5089–5092 (2012)
22. Janin, A., Baron, D., Edwards, J., Ellis, D., Gelbart, D., Morgan, N., Peskin, B., Pfau, T., Shriberg, E., Stolcke, A., Wooters, C.: The ICSI Meeting Corpus. In: Proceedings of International Conference on Acoustics, Speech and Signal Processing (ICASSP), vol. 1, pp. 364–367 (2003)
23. Hillard, D., Ostendorf, M., Shriberg, E.: Detection of Agreement vs. Disagreement in Meetings: Training with Unlabeled Data. In: Proceedings of HLT/NAACL, vol. 2, pp. 34–36 (2003)
24. Kalimeri, K., Lepri, B., Aran, O., Jayagopi, D.B., Gatica-Perez, D., Pianesi, F.: Modeling dominance effects on nonverbal behaviors using granger causality. In: Proceedings of the 2009 International Conference on Multimodal Interfaces (ICMI), pp. 23–26 (2012)
25. Rienks, R., Heylen, D.: Dominance Detection in Meetings Using Easily Obtainable Features. In: Renals, S., Bengio, S. (eds.) MLMI 2005. LNCS, vol. 3869, pp. 76–86. Springer, Heidelberg (2006)
26. Wang, W., Precoda, K., Hadsell, R., Kira, Z., Richey, C.: G. Jiva, G.: Detecting leadership and cohesion in spoken interactions. In: Proceedings of International Conference on Acoustics, Speech and Signal Processing (ICASSP), pp. 5105–5108 (2012)
27. Hall, M.A.: Correlation-based feature selection for machine learning. Ph.D. thesis, The University of Waikato (1999)
28. Yu, L., Liu, H.: Feature selection for high-dimensional data: A fast correlation-based filter solution. In: Proceedings of Machine Learning-International Workshop Then Conference, vol. 20, p. 856 (2003)
29. Burges, C.J.C.: A tutorial on support vector machines for pattern recognition. In: Data Mining and Knowledge Discovery, vol. 2(2), pp. 121–167 (1998)
30. Sarda, S., Constable, M., Dauwels, J., Dauwels (Okutsu), S., Elgendi, M., Mengyu, Z., Rasheed, U., Tahir, Y., Thalmann, D., Magnenat-Thalmann, N.: Real-Time Feedback System for Monitoring and Facilitating Discussions. In: Mariani, J., Devillers, L., Garnier-Rizet, M., Rosset, S. (eds.) Natural Interaction with Robots, Knowbots and Smartphones, pp. 375–387. Springer, New York (2013), doi:10.1007/978-1-4614-8280-2, ISBN: 978-1-4614-8279-6
31. Basu, S.: A linked-hmm model for robust voicing and speech detection. In: Proceedings of International Conference on Acoustics, Speech, and Signal Processing (ICASSP), vol. 1, pp. I-816–I-819 (2003)
32. Eyben, F., Wollmer, M., Schuller, B.: openSMILE - The Munich Versatile and Fast Open-Source Audio Feature Extractor. In: Proceedings of ACM Multimedia (MM), pp. 1459–1462 (2010)
33. Wang, J., Zucker, J.D.: Solving Multiple-Instance Problem: A Lazy Learning Approach. In: Proceedings of 17th International Conference on Machine Learning (ICML), pp. 1119–1125 (2000)
34. Haykin, S.: Neural Network, A comprehensive foundation. Neural Networks 2 (2004)
35. Rish, I.: An empirical study of the naive Bayes classifier. In: Proceedings of IJCAI 2001 Workshop on Empirical Methods in Artificial Intelligence, pp. 41–46 (2001)

VIP: A Unifying Framework for Computational Eye-Gaze Research

Keng-Teck Ma, Terence Sim, and Mohan Kankanhalli

National University of Singapore,
13 Computing Drive,
Singapore 117417
{ktma,tsim,mohan}@comp.nus.edu.sg

Abstract. Eye-gaze is an emerging modality in many research areas and applications. We present our VIP framework, which captures the dependence of eye-gaze on Visual stimulus, Intent, and Person. The unifying framework characterizes current eye-gaze computational models. It allows computer scientists to formally define their research problems and to compare with other work. We review the state-of-art computational eye-gaze research and applications with reference to our framework. With the framework, we identify gaps in eye-gaze research and present our work on the new research problem of attribute classification. The accuracy of 0.92 is achieved for classification of Introvert/Extrovert.

Keywords: eye-gaze, framework, visual attention, classification.

1 Introduction

"The eyes are the windows to the soul," goes an old English proverb. We agree. In fact, the window acts both ways: as a portal into the person's mind, and as a lens to perceive visual stimuli. In this regard, eye-gaze can provide invaluable clues both to the viewer, and to the object being viewed. This is the exciting premise, and promise, of research using eye-gaze data (see Section 2 for formal definition). Eye-gaze not only permits a fresh approach to existing problems (such as image segmentation), but also throws open a brave new world in which new applications may be created, and new inferences made.

We further advance eye-gaze research by proposing, in this paper, a unifying framework with which to reason about eye-gaze. We review existing models used in current eye-gaze research, and show that, while they are appropriate for their given applications, they are, alas, incomplete. We then propose our VIP eye-gaze framework, which captures the dependence of eye-gaze on Visual stimulus, Intent, and Person. By *visual stimulus* we include any visual modality, such as traditional images and videos, and also novel mediums like 3D images and games. By *intent* we refer to the immediate mental states such as purpose of viewing the stimulus, the emotions elicited by the stimulus, etc. Finally, by *person* we mean the persistent attributes of the viewer of the visual stimulus, including identity, gender, age, and personality types. Because we have done careful survey of the

A.A. Salah et al. (Eds.) : HBU 2013, LNCS 8212, pp. 209–222, 2013.
© Springer International Publishing Switzerland 2013

field, we believe our VIP framework unifies and subsumes all existing eye-gaze models.

We illustrate the utility of our framework with the novel application of inferring the demographic and personality factors of the viewer. As far as we can tell, this inference of demographic profile and personality type for eye-gaze is pioneering; no one else has done this before. Indeed, the reader will quickly see, that given our VIP framework, many new research opportunities lie just ahead.

2   VIP Framework

In a controlled environment, eye-gaze information of a healthy subject is the automatic and mostly subconscious response of the the viewer's mental processes to the stimulus.

The *visual stimulus* can be an image, a video (with optional audio), a binocular image or an interactive stimulus such as video game. Over the past 25 years, there are extensive and active studies of the properties of the stimulus which affects the eye-gaze [5,12]. In visual saliency literature, this is known as the bottom-up cues which include colors, brightness contrast and orientations.

The immediate mental processes and conditions have strong and obvious influences [37,33,6]. These processes include the top-down influences (knowledge, expectations, reward, and current goals) in the visual saliency literature. Emotions and fatigue are other examples of immediate mental factors. These factors will be coined as *intent*.

Recent psychological research shows that personal attributes of the viewer can affect the eye-gaze. These attributes are stable characteristics of the viewer which persist over months, years or even lifetime. Some persistent attributes are the viewer's identity, gender, age and personality types etc. Goldstein et al. [14] noted that "there are some significant differences in the observation behaviors between gender and age groups" when watching movies. Chua et al. [9] demonstrated that there are cultural differences in eye-movements. Personality has also been discovered as important in gaze modulation [31]. Shen and Itti's work on visual attention shows that the top-down influences are modulated by gender [34]. There are also identification systems which uses eye-gaze information as a biometric [3,15,30]. In layman's terms, the "who" and the "type" of the viewer are the persistent attributes. These attributes will be referred to as *person's* attributes.

We then formally define the eye-gaze data, E, as follows:

$$E = g(\{t_i, x_i, y_i, p_i, q_i, d_i, s_i, b_i, c_i\}_L, \{t_i, x_i, y_i, p_i, q_i, d_i, s_i, b_i, c_i\}_R) \qquad (1)$$

where g is a function of a *sequence* of eye-gaze data which

- i: the sequence number, i=1,2,...,n where n is the number of samples.
- t_i: time-stamp of the eye-gaze is related to the sampling rate. Usually the intervals are fixed.

- x_i: horizontal coordinates of the eye-gaze.
- y_i: vertical coordinates of the eye-gaze.
- p_i: horizontal location of the eye in the camera image (video-based eye-tracker only).
- q_i: vertical location of the eye in the camera image (video-based eye-tracker only).
- d_i: distance of the eye to eye-tracker.
- s_i: pupil size of the eye. (diameter or area)
- b_i: eye's opening magnitude. if $b_i = 0$, x_i,y_i and s_i are undefined since the eye is shut.
- c_i: tracking quality. (e.g. 0 = bad, 1 = excellent)
- L/R: left or right eye. Disparity can be used to compute depth or motion.

Together with other auxillary data, such as position of eye-tracker relative to screen/object of interests, 3D position of the eye-gaze can be computed. Examples of g are fixations, saccades and scanpaths vectors. If g is the sequences of fixations, then each fixation u_j is defined as:

$$u_j = \{\bar{x}, \bar{y}, \bar{s}, \bar{b}, t_{start}, t_{end}\} \tag{2}$$

where $\bar{x}$ is the mean value of all x_i in the fixation respectively, t_{start} is the start time of the fixation and t_{end} is the end time of the fixation. Thus g is defined as:

$$g = \{u_j\} \tag{3}$$

Since eye-gaze is influenced by the visual stimulus, intent and person; E can also be defined as a function of the 3 factors:

$$E = f(V, I, P) \tag{4}$$

where V is the visual stimulus' feature vector, I is the immediate mental states feature vector and P is the set of persistent personal attributes. Examples of V are the color and contrast feature vectors. Examples of I are tasks, skill levels or emotion states and emotion intensity. Examples of P are identity and gender.

In the ideal situation, g and f are equivalent. However, due to sensor's noise, computational limitations and incomplete model etc., they are not the exactly the same. In the computational models which we review, the objective of the system is to minimize some application-specific error measure between the ground-truth and the system's results. Hence, "$\approx$" is taken to mean the minimization of the error measure on the both sides of the equation in this paper.

We called this the VIP framework. With this framework as a reference, the features, computational model and assumptions of applications and research problems can be formally described and compared. New research directions are also easier to be discovered by identifying gaps of existing models. We will next survey the current models and applications and how they are completely defined by our framework.

Without loss of generality, consider the special case of which E depends only on V and I. Then either P is a constant or that E is independent of P. If P is a constant c, then we can rewrite $f(V, I, c)$ as $\underset{P=c}{f}(V, I)$. If P is not a constant, then f can be simplified to $f(V, I)$. For both conditions, we will refer to the simplified equations as the VI model. Also, f^{-1} means the inverse dependency of eye-gaze and the VIP factors. It does not necessarily imply that a corresponding f must exist.

2.1   V Models

V models assume that without an explicit goal, attention is predominantly dependent on bottom-up cues [11,17]. In other words, E is independent of P. And I is generally assumed to be the *same* for all viewers. Thus $\underset{I=c}{f}(V)$ defines these models.

It is commonly established that eye-gaze is a reliable proxy for visual attention and the V model is used by current saliency inference algorithms as the ground-truth model. In studies whereby ground truth saliency maps were generated from gaze data as the reference for comparison against computational models, a *single average* ground-truth saliency map was generated for each image [7,17,24,22]. Hence, the reference model is $\underset{I=c}{f^{-1}}(\{E\})$ where $\{E\}$ is the set of the fixations for all human subjects and $\underset{I=c}{f^{-1}}$ is a function, e.g. Gaussian filter [16], which outputs the group-truth saliency map.

The image segmentation problem is another open research problem which has successfully exploited the eye-gaze data for better accuracy [28]. Based on the premise that the human eye invariably fixates within the interior of an object, the algorithm attempts to find the set of boundary contours surrounding the fixation. The segmentation problem can be effectively transformed to an energy minimization problem. By using multiple fixations, its performance is better than the single random fixation method proposed by Mishra et al. [23]. Mishra et al.'s method is in turn better than pure image-based segmentation algorithms [1,2]. The assumption is that humans *generally* fixate on the most salient objects. The segmentation algorithm $h(f^{-1}(E), V)$ such that $f^{-1}(E)$ localizes the most salient object in the visual stimulus.

The real-time surveillance video summarization system proposed by Vural and Akgul can mix actions from different frames into the same video for more compact videos [35]. A real-time automated algorithm will detect video sections which actions which has occurred. Filtering is performed on the detected video section based on the fixations of the human operator. The $\underset{I=surveillance}{f^{-1}}(E)$ computes the ROI within the video frames V. For this application, I is implicitly assumed to be the mental state of a security personnel at work which is termed *surveillance*. The *task* of general surveillance, e.g. looking for suspicious actions and *domain knowledge* such as familiarity about the monitored environment are expected to be part of *surveillance* state of mind.

Generally, the V applications improve upon image-based algorithms by integrating E into the algorithms. There are many other such problems which benefited from the eye-gaze information [28,23,27].

2.2 I Models

The *general* I models assume that some I can completely determined the specially selected E, i.e. $E \approx f(I)$. One such example is the activity recognition system by Bulling et al. [8]. They recorded saccades, fixations and blinks using a wearable electrooculography (EOG) device. It can classify 5 activity classes: copying a text, reading a printed paper, taking handwritten notes, watching a video, and browsing the Web. It opens up the wider applicability of eye-gaze data to other activities that are difficult, or even impossible, to detect using common sensing modalities. $f^{-1}(E)$ identifies the activities I from the eye-gaze features E. In this paper, both V (office environment) and P are assumed to be non-informative and are not included in their computational model.

Another example is the "Midas-touch" problem in gaze-based interactions systems. The problem is to infer I from E so that the systems can determine if an eye-gaze is observing or actioning (e.g. issuing a command). Bednarik et al. have used the features extracted from fixations, saccades and pupillary responses to determine the intentions of the user [4]. Their experimental results indicated that fixations and saccades features are more reliable than pupillary responses for predicting intentions.

2.3 P Models

As eye movements are counterfeit resistant due to the complex neurological interactions and the extraocular muscle properties involved in their generation, they have been proposed as a viable biometric by various papers [15,30]. In these papers, the stimulus and the tasks are the same during the training and testing phases. Hence, $E \approx \underset{V=c1, I=c2}{f} (P)$.

Kinnunen et al. [20] implement a stimulus V independent eye-gaze biometric. They identified the histogram of all angles the eye gaze travels during a short period, few seconds, as a potential predictor of a person's identity regardless of V and I. Hence, $f^{-1}(E)$ infers the person's identity P from the histogram E. Their methods are unlike those which use the same task and stimulus for identification.

Zhang et al. [38] uses the features extracted from videos of subjects talking to distinguish identical twins. Out of their 6 features, 3 of them are gaze data: gaze change, pupil movement and eye opening magnitude. In their system, the V varies from the bedroom, recording studios to convention halls filled with people. Therefore, the V is not of consequences to the accuracy. Their P ranges across different age, gender, ethnicity etc. Their system is able to distinguish between identical twins who have many common personal attributes.

To the best of our knowledge, other than biometric applications, there are no application which infers P from E. However, there are many advantages of using eye-gaze to infer other personal attributes as compared to conventional methods such as questionnaires and vision-based approach. Thus, we propose a novel attribute classification problem which is to accurately infer the personal attributes from the eye-gaze. It assumes that given the some stimulus ($c1$), viewers having common intents ($c2$) but differing personal attributes will have different eye-gaze patterns. Hence, $\underset{V=c1,I=c2}{f^{-1}}(E)$ will infer P. We achieve the accuracy of 0.92 with 52 subjects viewing 2 images for introvert/extrovert classification. Further details are presented in Section 3.

2.4   VI Models

This model assumes that eye-gaze is dependent on both the visual stimulus features and the immediate mental states of the viewer, e.g. tasks or emotions.

The fixation prediction algorithms which combine both top-down influences and bottom-up cues are examples of applications which uses VI model. The objective of these algorithms is to find some $f(V, I)$ such that the error measure between $f(V, I)$ and E is small. The main directions of research are the methods of combining the features V and I and using new features [12].

In implicit tagging applications, affectiveness of the stimulus is automatically assessed from the viewer's various physiological signals, including pupillary dilation (PD) [25]. The PD is known to be influenced by emotions (I) and light intensity (V). Gao et al. attempts to use Adaptive Interference (AIC), with H* time-varying adaptive (HITV) algorithm to determine the emotions of the viewer [13]. Hence, $I \approx f^{-1}(E, V)$.

Yadati et al. has proposed a novel method for interactive personalized advertisement insertion for a single user [36]. The proposed system fuses in real time, the emotion type (from facial expressions), emotion intensity (from PD) and the affective values (from affective analysis of the video). The most effective advertisements are then inserted accordingly. It has better brand recall rate than the referenced affect-agnostic method. $f^{-1}(E, V)$ infers the I (emotional intensity) from both E (PD) and V (image-based affective analysis of the video segment).

Samsung Galaxy S IV is a smartphone with eye-tracking capability [32]. It can detect whether the user is looking at the screen and adjusts its response according to the displayed task. The "Smart Stay" feature will turn off the screen if the eyes are not detected; the "Smart Pause" feature will pause a playing video if the user looks away. Thus, $I \approx f^{-1}(E, V)$.

2.5   Other Cases

The VP and IP models are not sufficiently explored by researchers. The VP model assumes that given some constant I, the eye-gaze are dependent on both the visual stimulus and the personal attributes. One potential research problem is attribute-specific fixation prediction.

The IP model assumes that E is either independent of V or that V is fixed. We do not know of any application or research problem with such assumptions. One potential research problem would be the co-inference of I and P from E that is $(I, P) \approx \underset{V=c}{f^{-1}}(E)$. For example, given some specially selected video and the eye-gaze features, the algorithm can infer gender *and* emotions.

From our extensive literature survey, there is no research problem which is formulated as the most general VIP model. This is clearly a big and interesting gap to be filled. One of the first step is to build a dataset which consists of all 3 factors. Much scientific insights can be gained from a comprehensive dataset which consists of all 3 factors. For example, new discoveries about the relationship and patterns can be found. Co-inference of 2 or even 3 factors may be possible. We have built a VIP dataset which is available at http://mmas.comp.nus.edu.sg/VIP.html.

Table 1 summarizes the features and applications for the various VIP models. From the table, it is clear that V models are well-researched and there are research gaps to be filled in the other models, especially the various combinations of P.

Table 1. Comparison of various VIP models. The underlined application: attribute classification is our contribution in this paper. We also make our VIP dataset which comprises of the 3 factors available at http://mmas.comp.nus.edu.sg/VIP.html. We also suggest open research problems for VP and IP model.

Model	Features	Examples of applications/problems	References
V	color, brightness, contrast, depth region of interests	fixation prediction, bottom-up saliency, image segmentation, image annotations	[5,21,7,17,24,22] [28,23,27]
I	tasks, fatigue, emotions	activity classification, fatigue detection, emotions classification	[37,8]
P	identity, demographic, personality	biometric, attribute classification	[3,15,30,20] Section 3
VI	features of V and I	saliency models, video summarization, interactive advertisement	[12,19,36]
VP	features of V and P	attribute-specific fixation prediction	Open area
IP	features of I and P	$(I,P) = f^{-1}(E)$	Open area
VIP	features of V, I and P	VIP dataset	Open area

3 Attribute Classification

From the VIP framework, we have identified the new problem of personal attribute P classification from eye-gaze information E. We define V to be constant for the training and the inferencing. I is assumed to be free-viewing. Thus, the problem is defined as:

$$P = \underset{V=c, I=free-viewing}{f^{-1}} (E) \qquad (5)$$

where P is the persistent personal attribute, e.g. gender. $\underset{V=c, I=free-viewing}{f^{-1}}$ is the classifier which was trained on eye-gaze information of other subjects when free-viewing the same stimulus. The information is labeled with their corresponding P. E is the eye-gaze information of the test subject. This problem is a P model since the V and I are constants.

Many of the personal attributes, such as gender, age, culture and personality types are routinely collected by many organizations. These attributes are collectively known as demographic/personality profile. The profiling is used for marketing, personnel screening etc. The advantages of eye-gaze over other modalities are low latency, no purposeful thoughts required and it is non-obtrusive.

Personal attribute classification is analogous to taking a survey. The eye-gaze information in response to an image is similar to taking a survey at a subconscious level. Instead of questions, visual stimuli are presented. Similar to the question in a survey, only eye-gaze data of purpose-selected stimulus can accurately determine the value of the intended attribute.

3.1 Experimental Setup

The images were selected from the NUSEF [28] dataset, which contains both neutral and affective images. Out of 758 images, 150 were randomly selected.

72 subjects were recruited from a mixture of undergraduate, postgraduate and working adult population. The male and female subjects are recruited separately to ensure an even distribution. They were tasked to view the 150 images in a free-viewing settings (i.e. without assigned task). Each image was displayed for 5 seconds, followed by 2 seconds viewing of a gray screen. The images were displayed in random order. Their eye-gaze data was recorded with a binocular infra-red based remote eye-tracking device SMI RED 250. The recording was done at 120Hz. The subjects were seated at 50 centimeters distance from a 22 inch LCD monitor with 1680x1050 resolution. This setup is similar to other ones used in eye-gaze research [28].

Before start of the viewing experiment, the subjects also provided their demographic data: gender, age-group, ethnicity, religion, field of study/work, highest education qualifications, income group, expenditure group and nationality. 3 personality type questions are posed based on the Jung's Psychological types [18].

The recorded eye-gaze data were preprocessed with the SMI SDK to extract the fixations from the preferred eye as chosen by the subjects. The recorded data of the 52 subjects, 27 females and 25 males, who have fixations for more than 100 images were used for the attribute classification problems. The number of subjects are comparable to similar studies in eye-gaze experiments [31,10].

3.2 Features Selection

As this is the first work on using eye-movement data to classify demographic and personality attributes, there is no prior research to directly leverage on. From our preliminary inspections of the fixation data, we select the potential 20 features as follows:

- mean value of the horizontal coordinates, x, of the fixations: $\bar{x}$
- mean value of the vertical coordinates, y of the fixations: $\bar{y}$
- mean value of the fixations' duration: $\bar{d}$
- triangle matrix of covariance of x and y: σ_x, σ_y and σ_{xy}
- standard deviation of duration: σ_d
- standard deviation of pupil size divided by mean value of pupil size: $\sigma_p/\bar{p}$
- 1st fixation: x_1, y_1, d_1
- 2nd fixation: x_2, y_2, d_2
- fixation with the longest duration: x_L, y_L, d_L
- total fixation duration: D
- number of fixations: N

To select the relevant features for classification, a correlation analysis method was applied. The analysis is performed for each image separately. As an example, for the image "dog.jpg', the analysis is applied to $\bar{x}$ of all subjects and the corresponding attribute of the subjects (female=1, male=0). The zeroth lag of the normalized covariance function is used to compute the correlation coefficients and the hypothesis of no correlation. Each p-value is the probability of getting a correlation as large as the observed value by random chance, when the true correlation is zero. The correlation is defined as *significant* if $p - value < 0.05$. This means that the probability of observing a correlation due to statistical fluke is only 5%.

We want to select the features which are highly correlated with the attributes' values and have low $p - value$ for many images. Since each pair (feature,image) has a 0.05 probability of being *significantly* correlated due to random coincidences, the number of expected correlated images for a feature is $0.05*150 = 7.5$ for the set of 150 images. Therefore, only features which *significantly* correlates with the attribute for more than 7.5 images are selected. The results are summarized in Table 2.

Hence, the features E selected are:

- *Male/Female*: σ_x, σ_y, $\sigma_p/\bar{p}$
- *Religious/None*: $\bar{x}$, $\sigma_p/\bar{p}$, x_1, x_2, d_2, x_L, D, N
- *Extrovert/Introvert*: σ_{xy}
- *Sensing/Intuition*: $\bar{d}$, σ_d, y_1, y_2, d_2, d_L, D
- *Thinking/Feeling*: $\sigma_p/\bar{p}$, y_2, d_2, x_L, y_L

The correlation analysis results shows that *Male/Female* have different variations of fixations and that their pupillary dilations are different. For religiosity, the 2 groups fixated on different parts of the images ($\bar{x}$, x_1, x_2). The fixation durations also differs. For *Extrovert/Introvert* groups, only the σ_{xy} is found to be significant. For *Sensing/Intuition*, the various fixation durations features, $\bar{d}$, σ_d, d_2, d_L, D, correlates positively with the *Sensing* group. This corresponds well with the characteristic of *Sensing* type who will spend more time to examine a stimuli before making a judgment. In *Thinking/Feeling* groups, the $\sigma_p/\bar{p}$ feature is a good indicator for emotions and it correlates positively with the *Feeling* group. In summary, the correlation analysis are reasonable and consistent with prior knowledge or research results [34].

Table 2. Correlation Analysis. The values in the table shows the number of images which $p-value < 0.05$ for the feature. The features which have less than 7.5 $(0.05*150)$ images are considered to be statistical coincidences, and are not selected. The features which are selected as underlined.

	$\bar{x}$	$\bar{y}$	d	σ_x	σ_y	σ_{xy}	σ_d	$\sigma_p/\bar{p}$	x_1	y_1	d_1	x_2	y_2	d_2	x_L	y_L	d_L	D	N
Male/Female	1	1	0	<u>18</u>	8	6	0	<u>14</u>	2	2	0	5	4	4	2	3	0	3	3
Religious/None	<u>17</u>	2	5	3	6	3	3	<u>8</u>	<u>17</u>	1	3	<u>9</u>	5	8	<u>12</u>	4	5	<u>68</u>	<u>46</u>
Extrovert/Introvert	2	0	0	3	6	<u>8</u>	1	3	1	3	3	1	5	2	3	1	1	0	2
Sensing/Intuition	0	7	<u>16</u>	3	2	4	<u>10</u>	7	0	<u>9</u>	7	3	<u>8</u>	<u>13</u>	4	3	<u>12</u>	<u>12</u>	4
Thinking/Feeling	6	6	3	0	2	0	4	<u>20</u>	3	7	5	7	<u>11</u>	9	<u>12</u>	<u>14</u>	5	6	7

3.3 Classifier and Training

We used the standard linear SVM classifier in the Matlab Biometric Toolbox, with the default parameters and auto-scaling.

For cross-validation, we applied the leave-one-out method. This method is most suitable as there are insufficient number of subjects per image for k-fold cross-validation, or train-validate-test division.

3.4 Empirical Results and Analysis

Table 3 summarizes the experimental results. Except for gender, the mean accuracies are lower than the prior distribution. This validates our claim that only certain images are useful for certain attribute classification. This also indicates that differences of gaze information of gender are greater and can be more accurately differentiated. The maximum accuracies are higher than the prior distributions for all factors, indicating that it is possible to classify the factors for using those images respectively. Male/Female, Religious/None and Extrovert/Introvert classifiers have many images which have higher accuracy than prior probability. Thus it is easier to select an appropriate image to suit the application requirements for these attributes. The Religious/None attribute has the highest maximum accuracy (0.78) while the Extrovert/Introvert the lowest (0.66). This suggests that religiosity has more influence on eye-gaze information compared to Extrovert/Introvert attribute.

3.5 Classification Using Eye-Gaze from Multiple Images

We further conducted a set of experiments in which attributes are classified by gaze information of *multiple* images. There are many methods of combining the

Table 3. Accuracy of the classifiers. Prior probability refers to the prior proportion of the majority group. In our dataset, there are 27 females and 25 males subjects, thus prior probability for gender is $27/52 = 0.52$. Images refers to the number of images which classifiers' accuracies are higher than prior probability.

	prior	mean	max	images
Male/Female	0.52	0.54	0.75	94
Religious/None	0.63	0.58	0.78	46
Extrovert/Introvert	0.52	0.51	0.66	80
Sensing/Intuition	0.62	0.52	0.76	26
Thinking/Feeling	0.63	0.54	0.73	24

classifiers from single image classification. We experimented on the voting and tree ensemble methods.

The voting ensembles classifier is implemented as follows. For each subject, the classification results from the single image classifiers vote for the final class. For example, if a subject viewed 5 images and the respective classifiers' results are male, male, female, female, female; then the final classification result is female (3 votes vs 2 votes for male). For this method, the selection of the classifiers is critical to the accuracy rate. The selected single-image classifiers should be also independent for high accuracy. There are 3 selection methods. Using the single best classifier: *single*, using all classifiers: *all* and using the top k classifiers, k is the optimal number of classifiers: *greedy*.

We also use construct an decision tree method where each internal node is a single-image classifier.

The experimental results are shown in Table 4. Clearly, using multiple images outperforms even the best single image classifier. The *all* ensembles have the worst accuracies. This is consistent with our observations that only some images are suitable for attribute classification. The *tree* ensembles are generally good and only a few images are required. Thus it is suitable for applications which the users may not be willing to view too many images.

Table 4. Mean accuracy of the multiple image classifiers. For *greedy* and *tree*, the number in the parentheses indicate the number of classifiers selected. The best accuracies for each factor are underlined.

	single	all	greedy	tree
Male/Female	0.75	0.58	<u>0.87</u> (3)	0.85 (3)
Religious/None	0.78	0.65	<u>0.88</u> (8)	0.84 (2)
Extrovert/Introvert	0.66	0.53	0.80 (12)	<u>0.92</u> (2)
Sensing/Intuition	0.76	0.52	0.80 (3)	<u>0.92</u> (5)
Thinking/Feeling	0.73	0.54	<u>0.90</u> (13)	<u>0.90</u> (4)

Table 5. Some examples of applications and their corresponding VIP models

Application	Formulation	f/f^{-1}	E	V	I	P
Saliency [7]	$E \approx \underset{I=c}{f}(V)$	Information Maximization	Gaussian Filter of Fixations	Colors	Free-view	–
Saliency [24]	$E \approx \underset{I=c}{f}(V)$	Conspicuity, Normalization, Summation	Gaussian Filter of Fixations	Colors, Orientation	Free-view	–
Image Segmentation [28]	$V \approx \underset{I=c}{f^{-1}}(E)$	Energy Minimization	Fixations	Most Salient Object	Free-view	–
Video Summarization [35]	$V \approx \underset{I=c}{f^{-1}}(E)$	Energy Minimization	Gaze	Motions	Surveillance	–
Activity Recognition [8]	$I \approx f^{-1}(E)$	mRMR [26], SVM	Saccades, Fixations, Blinks	–	Activity	–
Midas Touch [4]	$I \approx f^{-1}(E)$	Normalization, SVM	Fixation	–	Act/ Observe	–
Biometric [20]	$P \approx f^{-1}(E)$	UBM [29], GMM	Gaze	–	–	Identity
Twins Identification [38]	$P \approx \underset{I=c}{f^{-1}}(E)$	Alignment, GMM, SVM	Gaze, Pupil Movement, Opening Magnitude	–	Talking	Identity
Implicit Tagging [13]	$I \approx f^{-1}(E,V)$	AIC, HITV	Pupillary Dilations	Intensity	Emotions	–
Smart Pause [32]	$I \approx f^{-1}(E,V)$	Proprietary	Gaze	Video/ Other	Pause/ Play/Other	–
Interactive Ads [36]	$I \approx f^{-1}(E,V)$	Fusion	Pupillary Dilations	Affect	Emotions	–
Attribute Classification	$P \approx \underset{V=c1,I=c2}{f^{-1}}(E)$	Correlation, SVM	Fixations	Specific Images	Free-View	Demography, Personality

4   Conclusion

In conclusion, we proposed a novel and unifying VIP framework which formally defines the eye-gaze computational models. This framework will facilitate the advances of computational eye-gaze research as new problems can be more easily identified. Table 5 shows some examples of eye-gaze applications and their VIP formulations. Secondly, we identified the new research problem: attribute classification. Thirdly, we have built a complete VIP dataset and make it publicly available.

Acknowledgments. This work is funded by the A*STAR PSF Grant No. 102-101-0029 on Characterizing and Exploiting Human Visual Attention for Automated Image Understanding and Description.

References

1. Arbeláez, P., Cohen, L.: Constrained image segmentation from hierarchical boundaries. In: CVPR 2008, pp. 1–8. IEEE (2008)
2. Bagon, S., Boiman, O., Irani, M.: What is a good image segment? a unified approach to segment extraction. In: Forsyth, D., Torr, P., Zisserman, A. (eds.) ECCV 2008, Part IV. LNCS, vol. 5305, pp. 30–44. Springer, Heidelberg (2008)
3. Bednarik, R., Kinnunen, T., Mihaila, A., Fränti, P.: Eye-movements as a biometric. In: Image Analysis, pp. 16–26 (2005)
4. Bednarik, R., Vrzakova, H., Hradis, M.: What do you want to do next: a novel approach for intent prediction in gaze-based interaction. In: Proceedings of the Symposium on Eye Tracking Research and Applications, pp. 83–90. ACM (2012)
5. Borji, A., Itti, L.: State-of-the-art in visual attention modeling. IEEE Transactions on Pattern Analysis and Machine Intelligence 35(1), 185–207 (2013)
6. Bradley, M.M., Miccoli, L., Escrig, M.A., Lang, P.J.: The pupil as a measure of emotional arousal and autonomic activation. Psychophysiology 45(4), 602–607 (2008)
7. Bruce, N., Tsotsos, J.: Saliency based on information maximization. Advances in Neural Information Processing Systems 18, 155 (2006)
8. Bulling, A., Ward, J., Gellersen, H., Troster, G.: Eye movement analysis for activity recognition using electrooculography. Pattern Analysis and Machine Intelligence 33(4), 741–753 (2011)
9. Chua, H., Boland, J., Nisbett, R.: Cultural variation in eye movements during scene perception. Proceedings of the National Academy of Sciences of the United States of America 102(35), 12629–12633 (2005)
10. Dorr, M., Martinetz, T., Gegenfurtner, K., Barth, E.: Variability of eye movements when viewing dynamic natural scenes. Journal of Vision 10(10) (2010)
11. Elazary, L., Itti, L.: Interesting objects are visually salient. Journal of Vision 8(3) (2008)
12. Frintrop, S., Rome, E., Christensen, H.I.: Computational visual attention systems and their cognitive foundations: A survey. ACM Transactions on Applied Perception (TAP) 7(1), 6 (2010)
13. Gao, Y., Barreto, A., Adjouadi, M.: Monitoring and processing of the pupil diameter signal for affective assessment of a computer user. In: Jacko, J.A. (ed.) Human-Computer Interaction, Part I, HCII 2009. LNCS, vol. 5610, pp. 49–58. Springer, Heidelberg (2009)
14. Goldstein, R., Woods, R., Peli, E.: Where people look when watching movies: Do all viewers look at the same place? Computers in Biology and Medicine 37(7), 957–964 (2007)
15. Holland, C., Komogortsev, O.V.: Biometric identification via eye movement scanpaths in reading. In: 2011 International Joint Conference on Biometrics (IJCB), pp. 1–8. IEEE (2011)
16. Judd, T., Durand, F., Torralba, A.: A benchmark of computational models of saliency to predict human fixations. Tech. rep. MIT (January 2012)
17. Judd, T., Ehinger, K., Durand, F., Torralba, A.: Learning to predict where humans look. In: IEEE International Conference on Computer Vision (ICCV) (2009)
18. Jung, C.G., Baynes, H., Hull, R.: Psychological types. Routledge, London (1991)
19. Katti, H., Yadati, K., Kankanhalli, M., Chua, T.S.: Affective video summarization and story board generation using pupillary dilation and eye gaze. In: 2011 IEEE International Symposium on Multimedia (ISM), pp. 319–326. IEEE (2011)
20. Kinnunen, T., Sedlak, F., Bednarik, R.: Towards task-independent person authentication using eye movement signals. In: Proceedings of the 2010 Symposium on Eye-Tracking Research & Applications, pp. 187–190. ACM (2010)

21. Lang, C., Nguyen, T.V., Katti, H., Yadati, K., Kankanhalli, M., Yan, S.: Depth matters: influence of depth cues on visual saliency. In: Fitzgibbon, A., Lazebnik, S., Perona, P., Sato, Y., Schmid, C. (eds.) ECCV 2012, Part II. LNCS, vol. 7573, pp. 101–115. Springer, Heidelberg (2012)

22. Le Meur, O., Le Callet, P., Barba, D., Thoreau, D.: A coherent computational approach to model bottom-up visual attention. Pattern Analysis and Machine Intelligence 28(5), 802–817 (2006)

23. Mishra, A., Aloimonos, Y., Cheong, F.L.: Active segmentation with fixation. In: 2009 IEEE 12th International Conference on Computer Vision, pp. 468–475. IEEE (2009)

24. Ouerhani, N., Von Wartburg, R., Hugli, H., Muri, R.: Empirical validation of the saliency-based model of visual attention. Electronic Letters on Computer Vision and Image Analysis 3(1), 13–24 (2004)

25. Pantic, M., Vinciarelli, A.: Implicit human-centered tagging [social sciences]. IEEE Signal Processing Magazine 26(6), 173–180 (2009)

26. Peng, H., Long, F., Ding, C.: Feature selection based on mutual information criteria of max-dependency, max-relevance, and min-redundancy. IEEE Transactions on Pattern Analysis and Machine Intelligence 27(8), 1226–1238 (2005)

27. Ramanathan, S., Katti, H., Huang, R., Chua, T.S., Kankanhalli, M.: Automated localization of affective objects and actions in images via caption text-cum-eye gaze analysis. In: Proceedings of the 17th ACM International Conference on Multimedia, pp. 729–732. ACM (2009)

28. Ramanathan, S., Katti, H., Sebe, N., Kankanhalli, M., Chua, T.-S.: An eye fixation database for saliency detection in images. In: Daniilidis, K., Maragos, P., Paragios, N. (eds.) ECCV 2010, Part IV. LNCS, vol. 6314, pp. 30–43. Springer, Heidelberg (2010)

29. Reynolds, D.A., Quatieri, T.F., Dunn, R.B.: Speaker verification using adapted gaussian mixture models. Digital Signal Processing 10(1), 19–41 (2000)

30. Rigas, I., Economou, G., Fotopoulos, S.: Human eye movements as a trait for biometrical identification. In: 2012 IEEE Fifth International Conference on Biometrics: Theory, Applications and Systems (BTAS), pp. 217–222. IEEE (2012)

31. Risko, E.F., Anderson, N.C., Lanthier, S., Kingstone, A.: Curious eyes: Individual differences in personality predict eye movement behavior in scene-viewing. Cognition (2011)

32. Samsung Galaxy S4 - Life Task, http://www.samsung.com/global/microsite/galaxys4/lifetask.html#page=pausescroll (accessed April 2, 2013)

33. Schleicher, R., Galley, N., Briest, S., Galley, L.: Blinks and saccades as indicators of fatigue in sleepiness warnings: looking tired? Ergonomics 51(7), 982–1010 (2008)

34. Shen, J., Itti, L.: Top-down influences on visual attention during listening are modulated by observer sex. Vision Research 65, 62–76 (2012)

35. Vural, U., Akgul, Y.S.: Eye-gaze based real-time surveillance video synopsis. Pattern Recognition Letters 30(12), 1151–1159 (2009)

36. Yadati, K., Katti, H., Kankanhalli, M.: Interactive video advertising: A multimodal affective approach. In: Li, S., El Saddik, A., Wang, M., Mei, T., Sebe, N., Yan, S., Hong, R., Gurrin, C. (eds.) MMM 2013, Part I. LNCS, vol. 7732, pp. 106–117. Springer, Heidelberg (2013)

37. Yarbus, A., Haigh, B., Rigss, L.: Eye movements and vision, vol. 2. Plenum Press, New York (1967)

38. Zhang, L., Nejati, H., Foo, L., Ma, K.T., Guo, D., Sim, T.: A talking profile to distinguish identical twins. In: Proceedings of the 10th International Conference on Automatic Face and Gesture Recognition. IEEE (2013)

Head, Shoulders and Hips Behaviors during Turning

Nesrine Fourati and Catherine Pelachaud

LTCI, Telecom ParisTech, France
{nesrine.fourati,catherine.pelachaud}@telecom-paristech.fr

Abstract. Turning behavior is part of the basic library of motor synergies. It involves a complex interplay between the different body parts. In this study, we investigate the behavior of shoulders, hips and head during walking and turning tasks with various emotional states and different angles. We found that shoulders and hips follow a strong linear relationship during turning with different angles and styles of walk, while the head behavior is affected by these variables.

Keywords: Turning, Head behavior, Shoulders movement, Hips movement.

1 Introduction

The turning task, and more generally the change of direction in locomotion, was studied in many fields of research including clinical domain, neuroscience, computer animation, locomotion behavior annotation, analysis and synthesis. Turning can be considered as a part of the basic library of motor synergies characterized with an adaptive and stable behavior [1], [2]. Turning behavior involves a complex interplay between the different body parts. Previous researches revealed interesting founding that concern the interaction between the trunk, the head, the eyes [3], and also the coordination between lower body parts [2] during turning task. However, the coordination between shoulders and hips during turning movement has not been widely studied. The interaction between head and trunk movement during turn was mostly studied in turns within a restricted range around 90 °. Only few studies investigated the head and trunk behavior during turning task from different angles [4]. Since the head and trunk movement were studied on neutral turning behavior, it is still unclear whether they depends on the style of walk during turning task.

In the following section, we will discuss the different properties of turning task found in previous works. Section 3 is devoted to the description of the databases that we used in this study and the segmentation of walking sequences. In Section 4, we will investigate the relationship between shoulders and hips during turning with different angles along with different styles of walk. Finally we will study the head and trunk behavior during turning with different angles and walk styles.

A.A. Salah et al. (Eds.) : HBU 2013, LNCS 8212, pp. 223–234, 2013.
© Springer International Publishing Switzerland 2013

2   Turning Behavior Properties Studied in Previous Works

Turning behaviors have been studied from a biomechanical point of view. Several approaches studied the trajectory of one or several limbs (mainly pelvis and head) in the space. They focused on the curvature-velocity relationship. Based on the walking trajectories, these studies showed that a power law controls the relation between radius of curvature and velocity of the followed path in cyclic trajectories [5], [6]. This rule is probably the most known assumption used in turning behavior studies from curved trajectories, but it has recently been extended to a single turning task [1]. However, the displacement of the body in the space is not enough to understand the behavior of turning. Thus it is important to study the coordination between the different body parts during turning.

The coordination of lower body limbs has also received a high level of interest in the studies aiming to understand the turning task. This is because the locomotion behavior is mainly and not only based on the production of a motor pattern via lower limbs coordination. It has been shown that the coordination at the level of lower limbs shifts from a symmetric to an asymmetric mode when the person change the direction of walk [2]. The asymmetric mode of coordination at the level of the lower limb was explained with the stabilizing mechanisms for postural control [2].

Other studies focused on the properties related to upper body parts during turning task. It has been shown that upper body parts anticipate the movement toward the direction of turn before lower body parts and that the head systematically shifts toward turns direction before the trunk does [4]. This indicates the role of the head as an inertial guidance platform to which are referred the movements of the other body segments [2]. This anticipation turned out to be occurred at a constant distance rather than at a constant duration before a turn [4]. The anticipation of head direction change to the direction of turn has been used as a mean to detect turning onset and offset [7]. It was also found that there is a strong relationship between head, eyes and body orientation in the locomotion as well as turning behaviors [2], [3],[4].

Apart from the anticipatory orientation of the head, the stabilization of head orientation during turning is considered as a second main factor affecting head movement during turning behavior [4], [2], [3]. The anticipation and stabilization mechanisms are both combined in turning behavior [2]. It has been shown that the head can stabilize itself by looking toward the new direction of walk during turning task. Only few studies investigate the effect of different turning angles on the head behavior during turning [4]. Besides, the effect of the walk style on the head behavior is still unclear. In our work, we study the effect of the angle of turn and the style of walk on the head behavior during turning. Previous works described the head behavior during turning through the maximum orientation of the head around the yaw axis. Two references were used to determine this measure; the heading and the trunk [4]. We used these measure to study the head orientation during turning with respect to the trunk and to the trajectory of walk.

Although several properties of turn were studied previously, studying the relationship between lower and upper body parts to get some insights into how lower and upper body parts are coordinated received little consideration in the studies related to the analysis of walking and turning behavior. In this paper we also studied the relationship between shoulders and hips movement during walk and turning behavior with different angles and different styles of locomotion.

3 Databases Description

In this work, two different databases recorded with two different inertial motion capture systems were used [8], [9]. The first database (eNTERFACE08 3D) is devoted to the study of neutral turning behavior with different angles while the second database (Acted emotional walking database) is used to study the effect of the style of walk on walking and turning behavior with 180 ° turn angle.

In general, in databases of turning behaviors two types of turns are differentiated: Constrained [5] turns and Unconstrained [9] turns (See Fig. 1). In the first type of turn, the person is asked to follow a specific trajectory predefined in advance (See Fig. 1 a)). The advantage of this recording is that there are more accurate information about the angle of turn and the trajectory of the body limbs in space. However, it can result in a non-natural behavior of walking and turning tasks since the person is always looking at the predefined trajectory. In unconstrained turns recording, the person is asked to turn around some obstacles that define the turn angle(See Fig. 1 b)). Both databases that we used in our study are based on the recording of unconstrained turns.

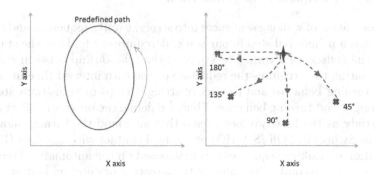

Fig. 1. Two types of turns: a) Constrained turn with predefined path, b) Unconstrained turns

3.1 eNTERFACE08 3D Database

The eNTERFACE08 3D database is described in details in [9]. The movement of the body was recorded through the inertial motion capture system

Animazoo [10]. This database contains, among others, walking sequences containing turning task with different turn angles for 41 subjects. A single turn was performed for each walking sequence. For turning task, the subjects were asked to walk straight starting from a point drawn on the floor until they reached a line (which was also drawn on the floor) from which they must change the direction of walk to reach another point (See Fig. 1 b)). The angles of the direction change were 45 °, 90 °, 135 ° and 180 °.

3.2   Acted Emotional Walking Database

The acted emotional walking database was recorded in order to analyze different styles of walking behavior. The intertial motion capture system Xsens [11] was used to record the movement of the whole body (ignoring fingers). The walking behavior of 11 actors (6 female and 5 male) were captured while they expressed 8 emotional states (Joy, Anger, Panic Fear, Anxiety, Sadness, Shame, Pride and Neutral) described with 3 scenarios. The database is described in details in [8].

In this study, only the walking sequences of seven subjects (4 female and 3 male) that are the more expressive among all the subjects were selected. Four styles corresponding to the expression of four emotions: Pride, Anger, Anxiety and Sadness were selected. Previous researches showed that the expression of those styles of walk has a significant influence on the head movement [12]. The actors were not aware of the study of turning behavior. They were rather focused on the style of walk.

3.3   Walking Sequences Segmentation

The segmentation of walking sequences into straight walks sequences and turning movement is a primordial step in our work. It requires to find out the start (onset) and end (offset) of a turn. The study of the relationship between shoulders and hips during turn requires the reduction of the turn interval time in order to focus on turning behavior and to remove straight steps or transitions steps between straight and turning behavior. Thus, we define the onset and offset of turn for this study as the first two foot events that surround the turning movement such as the Swing Heel Off (SW HO) or the heel contact with the floor [13]. The segmentation of walking sequences was first based on the automatic detection of turn instant, and second on the automatic detection of onset and offset of turn. Both the detection of turn instant and turn boundaries (onset and offset) were based on turning angles. Turning angles were measured from hips and shoulders vector orientation around the yaw axis (See Fig. 2).

- **Turn instant detection;**
  Since all the turns were performed with 180 ° in the emotional walking database, the turn instant was detected as the frame in which the turning angle reaches 90 °. Using the prior knowledge that there is only one turning task in each walking sequence of eNTERFACE08 3D database, the turn instant was defined as

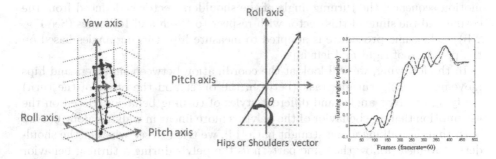

Fig. 2. The measure of Turning angles from hips and shoulders vector orientation around the yaw axis : a) Hips and shoulders vectors based on global positions of joints, b) Turning angle of Hips or Shoulders vector measured at a specific frame, c) Turning angles of hips and shoulders vector for all the sequence

the frame corresponding to the average of turning angle values related to shoulders or hips vector orientation.

- **Turn onset and offset determination;**
  The determination of turn onset and offset is based on the turn instant:
  - First we detect the occurrence of all the foot events in the walking sequence,
  - Second we detect the turning boundaries frames defined as the first local maximum/minimum of turning angles that occur before and after the turn instant,
  - Finally we define the turn onset as the foot event that occurs before the first turning boundary and the turn offset as the foot event that occurs after the second turning boundary. Only few false detection of turn offset and onset instant were detected and corrected by hand (the percentage of false detection was: 24% for 45°, 4.87% for 90°, 2.43% for 135° and 0% for 180°).

4   The Relationship between Shoulders and Hips during Walk and Turn

The relationship between upper and lower parts and their coordination received little consideration in the studies related to walking and turning behavior. In this section, we investigate the relationship between shoulders and hips during walking and turning with different angles and different emotions. We focus on the movement of shoulders and hips in the horizontal plane, that is the orientation of the vectors around the yaw axis. We use the global positions defined in the spatial coordinate system (that reflects the real world) to measure the orientation of the shoulders and hips vectors defined respectively with left and right shoulders positions and left and right hips positions (See Fig. 2 a)). At each frame of the motion sequence, the turning angle of the shoulders vector is deduced from the cosine and the sinus of this vector with respect to Pitch and Roll axes (See Fig. 2 b)). The same procedure is adopted to measure hips turning angles based on the positions of right and left hips.

In the following, we will look at the coordination between shoulders and hips movement during turning task (between the onset and the offset of the turn) studying different angles and different styles of turning behavior. Based on the assumption that the behavior of the pelvis is more linear in walking along curved path than in walking along straight path [14], we tried to see whether the shoulders movement follow the same pattern as the pelvis during a turning behavior and if maintains the same properties for different angles and different styles of walk.

4.1   Shoulders and Hips Relationship during Walk and Turn with Different Angles

We used the eNTERFACE08 3D database to study the behavior of shoulders with regards to the behavior of hips in turning task with different angles. We tried to see whether there is a linear relation between those two different body parts for different turn angles. Using the results of motion sequences segmentation, we fit a linear model to the data projected in shoulders and hips turning angle space between the onset and offset of turn. We found that the shoulders and hips movement are related through a positive linear relationship during turning behavior (see Fig. 3). The coefficient of determination (R^2) was measured for each linear model fitted to the relationship between shoulders and hips between turn onset and turn offset. After applying One-way Anova, we found that the angle that characterized the turning movement had a significant effect on the value of R^2 ($p < 0.001$). The higher is the turning angle, the higher is the average value of R^2 for all the samples (See Table 1).

To measure the global properties of the linear relationship between shoulders and pelvis movement, we fitted the linear model to all the samples of the eNTERFACE08 3D database for each of the four sets of turning behavior (related to 45°, 90°, 135° and 180° angles). Figure 3 illustrates the linear regression models for the samples related to each set of turning behavior. The corresponding R^2 for each linear model are shown in Table 1. They indicate a strong linear relationship between shoulders and hips movement during turning task with different angles. The low value of R^2 related to 45° turns is mainly due to the variation of turning behavior with 45° among the subjects ; since the turning task was unconstrained, subjects tend to turn with angles different from 45° (mostly lower than 45°). Overall, the higher was the turn angle the stronger was the relationship between hips and shoulders with slight differences in the coefficient of the model between 90°, 135° and 180° (See Fig. 3 where the 95% interval of confidence diminishes as turn angle increases).

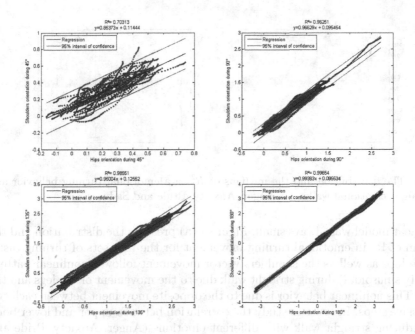

Fig. 3. Positive linear relationship between hips and shoulders movement for a) 45 ° turn angle, b) 90 ° turn angle, c)135 ° turn angle, d)180 ° turn angle

Table 1. The results of fitting a linear model to the shoulders-hips relationship in eNTERFACE08 3D database

Parameters	45 °	90 °	135 °	180 °
Average of R^2	0.9057	0.9783	0.9927	0.9973
Linear model coefficients	(0.8537,0.1144)	(0.9963,0.0955)	(0.95,0.1255)	(0.9938,0.0855)
R^2 of the linear model fitted to all the samples	0.7031	0.9625	0.9855	0.9965

4.2 Shoulders and Hips Relationship during Walk and Turn Back with Different Emotions

Although we previously showed the strength of the linear relationship between shoulders and pelvis movement during turning with different angles and especially for 180 °, it is important to see whether we obtain the same results when studying different styles of walking and turning behavior. The acted emotional walk database was used for this purpose. After applying One-way Anova, we found that there was a significant effect of the emotions and all the subjects on the coefficient of determination R^2 and on the slope of the linear model (P<0.001). However, the standard deviation of R^2 for all the samples was 0.0047 (R^2 ranged from 0.9526 to 0.9999) which means that the variance that explained

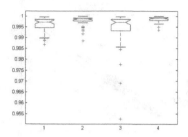 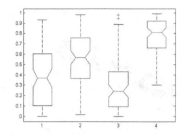

Fig. 4. The distribution and the medians of R^2 in a)emotional turning behavior and b) straight emotional walks, for Anger, Anxiety, Pride and Sadness

the linear model was always small. Figure 4 (a) presents the distribution and the median of R^2 in emotional turning movement for the four sets of turning task.

The hips as well as the shoulders vector movement follow a nonlinear pattern (mostly sinusoidal) during straight walk due to the movement of the legs and the arms. This nonlinear behavior is due to the opposite movement between each two successive steps. In order to study the correlation between upper and lower body parts during straight walk with different emotions (Anger, Anxiety, Pride and Sadness), we applied One-way Anova on the coefficient R^2 for the four emotions studied in our database. We found that emotions have a significant main effect on the correlation between shoulders and pelvis movement during straight walks. Figure 4 (b) shows that the differences between the medians and the distribution of R^2 between emotions are highly significant. The higher median value of R^2 was assigned to the sad emotional walks while the lower median value of R^2 was related to the pride emotional walks. This can be explained as actors tend to walk slowly with less variability of upper body parts and small foot strides. This behavior results in similar patterns between shoulders and hips. Unlike sadness expression, the actors express pride with large foot strides and a large amount of arms swings which leads to an opposite pattern of shoulders with respect to the hips. Anger and Anxiety expression included a significant change at the level of upper body parts as well as lower body parts.

5   Head Behavior during Turning

To be able to compare our results with the results found in previous works, we employ the same parameters used to study the stabilization of head during turn [4]. Thus, the analysis of head behavior was based on three features. The first and second feature represent the relative maximum relative head yaw during turning with respect to two references: heading and trunk yaw. Heading was measured based on the trajectory of body center of mass (CoM) in the space as described in [3]. In the following sections we use the term head-trunk yaw and head-heading yaw to refer respectively to the maximum orientation of the head with respect to the trunk and the heading. The third feature corresponds to the occurrence of the maximum relative head yaw (in seconds) with respect to the onset of turn. As the SW HO is considered as the first event that occurs during a step, it was used as a common reference that represents the onset of turn in this study. We conduct two studies; the first one is focused on the head behavior during turning with different angles while the second one is devoted to the analysis of head behavior during turning with different styles of walk.

5.1   Head Behavior during Turning with Different Angles

In this study, we focus on the orientation of the head around the yaw axis between the onset and the offset of the turn. We measured the maximum head orientation that occur between turn boundaries with respect to the trunk and the heading as explained in section 5. After applying One-way Anova, we found that the turn angle had a significant effect on the relative head orientation (P< 0.001) both for heading-head and trunk-head). Similarly to the results presented in [4], we found the same pattern of results for heading and trunk references. The relative head orientation using the trunk or heading as a reference shows a continuous increase for the turn angles up to 135 ° and a leveling off after that. The estimation of the magnitude of the relative head orientation was different between the two references. The average of the head orientation measured respectively using the heading and the trunk as references are shown in table 2. The trunk-head turned out to be smaller than the heading-head for all the turn angles (See table 2). This is explained by the orientation of the trunk that occurs with the orientation of the head during turning task.

Table 2. Head behavior stabilization measures in eNTERFACE08 3D database

Parameters	45 °	90 °	135 °	180 °
Heading-head	10.1 °	16.1 °	23.4 °	21.6 °
Trunk-head	5.9 °	9.9 °	15.1 °	14.7 °
The average of the occurrence of maximum head yaw (in seconds)	0.4375	0.7047	0.9613	1.1812

We also measured the instant when the head orientation reaches the maximum value relative to the SW HO event involving in the first turning steps. The main effect of of turn angle was significant (P<0.001) leading to a linear increase from 45 ° to 180 ° (See Table 2). This indicates that the instant in which occurs the maximal head orientation toward the turn direction with respect to the onset of turn is also affected by the turn angle.

5.2   Head Behavior during Turning with Different Emotions

The trunk-head and heading-head features were measured between the onset and the offset of 180 ° turns detected in the emotional walks. The expression of emotions through walking action had a significant effect on the head-trunk orientation as well as on the heading-head orientation (P<0.001). Similarly to the study presented in [4], we found that the head orientation relative to the trunk was smaller than with the heading as a reference. This result shows that the trunk was also rotated to the turn direction regardless of the style of walking and turning actions. Since the heading reference strongly depends on the trajectory of the CoM, we focus only on the maximum head yaw relative to the trunk to compare the head behavior between the different styles of walk and turn.

No significant difference was found between the trunk-head in turning related to the expression of Anger and Pride (P=0.33). The maximum head yaw relative to the trunk ranged from 0.22° to 35.22°. The effect of the expression of emotion on the trunk-head yaw increase while taking into account Anxiety expression (P<0.001) but the expression of Sadness showed the most significant difference among the other emotion expressions. The median (4.94°) as well as the range (from 0.1° to 14.8°) of trunk-head yaw in turning while expressing sadness turned out to be smaller than with the other emotion expressions. These results showed that the maximum head orientation relative to the trunk during turning task is not only depending on the angle of turn but also on the style of walk.

Studying the effect of emotions on the occurrence of maximum head yaw (in seconds) with One-way Anova showed a significant differences (P<0.001) among the four groups representing the four emotional behavior. Interestingly, the median related to the occurrence of maximum head yaw showed higher values for Pride ans Sadness (1.5s and 2.1s) and lower values for Anger and Anxiety (1.2s and 1.1s). That means that the maximum head yaw occur earlier with Anger and Anxiety expression than with Pride and Sadness expression. This result is congruent with the activation dimension of the studied emotional states; head orientation is slower for less active emotional states and faster for active emotional states.

6   Conclusion and Future Work

In this paper, we investigate the relationship between upper and lower body parts through the relationship between shoulders and hips movement. We found that those two modalities follow a strong linear relationship during turning task for different turn angles (45°, 90°, 135° and 180°) and different styles of walk and turn (while expressing Anger, Pride, Anxiety and Sadness). We found that the linear relationship is stronger for higher turn angles. In the future work, we aim to study whether this relationship is maintained for turn angles lower than 45°. The relationship between shoulders and hips movement must also be studied in cyclic curved trajectories to see whether it follows the same linear behavior found in turning around a corner. Like hips movement, shoulders movement is characterized with a non linear (sinusoidal) behavior during straight walk. However, shoulders and hips are in opposite of phase, mainly due to arm swings. But we showed that this opposite behavior strongly depends on the style of walk for Anger, Anxiety, Pride and Sadness expression through walking. That is the relationship of phase opposition between shoulders and hips is no more maintained during the sad expression as the body movement is less energetic and arms balance less.

In our work, we also investigate head behavior during turning with different angles and different styles of walk. We found that the maximum head yaw relative to the trunk and heading shows a continuous increase for the turn angles up to 135 ° and a leveling off after that. This result was found previously in [4] with similar values of maximum head yaw for the different angles. The occurrence of the maximum head yaw was also affected by the turn angle leading to a linear increase from 35 ° to 180 °. However, this behavior was not stable while changing the style of walk. The head orientation with respect to the trunk showed a significant decrease in turning task while expressing Sadness than while expressing more active emotional states like Anxiety and Anger. We showed that the occurrence of the maximum head yaw during turning task is also affected by the expression of emotion. The maximum head yaw occurs earlier for active emotional states (Anger and Anxiety) and later for less active emotional states (Pride and Sadness).

Acknowledgments. This research is supported by the National project Anipev1 (FUI Acteur Virtuel).

References

1. Olivier, A.H., Cretual, A.: Velocity/curvature relations along a single turn in human locomotion. Neuroscience Letters 412(2), 148–153 (2007)
2. Hicheur, H., Berthoz, A.: How do humans turn? head and body movements for the steering of locomotion. In: 5th IEEE-RAS International Conference on Humanoid Robots, pp. 265–270 (2005)
3. Imai, T., Moore, S.T., Raphan, T., Cohen, B.: Interaction of the body, head, and eyes during walking and turning. Experimental Brain Research 136(1), 1–18 (2001)
4. Sreenivasa, M.N., Frissen, I., Souman, J.I., Ernst, M.O.: Walking along curved paths of different angles: the relationship between head and trunk turning. Experimental brain research. Experimentelle Hirnforschung. Expérimentation Cérébrale 191(3), 313–320 (2008)
5. Hicheur, H., Vieilledent, S., Richardson, M.J.E., Flash, T., Berthoz, A.: Velocity and curvature in human locomotion along complex curved paths: a comparison with hand movements. Experimental brain research. Experimentelle Hirnforschung. Expérimentation Cérébrale 162(2), 145–154 (2005)
6. Vieilledent, S., Kerlirzin, Y., Dalbera, S., Berthoz, A.: Relationship between velocity and curvature of a human locomotor trajectory. Neuroscience Letters 305(1), 65–69 (2001)
7. Li, F., Zhao, C., Ding, G., Gong, J., Liu, C., Zhao, F.: A reliable and accurate indoor localization method using phone inertial sensors. In: Proceedings of the 2012 ACM Conference on Ubiquitous Computing, UbiComp 2012, p. 421 (2012)
8. Fourati, N., Pelachaud, C.: A new acted emotional body behavior database. In Multimodal Corpora: Beyond Audio and Video (IVA 2013 Workshop) (2013)
9. Tilmanne, J., Sebbe, R.: Dutoit: T.: A Database for Stylistic Human Gait Modeling and Synthesis. In: Proceedings of the eNTERFACE 2008 Workshop on Multimodal Interfaces, pp. 91–94 (2009)

10. IGS-190. Animazoo website, http://www.animazoo.com
11. MVN BIOMECH system. Xsens website, http://www.xsens.com/
12. Dael, N., Mortillaro, M., Scherer, K.R.: Emotion expression in body action and posture. Emotion 12(5), 1085–1101 (2012)
13. Mickelborough, J., van der Linden, M.L., Richards, J., Ennos, A.R.: Validity and reliability of a kinematic protocol for determining foot contact events. Gait & Posture 11(1), 32–37 (2000)
14. Olivier, A.-H., Kulpa, R., Pettré, J., Crétual, A.: A Velocity-Curvature Space Approach for Walking Motions Analysis. In: Egges, A., Geraerts, R., Overmars, M. (eds.) MIG 2009. LNCS, vol. 5884, pp. 104–115. Springer, Heidelberg (2009)

Towards Real-Time Continuous Emotion Recognition from Body Movements

Weiyi Wang[1], Valentin Enescu[1], and Hichem Sahli[1,2]

[1] Dept. Electronics & Informatics (ETRO), Vrije Universiteit Brussel (VUB),
Belgium
[2] Interuniversity Microelectronics Center (IMEC), Leuven, Belgium
{wwang,venescu,hsahli}@etro.vub.ac.be

Abstract. Social psychological research indicates that bodily expressions convey important affective information, although this modality is relatively neglected in the literature as compared to facial expressions and speech. In this paper we propose a real-time system that continuously recognizes emotions from body movements data streams. Low-level 3D postural features and high-level kinematic and geometrical features are through summarization (statistical values) or aggregation (feature patches), fed to a random forests classifier. In a first stage, the MoCap UCLIC affective gesture database has been used for training the classifier, which led to an overall recognition rate of 78% using a 10-fold cross-validation (leave-one-out). Subsequently, the trained classifier was tested with different subjects using continuous Kinect data. A performance of 72% was reached in real-time, which proves the efficiency and effectiveness of the proposed system.

Keywords: emotion recognition, real-time, bodily expressions.

1 Introduction

In real life, humans interact with each other and the environment with multi cues including facial expressions, gestures and voice. These cues together convey not only part of the content in the interactions, but also the information of affective states. In the past decades, a great effort has been made to automatically recognize emotions and affective states through different cues or their combinations. According to De Gelder [11], 95% of the research was conducted with face stimuli, the majority of the remaining 5% with audio, followed by bodily expressions. Supported by psychological studies, bodily expressions recently started to attract increasingly more research interest [11][14][30][2].

In this paper we propose an approach for real-time continuous recognition of expressive gestures from body movements. In the proposed metodology, both 3-dimensional low-level postural features and high-level (kinematic and geometrical) features are estimated, from which statistical cues or temporal patches, representing the dynamics of body movements, are calculated. The UCLIC affective gesture database [22] has been employed to train a random forests classifier,

A.A. Salah et al. (Eds.) : HBU 2013, LNCS 8212, pp. 235–245, 2013.
© Springer International Publishing Switzerland 2013

then both sequence-based (one single emotional gesture sequence) and continuous input tests were conducted to validate the recognition capabilities of the proposed approach. The obtained recognition rate, around 78%, outperformed the best result of apex posture-based recognition on the UCLIC database. Finally the trained random forests classifier has been used on continuous Kinect sensor data to provide real-time recognition of emotional gestures.

The rest of this paper is organized as follows: Section 2 introduces the research background, state-of-the-art and the trends that are related to the scope of this paper. Section 3 gives details of our proposed system, including feature extraction, recognition framework, as well as the introduction of the UCLIC database we used to test our system, followed by Section 4 of experimental results and comparison. Finally, in Section 5, we discuss the proposed approach.

2   Background

In [16], a survey of recent representative research work on automatic emotion analysis found the bodily information as an important modality to predict affective states. Berthouze and Kleinsmith [7][22] chose the most representative static postures that were acted by participants to analyze both categorical emotions and affective dimensions. A motion capture (MoCap) device was used to capture the body movements and low-level geometric features were calculated. They continued their work to spontaneous affects analysis in a body-controlled game scenario with a similar representation of selected postures [21], while the body's dynamics was not considered. Metallinou et. al in [25] described an emotional trends tracking system in a dyadic scenario performed by professional actors. The body movements were represented by both individual features and relative ones between two persons in dyadic interactions, in three dimensionalities. Gaussian Mixture Models and Long-Short Term Memory regression were used to continuously track the changes of three affective dimensions: *Activation*, *Valence* and *Dominance*. Convincing tracking results were reported for *Activation* and *Dominance*, while *Valence* was less tracked by the proposed feature sets. Castellano et. al [10][9] conducted categorical emotion recognition based on pre-segmented sequences. High-level features, such as quantity of motion, contraction index, velocity and acceleration, were calculated on a per-frame basis for each sequence. Then sequence-based statistical indicators such as initial/final slope, centroid of energy, etc... were computed for each feature sequence as inputs for the used machine learning algorithms. Due to the nature of proposed body movement descriptors, it is not easy to perform the recognition in real-time. Indeed the approach requires the complete expressive gesture sequence before recognition. Glowinski et. al [13] used similar body motion descriptors to investigate a minimal representation of expressive gestures. In their approach, Principal Component Analysis (PCA) revealed four components (roughly indicating motion activity, temporal and spatial excursion of movement, spatial extent and postural symmetry and motion jerkiness respectively) which could represent the expressions efficiently. Piana et. al [27] proposed a set of features to differentiate emotions, which includes both 3D movement information from RGB-D cameras or MoCap devices, and 2D features from the image segmentation of the shape of the users. Sparse Coding and Dictionary Learning were employed to combine the feature vectors in an unsupervised manner, followed by the normal SVM for classification. Similar feature set was used in [29] as a component of the social active music systems to analyze listener's affective states and then to control the music processing and playing. Some other studies were also conducted either by using bodily information as a complementary cue to facial expressions and speech [3][26], or in a constrained context [5][24]. Generally speaking, emotion recognition from bodily information is still an unsettled research question due to the differences in individual expressions, body movement sensors, as well as affective model definition. Wallbott [30] conducted comprehensive experiments and tried to reveal certain connections between the emotion categories and specific body movement patterns and postures. However, unlike Facial Action Coding System (FACS and its variants EMFACS and FACSAID for emotion analysis) [30] that is widely used in facial expression studies, there still is no agreement on affective bodily expressions within the research community.

3 Methodologies

3.1 Body Representation

The way to acquire and represent human bodily information influences directly the approaches to model the body movements and postures, and hence the affective analysis. Color cameras were widely used either to track the positions of certain parts of body (mostly hands and head) [13][26] or to abstract high-level body motions [10][17]. In contrast, marker-based motion capture devices give the positions or angular values of body joints, which are considered to be more precise and easier to process. However, participants are required to wear the marker suits. With the advent of increasingly mature RGB-D sensors (e.g. Microsoft Kinect sensor), depth information and body skeleton could nowadays easily be extracted from these devices and provide similar accuracy to the motion capture ones.

There exist several databases consider bodily stimuli as one of the modalities for affective analysis, such as the GEMEP (Geneva Multimodal Emotion Portrayals) corpus [4] and UCLIC affective gesture database [22]. In this work, we use the UCLIC database to train and evaluate our approach. Moreover, the trained classifier has been applied to continuous Kinect data. To build the UCLIC database, 13 candidates, from different cultural regions, were asked to act certain emotions (*Anger, Fear, Happiness,* and *Sadness*) with body languages [22]. A MoCap device with 32 markers attached on different segments of the body was used to obtain the joint positions. Although affective postures were the main research target of the UCLIC database, the acquired continuous frames make it also valuable for dynamic analysis. Fig. 1 depicts few frames of a sample sequence of 'fear' emotion.

Fig. 1. An example of fear emotion at four time points from the UCLIC database

3.2   Feature Extraction

Inspired by the results of psychological experiments conducted by Wallbott [30], both low-level postural features and high-level kinematic and geometrical features are extracted.

Postural Features: Some specific postures are generally bound to certain emotional expressions according to social psychological research. [30] has shown that upper body, especially arms and head, plays the most important role for expressions. Based on this observation, we calculate the spatial distances among hands, elbows and shoulders in each of the three dimensions, as well as the angles of two elbows. Moreover, we calculate the distance between feet, the orientation of feet and the orientation of shoulders. All these lead to 28 postural features in total. Note that, in contrast to the approaches proposed in [6][20], we assume that expressive postures are evolving both spatially and temporally rather than being static, which had been investigated and supported in previous work indicating that bodily expressions could also be segmented to *onset*, *apex*, *offset* as facial expressions [15]. Therefore, the 28 low-level postural features are calculated on a per-frame basis.

High-Level Features: These features are designed to represent the abstract characteristics of bodily expressions, such as *movement activity*, *movement power*, *body spatial extension* and *body bending*.

Body movement activity and power: Human motions could be thought of as being composed of different physical segments and each segment can move independently and exhibit an independent degree of activity [1]. As illustrated in Fig. 2, these body segments have a hierarchical structure, which allows estimating the body movement activity and power composed of three parameters: *force*, *kinetic energy* and *momentum* calculated hierarchically (from the bottom to the top) [19]:

$$segment\_Force = segment\_Mass \times segment\_Acceleration \qquad (1)$$

$$segment\_KineticEnergy = 0.5 \times segment\_Mass \times segment\_Velocity^2 \quad (2)$$

$$segment\_Momentum = segment\_Mass \times segment\_Velocity \qquad (3)$$

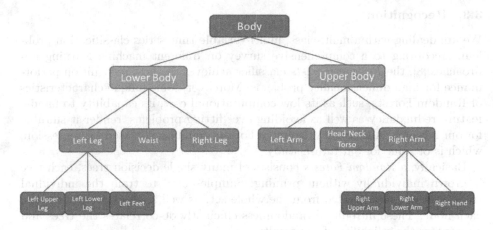

Fig. 2. Hierarchical representation of human body

where *segment_Mass* are estimated according to ergonomic definitions, which relate the body weight to the masses of different body segments (refer to [23] for details).

Body Spatial Extension: From the positions of body joints, we extract the body bounding box at each frame. Then three spatial extent indexes are calculated in x, y, z axis separately:

Symmetry: Spatial symmetric indexes are considered for the two hands in three coordinates. A relative coordinate system is used to make sure these indexes are position independent.

Body Bending: This feature is designed to catch full body bending forward or backward (mostly happens in fear and disgust emotions) movements.

Thus, ten high-level kinematic and geometrical features are extracted, together with the postural feature a frame-based38-dimensional feature vector is obtained. Note that, most of the above defined features are body size dependent, which means the height of the body will affect the feature values. This adverse effect could be practically eliminated by normalizing the feature values with the body size.

Statistical Features: In order to capture the gist of the body motion, we further calculate 6 statistical cues, *mean, standard deviation, min, max, kurtosis* and *skewness*, within a fixed-size time.

Temporal Patches: We also create temporal feature patches that concatenates, for the considered time window, the 38 per-frame features. Such temporal feature patch could catch not only the current states of the features, but also how they evolve within the time window.

3.3   Recognition

We are dealing with a multi-class, multi-variable time series classification problem. According to a comprehensive survey on different machine learning approaches [8], the *Random Forests* classifier achieves the best recognition performance for high dimensionality problems. Moreover, some unique characteristics of Random Forests, such as its low computational cost, its capability to handle feature redundancy as well as avoiding over-fitting problems, render it suitable for our research. Additionally, Random Forests could also be used for regression, which is of value for our future study.

Basically, a *Random Forests* consists of many single decision trees, each tree is grown individually without pruning. Samples used to train the individual trees are randomly selected from the whole set, as well as the variables used in each node. These introduced randomness efficiently de-correlates the trees and guarantees the reliability of the results.

4   Experiments

Baseline Classifiaction: We firstly estimated the 27 postural features proposed in [20], for which the UCLIC database was originally designed, for the apex frame of each affective gesture motion in the database, and used the WEKA toolbox [18] to run a 10-fold cross validation with leave-one-out strategy using different classifiers. The best results were achieved by the Random Forests classifier with an overall recognition rate of 75.41% (138 correctly classified out of 183). This result has been used as the baseline of our experiments.

Sequence Testing: Pre-segmented (single expression) gesture sequences from the UCLIC database were used to test the proposed features and classifier. We borrowed the idea from *Random Forests* to randomly sample a certain percentage of frames (e.g. 50 percent) within a testing sequence with replacement. Features with statistical cues and/or temporal patches were calculated for these frames. Then, we summed up the classification results of these frames and the mostly occurred label has been assigned to the considered sequence. Two evaluations were conducted:

Feature set comparison: we compared the contribution of low-level and high-level features, respectively. We conducted 10-fold cross validation with leave-one-out strategy for the 183 single expression gesture sequences. 100 trees were grown without pruning in the forest during training.

The recognition performance is presented in Table 1. When using only postural features, we could reach a higher classification accuracy as compared to high-level features, and the high-level ones are not sufficient to differentiate expressive gestures. This conclusion was also supported by a χ^2 *ranking* on all these features. It could be, on the other hand, partly explained by the *acted nature* of the UCLIC database.

Table 1. Recognition accuracy when using postural features and high-level features separately. The last row gives the baseline recognition rate with apex frames.

	Postural Features				High-level Features			
	Fear	Happy	Angry	Sad	Fear	Happy	Angry	Sad
Fear	28	10	8	3	21	15	8	5
Happy	6	36	4	1	11	32	1	3
Angry	5	3	28	5	4	14	16	7
Sad	1	5	6	34	4	3	3	36
Rate	68.85%				57.38%			
Baseline	75.41%							

Statistical cues and temporal patches comparison: we then analyzed the recognition rate when adding either statistical cues or temporal feature patches. The window size introduces an extra parameter to the system. A larger value would comsume too much calculation power, and on the other side if this size is too small, it would not be sufficient to capture the dynamics. Analyzing the UCLIC sequences, we observed that for most gestures, the motion lasts for $0.5s$ to $2s$. By taking into account the affordable latency (i.e., how fast we have to provide a classification result), we set the size of the time window to 30 frames ($0.5s$). Table 2 summarizes the the classification results.

Table 2. Recognition accuracy using the frame-based feature set, plus either statistical cues or temporal feature patches. The last row gives the baseline recognition rate with apex frames.

	Frame-based Features				+Statistical Cues				+Temporal Patches			
	Fear	Happy	Angry	Sad	Fear	Happy	Angry	Sad	Fear	Happy	Angry	Sad
Fear	31	11	4	3	34	5	5	5	35	7	3	4
Happy	5	36	4	2	4	38	2	3	4	39	3	1
Angry	4	5	29	3	4	3	30	4	3	4	30	4
Sad	2	3	4	37	3	2	3	38	2	2	3	39
Rate	72.68%				76.50%				78.14%			
Baseline	75.41%											

We can see that adding statistical cues or concatenating previous frames on the original frame-based feature set (temporal feature patches) could, to a certain extent, improve the recognition performance. Note that, although the feature set dimensionality would largely increase (6 times for statistical cues and 30 times for temporal patches), the *Random Forests* classifier delivers results in real-time due to its efficient tree-searching nature. Another conclusion from this experiment is that statistical cues and temporal patches reach very similar recognition rates. This is because statistical cues could be considered as abstract descriptions of the temporal evolvement of features, which convey similar information with temporal feature patches.

In this experiment, we also proved our proposed features and recognition framework outperform the baseline result. Manual expressive apex frame selection is not necessary in our system, thus it is feasible to be run with continuous, un-segmented data streams.

Continuous Recognition: Owing to the computational efficiency of *Random Forests*, the continuous prediction result could be given for each incoming frame in soft real-time (statistical cues or the temporal patches will introduce latency depending on the window size). We used a Kinect sensor to capture the body skeleton and feed the classifier trained with the UCLIC database sequences. It has to be noted that there are slight differences between the definition of joints in Kinect SDK and the ones defined in the UCLIC database, while during our experiments we observed it is not necessary to match them perfectly since the system has a certain tolerance. We asked six participants to *act* randomly the four emotions contained in the UCLIC database as naturally as possible (some examples of each emotion category in the UCLIC database were presented to provide some hints. However, the participants could freely act as their own understanding). To avoid nervousness and "over-acted" artifacts, the participants rehearsed as many times as they needed before the real experiments. In total 82 expressive segments, in which seven were not usable due to the errors in skeleton extraction, were collected. The recognition system was running in real-time giving the feedback of *neutral state* or recognized emotions. In the UCLIC database, the neutral gesture was defined to be a *T-Pose*, and could be simply detected by measuring both the body energy and body spatial extension. More sophisticated approaches could be introduced, but it is out of the scope of this paper. A simple window-based smoothing filter was applied to remove sharp errors. For the 75 expressive segments, 54 were correctly recognized, giving the recognition rate of 72%. Fig. 3 depicts the recognition results for a long sequence containing a random repetition of the four emotion segments.

From this experiment, one can see that even the subjects did not appear in the training data, the expressive gestures could still be well classified.

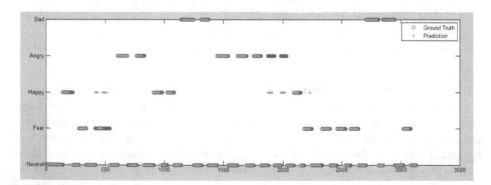

Fig. 3. Continuous recognition result of a sequence recorded by Kinect sensor. Red bars are labels and green bars are predicted results. Overlaps represent correctly recognized frames.

5 Discussion and Future Work

There are three important criteria of creating automatic affect analyzers: *correctness* (to match human observers labeling), *robustness* (not too sensitive to changing conditions) and *efficiency* (real-time processing and responsiveness) [16]. In this paper we proposed a real-time expressive gesture recognition system to meet those criteria. The system continuously calculates postural and high-level bodily features, as well as statistical cues. A random forests classifier is applied to make efficient predictions. The UCLIC affective gesture database was employed to train and test our model. Kinect sensor recordings were also used for testing in both offline and online recognition mode. Overall results are convincing and outperform the affective posture recognition conducted on the same database, which requires manual frame selection and is not suitable for continuous analysis. Obviously, when using Kinect skeleton streams as the inputs, the quality of the skeleton extraction directly influences the recognition performance. Moreover, due to the lack of available public 3D affective gesture corpus, our experiments were constrained to *acted* expressions and limited to four emotion categories. In the future, we will conduct other experiments that aim at eliciting and recording *spontaneous* affective expressions in multi-modalities. To have better body tracking quality, these recordings will be made using multiple RGB-D cameras (e.g. 2 Kinects placed with a certain angle), and the tracking will be implemented following the ideas from Girshick et. al [12] and Taylor et. al [28]. This system could be naturally extended to dimensional affective analysis (e.g. *Valence, Arousal, Dominance etc.*) using random forests regression, this being another part of our future work. Last but not least, we are planning to employ the approaches and system proposed in this paper to study the emotional expressions and perception of children in child-robot interaction scenarios, within the EU FP-7 Aliz-E project (www.aliz-e.org).

Acknowledgements The research work reported in this paper was supported by the EU FP7 project ALIZ-E grant 248116, and by the CSC-VUB scholarship grant. We also would like to thank the referees for their comments and suggestions, which helped improving the paper.

References

1. Aggarwal, J., Cai, Q.: Human motion analysis: a review. In: Proc. of Nonrigid and Articulated Motion Workshop, pp. 90–102 (1997)
2. Alaerts, K., Nackaerts, E., Meyns, P., Swinnen, S.P., Wenderoth, N.: Action and emotion recognition from point light displays: an investigation of gender differences. PLoS One 6(6), e20989 (2011)
3. Baltrusaitis, T., McDuff, D., Banda, N., Mahmoud, M., el Kaliouby, R., Robinson, P., Picard, R.: Real-time inference of mental states from facial expressions and upper body gestures. In: Proceedings of 2011 IEEE International Conference on Automatic Face Gesture Recognition and Workshops (FG 2011), pp. 909–914 (2011)

4. Bänziger, T., Mortillaro, M., Scherer, K.R.: Introducing the Geneva Multimodal expression corpus for experimental research on emotion perception. Emotion (Washington, D.C.) 12(5), 1161–1179 (2012), http://www.ncbi.nlm.nih.gov/pubmed/22081890
5. Bernhardt, D.: Emotion inference from human body motion. Tech. Rep. 787, Computer Laboratory, University of Cambridge, Cambridge (2010)
6. Bianchi-Berthouze, N., Cairns, P., Cox, A.: On posture as a modality for expressing and recognizing emotions. In: Emotion in HCI: Joint Procs. of the 2005, 2006, and 2007 Intl. Workshops, pp. 74–80. Citeseer (2008)
7. Bianchi-Berthouze, N., Kleinsmith, A.: A categorical approach to affective gesture recognition. Connection Science 15(4), 259–269 (2003)
8. Caruana, R., Karampatziakis, N., Yessenalina, A.: An empirical evaluation of supervised learning in high dimensions. In: Proceedings of the 25th International Conference on Machine Learning, ICML 2008, pp. 96–103 (2008), http://portal.acm.org/citation.cfm?doid=1390156.1390169
9. Castellano, G., Kessous, L., Caridakis, G.: Multimodal emotion recognition from expressive faces, body gestures and speech. Affective computing and intelligent interaction 4738, 71–82 (2007)
10. Castellano, G., Villalba, S., Camurri, A.: Recognising human emotions from body movement and gesture dynamics. In: Paiva, A.C.R., Prada, R., Picard, R.W. (eds.) ACII 2007. LNCS, vol. 4738, pp. 71–82. Springer, Heidelberg (2007)
11. de Gelder, B.: Why bodies? Twelve reasons for including bodily expressions in affective neuroscience. Philosophical Tran. of the Royal Society B: Biological Sciences 364, 3475–3484 (2009)
12. Girshick, R., Shotton, J., Kohli, P., Criminisi, A., Fitzgibbon, A.: Efficient regression of general-activity human poses from depth images. In: 2011 International Conference on Computer Vision, pp. 415–422 (November 2011), http://ieeexplore.ieee.org/lpdocs/epic03/wrapper.htm?arnumber=6126270
13. Glowinski, D., Dael, N., Camurri, A., Volpe, G., Mortillaro, M., Scherer, K.R.: Toward a Minimal Representation of Affective Gestures. IEEE Transactions on Affective Computing 2(2), 106–118 (2011)
14. Gross, M.M., Crane, E.A., Fredrickson, B.L.: Methodology for Assessing Bodily Expression of Emotion. Journal of Nonverbal Behavior 34(4), 223–248 (2010), http://www.springerlink.com/index/10.1007/s10919-010-0094-x
15. Gunes, H., Piccardi, M.: Automatic temporal segment detection and affect recognition from face and body display. IEEE Transactions on Systems, Man, and Cybernetics. Part B, Cybernetics: A Publication of the IEEE Systems, Man, and Cybernetics Society 39(1), 64–84 (2009)
16. Gunes, H., Schuller, B.: Categorical and dimensional affect analysis in continuous input: Current trends and future directions. Image and Vision Computing (July 2012), http://linkinghub.elsevier.com/retrieve/pii/S0262885612001084
17. Gunes, H., Shan, C., Chen, S., Tian, Y.: Bodily Expression for Automatic Affect Recognition. In: Advances in Emotion Recognition (2012)
18. Hall, M., Frank, E., Holmes, G., Pfahringer, B., Reutemann, P., Witten, I.H.: The WEKA data mining software: an update. SIGKDD Explor. Newsl. 11(1), 10–18 (2009)
19. Kahol, K., Tripathi, P., Panchanathan, S.: Gesture Segmentation in Complex Motion Sequences. In: Proc. of International Conference on Image Processing (ICIP 2003) (2003)

20. Kleinsmith, A., Bianchi-Berthouze, N.: Recognizing affective dimensions from body posture. In: Proceedings of the 2nd International Conference on Affective Computing and Intelligent Interaction, pp. 45–58 (2007)

21. Kleinsmith, A., Bianchi-Berthouze, N.: Automatic recognition of non- acted affective postures: A video game scenario. IEEE Trans. on Systems, Man, and Cybernetics Part B 41(4), 1027–1038 (2011)

22. Kleinsmith, A., De Silva, P.R., Bianchi-Berthouze, N.: Cross-Cultural Differences in Recognizing Affect from Body Posture. Iteracting with Computers 18(6), 1371–1389 (2006)

23. Kroemer, K.H.E., Kroemer, H.B., Kroemer-Elbert, K.E.: Ergonomics: how to design for ease and efficiency. Prentice Hall (1994)

24. Leite, I., Castellano, G., Pereira, A., Martinho, C., Paiva, A.: Modelling Empathic Behaviour in a Robotic Game Companion for Children. In: Proceedings of the ACM/IEEE International Conference on Human-Robot Interaction (HRI 2012) (2012)

25. Metallinou, A., Katsamanis, A., Narayanan, S.: Tracking continuous emotional trends of participants during affective dyadic interactions using body language and speech information. In: Image and Vision Computing (September 2012), http://linkinghub.elsevier.com/retrieve/pii/S0262885612001710

26. Nicolaou, M.A., Member, S., Gunes, H., Pantic, M., Member, S.: Continuous Prediction of Spontaneous Affect from Multiple Cues and Modalities in Valence Arousal Space. IEEE Trans. on Affective Computing, 1–15 (2011)

27. Piana, S., Staglianò, A., Camurri, A., Odone, F.: A set of Full-Body Movement Features for Emotion Recognition to Help Children affected by Autism Spectrum Condition. In: IDGEI International Workshop (2013)

28. Taylor, J., Shotton, J., Sharp, T., Fitzgibbon, A.: The Vitruvian Manifold: Inferring Dense Correspondences for One-Shot Human Pose Estimation Optimization of Model Parameters, pp. 103–110 (2012)

29. Volpe, G., Camurri, A.: A system for embodied social active listening to sound and music content. Journal on Computing and Cultural Heritage 4(1), 1 23 (2011), http://dl.acm.org/citation.cfm?doid=2001416.2001418

30. Wallbott, H.G.: Bodily Expression of Emotion. European Journal of Social Psychology 28(6), 879–896 (1998)

Human Behaviour in HCI: Complex Emotion Detection through Sparse Speech Features

Ingo Siegert, Kim Hartmann,
David Philippou-Hübner, and Andreas Wendemuth

Cognitive Systems Group, IIKT, and Center for Behavioral Brain Sciences,
Otto von Guericke University Magdeburg, Germany
ingo.siegert@ovgu.de

Abstract. To obtain a more human-like interaction with technical systems, those have to be adaptable to the users' individual skills, preferences, and current emotional state. In human-human interaction (HHI) the behaviour of the speaker is characterised by semantic and prosodic cues, given as short feedback signals. These signals minimally communicate certain dialogue functions such as attention, understanding, confirmation, or other attitudinal reactions. Thus, these signals play an important role in the progress and coordination of interaction. They allow the partners to inform each other of their behavioural or affective state without interrupting the ongoing dialogue.

Vocal communication provides acoustic details revealing the speaker's feelings, believes, and social relations. Incorporating discourse particles (DPs) in human-computer interaction (HCI) systems will allow the detection of complex emotions, which are currently hard to access. Complex emotions in turn are closely related to human behaviour. Hence, integrating automatic DP detection and complex emotion assignment in HCI systems provides a first approach to the integration of human behaviour understanding in HCI systems.

In this paper we present methods allowing to extract the pitch-contour of DPs and to assign complex emotions to observed DPs. We investigate the occurrences of DPs in naturalistic HCI and show that DPs may be assigned to complex emotions automatically. Furthermore, we show that DPs are indeed related to behaviour, showing an age-gender specific usage during naturalistic HCI. Additionally, we prove that DPs may be used to automatically detect and classify complex emotions during HCI.

Keywords: Prosodic Analysis, Companion Systems, Human-Computer Interaction, Discourse Particle, Pitch Contour Classification.

1 Introduction

Verbal human communication consists of several information layers, revealing details beyond the pure textual information given. These details are normally provided by humans to enhance human-human interaction (HHI) and to increase the likelihood of a positive interaction outcome. Human-computer interaction (HCI) systems have failed to note and respond to these details so far, resulting in users

A.A. Salah et al. (Eds.) : HBU 2013, LNCS 8212, pp. 246–257, 2013.

trying to cope with and adapt to the machines behaviour. This adaptation of the user leads to the typical Human-Machine Interaction patterns and results in a loss of information, lowering the chance of positive HCI. In order to enhance HCI, an adaptation to the user's behaviour and the integration of a general human behaviour understanding is indispensable [22]. Vocal communication provides acoustic details revealing the speaker's feelings, believes, and social relations. These acoustic features are commonly used to detect so called basic emotions from speech. However, incorporating acoustic feature and human behaviour analysis may even allow the detection of complex emotions, which are currently hard to access. Amongst these especially the users' affective states and their attitudes towards the ongoing dialogue are of interest. These can be favourably inferred from the speaker's intonation.

As the intonation is influenced by semantic and grammatical information, it is advisable to investigate the intonation of so-called discourse particles (DPs) e.g. "hm" or "uhm" [1]. These speech fragments cannot be inflected, but emphasised. DPs have the same intonation curves (pitch-contours) as sentences and may thus indicate the same affective meaning.

To determine the role of DPs within the dialogue, methods are needed that are feasible to assign defined form-prototypes. Furthermore, it must be investigated which pitch-contours occur in naturalistic HCI and whether these contours are congruent with the findings by linguists.

In this paper we present methods allowing to extract the pitch-contour of DPs and assign complex emotions to observed DPs. We investigated different form-function-relations (for the occurrence of DPs) within the naturalistic LAST MINUTE corpus and derive generally expectable form-function relations for naturalistic HCI. This paper provides a significant extension of [20] as further DPs are investigated and relations between DPs and complex emotions are deduced. The paper may include similar descriptions for technical definitions as in [20].

1.1 Discourse Particles

During HHI several semantic and prosodic cues are exchanged among the interaction partners and used to signalize the progress of the dialogue [1]. Especially the intonation of utterances transmits the communicative relation of the speakers and their attitude towards the current dialogue.

As known from literature, specific monosyllables (e.g. DP) have the same intonation curves as complete sentences and represent a similar functional relation [10]. These DPs cannot be inflected but may be emphasised and occur at crucial communicative points. The DP "hm" is seen as a "neutral-consonant" whereas "uh" can be seen as a "neutral-vocal" [18]. The intonation of these particles are largely free of lexical and grammatical influences. Schmidt presented an empirical study where he determined seven intonation specific form-function relation classes of the DP "hm", see Table 1 and [18]. The form function relation refers to the assignment of a form (pitch contour) to a specific function (meaning). An investigation for English DPs and the features syllabification, duration, loudness, pitch slope, and pitch-contour is presented in [21]. Unfortunately, loudness

Table 1. Form-function relation of DP "hm" according to [18], the terms are translated into appropriate English ones. DP-D can be seen as a combination of DP-R and DP-F.

Name	idealised pitch-contour	Description
DP-A	⌐‾\	attention
DP-T	—	thinking
DP-F	\	finalisation signal
DP-C	∨	confirmation
DP-D	∧\	decline
DP-P	∕∖	positive assessment
DP-R	∕	request to respond

cannot be measured perfectly for realistic scenarios, as the distance speaker-microphone is varying, see Section 2.1. Syllabification can be splitted into single particles, whereas the contour is more exact than the slope. In [2] American English feedback cues are investigated and several DPs are annotated using eleven categories. Further information on the semantics of DPs can be found in [1].

The previously described experiments are made on isolated recorded particles, hence, it must be investigated if these prototypical form-function relations can be found within naturalistic HHI.

The authors of [7] examined the data of four different conversational styles in German: talk-show, interview, theme-related talk, and an informal discussion, with an overall length of 179min. They extracted 392 particles from the material and confirmed the form-function relation.

A further observation is that the occurrence of the different form-function relations is depending on the conversation type, [14]. The author examines 2913 variants of the DP "hm" in 11 different conversations from different styles. In conversations of narrative or cooperative character confirmation signals are dominating, whereas turn holding signals dominate argumentative conversations [14].

As the considered DPs have a specific function within the conversation, the use of these particles requires both conversational partners to understand the meaning. Hence, it may be assumable that DPs do not occur during HCI. A study investigating this hypothesis is presented in [4]. The authors conclude that while the number of partner-oriented signals are decreasing during HCI, the number of signals indicating a talk-organising, task-oriented, or expressive function are increasing. However, [4] are not employing an automatic method to assign the DPs characteristic to a specific meaning. In [20], we showed that the findings for task-oriented signals presented by Schmidt in [18] are valid for HCI as well, investigating the "neutral-consonant" "hm". Among these signals, the functional

DP-T ("thinking") is occurring most frequently. These signals encode an affective state of the user and are hence worth to be decoded by a technical system.

This paper focusses on the phenomenological inspection of the "neutral-vocal" "uh" and the combinational DP "uhm"[1] and the utilization of the pitch contour of DPs for complex emotion recognition.

1.2 Complex Emotions in HCI

A general definition of emotions is difficult to provide as it is subject to discourse within the research community. However, emotions are generally considered as psychophysiological experiences related to events in time and to the individuals' assessment of an event. According to the individual reaction stereotypes formulated by [9], an individual will always respond with the same psychophysiological pattern to a psychological stimulus. Applying this knowledge to emotion detection from speech implies a high relevance of feature variations related to vocal tract deformations as investigated and suggested in [15]. The individual reaction stereotypes allow HCI researchers to assume a machine learnable correlation between an individual's physiological reactions and his psychological assessment.

In the LAST MINUTE corpus, knowledge about the individual's emotion specific physiological speech reaction patterns are not annotated, but could be by an assessment process. The emotions generally considered within the HCI research community are so called basic emotions, referring to [3]. Although the expression of emotions is generally considered as culture dependent, [3] found that certain physiological expressions are universally categorized as specific emotions. From these observations, [3] derived a set of six emotions regarded as "basic" emotions in humans: anger, disgust, fear, happiness, sadness and surprise.

Opposing to basic emotions, complex emotions are considered as combinations of basic emotions [12] or as states located between basic emotions in the emotional space [16]. Due to the observations of [3], complex emotions are also considered as complementary to basic emotions. Hence, complex emotions are those emotions not universally recognised by similar physiological reaction patterns and are hence believed to arise from cultural conditioning or individual associations of the combined basic emotions, making complex emotions highly specific to an individual's behavior, cf. Fig. 1, instead of a combination of basic emotions as suggested in [12].

However, as the goal in HHI is the advancement of a positive interaction outcome, it is observed that certain complex emotions crucial to the interaction is additionally given non-literally to compensate possible textual misunderstandings. These information are encoded through purely acoustical fragments being independent of grammatical or linguistic considerations. These fragments are used to communicate certain complex emotions universally.

Due to their specific role, the form (pitch contour) function (meaning) relation of DPs (assigned complex emotions) may be learned on a general basis and

---

[1] As we perform our investigations on German material, we decided to rely on a perceptional translation: "ähm" is translated as "uhm", to be consistent with German soundness, we translated "äh" as "uh".

Fig. 1. Localisation of basic and complex emotions in emotional space

applied user-independently although being behaviour specific. DPs are especially used to communicate non-literal signals to enhance dialogue conformity, such as "confirmation", "rejection", "irritation" and "consideration"/"thinking", each yielding specific behavioural reaction patterns. Hence, DPs represent a promising approach to incorporating human behaviour understanding in technical systems for specific complex emotions and their associated behaviour.

As variations in the expressions of DPs during HCI are only observed quantitatively, not qualitatively, cf. [18], the detection of human behaviour related to complex emotions transmitted through DPs may be implemented on a general basis. However, this is not true for other complex emotions due to their highly individual specific nature. As complex emotion detection is crucial to human behaviour understanding, concepts for the integration of complex emotion detection in modern HCI systems have to be developed. The difficulties in the detection of complex emotions arise due to the close relation between complex emotions, human behaviour and the individual reaction stereotypes. Utilizing the usual approach to emotion detection from speech, this combination implies the need of user specific learning and labelling of complex emotions not expressed through DPs. This approach is highly inefficient and impractical.

We therefore suggest an approach to the general incorporation of complex emotions in HCI systems through the utilization of the understanding of complex emotions as interstates of basic emotions in the emotion space, see Fig. 1. However, this approach implies the need of an emotion representation not based on learning and labelling, but rather on the basic emotion locations in the emotional space and measured individual physiological reaction patterns. Currently few models exist that allow this approach to emotion representation and analysis, one being described in [6].

2 Methods

2.1 Dataset

The conducted study of this paper utilizes the LAST MINUTE corpus [17], containing multi-modal recordings of 133 German speaking subjects in a so called Wizard-of-Oz experiment. The setup revolves around a journey to the unknown place "Waiuku", which the subjects have won. Each experiment takes about 30min. Using voice commands, the subjects have to prepare the journey, equip the baggage, and select clothing. Most of the experiments are transliterated, enabling the automatic extraction of speaker utterances. Details regarding the design of the corpus can be found in [17]. The LAST MINUTE corpus was chosen as it presents a naturalistic HCI [19]. The corpus was designed to have an equal distribution of age and gender of the subjects. The subjects are divided in two subgroups according to their ages. The younger group ranges from 18-28 years, the elder group consists of subjects being over 60 years.

The experiment is divided into two phases, a personalisation and a problem solving phase. During personalisation, the subject gets familiar to communicating with a machine. The subjects are guided to talk freely. During the problem solving phase, the conversation is more task focused and the subjects talk in a command-like style. Additionally, interviews were done with roughly half of the subjects. A conclusion drawn from the interviews was that the subjects experienced the exper-imental interaction with the technical system as a hybrid between human-human and human-computer interaction [11]. As the system was designed as a Wizard employing a rather technical and synthesised voice, this observation supports the claim that the investigated technical system has companion-like abilities.

We used a subset of 56 subjects with a total duration of 25h, where a pro-fessional neckband headmicro was utilized. The group distribution of age and gender is as follows: young males and young females are each represented by 16 subjects, old males and old females by 12 subjects each. As the DPs are translit-erated, we conducted an automatic alignment with a manual correction phase for the extraction. This results in 1925 DPs extracted in the described subset. Within these 1925 DPs, the DPs "hm" was counted 273 times, "uh" 485 times and "uhm" 1167 times. A detailed description can be found in Section 3.1.

As a first measure for loudness, we calculated the mean short time energy over centred means per speaker resulting in a normalised energy of 0.52 ± 0.12. The smallest averaged value is 0.21 ± 0.22 and the highest averaged value is 0.75 ± 0.10 for one speaker respectively. As the loudness correlates with the signal energy, this values indicated that the loudness is not a suitable measure for this naturalistic database, because the energy varies too much along the subjects.

We performed a function labelling of the DPs, utilizing the form function types according to Schmidt, cf. Table 1 and could reproduce the findings by Schmidt within the context of longer conversations. The calculated reliability coefficient is 0.50 using Krippendorff's alpha, for details see [20].

2.2 Automatic Pitch Extraction

As we have seen in Section 1.1, DPs fulfil an important function within the conversation for both HHI and HCI. The feature *pitch-contour* together with *duration* allows to derive a form-function relation. Therefore, a reliable method to extract and classify the pitch-contour should be developed. To extract the pitch, we rely on commonly used methods, presented in detail in [5]. The extracted DPs are windowed using a Hamming window with a width of 30ms and a stepsize of

5ms. Then, we calculated the short-time energy, this is later used, to perform the voiced/unvoiced decision. After windowing, we applied a low-pass filter with a pass-band frequency of 900Hz and center-clipping. The autocorrelation method is used afterwards, to extract the pitch values for each frame. Having extracted the pitch for all windows of one utterance, a smoothing using a median filter utilizing five values is applied to suppress outliers.

As these frame-wise extracted values do not model the pitch-contour, we generate the temporal characteristics by calculating the delta (Δ), double ($\Delta\Delta$) and triple ($\Delta\Delta\Delta$) regression coefficients of the static values, by [24]:

$$d_t = \frac{\sum_{l=1}^{L} l(c_{t+l} - c_{t-l})}{2\sum_{l=1}^{L} l^2} \tag{1}$$

with d_t being the (delta) regression coefficient at time t of the static coefficient c_t (e.g. pitch) and the shift length $L = 2$. To obtain the double coefficients, the formula is applied to the delta coefficients, similarly the third coefficients are obtained using the double coefficients. This kind of calculation implies that when using the double coefficients, the delta coefficients have to be calculated as well. This results in up to three more coefficients per static feature coefficient.

In [8] the authors show the importance of much broader temporal information by incorporating the so called Shifted Delta Cepstra (SDC). These coefficients utilize a much broader temporal context. For calculations, the authors of [8] suggest an index i in the range of $[-3, 3]$, a shift factor of $P = 3$ and a shift length of $L = 1$. This adds seven coefficients per static coefficient and results in an incorporation of $\pm$ 10 frames, see Fig. 2.

$$sdc_t = c_{(t+iP+L)} - c_{(t+iP-L)} \tag{2}$$

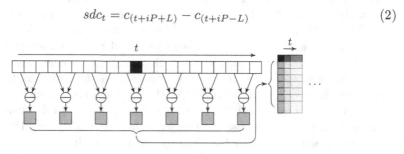

Fig. 2. Computation of SDC features. By using the previously defined values $i = [-3, 3]$, $P = 3$, and $L = 1$, a 7-dimensional SDC vector (▨) is gathered from a temporal context of 21 consecutive frames around our actual frame (■).

2.3 Automatic Emotion Detection

As it is suggested by Schmidt, our featureset only relies on the extracted pitch contours, which results in a feature vector containing only the pitch values of the utterance. The extracted pitch contours are not always congruent with the defined prototypes in Table 1, cause of different pronunciation lengths or attachments to surrounding expressions. Hence, a pure prototypical correlation would not be sufficient. Additionally the pronunciation length is varying. To compensate this fact, we applied a Hidden Markov Model (HMM) algorithm. These models are commonly used to deal with temporal pattern recognition. HMM are the successor of the Dynamic Time Warping algorithm used in speech recognition, cf. [13,23]. We utilized a commonly used 3-state left-right HMM to incorporate the different length of the DPs. The input features are modelled as Gaussian mixture models with a number of mixtures, which is yet to be fixed and which is investigated in Section 3.2. For training and testing we use the HTK Speech Recognition Toolkit, see [24].

To incorporate the temporal context, we utilize Δ, $\Delta\Delta$, $\Delta\Delta\Delta$, and SDC coefficients. This results in a feature vector with a length between 2, using only pitch plus deltas, and 11, using pitch plus all temporal context coefficients.

Currently, we are only confident to define a functional meaning for the DP "hm", as this DP and the functional meaning ("thinking") is investigated and approved [7,14,18]. Hence, within this work we solely utilize the DP "hm" for our complex emotion recognition.

We formulate the two-class problem *thinking* vs. *non-thinking* and distinguish between DP-T and all other functionals. The labels of the subset of the LAST MINUTE Corpus are gathered via a manual labelling process and described in [20]. This results in the unbalanced distribution of 211 samples for the class *thinking* and 63 samples for the class *non-thinking*.

3 Results

In addition to [20], we investigate the DPs "uh" and "uhm". Furthermore, we examine the automatic classification of the DP "hm" to its form-function relation and herewith assign the DP to a human behaviour associated complex emotion.

3.1 Phenomenological Inspection

Within our subset of 56 subjects, only one subject does not use any DP. The overall mean for all particles is 20.84 with a standard deviation of 9.66 per conversation. One subject, a young female, uses a maximum of 93 particles. The occurrence of DPs is not equally distributed among the four age-gender groups, as shown in Fig. 3. While the occurrence of the DPs is equally distributed among the two young aged groups (my and fy), we observed that females (fo) from the older group use the DPs twice as often as males (mo) from the older group.

Regarding single DPs, we noticed divergent behaviour. The use of "hm" is more frequent for female than for male subjects for both age groups. Whereas the subjects age does not influence the occurrence of "hm", the use of "uh" and "uhm" is more frequent for elderly subjects.

The next aspect we want to investigate is the occurrence of the DP within the two different experimental phases. Fig. 4 gives a plot considering the DPs for both phases individually regarding the different speaker groups. Comparing the total frequencies for all DPs, we gathered a mean occurrence of 11.8 for personalisation and a mean of 9.04 for the problem solving module. Furthermore, it can be observed that all speaker groups use DPs 1.3 times as often during the personalisation phase as in the problem-solving phase.

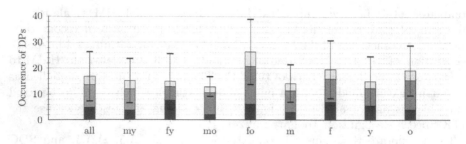

Fig. 3. Mean occurrence of DP types "hm" (■), "uh" (■) and "uhm" (■). Furthermore, different subject groups in the case of gender (male, female) and age (young and old) are compared. The standard deviation is calculated form a combination of all three DPs is given. For comparability the group independent occurrence (all) is given.

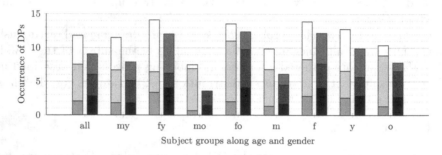

Fig. 4. Mean occurrence of the considered DPs per experimental phase (personalisation: ■ ■ □, problem solving: ■ ■ ■) regarding different subject groups (male, female, young and old). For comparability the group independent occurrence (all) is given.

Investigating the mean occurrences per experimental phase in 4 one can observe that the DPs "uhm" and "uh" occur more frequently during the personalisation than during the problem solving phase. This observation is exactly opposite for the DP "hm". During the personalisation phase, the DP "hm" occurred approx. 1.5 to 2 times less than during the problem solving phase. As the conversation style is much more restricted in the second phase, we did not expect this observation. Incorporating the labels from a manual annotation process shows that 77% of the "hm" are labelled as functional DP-T (thinking), cf. Table 1, which is a complex emotion. Furthermore it can be seen that the use of "hm" is more frequent for female and elderly subjects for the second phase.

The age-gender dependent variations were observed during our investigations, but are not relevant for our automatic form function assignment to complex emotions, as DPs are generally considered universal. The observations indeed show an age-gender specificity as expected for behaviour associated results.

3.2   Utilizing a Complex Emotion Detection

The phenomenological investigation of the naturalistic material reveals that the DPs occur frequently enough, to be used as an indicator for complex emotions.

Especially the affect "thinking" is occuring very frequent. As we have shown in Section 1.2, this affective state is important for the ongoing of the interaction.

However, the assignment of form function relations to DPs must be conducted through interdisciplinary investigations, combining psychological and linguistic considerations. Currently, the DP "hm" is the only DP having a generally accepted and academically substantiated form function assignment.

In order to allow a logically repeatable classification of complex emotions based on DPs, we divide the set of extracted DPs into the classes "thinking" (being assigned to the DP "hm") and non-thinking (representing all other form functions of the DP without a form function assignment).

To perform a classification of the DPs types "hm" into *thinking* and *not-thinking*, we performed several experiments utilizing pitch contour as the only feature enhanced with different temporal context information, as defined in Section 2.3. The DPs are extracted automatically based on aligned time informations from the translation. Furthermore, we varied the number of mixtures for the Gaussian mixtures. The results can be found in Table 2. We iterated the training six times for each additional mixture.

Table 2. Weighted average accuracy of our experiments with different features and mixtures. The best result for each fetureset is marked underlined, the overall best result is marked **bold**.

# Features	Mixtures					
	12	18	24	30	36	39
2 Pitch + Δ	0.35	0.38	0.43	0.44	0.50	<u>0.51</u>
3 Pitch + $\Delta\Delta$	0.37	0.39	0.47	0.47	0.61	<u>0.66</u>
4 Pitch + $\Delta\Delta\Delta$	0.40	0.45	0.58	0.69	0.78	<u>0.80</u>
8 Pitch + SDC	0.42	0.49	0.63	0.73	0.87	**0.89**
11 Pitch + all	0.56	0.63	0.66	0.71	0.84	<u>0.86</u>

When appending temporal context information, the accuracies are increasing up to 89% weighted average accuracy utilizing SDC coefficients. As we have shown in Section 1.1, the prototypical pitch contour characterises the different functional meanings. So a longer temporal context allows to model the pitch contour and thus leads to an improved accuracy. If we consider the misclassification rate for both classes, we observe a rather small rate for the thinking class (30%) and a big rate for the *non-thinking* class (up to 50%). We assume that this fact arises from to the highly unbalanced training set with small samples for the *non-thinking* class.

4   Conclusion

This paper presents results on the usage of functional meanings of DPs within HCI to allow complex emotion recognition and human behaviour understanding.

Starting with an overview of the form-function relation of DPs within HHI, we investigated the occurrence of different DPs for HCI. We rely on work presented in [18] and [20], stating that DPs are universal. As DPs are assignable to complex emotions and therefore related to human behaviour, this statement seems contradictory as human behaviour is especially age and gender specific and hence not universal. We were able to show that DPs are indeed universal, however the usage of DPs is gender-age specific.

We could observe that females from the older age group use the DPs most frequently and that female subjects generally tend to use the DP "hm" more often than male subjects. Investigating the two experimental phases, we noticed that the DPs "uh" and "uhm" are occurring more frequently in the personalisation phase than in the problem solving phase. This observation is exactly opposite for the DP "hm". This may be related to the identified form function relation "thinking" for some form functions of "hm". However, further investigations regarding both the assignment of further form function relations and the behavioural aspects of the age-gender specific usage of DPs should be conducted.

We used the extracted form function relation of the DP "hm" to determine complex emotions within the HCI. Therefore, we presented methods to extract the pitch contour and its temporal context. These features were used to train HMMs, to distinguish the assigned meaning, *thinking*, from other form functions of the DP. The best weighted average performance of 89% could be achieved using the pitch contour with SDC coefficients training a HMM with 39 mixture components. This exemplary shows that DPs are indeed employable for the detection of complex emotions and significantly contribute to the understanding of human behaviour in HCI systems.

Acknowledgement. This work was supported by the Transregional Collaborative Research Centre SFB/TRR 62 (www.sfb-trr-62.de) "Companion-Technology for Cognitive Technical Systems" funded by the German Research Foundation (DFG).

References

1. Allwood, J., Nivre, J., Ahlsén, E.: On the semantics and pragmatics of linguistic feedback. Journal of Semantics 9(1), 1–26 (1992)
2. Benus, S., Gravana, A., Hirschberg, J.: The Prosody of Backchannels in American Englisch. In: Proceedings of the 16th International Congress of Phonetic Sciences, pp. 1065–1068. Saarbrücken, Germany (2007)
3. Ekman, P.: Basic Emotions, pp. 45–60. John Wiley & Sons, Ltd., Sussex (2005)
4. Fischer, K., Wrede, B., Brindöpke, C., Johanntokrax, M.: Quantitative und funktionale Analysen von Diskurspartikeln im Computer Talk. International Journal for Language Data Processing 20(1-2), 85–100 (1996)
5. Gerhard, D.: Pitch Extraction and Fundamental Frequency: History and Current Techniques. Tech. Rep. TR-CS 2003-06, Regina, Saskatchewan, Canada (2003)
6. Hartmann, K., Siegert, I., Philippou-Hübner, D., Wendemuth, A.: Emotion-Detection in HCI: From Speech Features to Emotion Space. In: Proc. of 12th IFAC/IFIP/IFORS/IEA Symposium on Analysis, Design, and Evaluation of Human-Machine Systems (in press, 2013)

7. Kehrein, R., Rabanus, S.: Ein Modell zur funktionalen Beschreibung von Diskurspartikeln. In: Neue Wege der Intonationsforschung, Germanistische Linguistik, vol. 157-158, pp. 33–50. Georg Olms, Hildesheim (2001)
8. Kockmann, M., Burget, L., Černocký, J.H.: Application of speaker- and language identification state-of-the-art techniques for emotion recognition. Speech Commun. 53(9-10), 1172–1185 (2011)
9. Lacey, J.I.: Somatic response patterning and stress: Some revisions of activation theory. In: Appley, M.H., Trumbull, R. (eds.) Psychological Stress: Issues in Research. Appleton-Century-Crofts, New York (1967)
10. Ladd, R.D.: Intonational Phonology. Studies in Linguistics, vol. 79. Cambridge University Press (1996)
11. Lange, J., Frommer, J.: Subjective experience and intentional setting within intervies of User-Companion-Interaction. In: Informatik Schafft Communities, Beiträge der 41. Jahrestagung der GI. Lecture Notes in Informatics, vol. 192, p. 240 (2011)
12. Martin, J.C., Niewiadomski, R., Devillers, L., Buisine, S., Pelachaud, C.: Multimodal complex emotions: Gesture expressivity and blended facial expressions. I. J. Humanoid Robotics (3), 269–291 (2006)
13. Müller, M.: Information Retrieval for Music and Motion. In: Dynamic Time Warping. Springer, Heidelberg (2007)
14. Paschen, H.: Die Funktion der Diskurspartikel HM. Master's thesis, University Mainz (1995)
15. Patel, S., Scherer, K.R., Björkner, E., Sundberg, J.: Mapping emotions into acoustic space: the role of voice production. Biological Psychology 87(1), 93–98 (2011)
16. Plutchik, R.: Emotion, a psychoevolutionary synthesis. Harper & Row (1980)
17. Rösner, D., Friesen, R., Otto, M., Lange, J., Haase, M., Frommer, J.: Intentionality in interacting with companion systems an empirical approach. In: Jacko, J.A. (ed.) Human-Computer Interaction, Part III, HCII 2011. LNCS, vol. 6763, pp. 593–602. Springer, Heidelberg (2011)
18. Schmidt, J.E.: Bausteine der Intonation. In: Neue Wege der Intonationsforschung, Germanistische Linguistik, vol. 157-158, pp. 9–32. Georg Olms, Hildesheim (2001)
19. Siegert, I., Böck, R., Wendemuth, A.: The influence of context knowledge for multimodal annotation on natural material. In: Joint Proc. of IVA 2012 Workshops (Multimodal Analyses Enabling Artificial Agents in HCI) (2012)
20. Siegert, I., Prylipko, D., Hartmann, K., Böck, R., Wendemuth, A.: Investigating the form-function-relation of the discourse particle "hm" in a naturalistic human-computer interaction. In: 23rd Italian Workshop on Neural Nets. Smart Innovation, Systems and Technologies. Springer, Heidelberg (accepted 2013)
21. Ward, N.: Pragmatic functions of prosodic features in non-lexical utterances. In: Proceedings of Speech Prosody 2004, pp. 325–328. Nara, Japan (2004)
22. Wendemuth, A., Biundo, S.: A Companion Technology for Cognitive Technical Systems. In: Esposito, A., Esposito, A.M., Vinciarelli, A., Hoffmann, R., Müller, V.C. (eds.) COST 2102. LNCS, vol. 7403, pp. 89–103. Springer, Heidelberg (2012)
23. Xuedong, H., Jack, M., Ariki, Y.: Hidden Markov Models for Speech Recognition. Edinburgh University Press, Edinburgh (1990)
24. Young, S., Evermann, G., Gales, M., Hain, T., Kershaw, D., Liu, X., Moore, G., Odell, J., Ollason, D., Povey, D., Valtchev, V., Woodland, P.: The HTK book (for HTK Version 3.4). Cambridge University Press, Cambridge (2006)

Author Index